KT-216-979

MEDITERRANEAN

FRANCE
& CORSICA

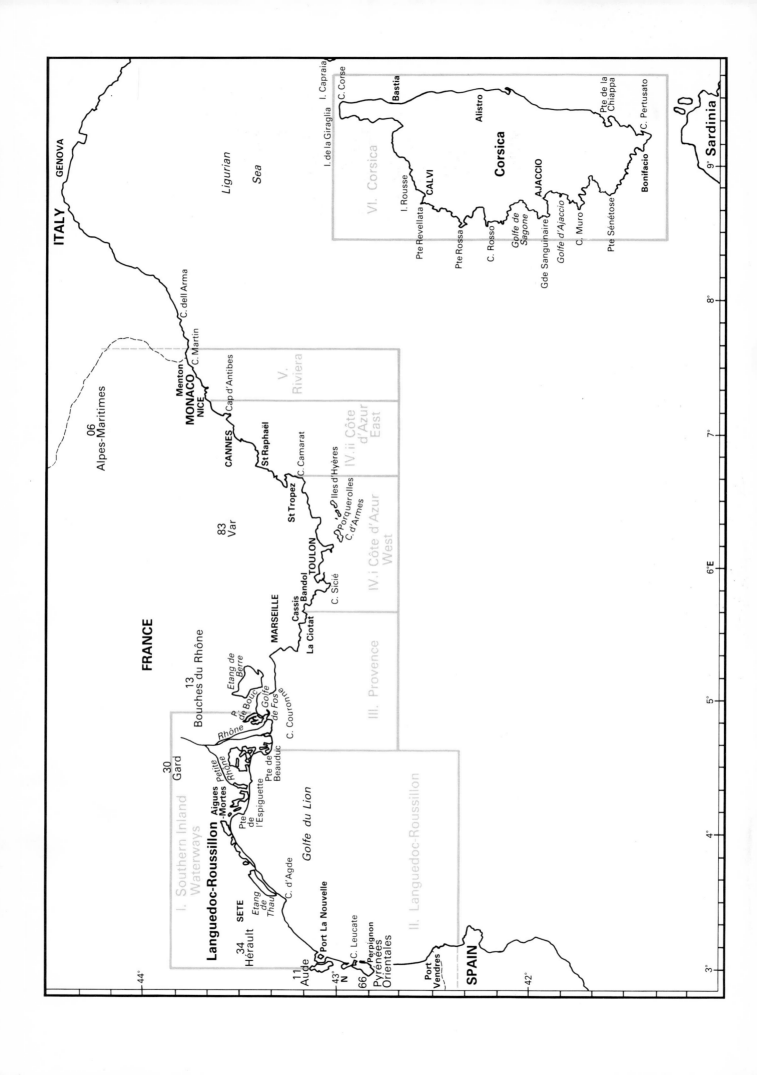

MEDITERRANEAN FRANCE & CORSICA

A sea guide

ROD HEIKELL

Imray Laurie Norie & Wilson Ltd
St Ives Cambridgeshire England

Published by
Imray, Laurie, Norie & Wilson Ltd
Wych House, St Ives, Huntingdon,
Cambridgeshire, PE17 4BT, England.

All rights reserved. No part of this publication may be reproduced, transmitted or used in any form by any means – graphic, electronic or mechanical, including photocopying, recording, taping or information storage and retrieval systems or otherwise – without the prior permission of the Publishers.

© Rod Heikell 1990

British Library Cataloguing in Publication Data

Heikell, Rod
Mediterranean France and Corsica
   1. France. Southeastern France. Coastal waters. Pilots' guides.
   I. Title
   623.89′29449

   ISBN 0 85288 141 X

CAUTION
Whilst every care has been taken to ensure accuracy, neither the Publishers nor the Author will hold themselves responsible for errors, omissions or alterations in this publication. They will at all times be grateful to receive information which tends to the improvement of the work.

PLANS
The plans in this guide are not to be used for navigation. They are designed to support the text and should at all times be used with navigational charts.

The last input of technical information was October 1990.

Printed at The Bath Press, Avon

Contents

Preface

The south of France conjures up a lot of images. The yachting mecca of the Mediterranean. Some of the most stylish marinas in the world. Sympathetic harbours in chic resorts. Cuisine ashore that is not only superb, sometimes superlative, but also offers excellent value for money. Good wine. Sandy beaches where topless nymph-like creatures and their macho escorts soak up the sun. Hot cloudless days. And the translucent blue Mediterranean. You will notice that descriptions of the south of France rarely include solitary anchorages, small fishing harbours, solitary days sailing along the coast, or solitary anything for that matter. If you expect to find relatively undiscovered little coves or uncrowded fishing harbours from the halcyon days of Hemingway and F. Scott Fitzgerald – they don't exist anymore.

To get the most out of the south of France you will need to adopt that certain style of cruising which accepts that there is as much to see and do ashore as afloat. Most of the towns along the coast have summer festivals with all sorts of things going on. Carnivals with a lot of all-night revelry. Music from organised jazz or classical concerts, often free, or from buskers who frequent the south of France in the summer. Exhibitions of everything from local folklore to local artistic talent. Fireworks displays whether for a local saint or just to celebrate summer. *Pétanque* played in dusty village squares. Permanent exhibitions in local museums – in the south of France there must be one of the greatest concentrations of post-impressionist art in the world. Along the coast there is a celebration of summer that you can join in or sit back and watch from a bar or restaurant – the eating and drinking bit is after all essential to cruising in France.

The French themselves should not be forgotten in all this. While over a third of the British population have visited France – it is the most visited foreign country – according to Theodore Zeldin only 2% say they admire the French. The Americans, who were helped by the French to gain independence, do little better. There are a lot of stereotypes around which complicate relations with the French right from the start and the British hold more than anyone else. The French themselves do little to help the situation. While the tourists are looking for the typical 'Jacques' or 'Henri', the French are fast turning themselves into the part. 'The stereotype thus lives on inextinguishably, turning out to be a hoax that the French play on foreigners, so successfully that they are taken in by it themselves. If you are a foreigner, you will be told that you can never know them properly; but if you are a Frenchman you can never understand yourself fully.' (Theodore Zeldin *The French*.)

To some extent the traveller on a yacht escapes from the unstated compact between local and tourist, since travelling on the water is often a passport to acceptance by the local boating community and you at least have to do practical things like buying groceries and fuel, which brings you closer to local life compared with the package holiday tourist. After that it is a matter of slowly picking away at the stereotypes, both your own and theirs, a process which can take some time.

One mistake that should not be made is to confuse the south with the north. There are essential differences between the north and south of France, in life style, attitudes, culture, and the language which can be impossible to understand when spoken in a thick local accent. Most of the French we learn is spoken with a northern or Parisian accent. In the south the accent is quite different and though you will be understood, it can be difficult to understand them. Along with the accent go the hand and facial gestures typical of the Mediterranean from Spain to Turkey and unless you are familiar with them it can add further to misunderstandings. If you understand the sign language of the face and hands it is just about possible to have a conversation without speaking.

Getting to know the French is worth the effort. The inanimate things you see along the coast, the monuments and cultural artifacts, and the landscape itself, are after all a remembrance of the things that shaped the people. And the life has a lot to recommend it. There is both a vibrancy and a languidness here and you should let it touch your life afloat. However I counsel caution. I ended up marrying one of them and so I am inexorably drawn into the life and the culture. This book is dedicated to my wife, Odile Marie Susanne Heikell.

Rod Heikell
Aix-en-Provence 1990

Acknowledgements

My thanks to Odile for crewing and deciphering the south of France; to Graham Sewell for crewing from Italy and around Corsica and to Katrina – Lavezzi will be long remembered; to Colin Michell and Yvette for crewing from Greece and remembering two trawlers going backwards!; to Joe Charlton for shelter and getting *Tetra* going again after the panic craning-out in Levkas; to Robyn for shelter; to Neil for woodwork and the latest music; to Adonis for his kindnesses; to Christo and Mila; to Madame Marguerite Bertolotti for shelter and forbearance in Martigues; to Madame Odette Meni for her *bouillabaisse*; to Eliane for some of the finest French cuisine I have tasted; to Dave and Claire Elderkin; to Olivier and Louise of S.Y. *Ariège*; to Alan Walker; to Nell and Rob for my introduction to the world of RAM and bytes; and to William Wilson and the staff of Imrays for their care and attention, as always, in putting this book together. Unfortunately the mistakes are mine alone.

Louise Grose drew the pen and ink sketches for the book – my thanks.

Elizabeth Cook compiled the index.

Bathing fashions then ...
Postcard c. 1900.

Narbonne. In this postcard c. 1920 it all looks remarkably similar to today, right down to the 'photographie' sign on the house on the bridge. (Author's collection.)

Nautical jousting at Toulon c. 1900.

Introduction

What to expect

The south of France has a relatively short stretch of coastline, some 350 or 400 miles depending on how many bumps and bays you measure, but along this short coast there are concentrated more marinas and harbours than anywhere else in the Mediterranean. The longest passage you will have to make between harbours is just over 30 miles around the mouth of the Rhône. By contrast along a five mile stretch of coast in the Golfe de Napoule there are four large marinas, two 'inland marinas' on the Rivière La Siagne, and three smaller harbours that pleasure craft use. Around 6000 berths by my reckoning. Most of the marinas and harbours offer excellent facilities for yachts and on the whole you need never worry about where to get fuel and water, hook up to electricity, get a weather forecast, shop for provisions, or find a restaurant.

The island of Corsica, lying just over a hundred miles off the coast, is in many ways another country. The national flag, a black Moor's head on a white background, is in striking contrast to the French tricolour. There are marinas dotted around the Corsican coast that provide good facilities for yachtsmen, but there are longer distances between them compared to the south of France. Between the marinas are numerous bays and coves, often in magnificent mountainous surroundings.

The concentration of marinas in the south of France also means a concentration of yachts and there is no getting away from the fact that when the French go on holiday in July and August, the entire coastline resounds to the flapping of sails and grinding of winches, and to the roar of engines, from Cerbère to Menton. Weekends are the worst and even outside July and August there are large numbers of craft out at the weekend. At the height of summer there may be some difficulty getting into the more popular marinas, especially for very large yachts, but generally you get squeezed in somewhere. Larger yachts, over 15 metres, should call up on VHF to reserve a berth; and craft over 25 metres should reserve berths in advance for the summer. If a marina is full to bursting and you are turned away, there will be another marina not too far away that you can get to.

Anchorages along the coast are invariably crowded by day in the summer, but by evening are comparatively deserted after everyone has departed for a marina. I understand now why some French yachtsmen will anchor just about anywhere and why they are so adroit at utilising tiny coves and bights for shelter so successfully – in the south of France the only way to get away from the crowds is to utilise just about any nook or cranny as an anchorage. I also understand why some of their compatriots are so maladroit at anchoring, even in a flat calm on good holding, when they normally spend every night in a marina berth.

In recent years France has taken to messing about in boats in a way no other nation has. There has been a proliferation in boating that has seen a boom in boat building, the two biggest boat-builders in the world are French, and in the ancillary services for the care and repair of boats. For craft based permanently or semi-permanently in the Mediterranean, the south of France has better facilities for repairs and maintenance, especially if a major refit is being considered, than anywhere else. The cost of the work is not cheap, but it is on the whole good quality work carried out with care.

MARINAS

Strictly speaking the term 'marina' applies only to purpose-built pleasure-craft harbours with an associated complex and facilities ashore. Over time the term has become blurred to mean almost any harbour, whether purpose-built or not, that deals almost exclusively with pleasure craft and offers facilities of a certain standard. The pedantic use of the term in its original sense is no longer useful and indeed is confusing, so I have used the term marina in its looser sense to include most of the pleasure-craft harbours along the French Mediterranean coast and around Corsica.

When you enter a marina or harbour, there is usually a *quai d'accueil*, a 'reception quay', where you berth temporarily to report to the *capitainerie* for a berth. In some marinas you may be allotted a berth on the *quai d'accueil* itself. In the height of summer you will often be waved to a berth directly by one of the marina staff. Yachts over 15 metres should call up on VHF to reserve a berth, especially in July and August when the marinas are crowded. There is no reason why smaller yachts should not also call up on VHF. Most of the *capitaineries* listen out on channel 9; alternatively try channels 16 or 12. In most marinas there is a speed limit of 3 knots which will at times be strictly enforced by the harbour authorities.

Various systems of laid moorings, posts, buoys, or finger pontoons are employed in the marinas and I have outlined their use below. It is prohibited to anchor in nearly all of the marinas.

BERTHING

In the majority of the marinas and harbours along the south of France and in Corsica you must berth stern or bows-to using a variety of methods to keep the boat off the quay or pontoon. It takes some skill to go stern-to, especially if there is a strong crosswind and a narrow gap to fit into between other yachts. Always have plenty of fenders out and when close to the quay warp the yacht into place rather than using the engine. For yachts up to 10 or 11 metres LOA. it is often easier to go bows-to as a yacht can be more easily manoeuvred into a berth when going forward. Moreover there is a gain in privacy as people on the quay cannot see into the cockpit or the cabin as they usually can when you are stern-to.

The common methods of berthing in a marina are outlined below, though there are of course minor variations from place to place.

Laid moorings

A chain sinker from a laid mooring is connected to a rope which is either tailed to the quay or to a small buoy. When you come in you must either pick up the small buoy or the rope and pull the mooring line tight, tying it off when the lines to the quay are made off. The lines are often dirty and may have sharp barnacles or coral worm on them, so wear gloves to prevent damage to your hands. If you get to the chain it is usually best to tie a line onto it (use a rolling hitch), or pass a line through a link if it is large enough, rather than cleating off the chain itself which can cause damage to the topsides and deck.

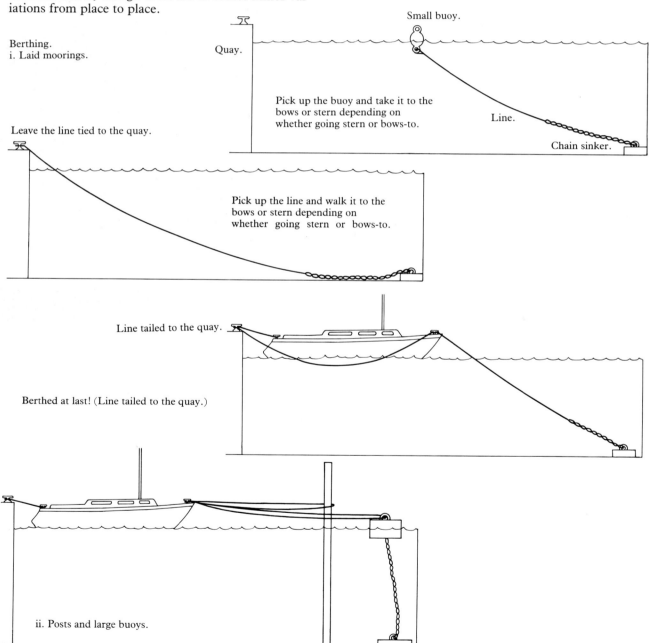

Berthing.
i. Laid moorings.

Quay.

Small buoy.

Pick up the buoy and take it to the bows or stern depending on whether going stern or bows-to.

Line.

Chain sinker.

Leave the line tied to the quay.

Pick up the line and walk it to the bows or stern depending on whether going stern or bows-to.

Line tailed to the quay.

Berthed at last! (Line tailed to the quay.)

ii. Posts and large buoys.

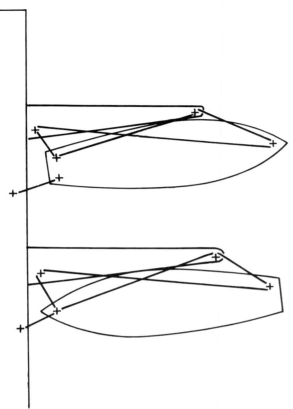

iii. Finger pontoons. Use springs to keep the boat off the quay.

Posts and large buoys

A line must be passed around a post or through the top of a large buoy and the ends tied off when the lines to the quay are made off. It is best to have a long line looped around the post or through the buoy rather than a single line tied off as the latter makes leaving difficult, especially in strong winds or crowded conditions.

Finger pontoons

Nose in and tie up alongside the pontoon with springs to keep the boat off the quay. Be careful when jumping down onto the pontoon as it will probably bounce down until there is enough buoyancy to support you.

ANCHORING

In many of the small bays and coves and in the *calanques* it is normal practice to anchor and take a long line ashore. This is principally because there are usually too many yachts in a given space to swing to an anchor or there is too little room in the smaller *calanques* between the sides. In some cases the practice of taking a long line ashore is useful to hold a yacht into the prevailing wind or swell in order to make life more comfortable on board.

Off most of the bathing beaches along the south of France and around Corsica, the bathing area is cordoned off by a line of yellow buoys. It is prohibited to enter the area marked by the buoys or to anchor within this area. In addition there will usually be a

Calvi

buoyed corridor for speedboats and water-skiers, water-bikes, and the like, to get from the beach to outside the bathing area. You should not anchor at the exit to the corridor or anywhere that obstructs boats entering or leaving it. Although not always observed, it is generally prohibited to exceed a speed of 5 knots within 300 metres of the coast and in some bays and small gulfs.

YACHT AND EQUIPMENT

Engines

A reliable engine is necessary for motoring through the inevitable calms a yacht will encounter. On other occasions a reliable engine will be necessary to motor against the strong winds and short seas of the Mediterranean to get into harbour. A petrol engine can be dangerous as in the high summer temperatures petrol vaporises easily and the risk of fire or an explosion is greater than in more northern latitudes. This risk applies equally to outboards, whether for the tender or as a backup on a motorboat, and it pays to think carefully about ventilation and petrol stowage. I have witnessed several explosions fuelled by petrol and the results have not been pretty.

Ventilation

Yachts built for northern climates will have inadequate ventilation for the hot Mediterranean. Extra skylights and vents and additional insulation can help solve the problem. Yachts with deckhouses and motorboats with large expanses of glass should have covers, normally in white canvas, made up to prevent a 'greenhouse effect' down below. An air-scoop to funnel air down the front or saloon hatch makes a big difference to life below and several commercially produced scoops are on the market.

Awnings

A good sun awning is a necessary piece of boat equipment. Much of your time will be spent in the cockpit and the awning should be designed to be a comfortable height above the cockpit seats and should have side curtains for when the sun is low in the evening. Make the awnings from dark-coloured canvas as light materials cause a glare and nylon and *Terylene* materials flap and crack in the slightest breeze. A permanent sun awning below the boom of a yacht or over the cockpit of a motorboat is well worth thinking about as it provides pleasant shade when at sea as well as in harbour. The bimini hoods often fitted to boats in the Caribbean are a good idea as they can be folded away when necessary.

Refrigerator

For those who can't do without cold drinks it is an essential piece of equipment. The heat-absorption and thermoelectric types do not work well in the high ambient temperatures. The type having a compressor working off the batteries (high current drain) or off the engine (expensive to purchase and install) work the best. Install a holding plate and get a top opening type of refrigerator so that the cold air does not fall out every time it is opened. And don't forget that ice is available in most harbours so that the humble ice-box can be used with the advantage that it costs virtually nothing and it never breaks down.

Shower

A shower is useful inside a yacht, but it is perhaps most useful if it can be used outside on deck or in the cockpit to wash off after swimming in the salty Mediterranean. Large water tanks or even a separate water tank may be required. Many modern craft have a shower installed on the aft swimming platform and this makes a lot of sense. The 'sun-shower' outfits, simply a black bag with a hose and shower rose attached, also work well though the water inside can get too hot if the bag is left in the sun for long at the height of summer.

Sails

Under the hot Mediterranean sun a yacht's sails suffer from ultraviolet degradation faster than in more northern climates. It is a good policy to cover the mainsail and bag any headsails when they are not in use. If you have a roller-reefing headsail then have a sacrificial strip on the luff and foot to protect it when furled.

Gang plank (passerelle)

This can be an elaborate affair or simply a plank. It is useful to have a pair of small wheels at the outboard end so that the board scraping over the quay does not annoy you or your neighbours. Some thought also needs to be put into where to stow the thing if you are not going to keep it permanently rigged on the stern.

Anchors

Preferences for different anchors vary with the individual, but the following information may be useful for coping with the different types of bottom found in the Mediterranean. In many bays and in the *calanques* it is very deep until close to the shore and it is standard practice to lay out an anchor and take a long line to the shore. Along much of the coast the bottom has thick weed covering it and some anchors have difficulty penetrating and digging in. If an anchor picks up a clump of weed it must be raised to clear it before trying again. If the water is clear enough, which it mostly is, pick a sandy patch to let the anchor down onto and then go astern to make sure it is well in. Afterwards you can cool off by snorkling over the anchor to see if it has dug in.

Bruce A good all-round anchor. It gets through weed well and once in holds well even on a short scope. It will sometimes collect a lump of weed and must be raised to clear it. It also stows easily on the bows of a boat. You will, though, need a much heavier anchor than the manufacturer's overly optimistic recommendations.

CQR A good all-round anchor. Use either a *Bruce* or *CQR* as the main bower anchor. It will often pick up a clump of weed, usually pulling up the whole plant by the fibrous roots, and must be raised to clear it.

Delta A new anchor, like the *Bruce*, of one-piece construction, though looking more like the *CQR*. The ability of the *Delta* to right itself to a holding position is a definite plus for the anchor and I look forward to trying one out in the 'rough'.

Danforth Good for getting through weed and holds well, but you need a substantially heavier anchor than the manufacturer recommends. My favourite for a kedge.

Fisherman Excellent for getting through weed and on difficult bottoms, especially rocky bottoms and hard sand. However the heavy weight of this anchor and it's awkwardness to handle are big disadvantages. A good alternative to the *Danforth* as a kedge or as an emergency anchor.

I do not favour the use of a *Danforth* or a *Fisherman* for the bower anchor as the chain easily fouls them when it swings over the top.

Grapnels Useful as dinghy anchors, but the folding types and the sort fabricated in the Mediterranean do not hold well except on rocky bottoms.

NAVIGATION

A yacht will require no more navigational equipment than would be used for offshore and coastal cruising elsewhere and in all probability will use less in practice. Much coastal navigation will be of the eyeball variety. Of the common or garden variety of equipment you will of course need a steering compass, hand-bearing compass, log, and depth-sounder. An RDF is useful as there is a good network of marine beacons and numerous air beacons. As the price of the silicon chip plummets I see more and more electronic position-finding aerials sprouting on craft and *satnav* and the newer *navstar* are as useful in the Mediterranean as they are elsewhere. Loran C is an alternative with good Mediterranean cover. Remember there is no Decca coverage in the Mediterranean and not likely to be in the future. Radar has become more compact and cheaper and is considered a priority over electronic position-finding equipment by some yachtsmen. Repair facilities for electronic equipment are the best in the Mediterranean along the French coast.

YACHT FACILITIES

Fuel

Where fuel is shown on the plans or mentioned in the notes I am referring in most cases to diesel fuel. However on many of the fuel quays in the marinas petrol is available as well. Almost without exception fuel is easily available in all of the marinas along the French coast. Around Corsica you may have to plan more carefully.

Gas

Camping gaz and propane and butane gas bottles are readily available in even the smallest villages and towns. *Calor Gas* bottles will not be filled. You can buy French bottles and an adaptor thread to connect them to your stove and other appliances. Because gas, whether *Camping gaz* or the other various brands of propane and butane are so commonly available, I have not listed the availability of gas in the notes – it was pointless since anywhere that has a few hundred souls or more has gas available.

Paraffin

Is difficult to obtain. Ask for *pétrole kerdane*. Wood alcohol, methylated spirits, without the blue dye used elsewhere, is commonly available in supermarkets – ask for *alcool à brûler*.

Water

Is safe to drink everywhere unless a notice saying *non potable* states otherwise. On the whole water quality standards are higher than in Britain where much of our water does not conform to EC standards.

Ice

Is available in most marinas either in block form or as ice cubes. Enquire at the *capitainerie* if you cannot see any obvious sign pointing the way.

Yacht spares

All types of yacht spares are widely available in France. At any of the larger marinas there will be several chandlers and agents for marine engines, outboards, and electronic equipment, including much equipment manufactured outside France. Boating bits and pieces are not cheap in France as they attract a luxury tax and even equipment manufactured in France will often cost more there than it does in Britain. Whether this situation will change in 1992 when taxes in the EC are rationalised remains to be seen.

Antifoulings

A yacht bottom fouls quicker in the warm waters of the Mediterranean than it otherwise would in more northern latitudes. A good antifouling is necessary since the absence of tides means you cannot give the bottom a quick scrub between tides. I have used the following with success: International *Micron*, Blakes *Tiger* (I believe the new tin-free equivalent is just as good), Hempels *Hard Racing*, and Veneziani hard antifouling. Remember antifoulings containing tin were first banned by the French. Soft copper-based antifouling is widely available, comparatively cheap and works well, though of course you cannot scrub it clean.

Hauling out

Nearly every marina has a yard or yards attached to it and most have travel-hoists which will get you in and out of the water quickly and efficiently. The new *Titre de Séjour* simplifies the paperwork for leaving a boat in France.

Gardiennage

In most of the marinas there are companies who will look after a boat for you in your absence. Leaving a boat in the water for the winter is perfectly feasible and all the normal services, running the engine(s), charging the batteries, checking mooring and berthing warps, airing the boat, checking covers, and any other work you detail, can be carried out. As elsewhere, if possible check out the credentials of the people who are going to do the work if you can, as successful *gardiennage* relies mostly on the person doing it rather than slick looking offices and glossy brochures.

Garbage

All marinas have garbage bins or large wheeled containers and rubbish belongs here and not in the sea. The French are beginning to clean up their backyard and marine reserves have been staked out around the coast. Visitors should do everything in their power to keep the waters they are sailing upon clean.

Rescue services

There are all-weather rescue craft dotted around the coast who will come to the aid of any yacht in distress. CROSS MED, the organisation responsible for maritime safety and security in the Mediterranean, keeps a 24-hour listening watch on VHF Ch 16. CROSS MED STE-MARGUERITE ☎ 94 27 27 11. S/CROSS AGDE ☎ 67 94 12 02. CROSS CORSE ☎ 95 20 13 63. As well there are numerous inshore rescue craft in many of the harbours. Having seen a lifeboat in action, going out in a force 9 *mistral*, I can vouch for the professionalism and courage of the service.

Charges

A charge is made at all of the marinas and most of the harbours. I have not included the actual charges as they fluctuate from year to year in no predictable manner. On the whole charges are less than in Britain for equivalent marinas. In nearly all of the marinas and harbours a yacht is permitted to go temporarily onto the *quai d'accueil* for a defined length of time, usually between 1 and 4 hours, to make enquiries, provision, or I suppose to have a bite to eat in a restaurant, but if you stay over the permitted maximum period you will be charged for the use of a berth.

General information

Tourist offices

In all of the villages and towns along the coast there are tourist offices, the *Syndicat d'Initiative*, where you can find out what there is to do and see ashore. Usually they have free maps and brochures on the area and will do their best to help you with any small problems you have.

Banks

Eurocheques, traveller's cheques, or hard currencies can be used at all banks offering *change* services. Only some banks will give cash advances on one of the two major credit cards, *Visa* or *Access*. Banks are generally open from 0830–1200 and 1400–1700, though hours vary from place to place and bank to bank. Some banks will not change money after 1500. The major credit cards, *Visa* and *Access*, and *American Express* are accepted by the majority of restaurants, boutiques, petrol stations, etc.

Public holidays

January 1	New Year's Day
May 1	Labour Day
July 14	Bastille Day
August 15	Festival of the Assumption
November 1	All Saints' Day
November 11	Armistice Day
December 25	Christmas Day

Movable holidays
Good Friday
Easter Monday
Ascension Day
Whit Monday

Most towns and villages have their own celebration days or saints' days as well, when not all services will be available.

Laundry

In a number of the marinas there are laundromats where you can do your own washing. Laundry services can be found in most of the larger marinas and towns, though the service is not cheap.

Security

Theft is an ever present problem in France as it is in the other developed western European countries. Normal precautions should be taken to keep the boat locked and any valuable gear should be removed from the deck if you are leaving the boat for a few days or longer. In many of the marinas a guard patrols at night and on the whole you will be unlucky to have anything stolen.

Health

Travellers from EC countries can get urgent treatment free or at a reduced cost in France. Get leaflet *SA 28/30 Medical Treatment During Visits Abroad* and fill in *Form CM1* at the back and send it in. You will be sent *Form E111* which you should carry with you. Medical treatment in France is excellent, but expensive if you are paying for it.

Mail

The French postal system is reliable if a little slow at times. Address your letters to *poste restante* or to a marina with the instruction to hold your mail. I prefer the latter and on the whole the marinas are helpful about keeping mail for you.

Provisioning

In general prices are reasonable in France compared to the rest of the Mediterranean. Though initially they might seem higher, this has to be traded off against the quality of the goods. French meat, for instance, normally contains little or no fat. Costs vary considerably between shops and it is best to do your shopping in one of the large supermarkets such as *Monoprix* or *Casino*. Imported goods are expensive and in any case are generally inferior to French brands.

Shopping hours in general are 0830–1200/1300 and 1400/1500–1800/1700 Monday to Saturday. Many shops also open on Sunday. Most shops are closed on Monday afternoons. Fresh produce can be obtained from local markets as well as cheeses and meat.

Meat Is expensive but the quality is excellent. Remember that the cuts of meat do not usually contain fat and bones so that what you are buying is all lean.

Fish A good selection of all types of fish at reasonable prices.

Fruit and vegetables Good selection throughout the year at reasonable prices.

Staples All the basics are widely available.

Cheese An excellent variety at comparatively cheap prices as you would expect. A camembert or brie with good French butter and a *baguette*, a bottle of local wine, and you have an excellent and cheap lunch.

Canned goods A good selection at reasonable prices.

Coffee and tea Instant coffee is comparatively expensive. Fresh coffee is excellent and you can choose the quality to suit your pocket. French tea is for 'infusions' and won't produce a British cuppa.

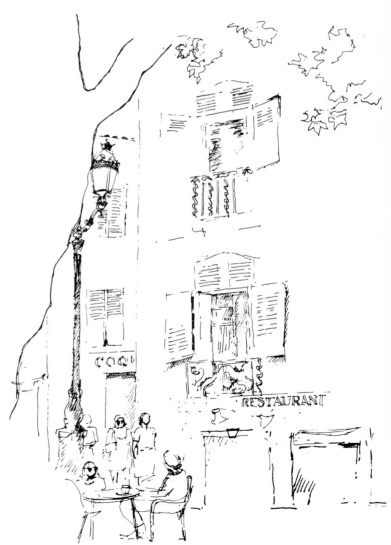

Wines, beers, and spirits Wine is of course excellent, cheap, and even a *vin de table* may bring a smile to your lips. If not better quality wines are available at very reasonable prices. French beer is of the lager type, eminently drinkable and very cheap to buy in the supermarkets. Spirits are comparatively cheap, especially cognacs as you would expect.

Formalities for entering and leaving France

When entering France it is no longer necessary to fly a 'Q' flag requesting customs clearance unless you have goods to declare. In practice you simply enter French waters and that is that. In 1986 the *Titre de Séjour*, a provisional resident's permit, was introduced along the Mediterranean coast. The permit is free and is issued by customs offices and will be ratified by them. If you are laying up a boat in France, the *Titre de Séjour* is issued in place of the old *Passeport du Navire Etranger*. The *Titre de Séjour* considerably simplifies matters, absolving the owner from checking with customs every time the yacht is visited or used.

An owner is allowed to use a yacht for 6 months in any 12-month period without being liable for TVA (French VAT). However you may not use the boat for any commercial purpose including chartering it. Although a co-owner or immediate family may use the boat, relatives and friends cannot. In the past there have been too many 'friends' and 'third cousins' using boats in disguised charters. The new *Titre de Séjour* means you can actually keep your boat in France as long as the *Titre de Séjour* is renewed with the relevant customs office every year. I quote from the information pamphlet issued: 'If usually your boat stays in France, show your resident permit to the office which ratified it in order to have it renewed.' And further: 'Any modification relative to either the boat, the owner or the user will imply a new provisional resident permit.'

In practice the regulations are interpreted with typical Gallic common sense by the authorities. Spot-checks are regularly carried out through the summer, though in a friendly fashion. The marine branch of the *Gendarmerie* also make spot-checks and will apprehend anyone exceeding speed regulations or behaving recklessly in a boat. Anyone infringing customs regulations or entering prohibited areas should not expect the normal Gallic charm to be turned on them – customs and the *Gendarmerie Maritime* take their work seriously.

Extracts from Article 196B of the Customs Code
1. Beneficiaries under the regulation: Free temporary importation is granted, for private use, to persons having their normal residence abroad according to the decree of 23 May 1975, which lays down the conditions applicable to the regime of free tempo-

rary importation of objects destined for the personal use of the travellers who are owners of a yacht and use it in a non-commercial way and, in particular, not for the transport of persons for remuneration, premium or any other material advantage or the industrial and commercial transportation of goods with or without remuneration.

2. Use of yachts placed under the regulation of free temporary importation: Yachts permitted to stay in French waters under the benefit of the privileged regulation of temporary free importation can only be used privately for the personal pleasure of the owners themselves.

Without prejudice to the statutory provisions the sale, rental, loan and generally speaking, the use of a yacht to a pecuniary end under the regulation are prohibited.

Customs duty

Foreign-flag boats whose owners or users reside in France are liable to French TVA (currently 18·6%) and in the case of some foreign flags, to an additional customs duty of between 3 and 5 times the normal rate. The following countries *are not liable* to the additional tax, though they are still liable to TVA if applicable.

Algeria	Mali
Austria	Morocco
Belgium	Mauritania
Benin	Monaco
Brazil	Netherlands
Burkino-Faso	Niger
Cameroon	Norway
Chad	Pakistan
Czechoslovakia	Poland
Congo	Portugal
Denmark	Central African Republic
Germany	Romania
Finland	Senegal
Gabon	Singapore
Greece	Spain
Iran	Sweden
Ireland	Thailand
Italy	Togo
Ivory Coast	Tunisia
Lebanon	United Kingdom
Luxembourg	United States of America
Madagascar	Yugoslavia
Malawi	Zambia

Boat documents

All boats entering France must have the boat registration documents on board at all times. Either full *Part 1* registration (the 'blue book') or the new *Small Ships Register* papers administered by the Royal Yachting Association are acceptable. Photocopies will not be accepted. In addition you should carry the boat's insurance papers and the owner should have a certificate of competence such as the Royal Yachting Association's *Yacht Master's* or, at the very least, a *Helmsman's* certificate.

Anyone who is not an EC national or Swiss must obtain a visa for France. You can obtain a three-year multi-entry visa for a cost little above the cost of a six-month visa. This visa must be obtained before you enter France. Everyone in France is required by law to carry their identification with them at all times, including visitors, though in practice not everyone does.

Food and wine

To write a page or so on the food and wine of France is a bit like trying to paraphrase the Bible into a page or two. So rather than attempt the impossible I've elected to list some commonly encountered dishes and if you want to know more you will have to buy one of the many books available on the subject. In the south of France the Provençal cuisine that influences much of the food was introduced to northern climes largely by Elizabeth David and she has written various books on the subject.

To experience the food, and drink the local wines is as good a reason as any other to go to France. The French take their food and wine seriously, sometimes a little pompously, but the national attitude means that you can eat better for less than anywhere else in Europe. Finding a good restaurant is an art which relies as much on your intuition as anything else. I have not listed restaurants in the pilotage notes as invariably restaurants change hands or the patron decides to cut corners or a new chef is employed and what was a good restaurant goes quickly downhill.

Soups (soupes)
Bouillon, a broth
Consommé, a clear soup
Aigo boulido, a Provençal garlic soup, may contain herbs, eggs, cheese, potatoes or fish, the garlic being the only essential ingredient. Very good for you and often used as a remedy following illness.
Aigo saou, a fish version of *aigo boulido* which can often be better than the more commonly known *bouillabaisse*.
Bouillabaisse, the fish dish of the south of France, not only a soup but a main meal. It is rarely found in its authentic form despite the number of restaurants that advertise a 'genuine' *bouillabaisse*. See Chapter III, page 128.
Soupe de poisson, usually better than imitation *bouillabaisse*. It is sieved and normally accompanied by dried bread and garlic, grated cheese, and *rouille*.
Soupe au pistou, a vegetable soup that both the Niçois and the Genoese claim as their own. It is a summer vegetable soup containing, ideally, three types of beans and importantly, basil.
Garbure, a thick vegetable soup from Languedoc-Roussillon

Hors d'oeuvre and salads
Crudités, raw seasonal vegetables sliced or chopped, usually accompanied by a mayonnaise dip.
Tapenade, a Provençal spread of puréed black olives, capers, tunny fish, and anchovies. Usually served on toasted bread.
Salade Niçoise with tomato, onions, olives, hard-boiled egg, and anchovies.
Salade aux lardons, usually a green salad with bits of cooked bacon.
Salade verte, exactly what it says, a green salad.
Salade de riz, a rice salad with tomatoes, green peppers, olives.

Eggs (les oeufs)
Omelettes can contain anything from a sprinkling of herbs to potatoes, ham, cheese, mushrooms; whatever the chef decides on.
Piperade, a dish of eggs and red peppers stewed, sometimes with cream, to form a sort of scrambled eggs – delicious.

Fish and shellfish (les poissons et les coquillages)
I will not list the different types of fish available that may be served grilled or fried with or without a sauce, rather the fish dishes for which the south is known.
Ailloli, a mayonnaise of vinegar, oil and crushed garlic, often eaten with fish dishes.
Bourride, a Provençal fish stew with *ailloli*, often the stew is thickened with egg yolks.
Brandade, a creamy dish of pounded salt cod.
Bouillabaisse, as much a main dish as a soup.
Friture, white bait deep fried.

Fish such as bream, sea bass, mackerel, flat fish, etc. are often cooked simply with fennel, basil, garlic, tarragon, or whatever herb or local variation a chef favours and as long as the fish is fresh, will usually be good.

Shellfish are eaten simply with a dash of lemon in most good *coquillage* restaurants and though I love oysters and mussels, I am only now getting used to *violets* and don't think I will ever get on with the *oursin* (sea urchin).

For those interested in Mediterranean fish cuisine, Alan Davidson's *Mediterranean Seafood* published as a Penguin paperback is invaluable.

Poultry and game (les volailles et le gibier)
Chicken may be stuffed with wild herbs, pine nuts, olives, lemon halves, whatever is considered suitable, and roasted. Capon is also popular.

Small birds like larks (*alouettes*), quail (*caille*) or guinea-fowl (*pintade*) are usually roasted with a sauce.

Rabbit (*lapin*) is often stewed with a thick sauce.

Meat (les viandes)
May be lamb (*agneau*), mutton (*mouton*), beef (*boeuf*), veal (*veau*), or pork (*porc*). Meat can be ordered very

rare (*bleu*), underdone (*saignant*), medium (*à point*), or well done (*bien cuit*).

There are a number of common dishes:

Daube, basically a stew. Also *pot-au-feu*.

Cassoulet, a stew of mutton and haricot beans. See Chapter II, page 82.

Basquaise with tomato and pimento.

Bercy with shallots and white wine.

Chasseur or *forestière* with mushrooms.

à la meunière, cooked in butter.

Provençale with tomatoes and garlic.

There are many many local dishes or variations.

Pastry and pasta (patés and pasta)

Quiche Lorraine, not quite Provençal, but popular nonetheless.

Tarte à l'oignon, an onion and cream tart.

Pissaladière Provençal, anchovy and onion pie.

Pizzas along the south coast are usually very good with the usual assortment of toppings.

Most of the pastas encountered in Italy are offered along the coast and are generally very good. In the early 20th century there was a considerable migration of Italians into the south of France and quite naturally many of them opened restaurants.

Vegetables (les légumes)

In addition to the inevitable French fries, though the French claim they were a Belgian invention that they made edible, and cooked individual vegetables, you will probably come across the following.

Ratatouille, the well known mixture of onions, tomatoes, aubergines, and peppers stewed together.

Gratin dauphinois, sliced potatoes baked in cream.

Tian, a baked vegetable dish with eggs and cheese.

Gratins, a baked dish with eggs, cream and cheese. It may be of tomatoes, courgettes, pumpkin, etc.

Beignets, deep-fried vegetable fritters, commonly aubergine or courgette.

Desserts (les desserts)

Commonly you will come across *mousse au chocolat, tarte aux pommes ou fraise, crème caramel, gâteaux* of one sort or another, and *glaces* and *sorbets*.

Crêpes are more often found in a crêperie where, with a variety of savoury and sweet fillings, you can have a complete meal.

Wines

Vines were introduced along the southern coast of France by the Phocaean Greeks who settled at Marseille around 600 BC. However it was under Roman rule that the expansion of vineyards began with new varieties of grapes introduced including the Syrah still cultivated today, and improved methods of wine production and storage. Julius Caesar was to be among the first in a long line to praise the vintages from the south of France. Through the Middle Ages they were much appreciated, with Good King René of Anjou a particular champion of Provençal wines.

In the 19th century the wines from the south became less popular and it was not until comparatively late in this century that they began to regain some popularity.

Along the coast various regions are known for particular wines and I have mentioned some of these in the text and wherever possible sampled the vintages, not scientifically I must admit, more in the spirit of enjoyable research. It may surprise some to know that the majority of the wines produced along the coast are rosés – the *Côtes de Provence* for instance are made up of approximately 60% rosés. For those like myself who do not normally choose a rosé, thinking it neither one thing or the other, the rosés produced in the south come as a pleasant surprise and along with 60% of the locals in Provence I am now a keen advocate of a crisp cool rosé on a hot summer's evening.

Starting from the west there are several *Apellation d'Origine Contrôlée* regions.

Côtes du Roussillon and Côtes du Roussillon Village are probably the best known, producing some excellent reds.

Les Corbières produce excellent reds and whites with *A.O.C. Fitou* probably the best known in the area.

Banyuls area produces excellent rosés and whites.

Côtes de Provence cover the area from the Rhône to as far along the coast as St-Raphaël. Only 45,700 acres have the right to *A.O.C.* status. The type of wines vary dramatically according to the location though the soil is much the same throughout the region – poor in topsoil, permeable and stony, sometimes so stony it is impossible to believe anything could grow there. In the region about 60% of the wines produced are rosés, 35% reds, and a miserly 5% whites. Of the latter the dry *Cassis* whites are probably my favourite. Of the reds I consider *Gigondas* better value for money than *Châteauneuf-du-Pape*. Of the rosés try what is on offer until you find what you like, though *Tavel* and *Lirac* are both worth sampling. The reds and whites of Bandol are worth sampling and the reds from La Croix-Valmer also merit attention.

Personally I usually disregard lists and years and tipple away until I find what I consider to be a reasonably priced acceptable wine. The '88 white from Pic de Picpoul in Bas-Roussillon was my own little find and at around 18 francs a bottle you couldn't go wrong.

Marine life

The marine life in the Mediterranean is at first disappointing. It is not as prolific or as diverse as you might imagine; there are fewer seabirds than you would see in more northern waters, good eating fish are more scarce and difficult to catch, and in places the sea bottom can be quite bereft of interest compared to say the Pacific or the Atlantic coast of France. There are a number of reasons for this relative paucity of marine life. The first is the non-tidal, or nearly so, nature of the sea which has two effects. First of all there is not the intertidal zone in which a varied and rich marine life lives and contributes to the ecosystem as it does in the Atlantic. The second effect from the absence of tides is that the sea is not turned over by the currents generated by the tides and the water is not, as it were, mixed up. This makes it difficult for plankton, the basis of all marine ecosystems, to live and multiply in great numbers and indeed the Mediterranean is a plankton-poor sea and therefore generally poor in marine life. It has always been so and it's much vaunted clarity is the result of the absence of 'soupy' plankton obscuring your vision. Add to this the fact that the Mediterranean has been fished far longer and more intensively than other seas and it is not surprising there are not as many fish around as you might have believed.

Although the marine life is initially disappointing, the yachtsman is in a unique position to discover and explore what there is in the Mediterranean. With a snorkel you can potter around the rocky coast and view the underwater life at leisure – at least the water is not so cold that you have to climb out every few minutes to get warm.

DOLPHINS AND WHALES

Dolphins are not as common around the south coast of France as in other parts of the Mediterranean, probably because of the noise and disturbance from waterborne traffic. However on passage to Corsica and around the Corsican coast you will most likely be visited by these lovely mammals. In the deep water off Corsica a number of sperm whales, said to be aging bulls from the Atlantic that had retired here with a few young cows for company, used to be seen. In 1977 I encountered one off here, but in recent years I have not heard any reports of them. Certainly there were a lot of dolphins around on my last crossing between Menton and Macinaggio in Corsica.

In the Mediterranean most of the cetaceans seen belong to the toothed whales which are fish eaters. The common dolphin (*Delphinus delphis*) will often be seen and is the most common of the cetaceans you will come across. These grow to 1·7–2·4 metres, weigh 75–85 kilograms, and are black or brownish-black on the back and upper flanks with a creamy white, often mottled, chest and belly. A distinctive tan or yellowish-tan hourglass pattern marks the flanks. Less common are the larger bottlenosed dolphin (*Tursiops truncatus*) and the common porpoise (*Phocaena phocena*). The pilot whale (*Globicephala*) is fairly common and relatively easy to identify.

EDIBLE FISH

The following list is not comprehensive, but includes most of the species you will come across in restaurants and the fish market. The assiduous fish gourmand should turn to Alan Davidson's *Mediterranean Seafood*.

Anchois – anchovies, usually salted and marinated.

Anguille – eel, rarely found in the south.

Bar – bass, excellent white flesh.

Barbou – brill.

Baudroie – angler fish.

Blanchaille – white bait, delicious deep fried as *friture*.

Calamars – squid, usually deep fried, sometimes with a black ink sauce.

Coquilles St-Jacques – scallops, good if fresh – they are usually frozen.

Crevettes – prawns or shrimps, likewise usually frozen.

Daurade – sea bream, excellent white flesh if a little bony.

Encornet – squid.

Espadon – swordfish, delicious as a steak with little else needed other than a squeeze of lemon.

Harengs – herrings, often in a cream sauce.

Homard – lobster.

Huîtres – oysters.

Langouste – lobster or crayfish.

Lotte – monk fish.

Loup – sea bass.

Maquereau – mackerel.

Merlan – whiting, commonly encountered with a cream or other sauce.

Mérou – brill.

Morue – salt cod.

Moules – mussels, cultivated in farms along the coast and, though smaller, are more tasty than their Atlantic cousins.

Mullet – grey mullet.

Omble-chevalier – char.

Palourdes – clams.

Poulpe – octopus, not as commonly encountered as in the eastern Mediterranean, but good when it is on offer.

Raie – skate, often served with a cream sauce or with *beurre noir*, black butter.

Rouget – red mullet, tasty but bony.

St-Pierre – John Dory.

Saumon – salmon, invariably imported.

Thon – tunny, firm flesh delicious grilled.

Truite – trout, usually farmed inland.

DANGEROUS MARINE ANIMALS

In the Mediterranean there are no more dangerous marine animals than you would encounter off the British coast, but the warm sea temperatures mean you are in the water more often and therefore more likely to encounter them.

Sharks Probably the greatest fear of a swimmer yet in all probability the least to be feared. Films such as

Jaws and *Blue Water, White Death* have produced a phobia amongst swimmers that is out of all proportion to the menace. After thirteen years of sailing around the Mediterranean I have positively identified a shark in the water on only a few occasions. Fishermen occasionally bring in sharks from the deep water, usually the mackerel shark or sand sharks. Compared to the waters in the Caribbean, around Australia and New Zealand, and in the Red Sea, the Mediterranean has a very low incidence of shark attacks. The last publicised attack, in the Bay of Naples in 1989, turned out to be a life insurance job. As far as I know there are no recorded shark attacks along the French Mediterranean coast and the total number of verified attacks for the Mediterranean as a whole is less than 20 in this century.

Moray eels Of the family *Muraenidae*, these eels are quite common in the Mediterranean and are often caught by fishermen. They inhabit holes and crevices and can bite and tear if molested. Usually they retire and are not aggressive unless wounded or sorely provoked.

Octopuses Are very shy and do not attack. They have much more to fear from man than man from them.

Stingrays The European stingray (*Dasyatis pastinaca*) is common in the Mediterranean. It inhabits shallow waters partially burying itself in the sand. If it is trodden on accidentally it will lash out with its tail and bury a spine in the offending foot. Venom is injected which produces severe local pain, sweating, vomiting and rapid heart beat, but rarely death. Soak the foot in very hot water and seek medical help.

Weeverfish Members of the family *Trachinidae*. The two most common are the Great Weever (*Trachinus draco*) and Lesser Weever (*Trachinus vipera*). The dorsal and opercular spines contain venom spines. When disturbed or annoyed the weever will erect its dorsal fin and attack. The venom injected produces instant pain which spreads to other parts of the body and is very painful. The victim may lose consciousness and death sometimes occurs. There are no known antidotes. Bathe the wound in very hot water and seek medical help as soon as possible. You are most likely to come across the weever in the fish market as it is considered an essential ingredient of *bouillabaisse*.

Note When walking in water where stingrays or weevers are thought to be, wear an old pair of plimsolls and shuffle along the bottom. Do not handle dead weevers or stingrays.

Jellyfish Of all the animals described the ones you are most likely to encounter are jellyfish. At certain times of the year and in certain places there will be considerable numbers of jellyfish in the water. All jellyfish sting for this is the way they immobilise their prey, but some species have more powerful stings than others and consequently deserve greater respect.

Aurelia aurita The common jellyfish. It has a transparent dome-shaped body with four purple-violet crescents grouped around the centre. Transparent or light violet mouth arms hang below. Up to

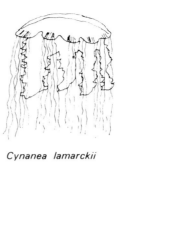

Cynanea lamarckii

Aurelia aurita

Pelagia noctiluca

25cm in diameter. A light contact with the stings is something like a stinging nettle, but prolonged contact can hurt.

Pelagia noctiluca A mushroom-shaped jellyfish up to 10cm in diameter. It is easily identified being light brown-yellow in colour and covered in 'warts'. It has long trailing tentacles and can inflict severe and painful stings.

Cyanea lamarckii A blue-violet saucer-shaped jellyfish up to 30cm in diameter. It can be identified by the frilly mass of mouth arms underneath. It has long tentacles which can inflict severe and painful stings. There is a brown variety (*Cyanea capillata*) which can grow up to 50cm in diameter.

Charybdea marsupialis Mediterranean sea-wasp. A transparent yellow-red box-shaped 'umbrella' up to 6cm long. Rarely seen but can inflict severe and painful stings.

Physalia physalis Portuguese man-of-war. Has a large conspicuous purple-red float (pneumatophore) above water growing to 30cm long and 10cm wide. Below it stream very long tentacles. Rarely seen but can inflict dangerous stings.

Rhizostoma pulmo Dome-shaped blue-white jellyfish up to 90cm in diameter. Its mouth and arms are fused in a grey-green 'cauliflower' mass below the body. It has no long tentacles and is not known as a vicious stinger.

There are no known antidotes to jellyfish stings, but there are a number of ways of obtaining relief. Antihistamine creams have proved useful in some, but not all, cases. Check with your doctor to see if you should use antihistamines. Dilute ammonium hydroxide, sodium bicarbonate, olive oil, sugar, and ethyl alcohol have all been used. In general use a weak alkali. A tip which I have not tried but which sounds promising is to use a meat tenderiser which apparently breaks down the protein base of the venom. Gloves should be worn when hauling up an anchor in jellyfish-infested water as the tentacles, especially those of *Pelagia*, can stick to the anchor chain.

Bristle worms In some locations numbers of bristle worms, probably of the family *Nereidae*, will be found. They are black and may grow up to 25cm long. The setae can produce a mild irritation similar to a stinging nettle if touched.

Sea urchins In some places on rocky coasts large colonies of sea urchins (*Paracentrotus lividus* and *Arbacia lixula*) will be found. While they do not have a venom apparatus, the spines penetrate and break off when the urchin is trodden on and are very painful. Wear plimsolls. Care must be taken not to get a secondary infection after the spines have been dug out.

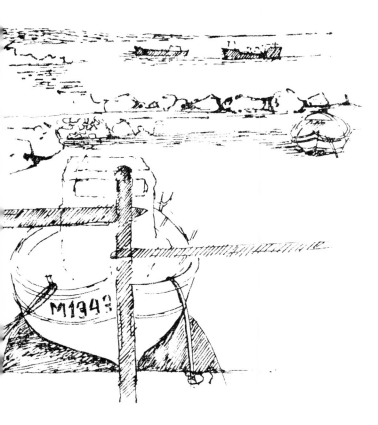

POLLUTION

The Mediterranean is a closed sea supporting a large population around its shores. About 120 million people live on the coastal region and this number multiplies considerably in the summer with the arrival of large numbers of tourists. The Mediterranean has a small tidal difference with about half the water coming from the Atlantic Ocean over the ledge at the Strait of Gibraltar – about one million cubic metres every second.

With most of the sewerage from the coastal population being pumped into the sea untreated, with tankers and oil installations causing hydrocarbon pollution, and with industrial waste being discharged directly into rivers and ultimately the sea, there has been considerable pollution of the waters in the western Mediterranean. The French, unfortunately, have lagged behind many other European countries in becoming environmentally conscious, but of late have established restricted zones along the coast where anchoring and fishing are prohibited, to allow marine life to return to normal, or at least to recover somewhat from the onslaught of pollution. Some controls are in place to restrict the dumping of industrial waste into the rivers and sea, and sewerage systems are being upgraded. Much more is still required.

Until recently nothing or little was being done about the increasing pollution in the Mediterranean. In 1975 a United Nations Environment committee decided to get together the culturally and politically diverse countries around the Mediterranean and work out a programme to clean up the sea. In 1980 all the countries (except xenophobic Albania) agreed to a programme. EC directives have also pushed authorities to clean up beaches and sewerage outlets to standards laid down by an EC committee (except for Britain which has some of the worst polluted beaches in the European community), though much more still needs to be done.

Some of the anti-pollution measures may affect the yachtsman. No thinking yachtsman should throw garbage into the sea, including organic rubbish, and especially not plastic. All of the marinas and harbours have garbage disposal bins and rubbish belongs here. Yachtsmen can be fined for dumping oil into a harbour or along the coast and again many of the marinas have special bins for waste oil. In the future it is possible that holding tanks will have to be fitted to private yachts. All harbours have toilets and showers and these should be used rather than the toilet or shower on board. The yachtsman may curse the extra cost and trouble involved with these regulations, but must acknowledge the necessity of such regulations when so much of the Mediterranean, and for that matter, the other seas and oceans of the world, are threatened by pollution of all types. More power to Greenpeace, Friends of the Earth, and anybody who picks up garbage carelessly discarded by users of the Mediterranean.

History

The following is a brief synoptic history relating to the south of France so you can put events and people into some sort of historical perspective. For more of an overview of French and European history John Bowle's *A History of Europe* is good, and on the 20th century Theodore Zeldin's *The French* is excellent. For more detail you will have to turn to some more scholarly works and wade your way through them.

BC
- *1000* The Ligurians occupy the coastal region and penetrate inland.
- *600* The Phocaean Greeks, from Phocaea (now Eski Foça) in Asia Minor, found Massalia, now Marseille. They are assumed to have introduced viniculture and the olive, though these may have already been introduced by the Phoenicians earlier. They expand and found other colonies along the coast and appear to have traded with the Ligurians.
- *540* The Carthaginians, a Phoenician colony, capture Massalia and hold it for 60 years.
- *5–4th century* Trading posts set up by the Phocaeans at Hyères, St-Tropez, Antibes, and Nice. Celts arrive from the north and war on and off against the Phocaeans.
- *340* Pytheas, a Phocaean navigator is believed to have sailed as far as England in search of amber and tin.
- *218* Hannibal, with elephants, crosses the Rhône and the Alps in his back-door attack on Rome.
- *125* Massalia asks Rome for help against the Celts.
- *122* The Romans defeat the Celts and found Aix-en-Provence.
- *102* Marius defeats the Teutons at Aix-en-Provence.
- *58–51* Julius Caesar completes his conquest of Gaul.
- *49* Julius Caesar sacks Massalia for siding with Pompey in the Civil War and founds Fréjus. Arles becomes an important centre.
- *10* Numerous Roman colonies are established and strengthened under the rule of Augustus. The coast is generally a prosperous area.

AD
- *1–3rd century* Roman civilisation spreads all along the coast. The Aurelian Way from Ventimiglia to Arles is the country's main land thoroughfare. Cities like Nîmes and Arles are rich and powerful.
- *313* Constantine grants the Christians freedom of worship and churches are established around the coast.
- *3–4th century* Christianity takes a firm hold along the coast and inland and many of the famous bishoprics and monasteries are established.

- *476* Fall of the Roman Empire.
- *5–6th century* Vandals, Alamans, Visigoths, Ostrogoths, and the Franks invade the south of France. Many of the cities are looted and burnt.
- *494* Clovis, King of the Franks, defeats the Alamans.
- *520* Arles made capital of Provence.
- *574* Saxon invasion.
- *7–9th century* Saracen and Moorish invasions all along the coast. Many of the communities retreat inland or build fortified towns.
- *800* Charlemagne crowned Emperor of the Holy Roman Empire.
- *843* Charlemagne's empire is divided between the three sons of Louis the Debonair. Provence is given to Lothaire, one of Charlemagne's grandsons.
- *855* Provence is made a kingdom by Lothaire for his son Charles.
- *859* Normans enter the Camargue.
- *884* The Saracens capture the region around the Maures *massif* and terrorise the adjacent coast.
- *10th century* Provence, after being shuffled around from hand to hand, becomes part of the Holy Roman Empire, but many towns retain their autonomy. Many of the coastal towns prosper and expand.
- *12th century* Provence passes to the Counts of Toulouse and then to the Counts of Barcelona. Aix-en-Provence is made the capital.
- *1246* Charles of Anjou becomes Count of Provence by marriage.
- *1248* St Louis leaves from Aigues-Mortes on the 7th Crusade.
- *1270* St Louis dies in Tunisia at the beginning of the 8th Crusade.
- *1308* Monaco bought by the Grimaldi family.
- *1309–1403* The popes and anti-popes at Avignon and the great divide of the west.
- *1337* Hundred Years' War starts, ends in 1453.
- *1343* Queen Jeanne becomes Countess of Provence.
- *1348* First great plague in the south of France.
- *1388* Count of Savoy acquires Nice and the surrounding territory.
- *1419* Nice officially ceded to the Count of Savoy.
- *1434* René of Anjou becomes Count of Provence. He is later known as Good King René and Provence enjoys a golden age.
- *1481* Provence becomes part of the Kingdom of France.
- *1501* Parliament is established at Aix-en-Provence.
- *1524–36* Provence invaded by Charles V, Holy Roman Emperor.
- *1543* Nice attacked by French and Turkish troops.

Marseille in the 15th century from
an old engraving.

- *1555* Nostradamus publishes his astrological predictions.
- *1560–98* Wars of Religion, end in 1598 with the Edict of Nantes allowing Protestants freedom of worship.
- *1610* Henri IV assassinated. He is succeeded by Louis XIII.
- *1629* Richelieu dismantles forts and castles in the south.
- *1643–1715* Reign of Louis XIV.
- *1685* The Edict of Nantes is revoked and Protestantism is outlawed. Three and a half million Huguenots flee to Protestant countries.
- *1691* Nice taken by the French.
- *1696* Nice returned to the Dukes of Savoy.
- *1707* Eugene of Savoy invades the south of France.
- *1720* Plague again spreads throughout the south of France.
- *1746* The Austro-Sardinian offensive is stopped at Antibes.
- *1787* Edict of Tolerance ends the persecution of Protestants.
- *1789* The French Revolution.
- *1792* The Marseille volunteers march to Paris singing the *Marseillaise*.
- *1793* Execution of Louis XVI on the 21st of January. Nice is reunited to France.
- *1799* Bonaparte lands at St-Raphaël on his return from Egypt.
- *1804* Napoléon crowned emperor.
- *1814* Abdication of Napoléon and exile on Elba.
- *1815* Napoléon lands at Golfe Juan on the 1st of March on his return from Elba. Battle of Waterloo on 18th June.
- *1830* Louis-Philippe accedes to the throne.
- *1852–70* Reign of Napoléon III.
- *1860* Nice restored to France.
- *1878* Monte-Carlo casino opens at Monaco.
- *1880* Phylloxera destroys many of the vines in France.
- *1940* Italians invade Menton.
- *1942* Germans invade Vichy France. The French Navy is scuttled in Toulon.
- *1944* Allied forces land on the coast. France liberated.
- *1970* Charles de Gaulle dies.
- *1989* Bicentenary of the French Revolution.

Technical introduction

Weather forecasts

At all of the marinas and most of the harbours a weather forecast is posted daily and in many, twice daily. In some marinas the weather forecast will be in English as well as French, but even if it is only in French it is easily understood. Often a map indicating wind strengths and the sea state over the local area will accompany the written forecast. In an increasing number of marinas the new *Antiope* video-text system is installed. General and local forecasts are continually updated and you can stop the information scrolling if you want to take your time looking at something. Weather forecasts are transmitted as follows:

France-Inter On 1829 kHz (164m) at 0645 and 2005 local time for all areas.

Marseille 1906 kHz (154m) at 0103, 0705, 1220 and 1615 UT.

Grasse 2649 kHz (113m) and 3722 kHz (81m) at 0733, 1233 and 1645 UT.

Monaco 4363·6, 8728·2, 8743·7, 13172·1, 17251·5, 22651·8 kHz at 0903, 1403, 1815, 0715 and 1715 in French and English.

Local radio

Nice-Radio France Côte d'Azur (FM) 103·8, 101·4 and 92·6 MHz at 0730/0830, 1000/1100, 1330/1400, 1500/1530, 1815/1830 local time.

Radio France-Marseille 96·7 and 103·1 MHz at 0715 for Grau-du-Roi to Ciotat and 1045 for Port Camargue to St-Raphaël local time.

Radio France-Roussillon 92·1 MHz at 0700.

Radio France Hérault-Montpellier 95·2 MHz and FM 101·2, 102 and 103·8 at 0845 Monday to Friday and 0755 on the weekends local time for Narbonne-Plage to Port Camargue.

Radio Riviera, an English language radio broadcasting on FM 104·1 and 106·5 which has a weather forecast for the land and sea at 0830 and 2030 local time. In addition it receives BBC World Service news via satellite on the hour.

VHF

Marseille Radio Perpignan channel 2
Sète channel 19
Martigues channel 28
Marseille channel 26
Toulon channel 62
Grasse Radio Cavalaire channel 4
Grasse channel 2
Bastia channel 24

Porto-Vecchio channel 25

Ajaccio (relay) channel 24 at 0733 and 1233 local time.

Radio Monaco transmits recorded weather forecasts in French and English for the coast between St-Raphaël and St-Remo continuously for 24 hours a day on VHF channel 23.

In addition to all these sources, the most comprehensive in the Mediterranean, there are also weather forecasts after the news on television on all six channels, around 2015 to 2045 in the evening, and weather forecasts in the local papers. In addition there are local telephone numbers, usually featured in the marinas and harbours, where you can ring the local meteorological service for a forecast, usually on tape.

At a number of harbours a light system operating in daylight hours signals strong winds. In normal conditions the lights are visible for 5 miles. The light characteristics are as follows:

- *LFl.8s* Winds of force 6 or greater forecast in the next 6 hours.
- *Fl* Local winds of force 6 or greater forecast in the next 3 hours.

At present the light signals for strong winds operate at the following harbours:

St-Cyprien-Plage
Canet-Plage
La Grande Motte
Pomègues (Ile du Frioul near Marseille)
Hyères-Plage
Bormes-les-Mimosas
La Garoupe lighthouse (Cap d'Antibes)

GLOSSARY OF METEOROLOGICAL TERMS

French	English
accalmie	lull
agité	moderate
amélioration	improvement
anticyclone	anticyclone
augmentation	increasing
averse	shower
avis	warning
avis de coup de vent	gale warning
basse pression	low pressure
beau	fine
belle (mer)	calm
brise	breeze
brise de mer	sea breeze
brouillard	fog
brume	mist

French	English
calme	calm
clair	fair
coup de vent	gale
courant	current
couvert	overcast
dépression	depression
direction	direction
en baisse	falling
en hausse	rising
éclaircie	bright interval
en formation	building
état de la mer	sea state
force du vent	wind force
fort	strong
forte	rough
fort coup de vent	strong gale
frais	fresh
fréquent	frequent
front	front
front chaud	warm front
front froid	cold front
grain	squall
grand frais	near gale
houle	swell
instable	unstable
léger	light
mauvais temps	bad weather
mer	sea
modéré	moderate
noeuds	knots
nuage	cloud
nuageux	cloudy
orage	thunderstorm
ouragan	hurricane
perturbation	disturbance
pluie	rain
pression	pressure
prévision	forecast
probabilité	probability
rafale	gust
région	area
situation générale	overall situation
stationnaire	stationary
tempête	storm
variable	variable
vent frais	strong breeze
zone	area
zone de haute pression	high pressure area

Coast radio stations

Marseille radio *Transmits* on 1906, 1939, 2182, 2628, 3722, 3795 kHz. *Receives* on 1988, 2009, 2049, 2083, 2153, 2160, 2182, 2321, 2449, 2477, 2506, 3168 kHz. *VHF* Ch 16, 24, 26, 01, 81, 62.

Grasse radio *Transmits* on 1834, 2182, 2649, 3722 kHz. *Receives* on 1988, 2009, 2023, 2049, 2056, 2153, 2167, 2182, 2286, 2321, 2449, 2477, 3168 kHz. *VHF* Ch 16, 2, 4, 5.

Monaco radio *Transmits* on 4363·6, 8728·2, 8743·7, 13172·1, 13141·2, 17251·5, 17267, 22651·8 kHz. *Receives* on 4125, 4100·2, 8257, 4069·2, 12392, 8204·3, 16522, 8219·3, 22062, 12401·3, 16478·6, 22055·8 kHz. *VHF* Ch 16, 28, 86.

CORSICA

Ajaccio VHF Ch 16, 24.
Bastia VHF Ch 16, 24.
Porto-Vecchio VHF Ch 16, 25.
Bonifacio VHF Ch 18.
Propriano VHF Ch 64.

Radiobeacons

MARINE BEACONS

West Mediterranean group 313·5 kHz
Cap Bon (Tunisia) *BN* 200M 37°04′N 11°03′E Seq. 1, 2.
Rax Caxine (Algeria) *CX* 200M 36°49′N 2°57′E Seq. 3, 4.
Porquerolles *PQ* 200M 42°59′N 6°12′E Seq. 5, 6.

South France group 287·3 kHz
Cap Béar *BR* 50M 42°31′N 3°08′E Seq. 1, 2.
Sète *SÉ* 50M 43°24′N 3°41′E Seq. 3, 4.
Ile du Planier *PN* 100M 43°12′N 5°14′E Seq. 5, 6.

West Corsica group 294·2 kHz
Pte de Sénétose *SNE* 100M 41°33′·5N 8°48′E Seq. 1, 2.
La Revellata *RV* 100M 42°35′N 8°44′E Seq. 3, 4.
La Garoupe *GO* 100M 43°34′N 7°08′E Seq. 5, 6.

East Corsica group 308 kHz
Ile de la Giraglia *GL* 100M 43°02′N 9°24′E Seq. 1, 2.
Pta di a Chiappa *CP* 100M 41°36′N 9°22′E Seq. 3, 4.

Other stations
Cap Couronne *CR* 305·7 kHz 50M 43°19′·58N 5°03′·25E.

AEROBEACONS

Istres *ITR* 390·5 kHz 43°31′·58N 4°55′·82E
Hyères *HYE* 322 kHz 70M 43°43′N 7°19′·3E.
Nice Mont Leuza *LEZ* 398·5 kHz 75M 43°43′·7N 7°20′·17E
Ajaccio Campo del'Oro *IS* 341 kHz 50M 41°53′·9N 8°36′·8E

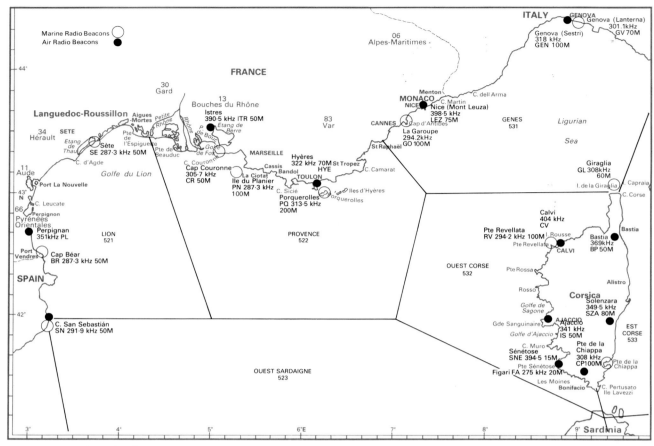

Radiobeacons and weather forecast areas.

Sénétose *SNE* 394·5 kHz 15M 41°33′·5N 8°47′·9E
Solenzara *SZA* 349·5 kHz 80M 41°55′·9N 9°23′·8E
Figari *FA* 275 kHz 20M 41°29′·9N 9°05′E
Bastia Poretta *BP* 369 kHz 50M 42°25′·7N 9°32′·2E
Calvi *CV* 404 kHz 42°34′·67N 8°48′·47E

Climate and weather

At the beginning of each chapter there is a description of the weather patterns for that stretch of coast. Here I will confine myself to general remarks.

WIND STRENGTH

All wind strengths in the text are described as a force on the Beaufort scale. To get the wind speed in knots from its force, multiply the force by 5 and then subtract 5 (up to force 8). See Appendix IV for a complete Beaufort scale of wind strength.

WINDS

It is convenient to divide up the coast at Toulon and talk about winds to the west and east of it.

To the W of Toulon the prevailing winds, summer and winter, are from the NW. Most gale force winds are also from the NW. Two winds dominate along this bit of coast. The *tramontane* blows from the Pyrénées as far as Sète. A *tramontane* is caused when a depression passes across the middle of France and the air bottled up over the land escapes through the gap between the Pyrénées and the Massif Central. The wind is funnelled down through the gap, known as the Toulouse gap, and escapes into the Mediterranean along the Languedoc-Roussillon coast. The other wind, the notorious *mistral*, blows when a depression passes over central France and the cold air over the land is blocked by the Alps and escapes along the Rhône valley. It blows out of the mouth of the Rhône with great force and over the coast as far as Toulon, although very strong *mistrals* can blow out over the coast as far as St-Tropez, Cannes, and even Nice.

The *mistral* has a notoriety that has been commented upon from early times. The Greek geographer Strabo said of it that it was 'an impetuous and terrible wind which displaces rocks, hurls men from their chariots, breaks their limbs and strips them of their clothes and weapons.' In 1786 Arthur Young in his *Travels in France* recorded that in January 'there was a mistral so furious, accompanied by so much snow, that flocks were carried four or five leagues

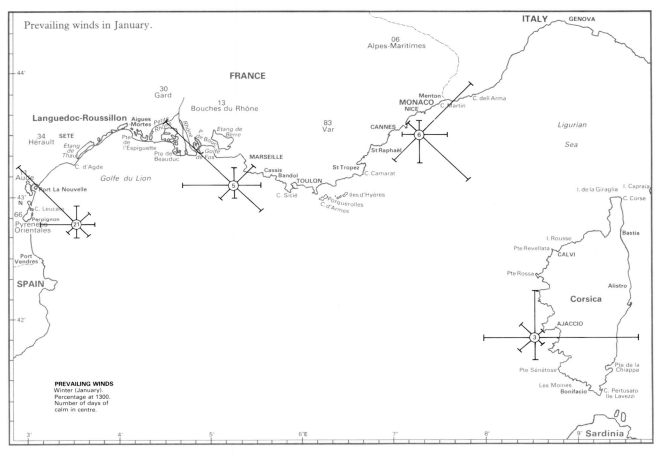

Prevailing winds in January.

PREVAILING WINDS
Winter (January).
Percentage at 1300.
Number of days of
calm in centre.

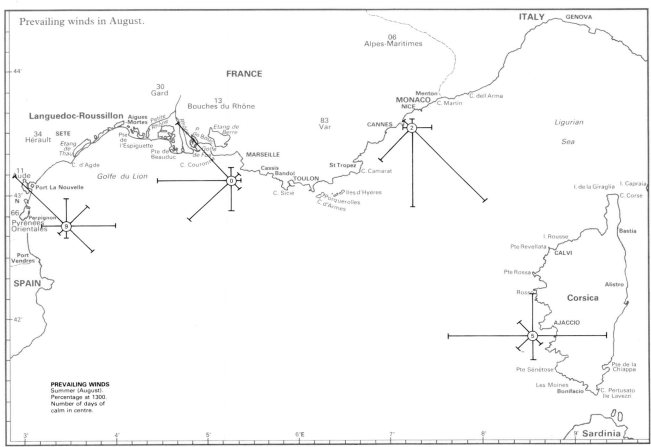

Prevailing winds in August.

PREVAILING WINDS
Summer (August).
Percentage at 1300.
Number of days of
calm in centre.

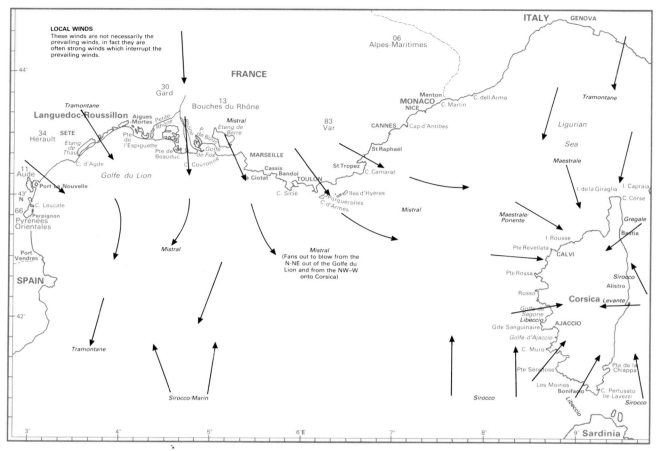

Local winds.

from their pasturages. Five shepherds were taking eight hundred beasts to Marseille; three of them and nearly all the sheep perished.' Another later tale relates how an unmanned locomotive was blown backwards from Arles to Marseille.

Although the *mistral* attracts the most comment, the *tramontane* is just as frequent and can be as fierce. It should not be underestimated. Local lore has it that the *mistral* and *tramontane* blow for multiples of 3 days. Though it commonly does blow for 3 or 6 days, it is just as likely to blow for anything from 1 day to 12 days. The *mistral* is usually preceded by long cigar-shaped clouds, though when it is blowing it is brilliantly clear with an almost electric atmosphere. It normally arrives in the early morning, at around 0500 hours in the summer. Local lore states that in the preceding evening the sunset will be very red, with long thin clouds at first red, becoming grey – the more quickly they turn grey, the stronger the mistral will be.

In the summer a full blown *mistral* or *tramontane* is rare. In spring and autumn the frequency increases, and in winter over 13% of all wind observations are of gale force winds, mostly from the NW. However in the summer what is called a local *tramontane* or *mistral* will often blow off the coast at around force 5–6, though its effect rarely penetrates more than 10 miles out to sea. The local *mistral* is strongest around the Rhône delta along to Marseille. Unlike a *mistral* proper it usually dies down in the late evening.

When winds from the NW are not blowing in the summer, there will normally be a SE–S sea breeze, the *marin*. The *marin* can get up to force 5–6, though usually it blows around force 4. Though it is well under gale strength, it can push quite a swell onto the coast. It dies down in the evening.

Apart from gales from the NW, there are also some southerly gales, mostly in the winter. These can cause a considerable swell to set onto the coast, especially difficult around the comparatively shallow water off the coast in the Golfe du Lion. Harbours here with south-facing entrances, of which there are many, can be dangerous to enter in these southerly gales.

To the east of Toulon the effects of the *mistral* are much moderated. There can be a gale force *mistral* at Marseille while at Nice there is a near calm. The normal summer wind here, especially east of St-Tropez, is a S–SE–E sea breeze that gets up around midday and dies down in the evening. It rarely blows more than force 4. On other occasions a NW–W wind will blow, though again rarely more than force 4–5. On the whole there are more days of calm along this coast than to the west of Toulon.

For winds around Corsica see the introduction to Chapter VI.

Local names for the winds

Bise Cold, dry northeasterly in the Languedoc-Roussillon region.

Libeccio West or southwesterly around the Corsican coast.

Maestrale Northerlies, not commonly used.

Marin Southerly sea breeze or other southerlies.

Mistral Cold, dry strong wind off the Rhône delta extending as far as the Balearics and Corsica.

Ponant A westerly blowing off the Côte d'Azur, commonly from midday to dusk.

Tramontane The strong NW–N wind blowing out of the Toulouse gap into the Golfe du Lion.

Vent d'Est The 'wind of the rain'. Preceded by heavy grey skies, the rain comes with the wind which can raise heavy seas on the coast.

DEPRESSIONS

The Golfe du Lion has the highest mean annual percentage of gales in the Mediterranean at 6·8%. Compare this to the Tyrrhenian Sea at 1·8%, the Ionian Sea at 4·5% and Corsica at 2·5–3%. Most of the gales in the Golfe du Lion occur in the winter, with just 1·3% in the summer. Close to 90% of the gales are from the N–NW (*tramontane* and *mistral*), though in my experience there seems to be a larger percentage of southerly gales than the 10% remaining allows.

Depressions enter the sea area off the south coast through the Toulouse gap, via the Strait of Gibraltar, and off the North African coast. The Golfe du Lion is an area where depressions are known to intensify before moving off. Depressions also intensify in the Ligurian to the east of the French Riviera. The figures speak for themselves and the lessons should be clear. The Golfe du Lion is an area which merits much respect and weather forecasts should be assiduously monitored before and during a crossing of the gulf.

THUNDERSTORMS

These are most frequent in spring and autumn. They are usually accompanied by a squall which can be very strong at times, but seldom last for more than an hour or two.

FOG AND VISIBILITY

Visibility is generally very good. Fog off the French coast is reported as highest in May at 5%. For all the other months it is less than 2%. In some areas where there is a concentration of industry, especially around the Golfe de Fos and Golfe de Marseille, smoke and emissions from industry can reduce visibility on windless days.

HUMIDITY

Humidity is on average moderate. To some extent it depends on wind strength and frequency. With a *mistral* for instance, humidity is low.

SEA

Sea temperature

Sea temperatures are lowest in January at around 12°C and highest in August at around 21°–24°C.

Swell

With strong southerlies, SW–SE, a heavy swell sets all along this coast. The swell is generally larger and lasts longer in the Golfe du Lion than it is east of Toulon.

Currents

In the winter there is a predictable WSW current along the coast. In the summer this current is appreciably weaker and can be stopped by the prevailing offshore winds. The current tends to cross the mouth of the Golfe du Lion and to pull a counter-current around the coast. While the current around the coast E of Toulon rarely exceeds 1 knot, currents in the Golfe du Lion can be accelerated by onshore winds up to 2 knots. This current is W-going off the Rhône, but has turned to the S and SE between Sète and Cap Creux.

Tides

In this area tidal heights are everywhere less than 0·3 metres (1ft) at springs. The tidal difference can be cancelled by strong contrary winds and for all intents and purposes tidal differences can be ignored.

Sea level

Differences in sea level can be caused by constant strong winds. Northerlies decrease the sea level and southerlies increase the sea level along the coast.

NAVIGATION

Buoyage

The IALA Buoyage System 'A' was introduced in 1980 and is well developed and consistent.

Lights

The coast is well lit and the lights are well maintained. A yacht will have no difficulty navigating along the coast at night although harbour lights will often be obscured by the bright lights of a town.

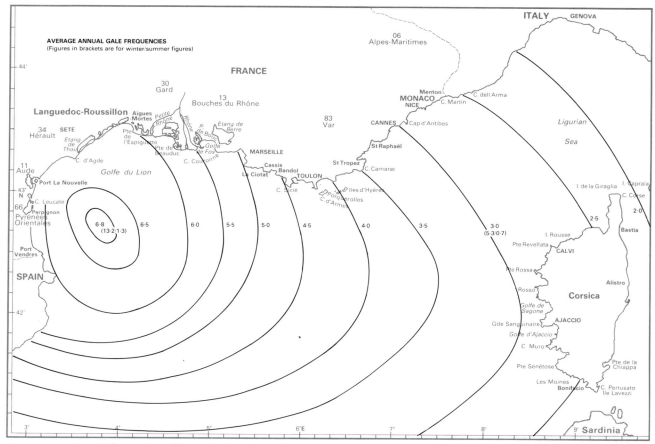

Average annual gale frequencies. Figures in brackets refer to winter and summer frequencies.

About the plans and pilotage notes

Nomenclature

For the most part I have used the French names and terms for all the places mentioned in this book. Many of the French words are similar to the English words and there should be no confusion for instance between Golfe de St-Tropez and the Gulf of St-Tropez or Port de Cannes and Port of Cannes. In Appendix III, in the glossary of useful words, there is a section on French words and terms used on charts which can be referred to if there are difficulties.

Abbreviations

In the pilotage notes all compass directions are abbreviated to the first letter in capitals, as is common practice. So N is north, SE is southeast, etc.

Harbour plans

The harbour plans are designed to illustrate the accompanying notes. It is stressed that many of these plans are based on the author's sketches and therefore should only be used in conjunction with official charts. They are not to be used for navigation. The author welcomes any corrections to the plans and pilotage information, which can be sent to the publishers. It is inevitable that I have overlooked things or made mistakes, though not, I hope, any major mistakes, and any help to make this book more accurate will be gratefully received.

Soundings

All soundings are in metres. I have checked all soundings where possible and in some cases may be over-cautious in defining shallow areas. With care you may be able to squeeze into places where slightly less depths are shown. It should also be remembered that some harbours are prone to silting, though most of these are dredged at fairly regular intervals.

For those used to working in fathoms and feet, the use of metres may prove difficult at first and there is the danger of reading the depth in metres as the depth in fathoms. For all practical purposes one metre can be read as approximately three feet and therefore two metres is approximately equal to one fathom. See Appendix V for comprehensive conversion tables.

Photographs

Most of the photographs were taken by the author. At the end of the year I drove along the coast of Mediterranean France to take other photographs to supplement those taken while sailing along the coast and, as it turns out, the majority of these photographs have been used. In the summer photographs taken from seaward are invariably fogged by the heat haze common in the day. When a *mistral* cleared the air I was safely tucked up in harbour and wasn't venturing out to take photographs in the good visibility it brings. Because the harbours along the coast are clustered closely together, photographs to help pilotage along the coast are not as necessary as in other countries around the Mediterranean, so I have used many of the photographs to give a 'flavour' of a place or stretch of coast. Around Corsica where the pilotage is more demanding I have used a larger percentage of photographs taken from seaward to help navigation – though the reader may moan that there are too many photographs showing yet another conspicuous Genoese tower.

Bearings

All bearings are in 360° notation and are true.

Key to symbols used on the plans

⚓   anchorage
   anchoring prohibited
   harbourmaster (*capitainerie*)
   fuel
   water
   showers
▶   yacht club

St-Jean-Cap Ferrat. Wooden eccentricity amongst all the
plastic. *Below* St-Jean-Cap Ferrat looking across to the
Alpes-Maritimes. *Opposite* The Esterel looking across from
Cannes.

Local produce in the markets is a delight – always fresh, varied, and not at all expensive. *Opposite* Autumn *étang*-scape on the Canal du Rhône à Sète. *Below* A strong *mistral* on the Etang de Berre – remember a photograph conveys little of the violence of the wind and sea.

I. Southern inland waterways

*CANAL DU MIDI FROM PORT LA ROBINE
  TO LES ONGLOUS
LA NOUVELLE BRANCH CANAL
ETANG DE THAU
CANAL DU RHONE A SETE*

*BEAUCAIRE BRANCH CANAL
PETIT RHONE
THE RHONE FROM ARLES TO PORT ST-
  LOUIS DU RHONE*

For many people France's inland waterways are looked at as a through route between northern Europe and the Mediterranean, a route that bypasses the Atlantic and particularly the perils of the Bay of Biscay. For dedicated brown-water cruisers the French inland waterways are an end in themselves, not a through route, but a system of interlinked routes of a huge arterial cruising ground. On several occasions I have used the French waterways to get down to the Mediterranean and each time I promised myself that I would spend a little longer looking around when I could. This time I could and pottered around the southern waterways described in this chapter. For craft within the restrictions on draught, air height, and beam, these waterways provide an interesting inland diversion from the sea, a spring or autumn mini-cruise. There is something inestimably pleasurable about gliding through the countryside on the water, puttering through towns and villages while cars sit at traffic lights or frenetically jump the amber light, mooring in the heart of villages or towns or at waterside restaurants, idly watching the wildlife in the jungle-like Camargue; in all an intimate sort of relationship with the interior that cruising on the sea, whatever its many and varied pleasures, rarely gives.

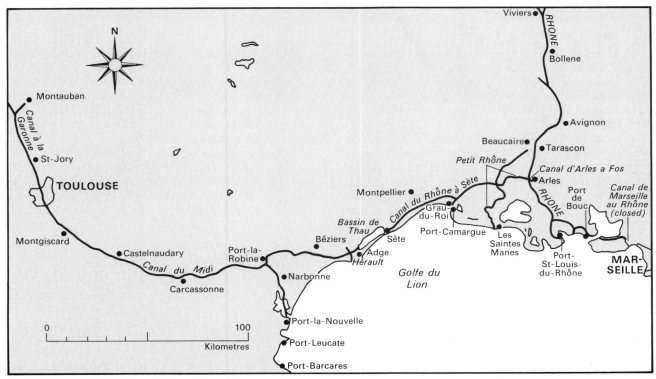

Southern inland waterways

One of the lowest bridges on the Canal du Midi immediately before Capestang. If you can fit through here you can fit under all of the bridges on the canal.

RESTRICTIONS ON CRAFT

The restrictions on draught, air height, beam and length effectively determine what sort of craft can use the waterways. The restriction on length is determined by the length of the locks and since most of them will take craft up to 30 metres long and the new European-standards locks can take craft up to 38 metres, it is the restrictions on draught, beam, and air height that matter. The maximum draught varies from 1·6 metres in the Canal du Midi to a minimum maintained depth of 3 metres in the Rhône. Air height also restricts craft that use the waterways, particularly the Canal du Midi. Here the old arched bridges have a maximum height in the middle of 3·3 metres, but only 2·4 metres at the edges. This means, for example, that motor cruisers with high wheelhouses may not fit through. The maximum beam, like length, is determined by the width of the locks. The smallest width is 5·5 metres in the locks on the Canal du Midi and this will only restrict some multihulls as air height and draught are likely to be the limiting factors for most other craft. The particular dimensions for the different waterways in this chapter will be found at the beginning of the section describing them.

Yachts using the waterways can raise or lower their masts at Port La Nouvelle, Agde, Sète, and Port St-Louis du Rhône. Most yachts based in the Mediterranean will not bother to raise or lower a mast just for a spring or autumn mini-cruise, but there are many motor-sailers and smaller yachts where raising or lowering a mast in a tabernacle is not a big deal and these craft can slip into the waterways for a few weeks or more without any trouble. Motor cruisers will have to check on air height, particularly in the Canal du Midi, considerations of draught and beam usually being secondary to the restrictions imposed by the height of the old bridges over the waterways.

HIRE BOATS

There are various boat hire firms dotted around the waterways. Most of these hire boats have been constructed with the waterways in mind, some with more aesthetic considerations than others, and normally come in anything from four berth up to ten berth size. As with all charter boats, the number of berths is not necessarily a good indication of the number of people who will comfortably fit for a holiday afloat. In addition to hire boats, there are several hotel boats operating on the southern waterways, converted *péniches* with comfortable accommodation and on-board cuisine, where you leave the skipper and crew to do the work while you relax and watch the countryside glide by.

Details of the various boat hire companies and their craft can be obtained from the French Government Tourist Office or perhaps more profitably from one of the monthly magazines devoted to inland waterways.

MOORING

Apart from the areas indicated for mooring on the plans or in the text, it is possible to moor alongside the bank where convenient as long as you do not obstruct passage along the canal or there is not a prohibition on mooring by the canal authorities. It is prohibited to stay overnight in locks. When mooring alongside the bank, the condition of the bank or wall and the depth of water at the edge of the waterway will of course determine whether it is possible or not.

The new water-slope at Fonserannes that now replaces the lock staircase. Efficient and technologically intriguing, it has considerably simplified the steep descent down to Béziers – or the ascent from Béziers if you are coming from the opposite direction.

Often there will be rubble from a collapsed wall or sticky mud composed of earth and organic matter that has been washed into the canal over the years so some care must taken when approaching the bank. Do it all delicately and if you can't get alongside at one spot try a little further along the bank. One thing to watch for is being dumped on the bottom when large craft pass and suck the water away from the bank – if there is rubble on the bottom the boat can be damaged if it gets dropped onto it.

LOCKS

Locks are either manned or automated. Although care is needed in the locks there is no trauma attached to passage through them and you will become quite blasé about it all after the first two or three.

On the old manned locks like those on the Canal du Midi the lock-keeper operates the lock, though it is normal to give him or her a hand. When ascending put someone ashore before the lock to take the lines from the boat. According to the inclination of the lock-keeper, your ascent or descent can be either smooth or turbulent depending on whether the sluice-gates are opened abruptly or gently. Most lock-keepers are friendly souls who will often have vegetables, eggs, or a bottle of local red or white for

sale. Occasionally you come across an eccentric one such as the lock-keeper who rushed off leaving us at the bottom of the lock with the gates closed and returned with a rifle, blasted away at a corner of the lock shouting 'Un rat! Un rat!' and then calmly put the rifle down and let us out.

Automated locks are operated either by what looks like a broom handle hanging from a wire across the canal, the handle must be pulled or twisted; or by a photoelectric cell that registers the boats presence. Traffic lights outside the lock tell you whether to wait or enter lock and another set of lights in the lock tell you when the cycle is complete. It is important to exit quickly when the gates are opened. A red button or cord inside the lock stops the cycle in an emergency.

On the large-scale waterways such as the Rhône, the European-standards locks are all manned with traffic lights or instructions over a loudspeaker telling you what to do and when. Commercial traffic has priority at all locks and pleasure craft should not attempt to get in before a barge or impede its passage.

ABOUT THE PLANS

The charts of the canals that accompany the text show the towns and villages, locks, bridges and any other pertinent features along the way. For some places a plan of the town or village is included with an indication of the services available.

All distances are measured in kilometres (km) as is common on European waterways.

The following symbols are used:

- *K*   kilometre number
-    lock
-    bridge
-    mooring
-    channel (Rhône and Petit Rhône)
-    fuel
-    water
-    electricity
-    shower
-    information
-    post office

TRAFFIC SIGNS

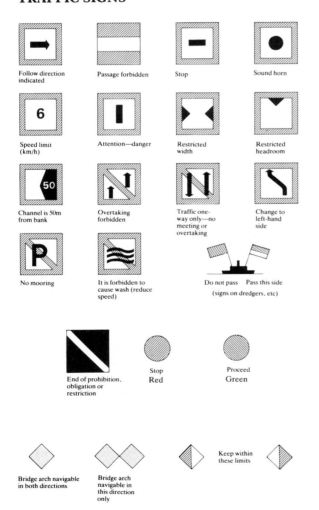

Follow direction indicated   Passage forbidden   Stop   Sound horn

Speed limit (km/h)   Attention—danger   Restricted width   Restricted headroom

Channel is 50m from bank   Overtaking forbidden   Traffic one-way only—no meeting or overtaking   Change to left-hand side

No mooring   It is forbidden to cause wash (reduce speed)   Do not pass   Pass this side (signs on dredgers, etc)

End of prohibition, obligation or restriction   Stop Red   Proceed Green

Bridge arch navigable in both directions   Bridge arch navigable in this direction only   Keep within these limits

Canal du Midi from Port La Robine to Les Onglous

Distance The overall distance of the Canal du Midi is 240 kilometres from Toulouse to Les Onglous on the Etang de Thau. At Toulouse the Canal du Midi connects with the Canal Latéral à La Garonne and thus with the Atlantic seaboard at Bordeaux. Distances (in kilometres) are measured from Toulouse with km0·0 at Toulouse basin and km240·1 at Les Onglous. Here I cover only the section from Le Somail at km166 to Les Onglous at km240·1. The La Nouvelle branch canal comprising the Canal de Jonction as far as the Aude and then the Canal de la Robine is dealt with separately.

Depth Minimum depth of 1·6 metres although silting has taken place in parts of the canal. In recent years drought has reduced the maximum amount of water available for the Canal.

Air height Maximum air height of 3·3 metres in the middle of the old arched bridges, but only 2·4 metres air height at the edges.

Width Maximum width of 5·5 metres.

Locks Eight locks between Le Somail and Les Onglous. This was formerly fourteen before the Fonserannes water slope replaced the old staircase of six locks here. Included in the eight locks is the flash-flood lock at Prades which is usually permanently open in the summer.

Bridges Lifting bridge at Fouga km210. All other bridges are fixed.

Traffic There is very little commercial traffic now, most of the traffic being hire boats from the hire firms dotted along the canal. Hotel *péniches* also operate on the canal.

Modernisation There have been plans to straighten some sections and increase the depth to 1·8 metres, but little has been done to date.

History From Roman times the idea of cutting a canal from the Mediterranean to connect with the River Garonne at Toulouse was dreamed of and various routes were plotted, but not until the l7th century did it become anything other than a fanciful idea. In the reign of Louis XIV the remarkable Pierre Paul Riquet was granted construction rights to begin work on the canal.

Pierre Paul Riquet was born in Béziers in 1604 and in 1623 married the wealthy Catherine de Milhau; the dowry from the marriage enabling him to purchase an estate near Toulouse. He was appointed collector of the salt tax for the Languedoc region, a job which meant he had to travel all over the region and not surprisingly his travels gave him an intimate knowledge of the country through which he was eventually to build the Canal du Midi. As well as his lucrative job as the salt tax collector, Riquet started a business supplying military hardware to the state. By the time he was fifty, Riquet was a rich man, but not yet ready to retire and the project for which he is remembered was yet to come. In his youth he had heard of a project to build a canal to link the Garonne to the Mediterranean; indeed his father had been on a committee that rejected the building of such a canal, and this project must have lodged itself in Riquet's brain. One of the principal problems of the early project was the lack of water to feed it during the hot rainless summers and it was to this problem that Riquet turned his mind.

The Languedoc is a dry region in the summer where the rivers are a mere trickle compared to the winter. In the winter the problem is too much water and the heavy downpours can turn them into dangerous torrents impracticable for navigation. The favoured system in the north of France of canalising rivers could not be employed here; and a canal had to be built on higher ground clear of the valley floors and winter torrents. To supply the water for the canal system Riquet devised a system of feeder canals from as far away as 60 kilometres and a reservoir to hold the winter rains for the dry summer. He was lucky to procure the services of a young engineer, François Andreossy, who as much as Riquet was responsible for the canal and the system of feeder canals bringing water to the reservoir at St-Férréol.

In October 1666 Louis XIV issued an edict granting the construction of the canal. The cost was to be borne by the state, by the Province of Languedoc, and by Riquet himself who was granted the profits from tolls levied on the canal. Construction began in 1666 and was to continue until 1681. Riquet died just six months before it was officially opened. The canal became something of an obsession for him and he managed to spend the entire family fortune on it without seeing a *sou* in return. Le Canal Royal, as it was first named, was designed and constructed to leave a lasting memorial to Louis XIV and this is reflected in the quality of the construction, not only in the locks and the canal itself, but also in the bridges and ancillary buildings.

The canal was not an immediate commercial success, mainly because of the difficulties in navigating the Garonne between Bordeaux and Toulouse. Not until the construction of the Canal Latéral à La Garonne was completed in 1856 did traffic on the Canal du Midi increase substantially. Unlike British canals which declined with the railways, traffic on the Canal du Midi increased right up through the 19th and 20th centuries, and even in the 1950s and 60s there was more traffic on the canal than in the 19th century. Although there is little commercial traffic today, the canal is far from dead, with large numbers of hire boats pottering along a canal that has changed little from the project Riquet planned and constructed over 300 years ago.

Note The description of the Canal du Midi is from Le Somail at km166 to Les Onglous on the Etang de Thau at km240·1. References to the left or the right bank are from the direction of Toulouse to the Etang de Thau.

km166 Le Somail. Mooring between the two bridges. Water nearby. Some provisions and restaurants. An attractive small village that was formerly the port for Narbonne until the branch canal was built in 1776. Until then passengers and freight were off-loaded here and continued on overland to Narbonne.

km168 Cesse Aqueduct. There is one-way traffic over the aqueduct and for a short distance before it. The aqueduct was constructed by Vauban in 1686 to replace a dam and level crossing, originally built by Riquet, that was prone to flooding. The aqueduct is one of the earliest surviving examples of its kind.

km168·3 Bridge (Truilhas).

km168·6 Port La Robine (left bank). This is the base for the Bateliers du Midi hire firm. Diesel fuel and water available.

km168·7 La Nouvelle branch canal on the right bank (see page 36).

km168·8 Railway bridge.

km171·4 Bridge.

km172 Argeliers. Moor on the left bank. The village is a short distance away. Provisions and a restaurant. There is a more convenient restaurant by the bridge.

km172·6 Bridge with restricted width. Restaurant.

km176·5 Bridge (Sériège).

km178·3 Bridge.

km180·6 Bridge.

km188·3 Capestang. Bridge with restricted width and air height. Quay on the left bank and moorings on the right bank after the bridge. Water. Good shopping for provisions and restaurants in the village.

Capestang can be identified from afar by the tall apse and choir of the unfinished 14th-century church, a vast edifice much too big for the village even in its unfinished state. The village is an attractive place, cut by narrow lanes with old houses hanging out crookedly over the lanes. At Capestang the worst disaster in the history of the canal occurred in November 1766 when a section of the canal bank collapsed after heavy rain and snow. The damage was repaired in three months, a masonry wall replacing the former earth bank, and to prevent it happening again a series of ingenious siphon pipes were installed that automatically started to siphon when water levels got too high.

km188·5 Bridge.

km191·7 Road bridge (Trézilles).

km194·1 Poilhes footbridge.

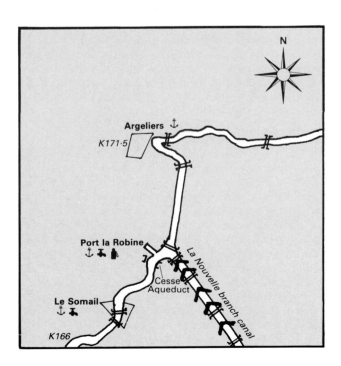

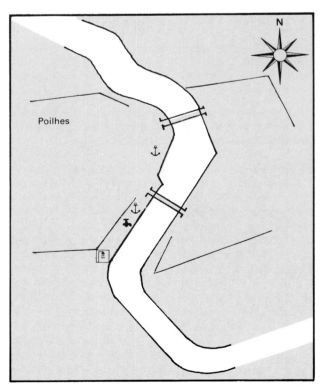

POILHES

Péniche 'hotel-boats' at Poilhes.   Capestang and the low bridge on the Canal du Midi.

Béziers basin.

km194·2 Poilhes bridge. Mooring between the two bridges. Water and public showers. Provisions and restaurants nearby in the village. There is a hire boat base near the footbridge. A friendly and attractive little village perched on a ridge overlooking the valley to the south.

km196·3 Bridge.

km198·8 Malpas tunnel. A 160 metre tunnel with one-way traffic. From either end it is easy to see if anyone is coming from the other direction and this is the only traffic control there is. The tunnel, cut through the soft sandstone, is the oldest existing canal tunnel known. The railway tunnel constructed in the 19th century was cut under this tunnel. Riquet had the Malpas tunnel constructed under the site of the 6th-century BC Iberian-Greek city, Oppidum d'Ensérune, which has now been excavated and a museum built to display the artifacts found. You can get to it along the road (D62) above. Also nearby is the unusual Etang de Montaldy, a shallow lake that was drained in the 13th century by the expedient method of putting a plug hole in the middle and drains to lead the water away. Drainage canals radiate from the central drain so that the fields look like a huge spoked wheel.

km200·5 Bridge. Colombiers village. Provisions and a restaurant.

km202 Canal narrows. One-way traffic in places until km204.

km204·4 Bridge.

km205·9 Bridge.

km206·6 Ecluse de Fonsérannes. Water slope and the celebrated lock staircase. Craft no longer use the lock staircase, but instead use the new water slope which is not as intimidating as it looks. A diesel-powered shunt pushes a wedge of water up the concrete slope or lowers it down. Traffic lights control entry to the slope; when they are green proceed into the wedge and tie up alongside the arm. A rubber screen at the back stops you running into the mechanism. Operation up or down the slope is smooth and you get an easier ride than in the old lock staircase.

When Riquet brought his canal to the slopes overlooking Béziers, he was generally reckoned by his critics to have committed a folly on a grand scale. To descend to the bottom he originally built an eight-lock staircase to the River Orb. Navigation on the Orb proved difficult, especially in the winter when it flooded, so in 1856 the new arm of the canal was built taking it over the river on the present elegant viaduct. The new canal reduced the number of locks to seven of which only six were used, the middle gates of the bottom lock remaining open. Although the Fonsérannes water slope makes things a lot simpler than the old system, when I traversed the

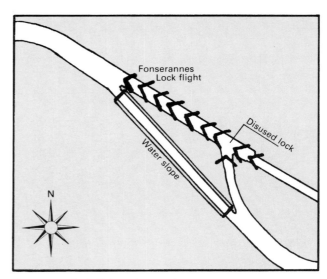

Fonserannes lock flight and water-slope.

staircase before the water slope was operational on my first trip on the Canal du Midi, it was all electrically operated so you arrived at the bottom painlessly although not as quickly as with the water slope.

km207·6 Orb aqueduct. Built by Mague in 1856 to bypass the Orb which was prone to silting and to flooding in the winter. The seven-spanned aqueduct gives the best view of Béziers straggling up the hillside to the cathedral and the palace on the summit. The best view of the aqueduct is at night when it is artfully spotlit.

km208 Ecluse d'Orb. Bridge.

km208·1 Béziers basin. Mooring on the left bank. Water and electricity. Fuel in the town. A hire boat base where a crane can haul boats onto the quay. Provisions and restaurants in the town. A bar and disco on a *péniche* in the basin.

BEZIERS

Béziers was the Celtic-Iberian settlement of Betera and under the Romans the city of Julia Beterrae. There was nothing outstanding to mark its early history up to the Middle Ages until 1208. In that year Pope Innocent III proclaimed his crusade against the heretical Cathars and so began one of the most bloody and grubby periods in the history of the Catholic church.

The south of France and particularly the Languedoc region was a stronghold of a Manichaean sect known as the Albigensians or Cathars. Manichaeism grafted the new Christian beliefs to older Babylonian and Persian beliefs to produce a dualistic religion where the world was seen in black and white terms, where good and evil were in a constant struggle, but where everything centred around the problem of evil. To the Cathars the world was created not by God, but by the Devil. They rejected most of the Catholic beliefs including the Old Testa-

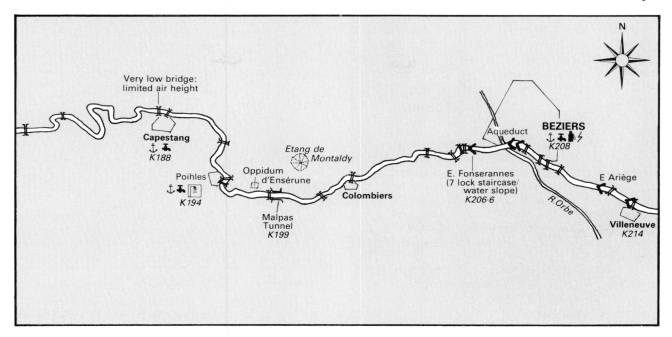

ment, churches, worship, and even the cross, but still considered themselves Christians. To the many poor in the region the sect had a strong populist appeal. The Pope evidently decided that the sect needed suppressing and on the 22nd of July 1209 the anti-Cathar crusade reached Béziers. It was led by Simon de Montfort and Arnald-Amaury, the latter the fanatical Abbot of Citeaux, and for both of them Béziers was a special target. Their target was Raymond Roger Trencavel, Viscount of Carcassonne and Béziers, who when ordered to suppress the heretical Cathars, had defiantly replied: 'I offer a city, a roof, a refuge, a loaf of bread and my sword to all the outcast men who will soon be wandering through the country.' The crusade took Béziers by storm and when the soldiers asked how they were to distinguish between Catholics and Cathars, the gory Abbot is said to have replied: 'Kill them all. God will know his own.' The entire population was slaughtered, estimates ranging between 20,000 and 60,000, with Catholic and Cathar dying together in the churches where they had sought shelter.

The Gothic cathedral and the Bishop's Palace that dominate Béziers today were built after the massacre, replacing the Romanesque structures that were burnt and pulled down in the crusade. Béziers seems to

have shrugged off the dark gloom of its past in the intervening years and in many ways it reminds me of a little Napoli – sunny and dark, grubby tenements with bright white washing drying between them, noisy and chaotic with calm corners like the canal basin.

km208·4 Ecluse de Béziers.

km208·5 Bridge.

km208·8 Floodgate. Bridge.

km209·5 Footbridge.

km210 Fouga lifting bridge.

km210·5 Bridge.

km212·5 Ecluse Ariège.

km212·7 Motorway bridge.

km213·8 Ecluse Villeneuve. Bridge. Mooring on the right bank. Provisions in Villeneuve village.

km215 Cers bridge.

km216·5 Bridge.

km218·3 Ecluse Portiragne. Bridge. Portiragne village nearby.

km221·6 Bridge.

km222 Port Cassafières. Basin on the right bank. This is a hire boat base with diesel fuel and water available and a restaurant nearby.

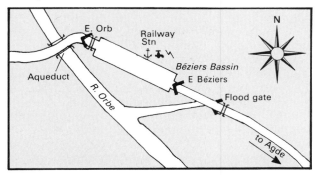

BEZIERS

The 'deep' lock at Béziers.

km225·2 Libron crossing. A sluice gate arrangement allows the crossing of the Libron river when it is in flood. Restricted passage.

km226·4 Bridge.

km228·2 Agde bypass bridge.

km229 Bridge.

km229·2 Railway bridge.

km229·7 Bridge.

km231·3 Ecluse Agde. The round lock here has three sets of gates, the extra gates allowing access into the Hérault river and to Agde and the Mediterranean via Grau d'Agde. Mooring upstream of the round lock.

km231·5 Agde (on the Hérault). Mooring alongside on the town quay or alongside in the canal connecting the Canal du Midi to the Hérault. Care needs to be taken as silting occurs along the sides of the Hérault. When the Hérault is in flood it is best to moor in the junction canal. Water and fuel at Agde. Good shopping for provisions, and numerous restaurants in the town.

Boatyard Just downstream of Agde there are several boatyards where you can moor on jetties. Fuel and water nearby. Craft can be hauled here, and there is a crane that can raise or lower masts, but remember there is only 12 metres air height under the bridge downstream. The yards are mostly devoted to fishing boats, but can do good work on pleasure boats. It is a short walk upstream to Agde.

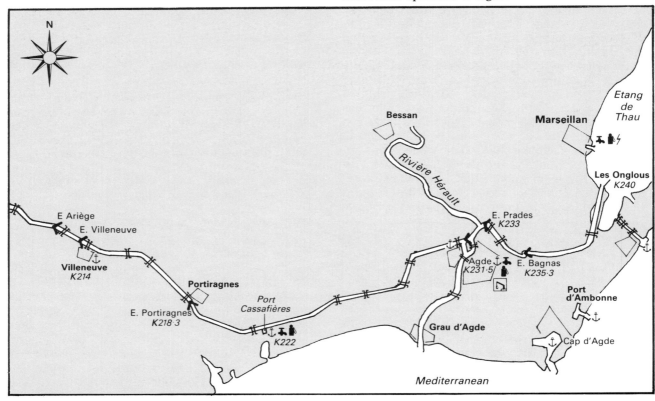

Agde on the banks of the River Hérault.

Note Yachts with masts longer than 12 metres should go to Sète via the Canal du Midi and the Etang de Thau as there are no good facilities for raising a mast at Grau d'Agde once past the bridge.

AGDE

Agde is one of the oldest towns in France. It was founded in the 6th century BC by the Greek Phocaeans from Marseille who established a trading port here called Agathe Tyché, 'the good place'. It was colonised by the Romans and was a bishopric from 400AD until the 18th century, although it was variously sacked by the Vandals, Visigoths, Ostrogoths and the Saracens. The huge cathedral that dominates the town was built in the 12th century with black basalt from nearby Mont Loup, an extinct volcano nearby. The cathedral is as much a fort as a place of

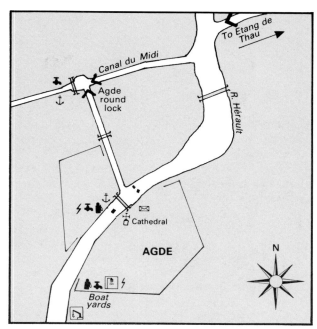

AGDE

worship with a crenellated top, arrow slits, a solid tower and a water reservoir; an architectural expression of the troubled times it was built in. Agde is dourly described by the *Blue Guide* as 'unprepossessing' and they go on to say it has changed little from a previous description of it as 'a dirty little fishing port'. It just goes to show you that you can't rely on guide books all the time, even the *Blue Guide*, as Agde is one of my favourite places in the region, a bubbling attractive town that while it boasts no important museums or monuments, although it does have a good small museum on local folklore, is well worth a visit for things simply French.

Navigation downstream

From Agde you can reach Grau d'Agde and the Mediterranean via the Hérault. There are normally depths of 2·5–5 metres in the river, with greater depths in the winter and spring. The bridge over the Hérault downstream of Agde has 12 metres air height in the middle of the span.

For Grau d'Agde see Chapter II.

km231·8 Canal du Midi enters the Hérault river. Proceed upstream for one kilometre until the Ecluse de Garde de Prades is seen on the right. The lock is only used when the river is in flood and is normally open in the summer.

The Rivière Hérault can be navigated for a further 5 kilometres upstream to Bessan. There is normally a minimum depth of 2·5 metres although silting occurs along the banks and there may be submerged logs about. This is a wild overgrown waterway with no waterside facilities although there are lots of possibilities to moor alongside the banks with due caution.

km233·2 Bridge.

km234·1 Bridge.

km235·3 Ecluse Bagnas.

km238·5 Onglous bridge.

km239·8 Les Onglous. There is a rough basin here, but it has silted making it useless for most craft.

km240·1 Les Onglous lighthouse: Oc(2)WR.6s14/10M. The white sector shows the safe approach from the Etang de Thau.

La Nouvelle branch canal

Canal de Jonction and Canal de la Robine

Distance 37 kilometres from the Canal du Midi (at km168·7) to Port La Nouvelle. Distances are measured from the Canal du Midi (km0·0) to Port La Nouvelle (km37·3).

Depth Minimum depth of 1·8 metres although silting has taken place in parts of the canal, and also where the Aude river is traversed. Depths in the Aude are much reduced at the end of summer.

Air height Maximum air height is determined by the Roman bridge at Narbonne where there is 3·3 metres in the middle of the arch, but only 2·3 metres at 5 metres either side. It is important to note that this bridge is a tighter squeeze than the lowest bridge on the Canal du Midi.

Width Maximum width of 5·5 metres.

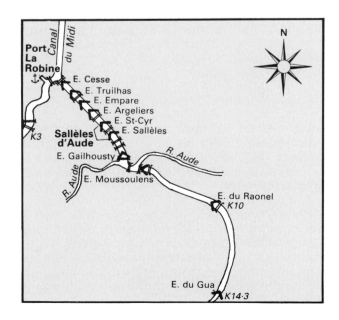

Locks Thirteen locks.

Bridges All fixed bridges.

Traffic There is light commercial traffic although even this seems to be decreasing.

Modernisation None planned.

History When the Canal du Midi was built, the good citizens of Narbonne were understandably miffed that their city was bypassed. Passengers and cargo were off-loaded at Le Somail and continued on to Narbonne by land. It was nearly a hundred years later that the Canal de Jonction was opened in 1776. This canal provided an abrupt descent via eight locks to the Aude river and then the Canal de la Robine to Narbonne. The Canal de la Robine was originally an open canal, really a secondary channel of the Aude, that wound from side to side to reduce the current. Later it was straightened and six locks built.

km0·0 Junction with the Canal du Midi.

km0·3 Ecluse (Cesse)

km1·0 Ecluse (Truilhas)

km1·6 Ecluse (Empare)

km2·3 Ecluse (Argeliers)

km3·0 Ecluse (St-Cyr)

km3·4 Bridge. *Sallèles d'Aude* village. Mooring downstream of the bridge. Provisions in the village.

km3·7 Ecluse (Sallèles). Formerly a double lock, now a single lock with a large rise and fall (5·4 metres).

km3·8 Bridge.

km4·9 Ecluse (Gailhousty). Bridge.

km5·1 Rivière l'Aude. The Canal de Jonction ends here and you must proceed across the Aude to the lock at the beginning of the Canal de la Robine. Care is needed as the river has silted in the middle behind the weir. At the end of the summer when water is short in the region, depths in the river are reduced. Once out of Ecluse Gailhousty proceed upstream into the Aude keeping close to the bank of the river and proceed to turn about 30 metres above the ferry cable across the river. From here go downstream keeping close to the opposite bank until you get to Ecluse Moussoulens.

km5·8 Ecluse (Moussoulens). Bridge.

km6·4 Bridge.

km9·8 Ecluse (Raonel). Bridge.

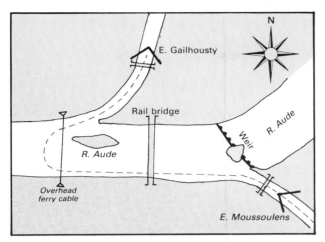

RIVIERE L'AUDE

km15·5 Bridge Marchands. The Roman bridge with the lowest air height on the canal. Old houses are built right across the bridge and it looks a bit like you are about to disappear down a big drain pipe.

km15·6 Footbridge.

km15·7 Narbonne. Quays on either side of the canal. Water and public toilets nearby. Here you are in the centre of Narbonne which is both good and bad. The good news is provisions and restaurants literally on your hatch-step. The bad news is that you are on public view from above and from the quay itself where the Narbonnais like to take their evening promenade.

km14·2 Ecluse (Gua). Footbridge. Quay downstream

km14·6 Footbridge.

km14·9 Footbridge.

km15·1 Bridge. Rail bridge.

km15·2 Two bridges.

km15·3 Ecluse de Narbonne. Care is needed of the side current coming in from the weir at the side of the lock.

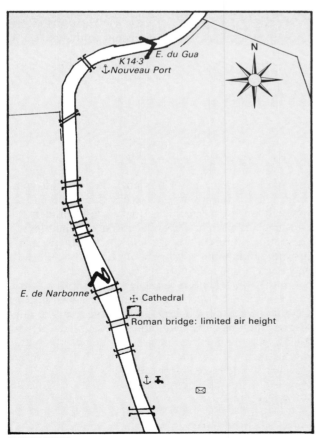

NARBONNE

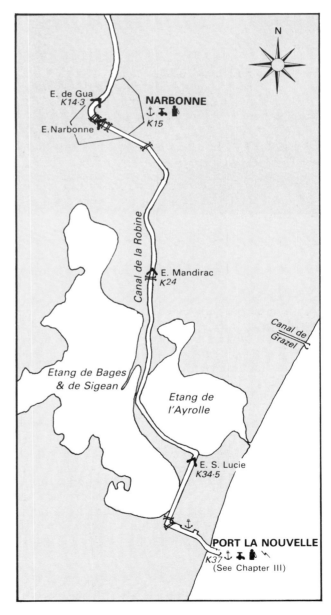

Ecluse de Narbonne in the middle of the city. Note the weir on the right.

NARBONNE

Narbonne has a long and prosperous history that is evident from even a cursory look at the town. The *centre ville* is lined by elegant old merchant houses and on the right bank are the palaces of the bishops and the towering cathedral, or at least part of it, for it was never finished. It was prosperous as far back as Roman times although little remained of the Roman city after the Vandals and Visigoths sacked it. Narbonne was founded around 600 BC and in the Roman period was the capital of the south until Lyon (then Lugdunum) eclipsed it in the 2nd century AD. It was then the principal port for the region and it continued as such right up into the Middle Ages. It was the seat of a bishop from the 4th century and was ruled jointly by both its bishops and its nobility. During the Albigensian Crusade it suffered a similar fate to nearby Béziers, though not all the population of Narbonne was put to the sword. The genocidal Arnald-Amaury who ordered both Catholics and Cathars alike to be slaughtered in Béziers was made archbishop here and set up a Court of Inquisition.

In 1340 one of those unimportant events that have grave consequences later on occurred. A dyke that had previously diverted the Aude river to scour the harbour and approaches was pulled down. The port soon silted bringing an end to the prosperity of the town. It was never again to rise to the prominence it had enjoyed earlier, being described by Champier in the 16th century as 'La Latrine du Monde', a fairly damning indictment that I should hasten to add in no way describes it today.

On the contrary, Narbonne is a thoroughly delightful town well worth a visit. The uncompleted Cathedral of St-Just should be visited if just to gape at the vaulting some 40 metres (130 feet) above. Nearby are the fortified palaces of the bishops with a monumental stone staircase up which the overfed prelates would ascend on the backs of mules. Also here is the Archaeological Museum that imaginatively displays finds from prehistoric to Roman times – well worth a look even if you normally can't be bothered with bits of old bone and artifacts.

km15·8 Bridge.

km16·1 Footbridge.

km24·1 Ecluse (Mandirac). Bridge.

km26·3 Bridge. On the right bank is the Etang de Bages et du Sigean though it is difficult to see very much because of the bank of the railway line.

km30 Etang de l'Ayrolle on the left bank.

km34·3 Ecluse (Ste-Lucie).

km37·3 The canal enters Port La Nouvelle under a bridge. Moor alongside on the right bank or at the pontoons if there is room. (See Chapter II, page 79, for details of Port La Nouvelle.)

Etang de Thau

The Etang de Thau, a large inland saltwater lake some 10 miles long by 2½ miles wide, is used to reach Sète or the Canal du Rhône à Sète from the Canal du Midi. The *étang* also has a channel to Marseillan-Plage at the southern end, though the low bridges with a maximum air height of 2·5 metres restrict craft able to use it. There are a number of harbours around the NW side of the *étang*.

Navigation in the Etang de Thau

The most conspicuous object in the étang is Mont de Sète (Mont St-Clair) at the SE end. Also conspicuous are: the lighthouse at Les Onglous, a white and red tower 10 metres high; the beacon on Rocher de Roquerôls, a red tower with a black band 6 metres high; and the green beacon off Pte du Barrou. In addition

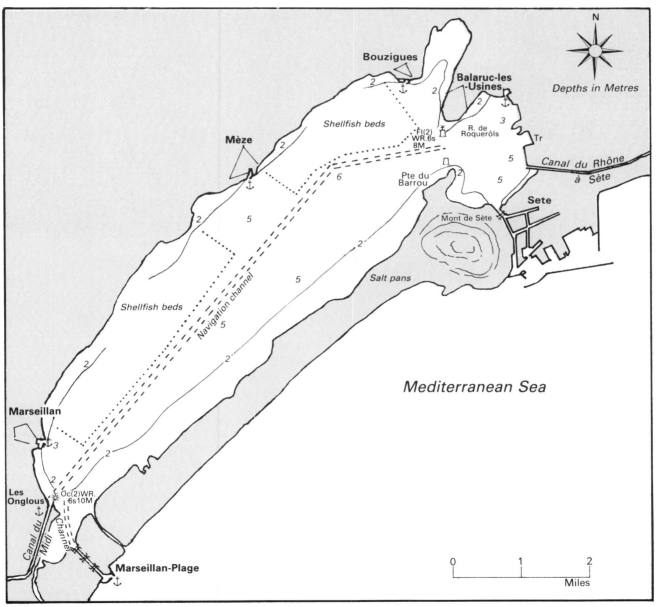

ETANG DE THAU

the chimneys and high buildings of the industrial complex at the E end of the *étang* are conspicuous.

Lights The principal lights for navigation are Les Onglous (Oc(2)WR.6s14/10M); Marseillan (Q.10M); Mèze (Fl.G.4s7M); Rocher de Roquerôls (Fl(2)WR.6s11/8M); and the Canal du Sète (Q.G.5M and Q.R.6M). In addition the flares at the oil refinery at Frontignan will be seen.

Dangers
● On the NW side of the *étang* shellfish beds obstruct navigation (see plan).
● Care needs to be taken on the SE side of the *étang* where there are extensive shallows.
● Care needs to be taken of strong northerlies in the *étang* as a particularly vicious sea is quickly whipped up on the shallow waters. Canal craft must take extra care and if there is any likelihood of a *tramontane* should stay in harbour or in the canal.

Note With prolonged strong northerly winds the water level in the *étang* can decrease by as much as half a metre. This can cause problems getting into harbours on the NW side and should be taken into account when calculating depths. An acquaintance who, tiring of the tides in his native Brittany, brought his yacht to the tideless Mediterranean and based it in Marseillan, now finds he sometimes runs aground after prolonged northerlies, something he fondly thought would soon be a distant memory.

Shellfish beds in the northwest of the *étang*.

HARBOURS

There are a number of harbours around the NW side of the *étang* and the harbours at Marseillan-Plage and Sète reached via short canals. None of the harbours on the NW side have any great depths and the note on water levels should be kept in mind.

Marseillan

Approach From the Canal du Midi the buildings of Marseillan will be seen. With strong SE winds there is a confused swell at the entrance.

Mooring Berth where directed or where convenient. There are poles around which you must take a line. Good shelter except from strong SE winds which cause a surge.

Facilities Water and electricity. Fuel in the town. Good shopping for provisions and restaurants ashore.

General An enchanting old town which, like Mèze and Bouzigues along the coast, is famous for its shellfish farmed right outside the harbour. A hire boat company is based here.

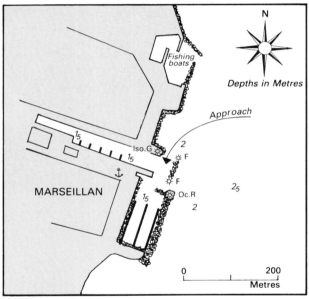

MARSEILLAN 43°21'·2N 3°32'·2E

Mèze

Approach The harbour must be approached between the shellfish beds to the SW and E. The buildings of the town and the light structure on the breakwater will be seen.

Mooring Berth where directed or where convenient. There are laid moorings tailed to a small buoy. Good shelter.

Facilities Water. Fuel on the quay. Good shopping for provisions and restaurants in the town.

General A small town of some antiquity. It was colonised by the Romans who called it Mezna and was a prosperous port right up to the 19th century – most of the wine of the Hérault region was exported from here until the railways came along. Today it is a

Mèze on the northwestern side of the *étang*. The town is renowned for its shellfish, particularly mussels, farmed on the beds that obstruct the waters around the approach.

lively place given over to the shellfish farms in the *étang* and a meal at one of the *coquillages* restaurants should be put on the list for those who enjoy their oysters and mussels with just a squeeze of lemon and a *soupçon* of the local dry white.

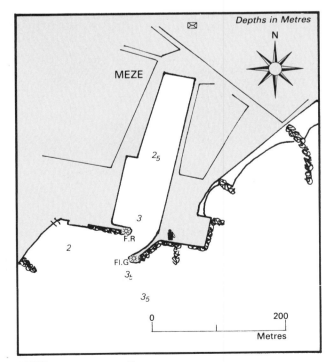

MEZE 43°25'·3N 3°36'·3E

Bouzigues

Approach A shallow harbour for craft drawing less than a metre. From the beacon on Rocher de Roquerôls the buildings of Bouzigues will be seen. Keep well clear of the shellfish beds to the W.

Mooring Head for the W basin and berth behind the breakwater. Care is needed as the harbour is prone to silting.

Facilities Water and fuel nearby. Provisions and restaurants in the village.

General A drowsy little village that like Mèze is famous for its shellfish. Mention Bouzigues to a Frenchman and he will reply *moules*.

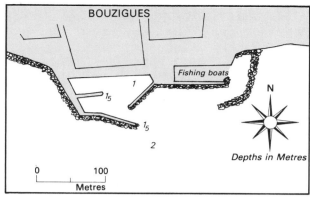

BOUZIGUES 43°24′·8N 3°39′·5E

Balaruc-Les Usines

A small pleasure-craft basin surrounded by industry. It is approached by a marked channel along the eastern end of the *étang*. Provisions in the village. There is not a lot to attract visitors here and the basin is mostly used by small fishing boats and local pleasure craft.

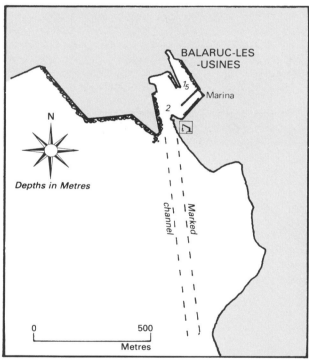

BALARUC-LES-USINES

TO SETE

From the *étang* the beacons on Rocher de Roquerôls and on Pte Barrou are easily identified. Closer in the lifting bridge and the white light towers at the entrance to the Canal Latéral and Canal Maritime linking the *étang* to the sea will be seen. The bridges between the Nouveau Bassin at Sète and the Etang de Thau open twice daily around 0800 and 1800. Enquire at the bridge office for the precise times and be ready to transit as soon as the bridges open. Moor alongside on the E quay of the canal entrance while waiting for the bridges to open. (For details on Sète see Chapter II, page 89.)

TO MARSEILLAN-PLAGE

This harbour is reached via a marked channel and a short canal. From Les Onglous a marked channel leads to the Canal de Pisse-Saumes which comes out at Marseillan-Plage. Access via the canal is restricted by the depth of 2 metres and a low air height of 2·5 metres. (For details on Marseillan-Plage see Chapter II, page 88.)

Lifting bridge on the Canal Latéral linking Sète to the Etang de Thau. Go like the clappers as the bridge doesn't stay open for long.

Canal du Rhône à Sète

Distance A total of 70 kilometres from the entrance at the Etang de Thau (km98·0) to Ecluse de St-Gilles (km28·0) at the entrance to the Petit Rhône. The distance was previously measured from the Etang de Thau to the old canal entrance at Beaucaire.

Depth Minimum depth of 2·2 metres.

Air height Maximum air height under the bridges of 4·1 metres.

Width Maximum width of 9·6 metres at the railway bridge at km97.

Locks One lock at the entrance to the Petit Rhône. The Ecluse de St-Gilles can take craft up to 175 metres long by 12 metres wide.

Bridges
km92·2 Lifting bridge at Frontignan which opens at 0700, 1100 and 1500.
km78 Mobile pedestrian swing bridge which opens on request.
km50·9 Swing bridge at Aigues-Mortes which opens on request.

Traffic There is little commercial traffic with only a few *péniches* using the canal. Hire boats use the canal from bases at Port Pérols and Aigues-Mortes as well as the bases on the Beaucaire branch canal.

Modernisation There are plans to modernise the Canal du Rhône à Sète so that the large barges using the Rhône can get to the Etang de Thau. The dredging of the canal to 2·2 metres from the original depth of 1·8 metres is nearly complete. A new section of canal to bypass Aigues-Mortes to the N and to bypass Frontignan are planned. In addition some bridges will be raised and some of the tight bends widened. Work started in 1983, but it looks like it will be some time before the planned improvements are completed at the present rate of progress.

History Before the Canal du Midi was finished in 1681, the idea of linking it to the Rhône was being planned and the states of Languedoc started the first stage of the canal by clearing and enlarging the medieval channels between the *étangs* around Aigues-Mortes. The link from the Etang de Thau to Aigues-Mortes was known as the Canal des Etangs and it was envisaged that work would start on a canal to the Rhône within a short time. Concessions were granted for the construction of the canal from Beaucaire, but nothing happened until the states of Languedoc took matters into their own hands again and started work on it in 1777. The Revolution interrupted the work and it was not finished until 1808. The old Canal des Etangs and the new Canal de Beaucaire became collectively known as the Canal du Rhône à Sète.

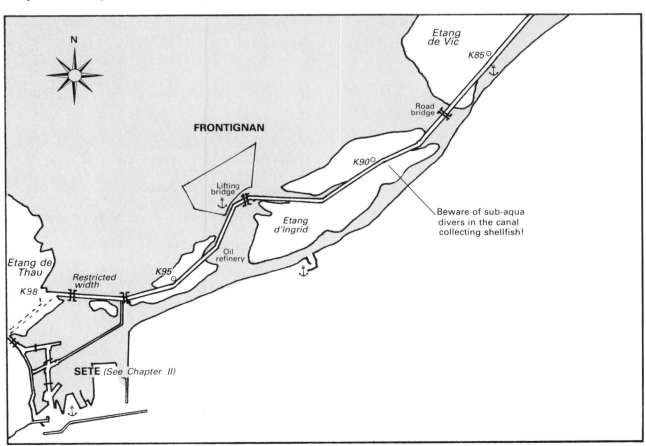

The vertical lift bridge at Frontignan. It opens only twice daily so you will more than likely have to stop for a few hours or overnight at Frontignan.

The canalisation of the Rhône this century so altered water levels that the Beaucaire lock connecting the canal to the Rhône was closed in the mid-1970s and the Petit Rhône canalised to a point close to the old canal just below St-Gilles. A lock to European standards was constructed to connect the Petit Rhône and the Canal du Rhône à Sète. In the diminutive *Roulette* I was one of the first pleasure boats through this relatively unknown section in 1977 and it surprised me in 1988 that a quick perusal of the log in the lock-keeper's office showed comparatively few boats using the Petit Rhône. In fact I didn't see another craft, commercial or otherwise, on the Petit Rhône.

Note Indication to the left or right bank is conventionally from the downstream direction (i.e. from the Petit Rhône to the Etang de Thau), but this would be confusing when describing the canal from the opposite direction so indications to the left or right bank are from the direction proceeding from the Etang de Thau to the Petit Rhône. There is much room for confusion here, though in practice it should prove straightforward.

km98 From Sète the barge canal to the entrance is marked by beacons though there are depths of 3–4 metres outside the channel. The entrance to the canal is difficult to see until close up to it.

At the entrance there is a scrappy old jetty on the N side previously advertised as the Marina du Flamant d'Or. It now appears disused and in any case the industrial surroundings with the petrochemical complex on the eastern side of the *étang* and at Frontignan don't do a lot to enhance the place.

km97·3 Road bridge. Railway bridge with limited width (9·6 metres).

km96·2 Junction with the Canal de la Peyrade, now disused. The basin is used by barges.

km96·1 Road bridge.

km92·3 Frontignan. Moorings on the left bank on a stone quay. Water. Provisions and several restaurants in the village. Despite the proximity of the oil refinery, Frontignan is a pleasant sleepy little village;

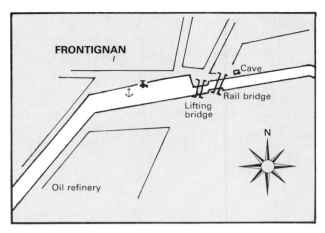

FRONTIGNAN

its soporific state perhaps induced by the sweet *Muscat* wine it is famous for. Just past the bridge there is a friendly *cave* on the left bank where you can taste the varieties of *Muscat*, as well as other local wines, before you buy. The creamy sweet *Muscat* was described by Colette as '... like a sun stroke, or love at first sight, or the sudden realisation of a nervous system'.

km92·2 Frontignan lift bridge. Opens at 0700, 1100 and 1500. Enquire at the bridge office to confirm times. Railway bridge immediately after and moorings on the left bank.

Note In the section of canal after Frontignan I encountered sub-aqua divers along the sides of the canal gathering shellfish, mussels and oysters I assume. There is usually someone on the bank assisting and watching for canal traffic, but care is needed not to shred any of these dedicated *coquillage* gastronomes with the propeller.

km86·6 Road bridge. On the left bank is Bois de la Fontaine and on the right bank Les Aresquiers, a popular stretch of deserted beach. In the *étangs* on either side there are large populations of the pink flamingos the region is noted for.

km85 Mooring possible on the right bank.

km78·6 Maguelone Abbey. The pine-clad knoll on which the abbey sits was once an islet with a large harbour behind it. This was the port for Montpellier until it silted and sand choked the harbour and joined the islet to the coast. A bishopric existed here from the 3rd century AD, though it was not until the 11th century when Bishop Arnaud rebuilt and enlarged the cathedral that it became the major structure we see today. In the 12th century the Pope sheltered from his enemies here and on his orders it was further enlarged and strengthened. Despite this there was little to keep a community here in this desolate spot, prey to the lightning raids of Corsairs from the Barbary Coast, and it slowly declined as the inhabitants moved elsewhere. In 1633 it was destroyed on the orders of Louis XIII because of the heretical

One of my favourite *cabanes*, 'feet in the water', on the Canal du Rhône à Sète.

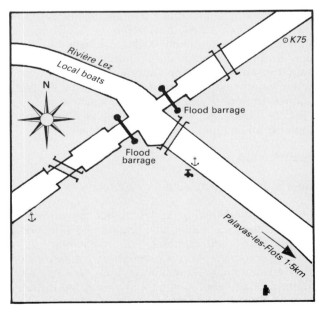

PALAVAS-LES-QUATRE-CANAUX

45

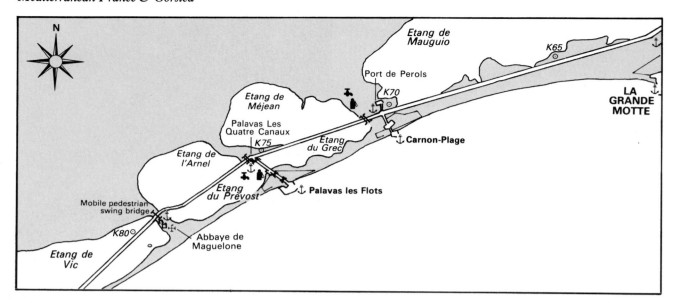

Protestant population that had migrated to it and the surrounding settlement was razed.

The abbey was partially rebuilt in 1875 and can be visited every day. The Romanesque church, basically a 12th century structure, has sturdy thick walls sprinkled with loopholes and topped with crenellations for the defence of the port and as a refuge for the population. Before you get to the abbey there is a massive stone gateway that appears to have been purely a ceremonial and not a defensive structure.

There are a few places to moor on the right bank near the abbey, but care needs to be taken of rocks under the water. Just past Maguelone there are numerous *cabanes* on the left bank and a floating pedestrian bridge that swings out of the way with the aid of an outboard motor. It opens on demand.

km75·5 Road bridge. Mooring on the right bank just before the bridge.

km75·2 Palavas-les-Quatre-Canaux. Where the river Lez crosses the canal there are sluice-gates over the canal that close when the river is in flood. In the summer this is rare. There is mooring on the Lez under the bridge though there is only 2·4 metres air height under it, less when the river is in flood. Water and electricity. A yard nearby and fuel on the road behind the yard. Craft drawing one metre or less can continue down the Lez to Palavas-les-Flots where there are all facilities (see Chapter II, page 93).

km75·1 Road bridge.

km71·5 Cabanes de Carnon.

km70·7 Carnon road bridge. Just past the bridge on the left bank is Canal du Hangar with mooring places. Water and electricity. A yard ashore. It is about a kilometre into Carnon-Plage for provisions and restaurants. Shallow-draught craft with less than 1·2 metres air height can proceed along the canal to Carnon-Plage (see Chapter II, page 93).

After Carnon there is the huge Etang de Mauguio on the left bank where lots of flamingos will be seen.

km70 Road bridge.

km61·7 Mooring on the right bank. It is about 1½ kilometres to the shops and restaurants at La Grande Motte.

km61 Cabanes de Roc.

km59 Canal de Lunel now disused.

km58·9 Road bridge.

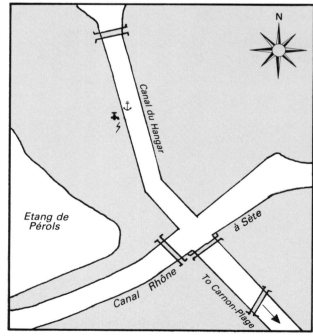

CARNON – PORT DE PEROLS

km55 Rivière Vidourle crosses the canal. There are sluice gates over the river on either side of the canal. The river can apparently be navigated down to Grau du Roi by shallow-draught craft and looks like an attractive detour.

km51·9 Road bridge. The Tour de Constance at Aigues-Mortes can be seen from here.

km51 Aigues-Mortes and the Chenal Maritime on the right bank. You can moor on the grassy right bank just before the entrance to the Chenal Maritime or in the basin in the Chenal Maritime under the bridge and the walls of Aigues-Mortes. Water and electricity in the basin. A charge is made. Good shopping for provisions and restaurants at Aigues-Mortes.

AIGUES-MORTES

Aigues-Mortes, the City of the Dead Waters, is a perfect example of a medieval fortified city. It was built by Louis IX as a base for his crusade to the Holy Land in the 13th century and has lain forgotten through the ages until its recent change in fortune with the tourist boom. The choice of Aigues-Mortes as a base was forced on Louis because France at this time had no port of its own on the Mediterranean. He negotiated the purchase of this tract of marshy land from a Benedictine abbey in 1240 and built the town and the Tour de Constance to protect his new port. A canal was dug through the salt marsh to connect it to the sea at Grau du Roi. If you are not happy about the taxes you pay today, to some extent blame Louis and his crusades. To pay for them a systematic system of taxation was introduced, the direct precursor of all our present ills. Ironically he attracted settlers to this marshy fever-ridden place by granting them tax exemptions.

Louis set sail from Aigues-Mortes on his first crusade in 1248. Joinville, a chronicler of the time, described the fleet setting sail: 'Our master-mariner called to his mariners in the prow of the ship and said "Is your task ready?" And they replied "Yes Sir, let the clerics and priests come forward." And when they arrived he called to them "Sing to the Glory of God" and they cried out with one voice "Veni, Creator Spiritus". And the master-mariner shouted to his men "Set sail for the love of God". Though Louis arrived in the Holy Land with some 1800 ships, he did not fare well against his infidel opponents and was ignominiously captured. It cost him the city of Damiette and 800,000 gold *bezants* for his own freedom and that of his fellow knights. He returned to France in 1256, and in 1270 set out from Aigues-Mortes on his second crusade. He was very ill by now '... cast down, with drawn features, hardly able to sit straight in his saddle', and on arriving in North Africa died within a day, of the plague.

St Louis, as he became known, left Aigues-Mortes as a purpose-made port protected by the Tour de Constance and a series of dykes and ditches around the town. The massive walls around the town were

Aigues-Mortes

Relief commemorating Louis IX's crusades from Aigues-Mortes.

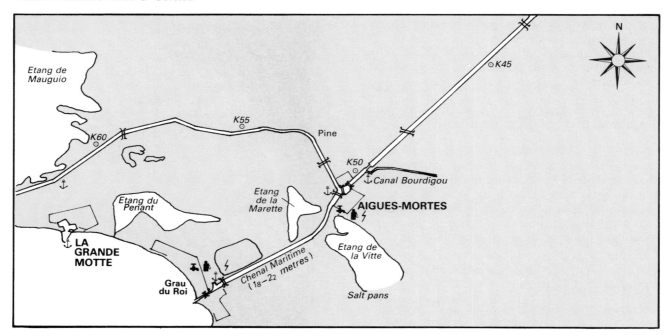

not built until later under Philip the Bold, though the real height of the walls is disguised today by the fact that the moat has been filled in. With the explosion of waterborne trade in the 14th century Aigues-Mortes prospered despite problems with the canal to the sea silting up. However by the late 15th and early 16th centuries the silting canal became virtually impassable for ships and Aigues-Mortes declined to such an extent that a report by François I stated that the inhabitants 'have great difficulty in keeping alive and in good health'. In the 19th century Alexandre Dumas more caustically commented that the inhabitants needed 'all their strength to keep alive'.

The forgotten city was put on the tourist map relatively recently, in the 1970s, and consequently still has much of the flavour of a Camargue town about it. Though it is a bit toy-town-like in places, it should not be missed. From the Tour de Constance, used as a political prison for everyone from the Knights Templar to Huguenot Protestants and anyone else who happened to be religiously or politically inconvenient, there is a panoramic view over the town and surrounding countryside to the Mediterranean beyond. There is a guided tour of the ramparts which can get a bit tedious and apart from the Tour de Constance, a wander around the back streets, with a drink or two in a café in the central square, is more rewarding.

CHENAL MARITIME

From Aigues-Mortes the Chenal Maritime runs for 6 kilometres down to Grau du Roi and the sea. There are several yards on the right bank near Aigues-Mortes and more at Grau du Roi where there is a crane for raising or lowering masts. There are two opening bridges, a sliding bridge above the town and a swing bridge in the town. There are limited moorings in Port de Pêche before the swing bridge. See Chapter II, page 97 for details on Grau du Roi.

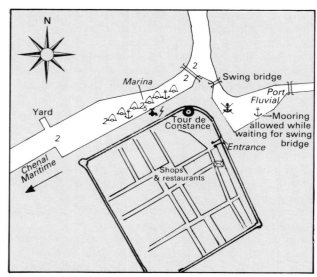

AIGUES-MORTES

km50·9 Railway swing bridge which opens on demand.

Port Fluvial

This basin can be used temporarily while waiting to pass the swing bridge. Care needs to be taken of the depths at the sides and of obstructions close to the bank. There is a pontoon that can be used if it is free.

km50·8 Fixed railway bridge.

km49·9 Lock permanently open. The lock was installed to control the ingress of sea water into the canal, but was found to be unnecessary and the gates were removed. The Canal Bourdigou is on the right bank, but it is not open for navigation. A number of *péniches* and local craft are usually moored in the entrance basin and there may be a space free here.

km48 Road bridge. The planned canal bypass is to cut across the corner from a point on the left bank just above the bridge to join up with the canal at a point clear of Aigues-Mortes.

km*43* Bridge with restricted width.

km39·2 Gallican bridge and Gallican village. Mooring on a grassy bank on the left. Water. Provisions and restaurant in the village.

On the right bank is the entrance to Canal des Capettes, a much overgrown canal which nonetheless looks an interesting proposition to explore.

km35·1 Franquevau bridge and Franquevau village. Mooring on a grassy bank on the left just before the bridge. Provisions and restaurant in the village.

From Franquevau to km30 there are numerous possibilities to moor on either bank in this Camargue wilderness.

km29·7 Bridge with restricted width.

km29 Junction of the Beaucaire branch canal on the left bank and a large turning area for barges.

km28 Ecluse de St-Gilles and entry to the Petit Rhône. Tie up on the left bank until the lock opens and the traffic lights turn green permitting entry. Once inside tie up and report to the lock office at the Petit Rhône end of the lock. Local wine is sometimes on sale here.

Beaucaire branch canal

Distance 28·4 kilometres from the junction with the Canal du Rhône à Sète at km29 to Beaucaire at km0·6.

Depth Minimum depth of 1·8 metres.

Air height Maximum air height under the bridges of 4·1 metres.

Width Maximum width of 8·7 metres although below Beaucaire the maximum width increases to 10 metres.

Locks One lock at km7·7. The Ecluse Nourriguier can take craft up to 80 metres long and 12 metres wide.

Bridges All fixed bridges.

Traffic Only pleasure craft and the occasional *péniche*. There are boat hire bases at St-Gilles and Beaucaire.

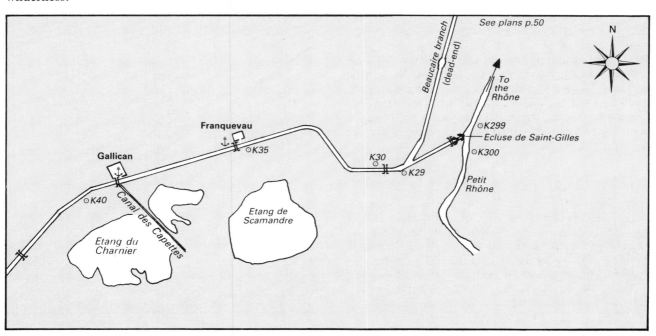

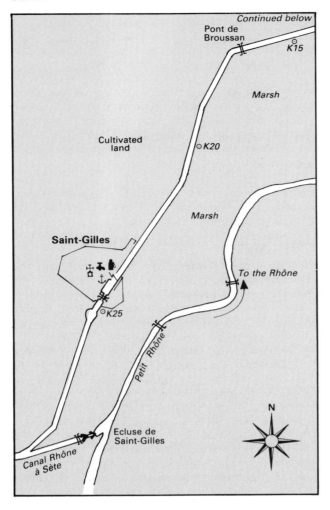

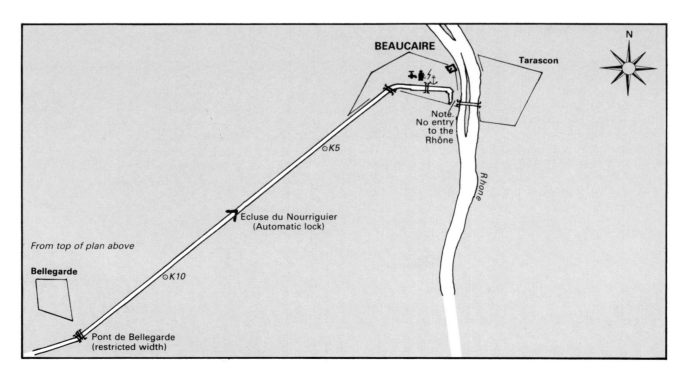

History The Beaucaire branch canal was originally part of the Canal du Rhône à Sète joining it with the Rhône at Beaucaire. The lock connecting the canal to the Rhône was closed in the 1970s when the new channel along the Petit Rhône was opened.

Note Indication to the left or right bank is from the direction going from the Canal du Rhône à Sète towards Beaucaire.

km29 Junction with the Canal du Rhône à Sète.

km24·9 Railway bridge.

km24·7 Road bridge with restricted width.

km24·5 St-Gilles basin. Moor on the left bank. Water, electricity, and diesel fuel nearby. A charge is made. Provisions and restaurants in the town. Uncharacteristically I will recommend a restaurant at Le Saint-Gilles Hotel, tucked away just off the main street, where someone cares a good deal for food.

ST-GILLES

Saint-Gilles was famous in the Middle Ages as a place of pilgrimage to the tomb of St Giles, or St Aegidius, who seems to have had some quite remarkable powers. In the 8th century St Giles gave away all his money to the poor and set off from Greece on a raft. Cast up in Provence, he saved a deer from a hunter's arrow by leaping out and grabbing the shaft in mid-flight, so amazing the aristocratic bowman that he founded an abbey to commemorate the miracle. An alternative version has St Giles being wounded by the arrow, reputed to have been fired by Childerac, king of France, and St Giles being crippled for life and

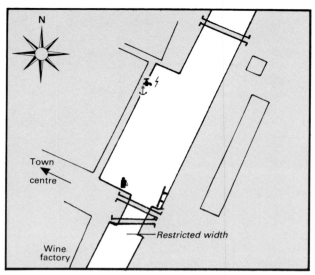

ST-GILLES

hence becoming the patron saint of cripples. St Giles set off for Rome to get recognition for his new abbey and was presented with two doors for it by the Pope. These he cast into the water and they were washed up on the shore in Provence at the same time and place as St Giles on his return. At this rate I'm surprised he was not made patron saint of sailors and navigators. He was buried in a simple church and the abbey built in the 12th century.

Apart from the abbey of the miraculous St Giles, the town was also an important river port for the region and in the 12th century boasted a population of over 30,000; today it has less than 4000. It suffered greatly during the Wars of Religion when the abbey was twice destroyed by the Protestants, though luckily on the second occasion the Catholic army arrived in time to stop them knocking down the west front of the church, which survives today and is a masterpiece of medieval stonework. There are scenes from the Old and New Testaments with examples of the rich imaginary bestiary that medieval monks peopled the world with.

The abbey is well worth a visit, but as for St-Gilles itself, I found so much traffic thundered through the town on its way west or east, that it was unbearable after the peace and quiet of the canal. One thing St-Gilles does have to help you get some peace is a number of *vinicole* plants producing some well respected wines. The largest is close to the left bank between the bridges.

km24 Bridge.

km16·6 Bridge.

km13·2 Bellegarde bridge with restricted width. Mooring downstream of the bridge and a snack bar. Shopping in Bellegarde village about one kilometre away.

km13·1 Road bridge.

km7·9 Road bridge.

km7·7 Ecluse de Nourriguier. The lock is automatic.

km3·4 Road bridge.

km2·2 Railway bridge with restricted width and a private bridge.

km1·3 Bridge with restricted width.

km0·9 Footbridge.

km0·6 Beaucaire basin. Mooring in the basin. Water, electricity, and fuel nearby. A charge is made. Good shopping for provisions and restaurants in the town.

BEAUCAIRE

Beaucaire on one side of the Rhône looks directly across to Tarascon on the other side and for centuries Beaucaire castle protected the Kingdom of France while Tarascon castle protected the Holy Roman Empire. Apparently river pilots would call out not 'port' or 'starboard', but 'Kingdom' or 'Empire'.

The river was an integral part of the local economy with Beaucaire the principal port on the river. From the 13th century right up until the 19th century Beaucaire was famous throughout Europe for its fair. Every July ships arrived from as far away as England, Germany, Turkey and the Levant for the huge fair on the banks of the Rhône, often seven or eight hundred ships were moored off the town. A sheep was slaughtered for the first ship to arrive and the fleece hung from the masthead. In the vast temporary city of canvas and wood, different 'streets' were given over to goods or countries so there were 'merchants of Marseille, who sold soap, oils and drugs; the traders in Moroccan leather; the turbaned Turks who sold carpets and pipes; the red-fezzed Greeks who dealt in sweet meats; the Persians with their precious attar of roses; the jewellers; the

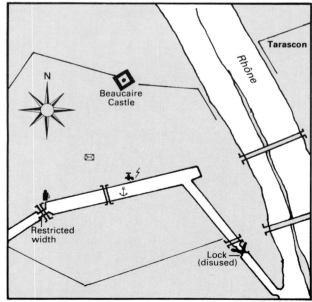

BEAUCAIRE

Guillotine flood-control gates at Gallician.

Leaving the lock that connects the Canal du Rhône à Sète to the Petit Rhône. The control tower is on the left of the picture.

spicers; the pastry cooks; the vendors of onions and garlic ...'. (Archibald Lyall paraphrasing Stendhal's description in *Mémoires d'un Touriste*.) The fair declined with the introduction of the railways in the 19th century which much reduced the role of river transport and river ports by building railheads on the coast.

Beaucaire remains a delightful town with the ruins of the castle on a pine-clad bluff behind. The castle was partially destroyed in the 17th century by Cardinal Richelieu, one of the many castles he knocked down to prevent insurrection in the south. Opposite Beaucaire is Tarascon and its castle, restored in 1926. You can walk across the bridge to visit it, though when the *mistral* is blowing wrap up well as it can be surprisingly chilly in the wind.

The Camargue

Just above Arles the Grand Rhône branches to form the Petit Rhône. Between the main course of the river and its tributary, is a vast region of wild river delta, overgrown with jungle-like trees and vegetation and divided up by shallow salt lakes, the *étangs*. In 1928 the French government declared a large part of it a nature reserve and in 1970 this area was further enlarged, thus preserving this unique environment.

The Camargue region has been built up by the silt brought down by the Rhône; around twenty million cubic metres of mud and sand that extends the delta by some ten to fifteen metres every year. In prehistoric times the area between the Rhône and Petit Rhône did not exist, in fact the Petit Rhône did not exist as the Rhône flowed into the sea at a point above where Arles now is. The alluvial soil soaks up salt from the sea as it is laid down and consequently the soil of the region is impregnated with salt. In the north of the Camargue this has not deterred man from draining the land, washing the salt out with fresh water diverted from the Rhône and growing crops on it. Much of the land has been used for rice fields which produce some 120,000 tons a year, nearly enough to supply France's needs. Most of it is short grain rice and this may account for the difficulty of finding long grain rice in France except for imported brands.

But it is not the rice fields the visitor to the Camargue comes to see. The wildlife is prolific. Many birds can be seen here that will not commonly be seen elsewhere. The Camargue and the adjoining Camargue-like areas are the last European breeding grounds of the greater flamingo. In addition the purple heron, osprey, plover, avocet, and various species of warblers are common. Smaller colonies of the little egret, night heron, squacco heron, red-crested pochard, and the bee-eater can be seen. Various birds of prey including the rare lesser kestrel may also be seen. As well as birds there are also foxes and the last colony of beavers in Europe, though more common and more famous are the Camargue horses and bulls.

The white Camargue horses, variously believed to be descended from a prehistoric type of horse whose bones have been found near Lyon or from ponies brought by the Saracens, are a tough, sure-footed species used by the local cowboys, the *guardians*, to get around this marshy land. The horses are born brown, but turn white in their fourth year. The Camargue bulls, black long-horned animals, are not raised for beef, but for the Provençal *courses à la cocarde*, the local type of bullfighting that has more in common with ancient Minoan bull-leaping than the bloody bullfights of Spain. Rosettes are attached to the horns of the bull and the bullfighters, dressed in white, must retrieve them. Since the bulls can wheel on the proverbial six pence and accelerate like a race horse, the young bullfighters need considerable skill to retrieve the rosettes. The bulls roam freely over the Camargue and though they are said to be docile in the wild, I've never approached close enough to find out.

On the Canal du Rhône à Sète and the Petit Rhône, you skirt the Camargue, though in parts it feels as if you are in the very heart of this wild region. On the Petit Rhône you will see as much and more in the way of bird life than you would do on the organised tours to the bird sanctuaries. If you cut the engine to an idle most of the birds seem unconcerned with your presence and you will be able to get quite close to them. To see the horses and bulls of the Camargue your best bet is to stand on the coach-roof so you can see over the banks on the Canal du Rhône à Sète between Aigues-Mortes and Ecluse de St-Gilles. If you can get down the Canal des Capettes, even for a short distance, you will likely see horses and bulls as well as a variety of bird life. Despite what some guide books say, you will see the pink flamingos virtually everywhere there is an *étang*.

Petit Rhône

Distance 21 kilometres from the junction with the Canal du Rhône à Sète at Ecluse de St-Gilles (km300) to the junction with the Rhône (km279·2).

Depth Minimum depth of 2·2 metres.

Air height Maximum air height of 4·75 metres.

Width Maximum width determined by the Ecluse de St-Gilles is 12 metres.

Bridges All fixed bridges.

Traffic There is some commercial traffic.

History The Petit Rhône was canalised and buoyed in the early 1970s to bypass the old Beaucaire branch canal to the Canal du Rhône à Sète.

Notes

• The channel is marked by beacons and buoys which show the starboard and port limits of the channel from the seaward direction, as is conventional. The channel is well marked as follows: starboard side – a black and white beacon post or a black buoy; port side – a red and white beacon post or a red and white buoy.

• There is an appreciable current varying from 1 knot at the end of summer to 2–3 knots in spring.

• Indication to the left or right bank is from the direction of Ecluse de St-Gilles towards the junction with the Rhône.

km30 Ecluse de St-Gilles. There is a quay you can moor up to on the left bank just outside the lock. From here follow the markers showing the channel. Beware of large logs and other debris which tend to gather in the entrance to the lock.

The Petit Rhône downstream of Ecluse de St-Gilles has only a limited depth of one metre and less and an air height restricted to 2·7 metres. From the lock it is 37 kilometres to the sea, but even shallow- draught craft need to take care of shifting sandbanks in the river. The channel is not buoyed, but the following may be helpful.

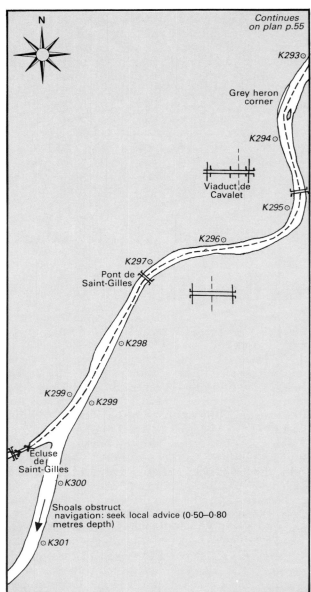

Continues on plan p.55

PETIT RHONE

km307 Albaron village. Restaurant and provisions.

km322 Bridge. Entrance and lock to Canal du Peccais à Sylvéréal.

km330·8 Cable ferry with a maximum height to the cable across the river of 2·7 metres. Café nearby.

km334·2 Port Dromar. A small pleasure-boat harbour. Water and a small hotel nearby.

km337 The mouth of the Petit Rhône on the Mediterranean. A sandbank obstructs the entrance. Port Gardian at Stes-Maries de la Mer is just over a mile to the E. (See Chapter III, page 104)

Upstream

km297·3 St-Gilles bridge. Pass under the middle where shown by the overhead diamonds.

The channel is clearly marked by beacons and buoys.

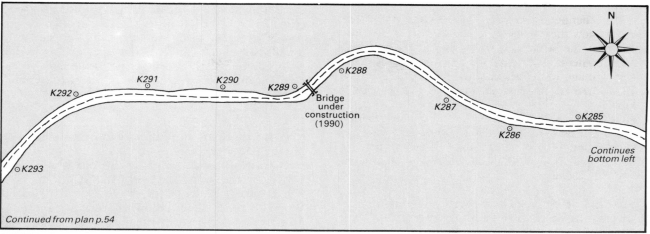

PETIT RHONE

km294·7 Viaduc de Cavalet. Pass under the right-bank arch where shown by the overhead diamonds.

km293·6 Grey heron corner. My name for one of the wildest stretches with water birds and birds of prey everywhere.

km288·7 New road bridge under construction.

km281·7 Fourques girder bridge. Pass under the wide span indicated by the overhead diamonds.

km281 Fourques suspension bridge. Pass under the wide span indicated by the overhead diamonds. Fourques village is nearby on the left bank.

km279·2 Entrance to the Rhône. Keep going well out into the stream and do not cut across the corner where training walls are submerged. Arles is approximately 3 kilometres downstream.

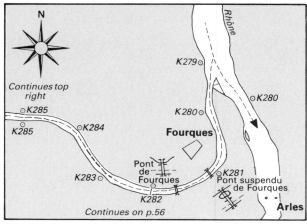

PETIT RHONE

The Rhône from Arles to Port St-Louis du Rhône

Distance 44·5 kilometres from the Petit Rhône at km279 to Port St-Louis du Rhône at km323·5. The Rhône from Port St-Louis du Rhône to its mouth on the Mediterranean is not navigable.

Depth A minimum depth of 3 metres is maintained although there is usually a greater depth than this.

Air height There is a minimum air height of 6 metres at the highest navigable water level.

Width The maximum width is determined by the locks at 12 metres, though the only lock on this stretch of the Rhône is at Port St-Louis du Rhône.

Locks Ecluse Maritime at Port St-Louis du Rhône with a length of 85 metres and a width of 12 metres.

Bridges All fixed bridges except for the lifting bridge at Port St-Louis du Rhône which opens when you lock through.

Traffic There is much commercial traffic ranging from small ships and large pusher barges up to 4500 tons as well as large 1500-ton barges, the latter mostly *pétroliers*. Commercial craft have right of way in the river and at locks.

Modernisation The planned canalisation programme for the Rhône ended with the completion of the Vaugris lock in 1980.

History The river has been used as a thoroughfare for 2000 years and more. The Phocaean Greeks from Marseille are reputed to have sailed up the river as did the Phoenicians on their wide-ranging voyages in search of trade. The Romans used it to supply their garrisons along the river and to ship wine from the hinterland. The use of the river continued into the Middle Ages with towns like Beaucaire becoming prosperous river ports. Nearly every town and vil-

Péniche on the Rhône at Arles.

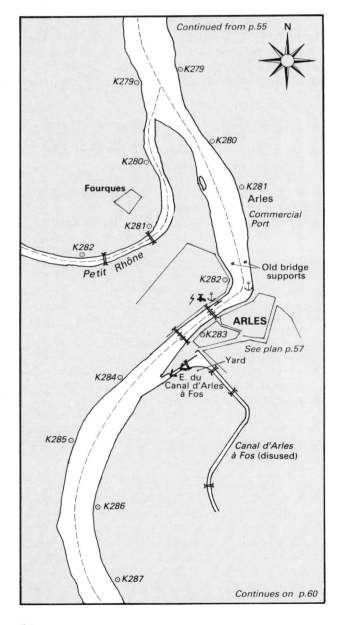

lage, no matter how small, had a port or landing and relied on the river for the transportation of goods and people. Regular goods and passenger services were established in the early Middle Ages and expanded right up until the 19th century when the railways arrived on the scene and the importance of river transport declined dramatically.

In 1934 the Compagnie Nationale du Rhône (CNR) was established with the aim of canalising the river for transport and just as importantly, harnessing the power of the river to produce electricity. The river was to be dammed in twelve places and locks built for river traffic on what was hoped to be a much tamed Rhône. Not until after the Second World War in 1948 did work start at Donzère-Mondragon and it continued right up until 1980 when the last of the dam and lock installations at Vaugris was finished. Ernle Bradford in *The Journeying Moon* described shooting the Donzère dam in his boat on his trip to the Mediterranean just after the war. He had taken a pilot, Monsieur Pacquet, at Lyon who steered the boat through the 'chute', the narrow gap left in the dam for boats to pass through:

'As *Mother Goose* dipped her bows into the 'chute', the propeller was flung, roaring, clear of the water. At the same moment, the wave which had built up in front of us broke like thunder on our bows. For a split second, as the water rolled over the fo'c'sle and swept aft along the upper deck and over the coach roof I thought it was certain to sink us. Warps and spars, boathooks and fenders rose up under the press of water and floated aft – as far as their lashings would allow them – in a confused heap. At one moment the propeller and rudder would be clear of the water. At another, they would be dug down into such conflicting currents that they were impotent.'

At the beginning of 1979 I took my former boat *Fiddlers Green* down the Rhône just before the Vaugris dam and lock were completed. While it was nothing like the river encountered by Ernle Bradford, it had a roar and a bite to it that was soon to be lost when the Vaugris installation was finished.

Note
• The channel is marked by beacons and buoys which show the starboard and port limits of the channel from the seaward direction as is conventional. Consequently when you are going down river the markers will be on the 'wrong' side. The channel is marked as follows: starboard side – a black and white beacon post, or a black or green buoy; port side – a red and white beacon post, or a red or red and white buoy.
• The current varies from 1–2 knots at the end of summer to 3–4 knots in the winter and spring. If you are going upstream it is obviously best to do so at the end of summer or beginning of autumn.
• Indication to the left or right bank is in the downstream direction from Arles to Port St-Louis du Rhône.
• The canalisation of the river shortened it by cutting out some bends, but most of the old kilometre markings have been kept. Consequently although the

Morning rush hour in Golfe de St-Tropez. *Opposite*
Pétanque, more a way of life than a mere game. *Below*
Béziers looking up to the cathedral and palace.

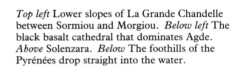

Top left Lower slopes of La Grande Chandelle between Sormiou and Morgiou. *Below left* The black basalt cathedral that dominates Agde. *Above* Solenzara. *Below* The foothills of the Pyrénées drop straight into the water.

river is now 310 kilometres long with km0·7 at Lyon, at Port St-Louis du Rhône the kilometre mark is km323 with the mouth a further 6 kilometres on.

km279·5 Junction with the Petit Rhône. The commercial port for Arles is on the left bank.

km281·9 Piles of the old bridge across the river. Pass in the middle of the two piles.

km282 Arles. Mooring on the left bank on the quay though along most of its length it has silted and good depths will only be found at the upstream end. You are close to the shops and the centre of Arles, but the best place to moor is a little further on the right bank.

km282·3 Arles. Mooring on a pontoon on the right bank. Water and electricity. Fuel is some distance away. A large supermarket behind the new church at Trinquetaille. It is a short and pleasant walk over Pont de Trinquetaille to Arles *centre ville*.

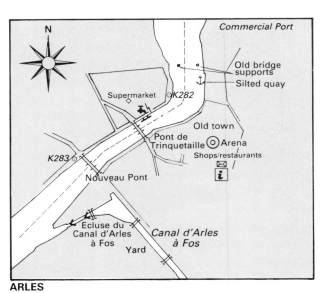

ARLES

Arles. The old town baking under the Midi sun.

ARLES

Arles' geographical position ensured its importance from very early on. The Phocaean Greeks established a small colony and a port here and later on, in the 2nd century BC, the Romans colonised it. The Consul Marius had a canal dug from the Golfe de Fos linking Arles directly to the sea and making it effectively an inland sea port. In 49 BC when Julius Caesar sacked Marseille for siding with Pompey, he made Arles the capital of Provincia. With the Aurelian Way passing through Arles it prospered, with everything that came by land or water going through the town. By 4 AD there was a bridge over the Rhône at Arles.

The monuments testifying to the importance of the city in Roman times are scattered around modern Arles. The huge amphitheatre is today used for the bullfights for which Arles is renowned. A theatre,

forum, temples, baths and the necropolis remain despite the best efforts of later Christian generations to pull them down. An aqueduct brought water some 75 kilometres to the town and a system of sewerage pipes kept it from getting smelly in the hot summers.

The necropolis by the Aurelian Way became famous throughout Europe as a place of burial for Christians. Anybody who was anyone, including kings, queens and generals as well as rich merchants planned to be buried in Alyscamps as it became known, probably after the Elysian Fields. Several odd legends are attached to it including one which relates how the dead were floated down the Rhône in wooden coffins with the burial fee enclosed, to be retrieved at Arles and deposited in Alyscamps. In the museum at Arles there is a good collection of some of the sarcophagi from the necropolis, though sadly

57

Alyscamps itself is now in an industrial zone between the railway line and the old Arles–Fos canal.

The importance of Arles continued into the Middle Ages. In the 9th century it was made the capital of the Kingdom of Arles which included Burgundy and part of Provence, and though it declined for a while after this, in the 15th century it was incorporated into the Kingdom of France and became the political capital. The medieval buildings around the old town, which once completely covered the amphitheatre, and the cathedral, remain to give a good idea of what Arles looked like at the time.

Like other river ports, Arles suffered a rapid decline with the arrival of the railways in the 19th century. In many ways what we see today are the sleepy remains of a 19th century river-port town left behind by the 20th century. In the afternoon heat Arles slumbers along with the old stones of its past by the shaded banks of the Rhône. Occasionally a pusher-barge will sweep down the river or push stolidly upstream, the present-day descendants of those early mariners who worked the river with a team of forty Charolais horses until steam ousted horse flesh, and the diesel engine, in turn, replaced steam.

VAN GOGH

Images of Arles, of the Rhône, of the Camargue, of Provence, are all coloured by Van Gogh's fiery canvases. His colours, his mad crows flying up from a cornfield, the bright *tartanes* at Stes-Maries de la Mer, the *Arlésienne* costumes, the *cafés* of Arles, the sunflowers that seem to reflect the buttery southern sunshine; these images crowd the senses in a way no other painter before or since has been able to do.

Van Gogh came to Arles from Paris in 1888 and lived in rooms over a bistro, La Civette Arlésienne, that he painted in his *The Yellow House*. The present bar, Civette Arlésienne, is behind the original house which he painted in his *The Yellow House*. The present bar, Civette Arlésienne, is behind the original house which was destroyed by a bomb in the Second World War. On his arrival he wrote happily to his brother about Arles: 'Of the town itself one sees only some red roofs and a tower, the rest is hidden by the green foliage of fig trees, far away in the background, and a narrow strip of blue sky above it. The town is surrounded by immense meadows all abloom with violet irises.'

His happiness was soon to disintegrate when his friend and fellow artist, Paul Gauguin, joined him at the end of the year. The artists quarrelled bitterly and often and it seems that Van Gogh was in the first throes of his illness, whether it was mental or spiritual. Gauguin later related how Van Gogh became 'excessively brusque and noisy, then silent' and how on one occasion Van Gogh 'was on the point of throwing himself on me with an open razor in his hand'. Van Gogh got progressively worse and at the height of his crisis with Gauguin, cut off his ear and delivered it to Rachel, a local lady of the night, with the instruction 'Gardez cet objet précieusement'. He

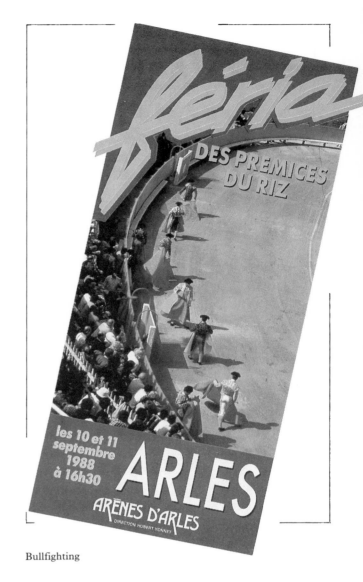

Bullfighting

painted his self-portrait later. In May 1889 he admitted himself to the asylum at St-Rémy-de-Provence where he painted at a frenzied pace, producing some 300 canvases, including most of those he is best known for.

Sadly there are few of Van Gogh's paintings in the south of France. Most of them are to be found in the large galleries in London, Amsterdam, Paris and New York. When they change hands, the sums make a mockery of the penurious life Van Gogh led in Arles. In July 1890 he committed suicide, shooting himself in the stomach after despairing of being cured of his madness; or was it despair at painting pictures no-one, including Gauguin, could understand and accept. Mervyn Peake, the author of the *Gormenghast* novels, paid this tribute to him.

an Gogh. His painting *Le Pont de
Anglois à Arles* immortalised the
ridge. It has been reconstructed
ear Arles.

Van Gogh

Dead, the Dutch Icarus who plundered France
And left her fields the richer for our eyes.
Where writhes the cypress under burning skies,
Or where proud cornfields broke at his advance,
Now burns a beauty fiercer than the dance
Of primal blood that stamps at throat and thighs.
Pirate of sunlight! and the laden prize

Of coloured earth and fruit in summer trance
Where is your fever now? and your desire?
Withered beneath a sunflower's mockery,
A suicide you sleep with all forgotten.
And yet your voice has more than words for me
And shall cry on when I am dead and rotten
From quenchless canvasses of twisted fire.

Arles. The amphitheatre was completely built over in the Middle
Ages as this 19th-century engraving shows.

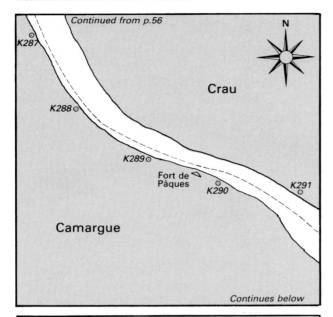

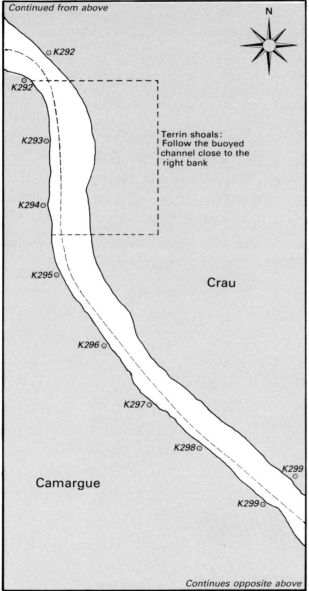

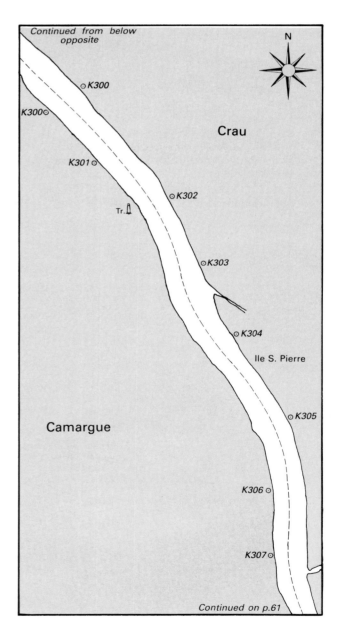

km282·5 Trinquetalle bridge. Pass under the centre span where indicated by the overhead diamonds.

km283 Nouveau Pont. Pass under the centre span where shown by the overhead diamonds.

km283·5 Entrance to the Canal d'Arles à Fos on the left bank. There is a lock, logically called Ecluse du Canal d'Arles à Fos, which leads to the now disused canal. There are a number of boatyards in the basin past the lock.

km292·5 Terrin shoals. The channel narrows and the current increases over the rocky shoals here. Follow the buoyed channel along the right bank closely.

km309 Ile des Pilotes.

km316 Salin de Giraud on the right bank.

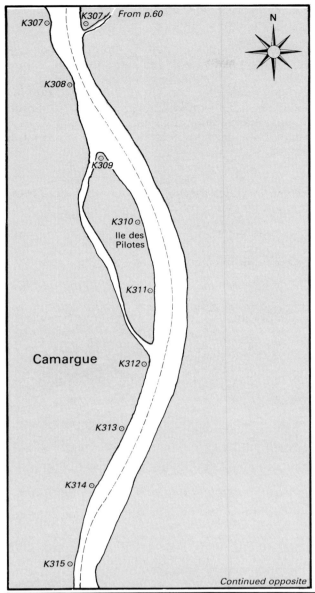

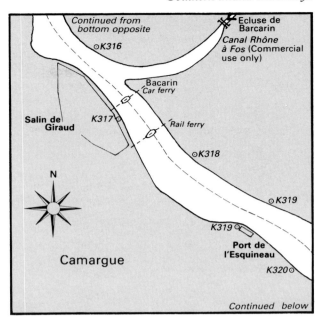

km316·5 Entrance to the Canal du Rhône à Fos on the left bank. The canal is for commercial craft only.

km316·7 Bacarin car ferry. The ferry will usually wait for you to pass, but care is needed not to obstruct its passage if it is leaving or has just left.

km317·5 Rail ferry.

km319 Port de l'Esquineau. Commercial use only.

km322 Port Abri du Rhône on the left bank. There are 1–1·5 metre depths inside, but most berths are permanently occupied by local boats.

km323 Tour de St-Louis. This large square tower on the left bank is conspicuous from upstream.

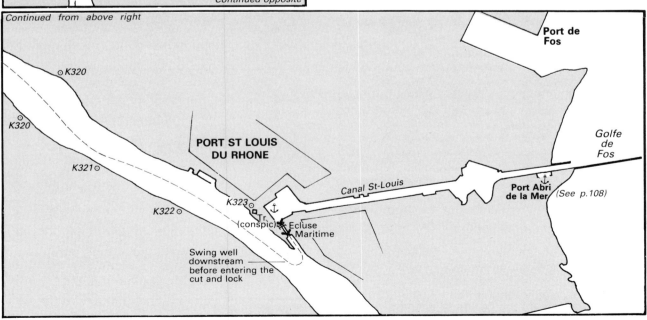

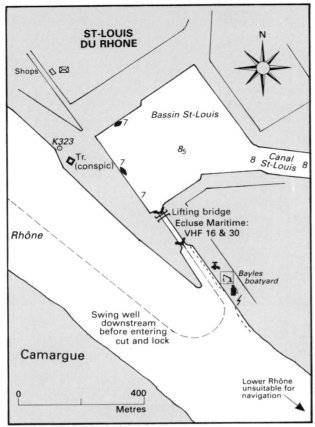

PORT ST-LOUIS DU RHONE

km323·5 Entrance to the Ecluse Maritime and Port St-Louis du Rhône on the left bank. Make a wide sweep downstream before entering the cut for the lock.

Care is needed before going alongside at Bayles Boatyard as silting has reduced depths to 1·5 metres and less in places, though fortunately it is all soft mud and you can plough your way through it if you touch bottom. Water, electricity and diesel fuel available here. A crane for raising and lowering masts. Bayles Boatyard has been putting masts up and down for years and so are qualified to get the job done quickly and efficiently. Chandlers ashore.

Ecluse Maritime VHF channel 16. The lock office will want particulars of your boat and will then let you into the lock. The bridge is raised when the lock cycle is complete and the gates into Bassin St-Louis are opened, or before you get into the lock coming from the other direction. Proceed into the basin and moor alongside. Bassin St-Louis and Canal St-Louis are dredged to 7–8 metres. Normally there is no objection to you mooring alongside in the basin, though if a cargo ship is due in the port, the harbourmaster will move you out of the way. There are shops for provisions and a few restaurants in the town. There is also a good local restaurant on the northeastern side of the basin.

Note The Rhône should not be navigated below Port St-Louis du Rhône and entry to the Mediterranean should be made only through the Canal St-Louis to the Golfe de Fos. (See Chapter II, page 107.)

The lifting bridge at Ecluse Maritime

Canal du Rhône–Fos–Port de Bouc

This canal running from km316·5 on the Rhône to the Port de Fos complex and then on to Port de Bouc is for commercial traffic only. There is in any case little advantage in using it since it is just 5 miles across the Golfe de Fos from the end of Canal St-Louis to Port de Bouc.

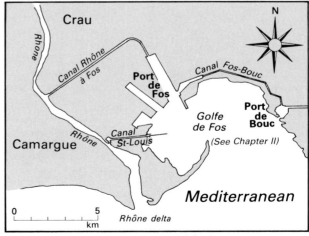

CANAL DU RHONE-FOS-PORT DE BOUC

II. Languedoc-Roussillon

This chapter covers the coast of Bas-Languedoc on the western side of the Rhône delta and the Plaine du Roussillon on the northern side of the Pyrénées. The long low sandy coast stretching around the Golfe du Lion has been christened the Côte d'Or though few bother to call it by any name other than Languedoc-Roussillon. The short section of rocky coast around the steep slopes of the Pyrénées close to the Spanish border, La Côte Vermeille, is also included here.

Unlike the coasts described in later chapters, Provence, the Côte d'Azur, and the Riviera, which immediately conjure up images and place names, Languedoc-Roussillon is little known except to Francophiles. Even ardent Francophiles will be hard pressed to tell you very much about the coastal region, their knowledge being confined to inland cities like Perpignan, Narbonne, and Montpellier. The reason for this is simply that until several decades ago there was very little on the coast apart for the old established harbour towns at Port Vendres, Port La Nouvelle, Agde, and Sète. The Phocaean Greeks from Marseille and later the Romans utilised these ports and established small colonies, but they must have dreaded the long stretches of empty sandy coast without shelter where an onshore gale or a *tramontane* could quickly wreck their unhandy ships. Right up until the 20th century it remained an empty coast.

All this changed several decades ago when the French government decided to construct purpose-built tourist cities and huge marinas along the coast, not one or two, but a whole chain of them stretching from the foothills of the Pyrénées to the Rhône delta. The first thing the government had to do was construct a trunk road along the coast, bring good fresh water to the area, and spray the stagnant lagoons to get rid of the mosquitoes that plagued the area. Six *unités* were planned for the Languedoc-Roussillon scheme, five of which have been built, and one, L'Embouchure de l'Aude, has been temporarily abandoned. From the south the five are: St-Cyprien (Argelès-Plage, St-Cyprien-Plage, and Canet-en-Roussillon); Leucate-Barcarès (Leucate-Plage and Port Barcarès); Gruissan (Gruissan-Neuf, Narbonne-Plage, and Valras-Plage); Cap d'Agde (Cap d'Agde, Ambonne, and Marseillan-Plage); and La Grande-Motte (Frontignan, Carnon-Plage, La Grande-Motte, and Port Camargue). In all of the *unités* work goes on improving and enlarging the apartment complexes and the marinas.

It is easy to decry this mass construction of instant tourist cities along the coast. Some of the architecture is appalling, some not so bad, and some really quite acceptable. For the yachtsman, there is now good shelter within short distances along what was a desolate and dangerous coast. No-one can deny that you get the feeling you have seen it all before. There is a homogeneity not found in resorts that developed more slowly. But as Archibald Lyall perceptively puts it in his *The South of France*, it could have been worse: 'It remains a hard fact that if this coast had been left to its own fragmented and unbridled devices, it would have become an ugly, uncontrolled rash of shacks, shanties and pestilential lagoons filling with garbage.'

Weather

The predominant wind along this stretch of coast is the northwesterly *tramontane*, which blows at force 6 and over for nearly 60% of observations. For over 11% of observations it blows at force 8 and above. It has been known to blow at hurricane force (force 12) on occasions. The *tramontane* is caused when a depression passes across central France and the air, bottled up between the Pyrénées and the Massif Central, escapes to the Mediterranean through the valley gap, known as the Toulouse Gap, between the high land on either side. The dangers of the *tramontane* are not just it's fury and the very real likelihood that you will encounter it, but also the fact that it can arrive very quickly, building up from a flat calm to force 6 or 7 in less than an hour. The *tramontane* whips up a vicious short sea and between the force of the wind and the force of the sea you can have very real difficulties making to windward for shelter. Since the *tramontane* is an offshore wind in this region, the only shelter will often lie to windward.

The frequency and mean wind strength of the prevailing NW *tramontane* does however vary dramatically along the coast. On the western side of the Golfe du Lion NW winds account for over 50% of the winds in the summer and over 60% in the winter, with gale force winds from this direction accounting for 13% of observations. Only 3% of the gales occur between June and August. In the NE corner of the Golfe du Lion, around Sète, there is a pocket of relatively less strong NW winds with mean wind strengths in the summer averaging force 4. In winter there is a higher chance of gale force winds from the south at Sète, whereas on the western side of the Golfe du Lion gale force winds are mostly from the N and NW.

Other winds along this coast are predominantly NE or SE. Strong onshore winds pose as much or more of a problem than does the *tramontane*. The coast is fringed by comparatively shallow water for

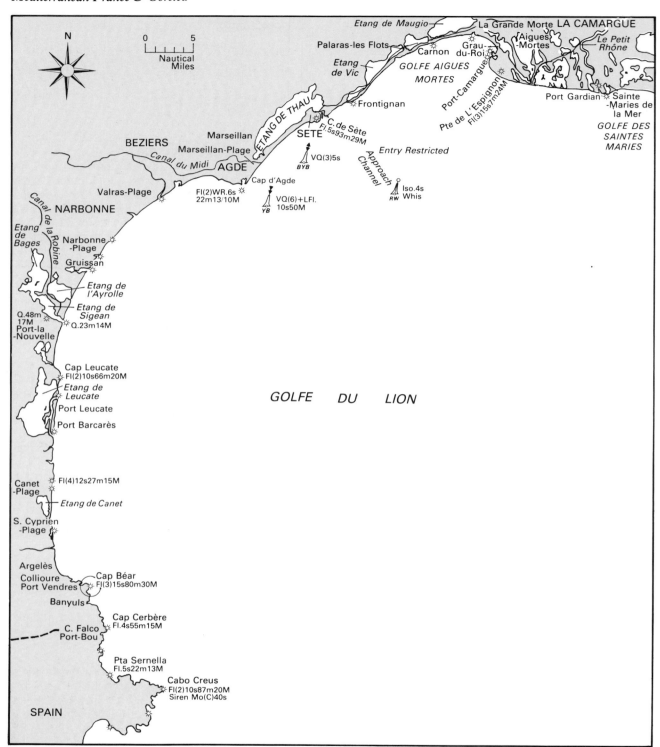

N

0 ⎸⎸⎸⎸⎸ 5
Nautical
Miles

Etang de Maugio
La Grande Morte **LA CAMARGUE**
Palaras-les Flots
Aigues
-Mortes
*Le Petit
Rhône*
Carnon
Grau-
du-Roi
*Etang
de Vic*
*GOLFE AIGUES
MORTES*
Port-Camargue
Frontignan
Pte de L'Espignon
Fl(3)15s7m24M
Port Gardian
Sainte
-Maries de
la Mer
ÉTANG DE THAU
C. de Sète
Fl.5s93m29M
SÉTE
*GOLFE DES
SAINTES
MARIES*
BÉZIERS
Marseillan
*Approach
Channel*
Entry Restricted
Marseillan-Plage
Canal du Midi
AGDE
VQ(3)5s
BYB
Cap d'Agde
Fl(2)WR.6s
22m13/10M
Iso.4s
Whis
RW
Valras-Plage
VQ(6)+LFl.
10s50M
YB
NARBONNE
*Etang
de
Bages*
Narbonne
-Plage
Gruissan
*Etang de
l'Ayrolle*
*Etang de
Sigean*
Q.48m
17M
Port-la
-Nouvelle
Q.23m14M
Cap Leucate
Fl(2)10s66m20M
*Etang de
Leucate*
GOLFE   DU   LION
Port Leucate
Port Barcarès
Fl(4)12s27m15M
Canet
-Plage
Etang de Canet
S. Cyprien
-Plage
Argelès
Collioure
Port Vendres
Cap Béar
Fl(3)15s80m30M
Banyuls
Cap Cerbère
C. Falco
Port-Bou
Fl.4s55m15M
Pta Sernella
Fl.5s22m13M
Cabo Creus
Fl(2)10s87m20M
Siren Mo(C)40s
SPAIN

some distance off and onshore gales can cause breaking waves and surf as far out as the 20-metre line. Since the majority of the new harbours have their entrances on the 5-metre line, strong onshore winds can make it dangerous to attempt to enter.

A yacht on passage along the coast or crossing the Golfe du Lion should always keep a listening watch on the radio for gale warnings. The Golfe du Lion has the highest frequency of gale force winds in the Mediterranean at an average 6·8% in the year with 13·2% in the winter and 1·3% in the summer. Like all official statistics, these figures do not seem to mirror the actual situation and suffice it to say that anyone who has cruised here will tell you that is a very windy corner of the Mediterranean. The *tramontane* can arrive quickly and within an hour you may have gale force winds. If a *tramontane* is forecast you should waste no time in making for a safe harbour – the alternative may be running off before it to Spain or the Balearics. Gales from the south take longer to arrive and are usually preceded by a long swell rolling in before the wind arrives, but it should be remembered that they will make the approach and entrance to some 80% of the harbours described here difficult and often dangerous.

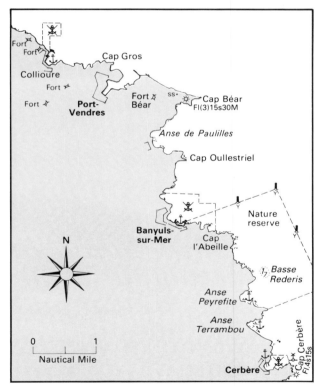

CERBERE TO COLLIOURE

CERBERE

A small harbour just along from the Spanish border on the N side of Cap Cerbère. It is tenable only in calm weather. Anchor under the breakwater or go onto one of the pontoons if there is room. There are no officials here for clearing in or out of France. Cerbère is the main border railway station and the tiny village is dominated by a huge railway station that would not disgrace a large city.

Note A mile N of Cerbère there is nature reserve extending up to a mile off the coast until Banyuls-sur-Mer. It is marked by four yellow buoys with the two outermost lit (Fl.Y.4s). Off Cerbère there is also a yellow buoy which is lit (Fl(3)Y.6s).

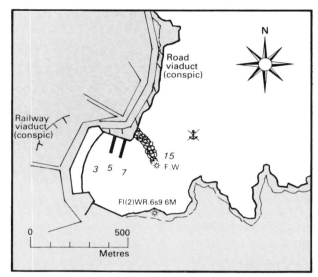

CERBERE 42°26'·5N 3°10'·2E

BANYULS SUR MER

Approach

Conspicuous Cap Béar with a tall lighthouse and old signal station on it is easily identified and Banyuls-sur-Mer lies 2 miles S of it. From the S the harbour and town will not be seen until around Cap l'Abeille. Closer in a viaduct on the N side of the bay and the oceanographic institute, a large white building behind the harbour, will be seen. The light structures at the entrance are easily identified.

By night Use the light on Cap Béar (Fl(3)15s30M) and the lights at the harbour entrance: Fl.WG.4s10/7M and Oc(2)R.6s. The white sector of the light on Ile Petite at the entrance shows the safe approach between 193° and 247°. The inner mole is also lit: Iso.4s.

Dangers
● With strong winds from the NE–E a heavy swell rolls into the bay making entry difficult and possibly dangerous. With a strong NW *tramontane* entrance can also be difficult.

Cap Oullestreil with Cap Béar in the distance looking N.

Banyuls sur Mer harbour looking SW.

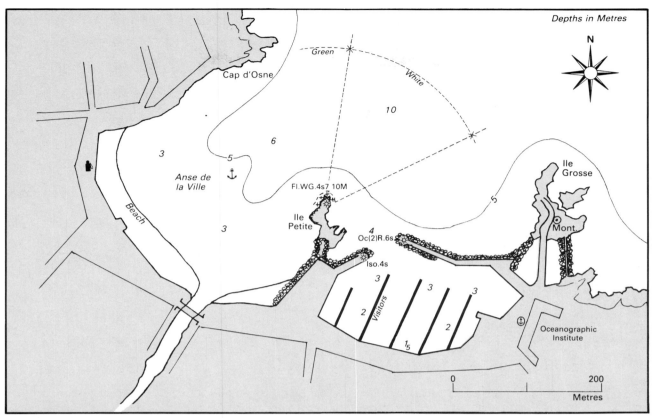

BANYULS SUR MER 42°28'·9N 3°08'·1E

- Give Ile Grosse a good offing in the approach from the S to clear the above and below-water rocks lying off it.

Mooring

Details 420 berths with 120 berths for visitors. Maximum LOA 25 metres. Go on the *quai d'accueil* just inside the entrance and report to the *capitainerie*. There are laid moorings tailed to buoys.

Shelter Good shelter although strong northerlies can make the harbour very uncomfortable.

Authorities Customs and port captain. A charge is made. This is the closest port to Spain with a customs office.

Anchorage In calm weather you can anchor in Anse de la Ville clear of the buoys marking the bathing area.

Facilities

Services Water and electricity at every berth. A shower and toilet block.

Fuel In the town about 200 metres away.

Repairs A 12-ton crane, but limited hard standing. Mechanical repairs and some GRP repairs possible. Chandlers.

Provisions Good shopping for provisions in the town. Ice available.

Eating out Numerous restaurants on the waterfront and in the town.

Other Post office. Banks. Buses and trains along the coast.

General

Banyuls is an old fishing village that has changed trades and is now a thriving tourist resort. Palms line the waterfront and the old houses straggling up the steep slopes make an attractive vista from the harbour. Aristide Maillol, the sculptor, was born in Banyuls and returned to live here after he tired of Paris. On Ile Grosse by the harbour there is one of his statues, a moving piece showing a dying man flanked by mourners. Also by the harbour is the Laboratoire Arago, an oceanographic institute mainly devoted to marine research, but with a large aquarium open to the public. Although not as well known as the aquarium at Monaco, the collection of Mediterranean and other marine life here is every bit as good and well worth a visit.

Banyuls is best known to the French not for a sculptor or the aquarium, but for its wines, flinty reds and dry fruity rosés. You can find them on sale in Banyuls and around the coast and they deserve sampling. The region also produces a sweet apéritif which tastes not dissimilar to an average ruby port to me.

Because Banyuls is an attractive place in a typically picture-postcard way, it attracts a lot of visitors in the height of summer, though in the harbour on the fringes of the town you are in the best place away from the worst of the noise and the crowds.

Port Vendres. The working side of the harbour.

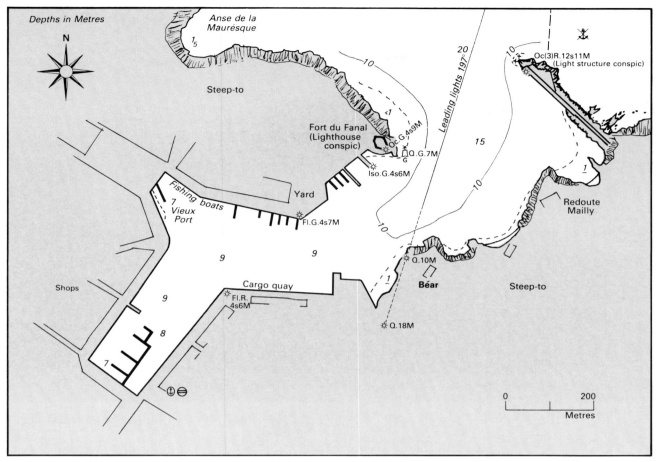

PORT VENDRES 42°31'·3N 3°06'·5E

PORT VENDRES

Approach

Conspicuous Cap Béar with its tall lighthouse and old signal station is easily identified. Fort St Elme to the W and Fort Béar on the summit of Cap Béar are also easily identified. The entrance to Port Vendres can be identified by the white lighthouse on the W side of the entrance and the high light tower on the outer breakwater.

By night Use the light on Cap Béar (Fl(3)15s30M) and the lights at the harbour entrance: Oc(3)R.12s11M, Oc.G.4s8M and Q.G.7M (beacon). The Avant Port is lit: Iso.G.4s6M and Fl.R.4s6M. There are leading lights into the harbour on 197·5°: Q.10M and Q.18M.

Dangers

● With strong winds from the N and E there is a confused swell around Cap Béar and in the approaches to Port Vendres. The steep-to rocky coast causes a nasty reflected swell and a yacht should keep well off Cap Béar in the approach from the S.

● With a *tramontane* there are strong gusts and breaking seas in the approaches. Even within the harbour there are gusts from the *tramontane*.

● Care needs to be taken of the shoal water on the W side of the entrance to the Avant Port.

Mooring

Details 243 berths with 30 berths for visitors. Maximum LOA 40 metres.

Berth on the E side of the Nouvelle Darse and report to the *capitainerie* for a berth. There are finger pontoons and laid moorings tailed to buoys.

Shelter Good all-round shelter although northerly gales cause a surge which can be uncomfortable.

Authorities Customs and port captain. A charge is made. Port Vendres is the last major port before Spain with a full complement of the relevant authorities for clearing in or out of France.

Facilities

Services Water and electricity at every berth. A shower and toilet block.

Fuel On the quay in the Nouvelle Darse.

Repairs A 150-ton travel-hoist and 60-ton crane. Limited hard standing when the fishing boats are out. Mechanical and engineering repairs. GRP and wood repairs. Chandlers.

Provisions Good shopping for all provisions nearby. Ice available.

Eating out Numerous restaurants in the town including good fish restaurants.

Other Post office. Banks. Buses and trains along the coast.

Collioure looking NW. The tower and the outer breakwater are conspicuous.

General

Port Vendres, the 'Port of Venus', was used by the Greeks and later the Romans. It was not fortified by either the Spanish or the French, to whom it variously belonged, until Vauban developed and fortified it in 1679. In the late 19th and early 20th centuries it became an important port for trade from North Africa and Spain. It was badly damaged in the Second World War, but revived after the war, with the trade from Algeria. When Algeria gained independence in 1962 trade dried up and now it mostly serves as the base port for a large fishing fleet.

Port Vendres is my favourite along this coast. Although Banyuls and Collioure are the good-lookers, they are also almost wholly devoted to tourism, whereas Port Vendres has its tourist appeal muted by the fishing fleet and the commercial port.

NOTE

Port Pierre-Méry In Baie de Paullites, S of Cap Béar, it is planned to build a 470-berth marina and associated residential complex on the site of an old explosives factory. At the time of writing work has yet to begin.

COLLIOURE

Approach

The last of the harbours on the Côte Vermeille before the long low coast of Languedoc-Roussillon.

Conspicuous From the N the steep slopes of the Pyrénées stand out prominently and Collioure lies some 2 miles along from the flat coast. From the S Cap Béar with its lighthouse and old signal station is easily recognised. In the closer approach the Château des Templiers and the tower at the root of the breakwater are conspicuous.

By night Use the Iso.G.4s8M on the breakwater. A night entry is not really recommended because of the difficulty in finding a spot to anchor in the dark. Often yachts at anchor do not display an anchor light.

Dangers There are severe gusts with the *tramontane*.

Note There is a military firing range to the N. When it is in use a red flag is displayed from Fort Carré on the coast.

Mooring

Details 90 berths in the small harbour with a maximum LOA of 6·5 metres, although slightly larger yachts may squeeze in.

Most yachts must anchor in one of the coves in the cloverleaf bay, clear of the buoys enclosing the bathing areas. Anchoring is prohibited in the sector between bearings of 095° and 110° from the tower at

The small-boat harbour at Collioure. Most yachts will have to anchor off.

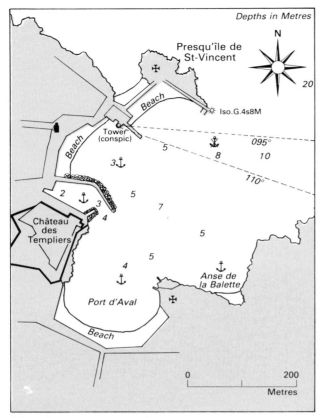

COLLIOURE 42°31′·7N 3°05′·3E

thers of modernism and the other art-isms of this century: Matisse, Dufy, Braque, Gris, Lhote and a whole host of lesser known artists. Fauvism, the -ism that used Van Gogh and his vital colours as an inspiration and whose leader was Henri Matisse, claims Collioure as its birthplace. At the Hôtel les Templiers in Collioure, the owner at the time accepted paintings as payment for board and lodgings and consequently has a superb collection of 20th-century art on display for most of the year.

Collioure has an ancient pedigree dating back to the Phocaean Greeks who established a colony here to trade with the Ibero-Ligurians. Later the Romans used it calling the harbour Cocoliberum. The sturdy Château des Templiers by the water was built by the Kings of Aragon in the 13th century and held by the Kingdom of Mallorca for some time. In the 15th century Louis XI took Collioure and so began a troubled period for the town on the border of the French and Spanish kingdoms. Not until Matisse and his friends discovered it was it prosperous again.

There is no denying the beauty of the old town set under the steep slopes of the bay, but in summer it can get very crowded. It also has what a local guidebook, quoted in *The South of France*, describes as 'beaucoup de snobisme', perhaps a legacy of all the egocentric artistic talent that was once concentrated here.

the base of the breakwater. The bottom is sand, rock, and weed; good holding once through the weed.

Shelter Reasonable shelter except from northerlies which send in a swell. In strong northerlies go to Port Vendres.

Facilities

Services Water from private sources ashore.

Fuel A petrol station on the waterfront.

Repairs No hauling facilities. A chandlers and hardware shop.

Provisions Good shopping for provisions in the town.

Eating out Numerous restaurants around the waterfront and in the town.

Other Post office. Banks. Buses and trains along the coast.

General

Long before the Languedoc-Roussillon *unités* were even dreamed of, Collioure was described as a 'pearl' of a resort by early travellers to the coast. In *West of the Rhône* Freda White describes it as the 'last of the beautiful villages of France – there is nothing beyond', which, if a bit harsh on Port Vendres and Banyuls, adequately expresses the feelings of those who came to Collioure and fell in love with it. In the early part of the 20th century it became something of an artists' colony and the list of names of those who came here reads like a roll call of the founding fa-

ARGELES-PLAGE

A small harbour at the mouth of La Massane river. It is still under construction and yet to be dredged so some care is needed when entering it.

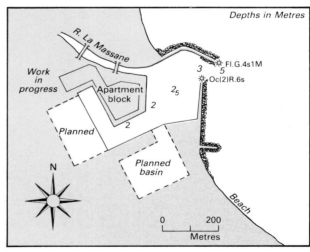

ARGELES-PLAGE 42°32′·7N 3°03′E

Approach

The harbour lies right where the foothills of the Pyrénées meet the flat coast. The apartment blocks of Argelès-Plage will be seen and the harbour is situated at the southern end of them. The entrance is lit (Fl.G.4s1M and Oc(2)R.6s), but a night entry is not advised.

Note Care needs to be taken of the depths inside as the bottom is uneven.

Mooring

Go where convenient on the unfinished section of the quay by the apartments on the middle 'island'.

Facilities

Water available, but little else.

General

Eventually the harbour will boast all amenities, though it is likely to be some time judging by the slow progress made since construction began in 1983.

ST-CYPRIEN-PLAGE

Approach

Conspicuous The harbour lies at the southern end of the apartment blocks of the resort. A water tower inland is conspicuous. Closer in the breakwaters and light structures on their ends show up well.

By night The harbour entrance is lit: VQ(4)R.2s10M and F.

Dangers With strong winds from the E and S there is a confused swell at the entrance. With gale force easterlies entry may be dangerous.

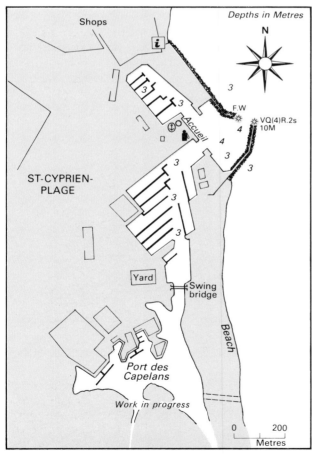

ST-CYPRIEN-PLAGE 43°37'·3N 3°02'·4E

Note Approximately 1½ miles ENE a yellow buoy with a X topmark is in position on the western limit of the area where anchoring is prohibited. It is lit: Fl(3)Y.

Mooring

Details 2200 berths with 440 berths for visitors. Maximum LOA 20 metres.

Berth at the *quai d'accueil* in the Avant Port and report to the *capitainerie* for a berth. There are finger pontoons or laid moorings tailed to buoys.

Shelter Good all-round shelter.

Authorities Port captain and marina staff. A charge is made.

Facilities

Services Water and electricity at every berth. A shower and toilet block.

Fuel On the quay in the Avant Port.

Repairs 27 and 50-ton travel-hoists and a 100-ton slipway. Mechanical and engineering repairs. GRP and wood repairs. Electrical and electronic repairs. Sailmakers. Chandlers.

Provisions Good shopping for provisions at the northern end of the marina. Ice available.

Eating out Numerous restaurants open in the summer.

Other Post office. Banks. Hire cars. Taxis. Internal and some international flights from Perpignan.

General

St-Cyprien-Plage, the first of the huge *unités* you encounter going north, is somehow the most architecturally dull of what is a fairly uniform architectural theme anyway. Perhaps I missed something. The marina is efficiently run, the yard well equipped to haul all types of yachts, large and small, there are two golf courses, tennis courts, a riding club and of course the beach complete with a statue by Maillol, *La Baigneuse à la Draperie*; but that is about all I can say of the place.

Note

Work is in progress developing the marina and associated apartment complex around the *étang* south of St-Cyprien. Eventually it is planned to link the *étang* directly to the sea by digging a channel across the beach, so access will be direct rather than through the basin to the north as it is at present.

OCCITANIE

In the Languedoc-Roussillon region you may see a badge on the back of local cars with not *F* for France, but *OC* for Occitanie. The Occitan movement is not as well known as say the Breton or Corsican movements for cultural and political autonomy, partly because they don't go around daubing Occitan graffiti everywhere, but they have a sizeable following in the south of France, though like most movements of this type nobody is saying what that means in numbers.

The name Occitanie comes from the old word in the south for 'yes', which was *oc*, hence the region of the language of *oc*, Languedoc. In the north the word for 'yes' was *oïl*, later *oui*, and the north was known as the language of *oïl*, *langue d'Oïl*. Many of the songs, poems and much literature of the Middle Ages was written in *langue d'Oc*. It was the language of the troubadours and was used outside the region as far away as Germany and the Hohenstaufen court in Sicily. When the language of the north became the dominant tongue, the *langue d'Oc* was broken up into different dialects of which only one, Catalan, is still common.

The Occitan movement does not seek political autonomy as the Catalan movement in Spain does, although it has a number of leading lights who envisage a sort of agricultural utopia removed from what is seen as the northern mercantile rat-race. One of the problems the movement faces is that those speaking one of the 'Oc' dialects in Nice for example, cannot understand the 'Oc' dialect of those in Toulouse, so there is no common unifying language for the movement. What the Occitan movement does do is preserve the culture and the old music and poetry that was written in the *langue d'Oc*. In Theodore Zeldin's *The French* an Occitan supporter describes his feelings for the music of 'Oc' like this: 'I want to be a musician of the people playing according to local traditions. I prefer playing at dances. We give concerts, we perform in the streets, at marriages, in church for Christmas, at funerals, at ceremonies. The most popular music we play is dance music, and also comic carnival music; we have songs for every moment of life, satirical and political, for engagement parties and for cuckolds, for work and bereavement.'

This attachment to the music and language of 'Oc' is the key to the Occitan movement. In its organisation and political effectiveness, Occitanie doesn't have a lot going for it, but once you understand the emotional feelings people have for it, it's efficacy as a movement can be seen as quietly powerful; a revolution of hearts and minds rather than a revolution of rhetoric and political change. The music and language grafted to what has been called the 'civilisation of the vine' makes up a sort of southern cultural consciousness at odds with the smooth cultivated politicians and their plans in Paris and the north. The Occitan supporter quoted earlier summarised his feelings about Occitan music with a statement that could equally apply to the Occitanie movement itself: '... everything is waiting to be invented.'

Van Gogh. *Tartanes* at Stes-Maries.

CANET-EN-ROUSSILLON
(CANET-PLAGE, PORT PERE NOEL)

Approach

Conspicuous The apartments of the resort and a water tower are conspicuous. Closer in the modern twin-pillared lighthouse just N of the harbour is easily identified. The breakwaters of the harbour and the light structure on the end of the outer breakwater show up well.

By night Use Canet-Plage lighthouse (Fl(4)12s16M) and the lights at the harbour entrance: Oc.R.4s9M and Fl(2)G.6s5M.

Dangers With strong winds from NE–SE there is a confused swell at the entrance and in gale force onshore winds entry would be dangerous.

Mooring

Details 977 berths with 117 berths for visitors. Maximum LOA 24 metres.

Berth on the *quai d'accueil* (a pontoon) just inside Bassin Le Gouffre and report to the *capitainerie* for a berth. There are laid moorings tailed to buoys or to the quay.

Shelter Good shelter although a strong *tramontane* can make some berths uncomfortable in the basin.

Authorities Customs, port captain and marina staff. A charge is made.

Facilities

Services Water and electricity at every berth. A shower and toilet block.

Fuel On the quay at the entrance to the basin.

Repairs A 27-ton travel-hoist and 80-ton slipway. Mechanical and engineering repairs. GRP and wood repairs. Electrical and electronic repairs. Sailmakers. Chandlers.

Provisions Good shopping for provisions nearby. Ice available.

Eating out Numerous restaurants nearby.

Other Post office. Banks. Hire cars. Taxis. Buses to Perpignan. Internal and some international flights from Perpignan.

General

Like St-Cyprien-Plage, less architectural effort seems to have been put into Canet-en-Roussillon than some of the other developments along the coast, with some pretty anonymous blobs of reinforced concrete doing duty as apartment blocks. Perhaps the directors of the marina feel this too since they put a good deal of effort into making the place run smoothly in a friendly sort of way. Visiting yachts get the use of a bicycle free of charge for an hour when they arrive. Close to the marina there is an aquarium with an interesting collection of marine life. If you concentrate on the ground-level view, the streets and squares are colourful and alive with the local *Canétois* and nearby *Perpignanais* enjoying themselves, and Canet-en-Roussillon slowly grows on you.

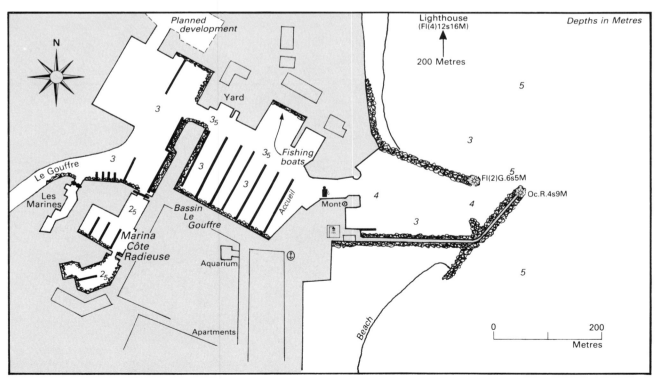

CANET-EN-ROUSSILLON 42°42'·2N 3°02'·6E

Etang de Leucate
(Etang de Salses)

This large inland lagoon has been developed along its eastern edge with the construction of the Leucate-Barcarès *unité*. The *étang* can be entered at Port Barcarès by craft with less than 3 metres air height or at the southern end of Port Leucate by craft with less than 18 metres air height. There are mostly 2–3 metre depths in the *étang* though its shores are fringed by depths of 1 metre and less for some distance off on the northern side. For shallow-draught craft it affords an interesting inland sailing area, but remember though it is inland, the *tramontane* still kicks up a vicious sea.

PORT BARCARES (GRAU ST-ANGE)

Approach

Conspicuous The *Lydia*, an old cruise boat on the beach 2 miles to the N is conspicuous. The apartment blocks at Barcarès will be seen and closer in the light structure on the breakwater and the brown tower-like *capitainerie* are easily identified.

By night The entrance is lit: Fl(2)R.6s10M and F (weak).

Dangers With strong easterlies and southerlies there is a confused swell at the entrance. With onshore winds over force 6–7 the entrance can be dangerous and a yacht should go to Leucate-Plage.

Mooring

Details 293 berths with 10 berths for visitors. Maximum LOA 13 metres.

Berth Go onto the *quai d'accueil* just inside the entrance and report to the *capitainerie* for a berth. There are laid moorings tailed to buoys or posts around which you take a line.

Shelter Good all-round shelter.

Authorities Port captain. A charge is made.

Facilities

Services Water and electricity at every berth. A shower and toilet block.

Fuel On the quay at the entrance to the basin.

Repairs A 9-ton crane and a slipway. Mechanical repairs. Specialist aluminium work can be carried out nearby. Chandlers.

Provisions Most provisions can be found in the summer. Ice available.

Eating out Restaurants on both sides of the harbour in the summer.

Other Post office. Bank. Hire cars. Taxis.

General

Port Barcarès is built on the original channel from the Etang de Leucate to the sea and was formerly

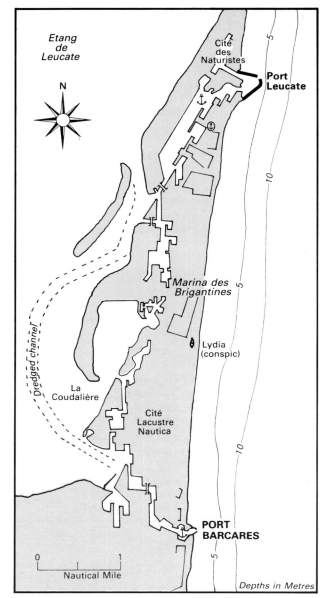

PORT BARCARES AND PORT LEUCATE

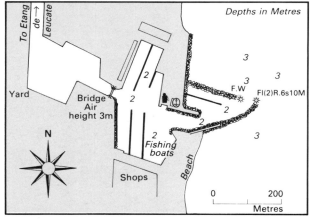

PORT BARCARES 42°47′·9N 3°02′·4E

known as Grau St-Ange before the construction gangs arrived. There has always been a fishing port here and it is good to see that the basin on the south side of Port Barcarès is reserved for the local fishing boats. The boats and bits of equipment and nets dumped on the quay add welcome colour and chaos to the harbour.

The *Lydia* on the beach to the north houses a casino and disco. It was stranded on the beach in 1967, though I couldn't find out whether this was intended or a fortuitous accident for the developers.

PORT LEUCATE

The largest of the Languedoc-Roussillon *unités*, though not yet the largest marina.

Approach

Conspicuous Cap Leucate, the only high ground near the coast, with a lighthouse and communications tower with a white dome on top, is easily identified just N of the harbour entrance. The *Lydia* on the beach 3 miles S of the entrance is conspicuous. Closer in the breakwaters and light structures at their ends show up well.

By night Use the light on Cap Leucate (Fl(2)10s20M) and the lights at the outer entrance: Fl.R.4s9M and Fl.G.4s3M. The inner entrance is lit (Oc.R.4s and Oc.G.4s) and the entrances to the various basins are also lit by occulting red or green lights.

Dangers In strong S and E winds there is a confused swell at the entrance and in onshore gale force winds entry could be dangerous. With a strong *tramontane* there can be a vicious chop in the Avant Port and the channel to the basins.

Note
● It is over a mile from the entrance to the basin and if a *tramontane* is blowing it seems much further.
● There is a speed limit of 5 knots within a band 300 metres off the coast and in the access channels to the marina.

Mooring

Details 1000 berths with 100 berths for visitors. Maximum LOA 20 metres. The total number of berths will eventually be expanded.

Berth on the *quai d'accueil* by the *capitainerie* and report for a berth. There are finger pontoons or posts around which you must take a line.

Conspicuous *capitainerie* at Port Barcarès.

Leucate-Plage looking N. Ultimately Leucate-Plage will link with Barcarès to form something like 11 kilometres of continuous marinas and associated apartment complexes.

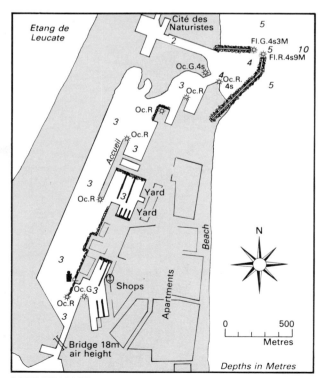

PORT LEUCATE 42°52′N 3°03′E

Shelter Good all-round shelter although some berths are exposed to the *tramontane* and can be uncomfortable.

Authorities Customs. Port captain and marina staff. A charge is made.

Facilities

Services Water and electricity at every berth. Several shower and toilet blocks.

Fuel On the quay in the southern basin.

Repairs A 45-ton travel-hoist. Covered storage ashore. All mechanical and engineering repairs. GRP and wood repairs. Electrical and electronic repairs. Sailmakers. Chandlers.

Provisions Good shopping for provisions in the summer.

Eating out Numerous restaurants and bars around the marina open in the summer.

Other Post office. Bank. Hire cars. Taxis.

General

Leucate along with Barcarès forms one of the largest single developments along the coast, extending from the Village Naturiste in the north above the harbour right down the sand spit on the east side of the Etang de Leucate to Le Barcarès de St-Laurent just south of Port Barcarès – some 11 kilometres of continuous resort. A channel around the Etang de Leucate connects Port Barcarès with Port Leucate and the harbours on the *étang* at Cité Lacustre Nautica, Marina des Brigantines and La Coudalière. When this whole project is completed I estimate there will be over 5000 yacht berths in the whole complex with a vast sprawl of apartments ashore. The existing architecture works tolerably well, with trees and shrubs softening the reinforced concrete, though a few *cabanes* and some irregular stonework would add a more human dimension to this huge resort city.

PORT LA NOUVELLE

A commercial port with a few berths for yachts near the seaward end of the La Nouvelle branch canal which connects with the Canal du Midi.

Approach

The harbour lies just over 6 miles N of Cap Leucate.

Conspicuous A tall chimney (white with red bands) and the buildings of a cement works inland of La Nouvelle are conspicuous. The tall light towers at the entrance and a number of oil storage tanks on the N side of the port are also conspicuous.

By night Use the light on Cap Leucate (Fl(2)10s20M) and the lights at the entrance: Q.14M and Iso.G.4s5M. The Q at the entrance in line on 292·4° with a Q.17M behind the entrance are the leading lights into the port.

Dangers With strong winds, force 6 and over, from the S and E, there are breaking waves at the entrance making entry difficult and often dangerous.

Caution
• Commercial vessels have right of way at all times in the approaches and in Port La Nouvelle itself.
• Depending on the wind direction there can be a current of up to 3 knots out of the channel.

Mooring

Details Yachts under 8–9 metres may find a berth on one of the pontoons near the bridge at the end of the harbour, but care needs to be taken of the depths close to the sides. Larger yachts can go alongside the S quay, though again care is needed.

Shelter Generally good, but the *tramontane* can kick up a chop and strong easterlies blowing against the current cause an uncomfortable ruckle.

Authorities Customs. Port captain. A charge is not normally made.

Facilities

Services A water tap on the quay by the pontoons.

Fuel Nearby on the S quay.

Repairs A 6-ton crane, but limited hard standing on the quayside. Masts can be raised or lowered here. Mechanical repairs. Chandlers.

Provisions Good shopping for provisions nearby in the town. Ice available.

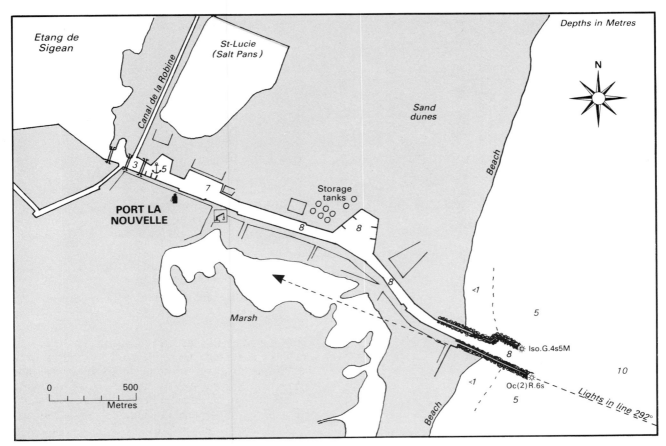

PORT LA NOUVELLE 43°01′N 3°04′E

Eating out Numerous restaurants in the town.

Other Post office. Banks. Taxis. Train to Narbonne and Perpignan.

General

Most descriptions of La Nouvelle dismiss it as a grubby little place to be avoided at all costs, but after the tourist cities on either side of it La Nouvelle comes as something of a relief, a real working port. It cannot be denied it is industrial, surrounded as it is by cement works and oil storage tanks, or that it smells alternately of acrid lime or rotting fish and weed from the nets of the fishing boats. And there are virtually no facilities for pleasure boats. What it does have are good fish restaurants with bargain-basement prices, down-to-earth cafés frequented by rough fishermen knocking back *pastis*. *Pastis* and a strawberry cordial was all the rage when I was there and it tastes better than it looks. And always there are the expanses of the *étangs* never far away.

GRUISSAN

A huge new marina carved out of the salt marshes by the old village of Gruissan. There is also the old harbour at Gruissan entered by the Canal du Grazel.

Approach

Visiting yachts should make for the new marina at Gruissan-Neuf to the NE of the entrance to the Canal du Grazel.

Conspicuous The old village of Gruissan on a small hummock and the ruined tower on its summit are conspicuous. Closer in the apartment blocks of Gruissan-Neuf will be seen. The breakwaters and the light towers on their ends at the entrance to Gruissan-Neuf are easily identified.

By night The entrance to Gruissan-Neuf is lit: Fl(2)R.6s7M and Fl.G.4s7M. The inner entrance and the beacons and buoys marking the dredged channel are lit: Fl.G and Fl.R. The entrance to the marina basin is also lit: Fl.G and Fl.R.

Dangers With strong onshore winds there is a confused swell at the entrance and with gale force winds

Gruissan. The old village and the conspicuous ruined Tour de Barberousse.

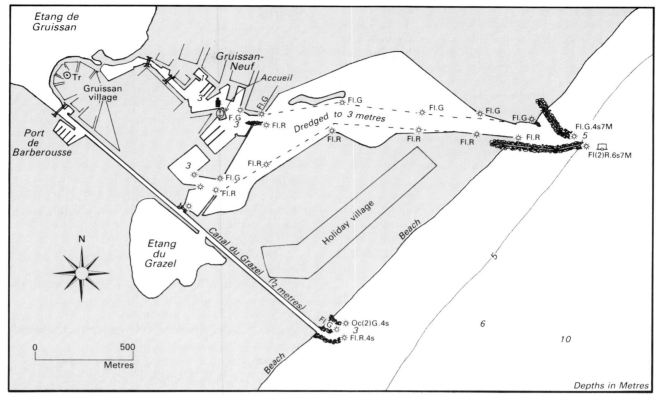

GRUISSAN 43°06'·5N 3°06'E

from the S and E entry could be dangerous. With a strong *tramontane* a considerable chop is kicked up in the dredged channel leading to the yacht basin.

Note
● It is around 1½ miles from the entrance to the yacht basin.
● There is a speed limit of 3 knots in the harbour and access channel, though local boats rarely seem to observe the limit.

Mooring

Details 750 berths with 150 berths for visitors. Maximum LOA 30 metres. Maximum draught: 2·5 metres. The total number of berths will eventually be expanded.

Berth at the *quai d'accueil* on the central pier and report to the *capitainerie* for a berth. The *capitainerie* is a conspicuous domed tower. There are finger pontoons or laid moorings tailed to the quay.

Shelter Good all-round shelter although some berths are uncomfortable in a strong *tramontane*.

Authorities Customs. Port captain and marina staff. A charge is made.

Facilities

Services Water and electricity at every berth. Several shower and toilet blocks around the marina.

Fuel On the central pier.

Repairs A 12-ton travel-hoist and a 50-ton crane. Mechanical and engineering repairs. GRP repairs. Electrical and electronic repairs. Sailmakers. Chandlers.

Provisions Good shopping for provisions in the marina or in the old village. Ice available.

Eating out Numerous restaurants around the marina and in the old village.

Other Post office. Banks. Hire cars. Taxis.

General

If you walk up to the ruined tower on top of the hummock that the old village sprawls over and around, you will be rewarded with a fine view over the *étangs* and the Montagne de la Clape. I was struck most by the loneliness of the flat horizons and sand dunes, broken only by the limestone ridge of La Clape, a landscape that has been catapulted into the mass tourism market by the huge development below. The village of Gruissan, with its narrow cobbled streets and the crumbling remains of the tower, has been left intact, still lapped on three sides by the waters of the *étang*. In older days it must have been an isolated and perilous place in this remote landscape.

The name of the ruined tower and of the small yacht basin in the old village, Barberousse, most likely refers to the famous corsair Khair ud-Din, nicknamed Barberossa for his red beard, the Bey of Algiers who terrorised the Mediterranean. Did he sack the town, or base his fleet here at some time, or is there another reason for the name?

GRUISSAN-VIEUX

Just over a mile SW of the entrance to Gruissan-Neuf is the entrance to the Canal de Grazel which leads to Port Barberousse at Gruissan-Vieux. The port can only be used by shallow-draught craft as there is a depth of just 1·2 metres in the canal. Entrance to the canal is dangerous in moderate to strong onshore winds when waves break on the bar at the entrance.

It is planned to dredge the canal in the future as it has been silting up for some time. Not so long ago there were 1·5 metre depths in the canal.

NARBONNE-PLAGE

Approach

Conspicuous A white radar dome on the high land behind and a water tower are conspicuous. Closer in the apartments of the small resort and the breakwaters of the harbour will be seen. A sculpted light tower on the end of the southern breakwater is conspicuous.

By night Use the light at La Pêche Rouge, Q(3)10s 2M, and the lights at the harbour entrance: Fl.G.4s and Fl.R.4s (weak). A night entry is not really recommended.

Dangers

● The harbour entrance is fringed by shoal water and in onshore winds of force 6 and over entry is dangerous. With onshore gale-force winds there are breaking waves and surf at the entrance. Although there are 2·5 metre depths, if there is any swell the depths are considerably reduced in the troughs of the swell and yachts drawing more than 1·5 metres should not attempt to enter.

● Yachts longer than 10–11 metres should not attempt to enter as a dogleg must be negotiated to get into the basin and there is little room inside for manoeuvring.

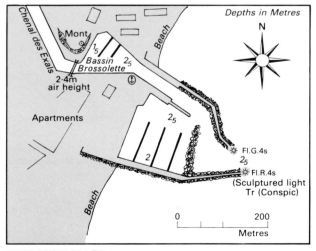

NARBONNE-PLAGE 43°10′N 3°11′E

Mooring

Details 600 berths with visitors' berths available. Many of these berths are in Bassin Brossolette and the canal off it and are for craft drawing less than one metre.

Berth where directed or on the W quay and report to the *capitainerie*. There are finger pontoons at most berths.

Shelter Reasonable shelter although strong southerlies and easterlies cause a surge.

Authorities Port captain. A charge is made.

Bassin Brossolette Craft drawing less than one metre may find a berth here where the shelter is excellent.

Chenal des Exals Craft drawing less than 0·8 metre and with less than 2·4 metres air height may find a berth here.

Facilities

Services Water at every berth. A shower and toilet block.

Fuel Close to Bassin Brossolette.

Repairs A 5-ton crane, but limited hard standing. Some mechanical repairs. Chandlers.

Provisions Limited shopping in the summer.

Eating out Restaurants open in the summer.

General

Narbonne-Plage lies at the edge of a limestone ridge, Le Montagne de la Clape, the only high land along this stretch of coast. It must have been a desolate place once, but now the up-market villas of the prosperous *Narbonnais* relieve the hard calcareous landscape. Above the inner basin there is a monument to Brossolette, a local leader of the French Resistance in the Second World War.

CASSOULET

Amongst the well known dishes of the south of France quoted in guidebooks, *cassoulet* always gets a mention. It has its origins in the Roussillon region with several places laying claim to the truly original recipe. The three towns vying for first place in the *cassoulet* league table are Toulouse, Carcassonne, and Castelnaudary, the latter generally being accepted as the true home of the dish. In many of the restaurants along this coast you will find *cassoulet* on the menu and it should be sampled.

Basically it is a *ragoût* with a base of white haricot beans to which is added various ingredients. Depending on which recipe you follow, a number of items are considered essential including mutton, goose fat (*graisse d'oie*) and goose jelly (*confit d'oie*) as well as the white haricot beans; but in reality *cassoulet* was originally a simple peasant dish designed to combine whatever was at hand – only later was the dish stuffed into a straitjacket recipe in a cookbook. Its ability to absorb all sorts of ingredients makes it a good one to cook on board and it has the advantage of all stew-type meals that it gets better the second time around, if, that is, it is not polished off in one go. Below I have simplified the recipe for cooking on board, though remember any similar or compatible ingredients can be used. I find it a good recipe for night passages as it can be prepared beforehand and then heated up later.

Simple Cassoulet (for four)
500g of mutton, preferably back, boned and cubed
200g of salami cut into chunks
100g of bacon or *lardon*
50g of goose fat (*graisse d'oie*), optional in my opinion and I never use it although all French recipes include it. If you want to go all the way get a small portion of *confit d'oie* as well – it is very expensive.
250g of white haricot beans. Soak them overnight or cheat and buy two medium-sized tins of them – they are readily available.
2 cloves of garlic, crushed
2 carrots, sliced
1 large onion, chopped
1 medium-sized tin of tomatoes, chop them up
Thyme
2 bay leaves
A small glass of cognac, optional
Salt and pepper to taste – for those who don't like a lot of salt remember the salami and bacon make it quite salty anyway.

Put a little oil (and the goose fat if you have it) in the bottom of a large pot or pressure cooker and gently brown the mutton, bacon and onion. Pour in a litre of water, less in a pressure cooker, and add all the other ingredients except the salami and cognac. Simmer for 2 hours, or 50 minutes in a pressure cooker. Add the salami and cognac and simmer for another half an hour, or 15 minutes in a pressure cooker.

Envoi Do not show this recipe to any French person and call it *cassoulet* or you will be in for a good hour's lecture on what the authentic dish should or should not include.

LES CABANES DE FLEURY

Just over 5 miles NE of Narbonne-Plage is the mouth of the Rivière l'Aude. Shallow-draught craft can cross the bar at the entrance and enter the river. Depths over the bar at the entrance vary from 1·5–2 metres and with even moderate onshore winds the entrance is dangerous with breaking waves over the bar. The NE side of the entrance is fringed by shoal water and rocks, and a yacht should approach the river on a course of around 300°. There are two leading marks, two white posts, behind the short breakwater on the SW side of the entrance. Once in the river proper there are depths of 1·5–4 metres in the channel. There is a basin on the W bank by the small resort of Cabanes de Fleury and another on the E bank.

At one time this area was earmarked as one of the Languedoc-Roussillon *unités*, l'Embouchure de l'Aude, with a huge marina for some 1500 yachts and an associated apartment complex ashore planned. For the time being the project has been dropped, but may be revived again some time in the future. At the moment there are local boats moored to rough wooden jetties, a few apartments and the *cabanes*, and wild salt marsh.

VALRAS-PLAGE

Approach

The harbour lies just inside the mouth of the River Orb.

Conspicuous It is difficult to see exactly where the harbour is. The apartment blocks of Valras-Plage will be seen and a water tower is conspicuous. Closer in the breakwaters and the light towers on the ends can be identified.

By night The entrance to the River Orb is lit: Fl.G.4s8M and Fl(4)12s9M. The entrance to the yacht basin is lit: Iso.G.4s and Iso.R.4s.

Dangers
● The coast is fringed by comparatively shallow water and a yacht should keep a prudent distance off.
● In strong southerlies and easterlies there is a confused swell at the entrance and in onshore gale-force winds the entrance can be dangerous.

Note When entering the mouth of the river keep closer to the W breakwater where there is deeper water.

Mooring

Details 185 berths with 20 berths for visitors. Maximum LOA 11 metres.

Berth at the *quai d'accueil* on the central pier until allocated a berth. There are finger pontoons or laid moorings tailed to buoys.

Shelter Good all-round shelter in the basin.

Authorities Customs. Port captain. A charge is made.

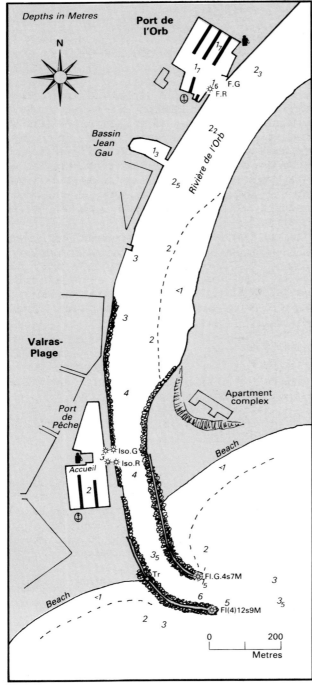

VALRAS-PLAGE 43°14'·8N 3°17'·8E

Facilities

Services Water and electricity at every berth. A shower and toilet block.

Fuel On the central pier.

Repairs A small crane at the basin, but there is limited hard standing on the quay. There is a yard further upstream that has good facilities. Mechanical repairs. GRP repairs. Chandlers.

Provisions Good shopping for provisions nearby. Ice available.

Eating out Numerous restaurants around the basin.

Other Post office. Bank. Taxis.

General

Valras-Plage is not part of the Languedoc-Roussillon scheme and hence has been developed in a more piecemeal fashion. The apartment blocks cannot be described as attractive, but the resort does have a more local feel to it reflected in the higgledy-piggledy mooring of boats along the river.

The Bassin Jean Gau just up the river is named after the pioneer French sailor who for years sailed his Tahiti ketch *Atom* around the world, stopping off in New York to work as a chef in a restaurant when he was short of funds. He was a much loved character who captured the imagination of the American public when he survived a hurricane that sank the German sail-training ship *Pamir* in mid-Atlantic with the death of all but six out of the eighty-six on board. It was feared that the tiny *Atom* was also lost, but a few weeks later Jean sailed into New York, and when asked about the hurricane, shrugged it off by saying he closed the hatches and went below to read and draw and sleep until things got better. He spent his last years in Valras-Plage, penniless and living on the goodwill of friends, a sad end for a grand old man of yachting.

PORT DE L'ORB

Just over a kilometre upstream of the yacht basin at Valras-Plage is Port de l'Orb. Although the basin is dredged to 1·7 metres, access is limited by 1·5 metre depths in the entrance, and yachts drawing more than 1·3 metres should not attempt to enter.

BASSIN JEAN GAU

A very small basin with 1·3 metre depths between Valras-Plage and Port de l'Orb.

GRAU D'AGDE

The village at the mouth of the Rivière Hérault. It is not really a harbour as such, with only a few berths along the banks of the river N of the village.

Approach

The breakwaters sheltering the entrance and the light towers at the ends are easily identified. The entrance is lit: Oc(2)R.6s7M and Oc.G.4s7M. With strong onshore winds waves break at the entrance making entry difficult and possibly dangerous.

Mooring

Where possible along the banks of the river just around the bend N of the village. When the river is in flood there is a strong current and attention must be paid to mooring lines and to whether or not what you are moored to is substantial enough.

Note Berths alongside the jetties off the village are reserved for local fishing boats.

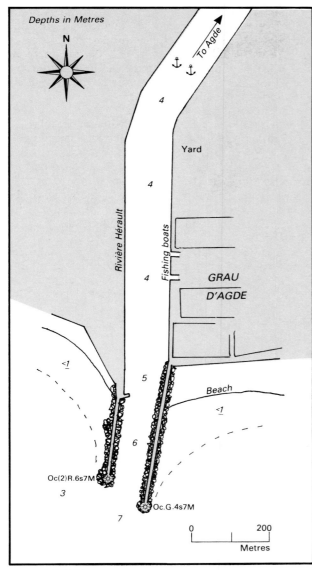

GRAU D'AGDE 43°17′N 3°27′E

Facilities

Provisions and restaurants in Grau d'Agde.

General

Grau d'Agde is not really a harbour as such, with berths wherever you are lucky enough to find one. Most yachts pass through here either coming or going from Agde and the Canal du Midi. (See Chapter I.)

CAP D'AGDE

Approach

This huge marina and shoreside complex lies under Mont d'Agde (Mont de Loup), the only high ground along this stretch of coast.

Conspicuous Mont d'Agde, which looks like an island from the distance, can be seen from some way off. A communications tower and the fort on the summit are conspicuous. Ile de Brescou lying in the approaches approximately 600 metres SSE of the entrance has a conspicuous fort and white lighthouse on it. Closer in the breakwaters of the Avant Port and the light towers on the ends are easily recognised. *La Lauze* beacon marking the shoal water off the entrance is also easily recognised.

Note The harbour should be approached through the channel between Ile de Brescou and *La Lauze* beacon, keeping at least 50 metres off *La Lauze*. Although local yachts cut across between Ile de Brescou and the coast and between *La Lauze* and the eastern breakwater, a visiting yacht should stick to the normal approach channel.

By night Straightforward. Use the light on Ile de Brescou: Fl(2)WR.6s13/10M. The red sector (113°-R-190°) covers only the dangers NW of the islet. A buoy Q(6)+LFl.15s marks the dangers to the S of Ile de Brescou. *La Lauze* light (Fl.G.4s6M) and the lights at the entrance to the Avant Port (Iso.G.4s9M and Fl.R.4s3M) show the way in. The knuckle on the breakwater is lit, Oc.G.

Dangers
● Ile de Brescou is fringed by shoal water. A rock with 0·5 metres over it lies approximately 200 metres NW of it and Roche de l'Ane, a rock with 0·4 metres over it lies approximately 150 metres S of the islet. A buoy, YB, with a ▼ topmark, is located about 350 metres S of Ile de Brescou on the 10 metre line. A yacht should keep to seaward of the buoy. It is lit: Q(6)+LFl.15s.
● *La Lauze* beacon, GW, marks an area of shoal water off the entrance. It is lit: Fl.G.4s6M. The beacon should be left to starboard on entry to the harbour.
● Numerous above and below-water rocks fringe the coast NE of Cap d'Agde and a yacht should keep at least 500 metres off.
● In strong southerlies and easterlies there is a confused swell at the entrance and with gale-force winds from this direction entry can be dangerous, with breaking waves across the entrance. With a strong *tramontane* a considerable swell is whipped up in the large Avant Port and care is needed.

Note There is a speed limit of 3 knots in the harbour.

Mooring

Details 2450 berths with 30 berths for visitors. Maximum LOA 20 metres. In practice there are more berths available for visitors when permanent berth-holders are absent.

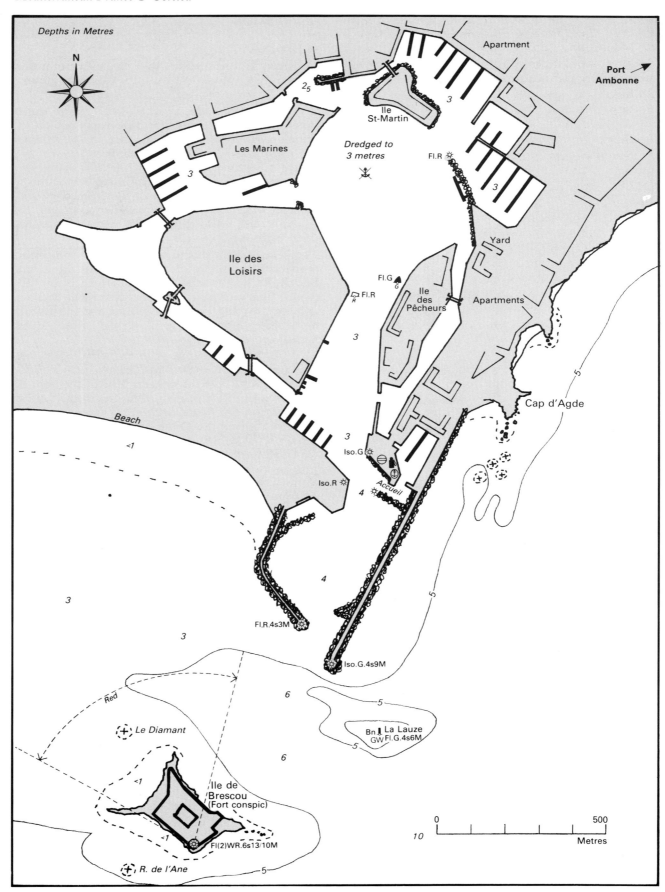

Depths in Metres

N

Port
Ambonne

Apartment

2₅

Ile
St-Martin

Les Marines

Dredged to
3 metres

Fl.R

3

3

Ile des
Loisirs

Yard

Fl.G
G

Fl.R
R

Ile
des
Pêcheurs

Apartments

3

3

Beach

<1

3

Iso.G

Iso.R

Accueil

Cap d'Agde

4

4

Fl.R.4s3M

3

5

Iso.G.4s9M

3

Red

6

5

Le Diamant

Bn
GW

La Lauze
Fl.G.4s6M

5

6

<1

Ile de
Brescou
(Fort conspic)

<1

Fl(2)WR.6s13/10M

R. de l'Ane

5

0   500

10   Metres

AGDE

Berth Go alongside on the *quai d'accueil* in the Avant Port and report to the *capitainerie* for a berth. There are laid moorings tailed to buoys or finger pontoons.

Shelter Good all-round shelter although some berths are uncomfortable in a strong *tramontane*.

Authorities Customs. Port captain and marina staff. A charge is made.

Facilities

Services Water and electricity at every berth. Several shower and toilet blocks around the marina.

Fuel On the quay in the Avant Port.

Repairs A 27-ton travel-hoist and slipways. Covered storage ashore. Mechanical and engineering repairs. GRP and wood repairs. Electrical and electronic repairs. Sailmakers. Chandlers.

Provisions Good shopping for provisions. Ice can be ordered.

Eating out Numerous restaurants of all categories around the marina.

Other Post office. Banks. Hire cars. Buses and taxis to Agde.

General

Cap d'Agde sprawls over much of the coast between Mont d'Agde and the sea, a huge purpose-built holiday city that can accommodate tens of thousands of visitors. The Quartier Nudiste at Ambonne alone caters for 20,000 sun-lovers. Cap d'Agde was one of the first of the Languedoc-Roussillon developments and, in addition to a more varied landscape amongst the dark volcanic basalt thrown up by the now extinct Mont d'Agde than the coast on either side, it benefits from a more human-scale architecture with a sort of sanitised Provençal theme to it. The pastel-coloured ziggurat apartments and villas work tolerably well and it is not at all an unpleasant place to wander around despite its vast scale.

The *étang* that was dredged for the construction of the vast marina was probably used by the Phocaean Greeks from Marseille. Richelieu is supposed to have started construction of a naval harbour here, but died before it was completed. He did manage to build the fort on Ile de Brescou and the fort on the summit of Mont d'Agde, presumably to protect the approaches to Agde on the Rivière Hérault which was the only centre of population here until construction began on Cap d'Agde.

PORT AMBONNE

A large but mostly shallow harbour, part of the naturist resort here. Only shallow-draught craft, drawing less than one metre, can use it. Whether or not you will have to divest yourself of garments to accommodate the spirit of the place I don't know.

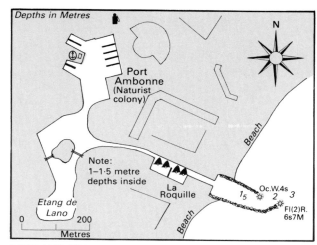

PORT AMBONNE 43°17'·6N 3°31'·8E

MARSEILLAN-PLAGE

A small harbour 2 miles NE of Port Ambonne. It is connected to the Etang de Thau by the Canal de Pisse-Saumes.

Approach

Conspicuous The apartments on the waterfront of Marseillan-Plage will be seen and the harbour lies at the NE end of the resort. Closer in the breakwaters and the light towers on their ends are easily identified.

By night The harbour entrance is lit: Fl.R.4s9M and Fl.G.4s5M. The entrance to the inner harbour is not lit.

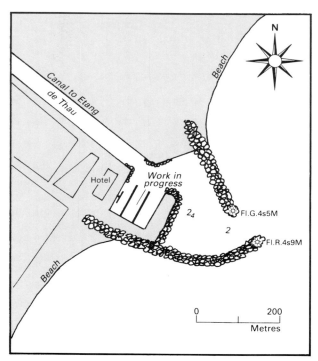

MARSEILLAN-PLAGE 43°19'N 3°33'·6E

Dangers
● With strong winds from the S and E there is a confused swell at the entrance and in gale-force winds from this direction entry would be dangerous.
● When entering keep close to the S breakwater as the depths decrease quickly near the N breakwater.

Mooring

Details 200 berths with 15 berths for visitors. Maximum LOA 15 metres.

Berth where directed or in a vacant berth and report to the *capitainerie*. There are posts around which a line must be taken.

Shelter Good all-round shelter in the inner basin.

Authorities Port captain. A charge is made.

Facilities

Services Water on the quay and electricity can be connected to most berths. A shower and toilet block.

Fuel Some distance away on the outskirts of the resort.

Repairs A small crane. Limited mechanical repairs.

Provisions Good shopping about a kilometre away in the resort.

Eating out Restaurants in the resort open in the summer.

Other Post office. Bank.

General

Marseillan-Plage is a slightly down-market resort, a poor cousin next to the more select resorts of Cap d'Agde and Ambonne. Perhaps because it is a smaller and more local resort, it is a friendly little place. The harbour is connected to the Etang de Thau by the Canal de Pisse-Saumes with a depth of around 2 metres though access is limited to craft with less than 2·4 metres air height. (See Chapter I, page 39 for further details on the canal and the Etang de Thau.)

SETE

Approach

Conspicuous Along this low sandy coast, Mont de Sète or Mont de St-Clair, along with Mont d'Agde, is one of the few high bits of land. From the distance Mont de Sète looks like an island and is easily identified from some way off. The lighthouse on the southern slope of Mont de Sète is conspicuous. From the E the oil refinery at Frontignan is conspicuous. Closer in the lighthouse in the middle of the outer breakwater and the lighthouse at the Vieux Bassin are conspicuous. The entrances to the harbour are easily recognised.

By night Use the light on Mont de Sète: Fl.15s29M. The western entrance is lit: Fl(2)R.6s7M and Iso.G.4s7M. The eastern entrance is lit: Q.R.10M and Fl(2)G.6s. The eastern pass inside the outer breakwater is lit: Oc.R.4s10M, Fl(3)G.12s5M, Oc(2)R.6s7M and Iso.4s. The lighthouse at the entrance to the Vieux Port has a sectored light: Fl(4)WR.12s15/11M. The white sector shows the safe approaches to the west and east entrances: 014°-W-054° for the west entrance and 260°-W-264° for the east entrance. From the E the flares at the oil refinery at Frontignan show up well. In practice a glance at the plan showing the approaches to Sète sorts out this muddle of lights and a night approach is straightforward.

Note In theory you should obtain permission via VHF channel 16 or 9 from the *capitainerie* to use the eastern entrance, but in practice few bother.

Dangers
● In strong southerlies there is a confused swell at both entrances. With strong SE winds the western entrance can be difficult. In southerly gales the eastern entrance is best as it is wider and has deeper water with the access channel dredged to 14·5 metres.
● Off the E side of the commercial harbour there are a number of unlit mooring buoys.

Caution Commercial traffic has right of way over pleasure craft at all times and on no account should you obstruct the passage of ships, especially inside the commercial port where there is limited room for manoeuvring. A good lookout should be kept as well for fishing boats which roar in and out of the harbour at speed.

Note When there has been heavy rain there can be a substantial outflow of water from the Etang de Thau via the Canal Maritime into Sète harbour. Normally this current is less than a knot, but after heavy rain it may be as much as 2–4 knots.

Mooring

Details The Vieux Port has 350 berths with 25 berths for visitors. Maximum LOA 20 metres.

Vieux Port Berth where directed or in a vacant berth and report to the club office. There are laid moorings tailed to buoys. Shelter here is good, but the wash from fishing boats coming and going at speed makes it uncomfortable. In the summer the Vieux Port is often full and you will have to go to the Nouveau Bassin.

Nouveau Bassin Go alongside the W quay keeping well clear of the S quay where the ferries to Morocco and the Balearics berth. Out of season it is polite to get permission from the *capitainerie* to berth here. In the summer yachts berth here without bothering to seek permission from the authorities, though if you are too close to the ferry berth, harbour officials will come around to move you on until the ferry has berthed. Shelter in the basin is good and generally more comfortable than the Vieux Port as you are not disturbed by the wash from the fishing boats.

Authorities Customs and immigration. Port captain. Staff from the Club Nautique administer the berths in the Vieux Port. A charge is made for berths in the Vieux Port.

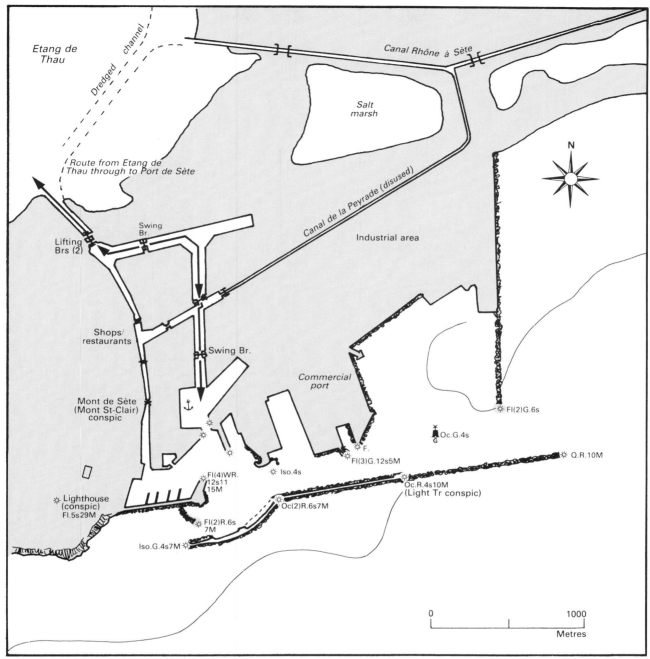

PORT DE SETE 43°24′N 3°42′E

Note

● There are also pleasure-craft berths at the entrance to Canal de la Peyrade. Most of the berths are occupied by local boats and there is no certainty that a free berth will be found.

● The bridges between the Nouveau Bassin and the Etang de Thau along the Canal Maritime and the Canal Latéral open twice daily around 0800 and 1800. Enquire at the *capitainerie* for the precise times and be ready to transit as soon as the bridges open – they won't wait for you so don't dawdle. (See Chapter I, page 39 for details on the Etang de Thau.)

Facilities

Services Water at every berth in the Vieux Port and several water points in the Nouveau Bassin. Electricity in the Vieux Port.

Fuel On the quay in the Vieux Port.

Repairs An 8-ton crane can haul yachts in the Vieux Port, but there is limited hard standing. In the Vieux Port there are two small cranes, 1½ and 2½ tons, suitable for raising or lowering masts, with operators used to doing the job. Mechanical and engineering repairs can be made. Electrical and electronic repairs. Sailmakers. Chandlers.

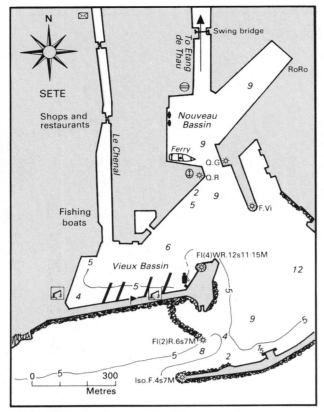

SETE: VIEUX BASSIN AND NOUVEAU BASSIN

region is caught by trawlers operating out of Sète and the harbour has that distinctive tang of drying nets and rotting fish and seaweed. Much of the wine of the Hérault is exported via Sète, with figures of around six hundred million litres per year quoted. But the mainstay of the port, which is now the second largest on the French Mediterranean coast after Marseille, is oil. Fortunately the huge petrochemical complex around Frontignan and the eastern side of the Etang de Thau does not intrude on Sète itself.

On Mont de Sète, or Mont de St-Clair as it is more commonly known to the Sètois, the poet Paul Valéry, who was born and lived in Sète for much of his life, is buried in the cemetery that figures in his well known poem, *Le Cimetière Marin*. On his tomb there is an inscription from the poem which ends: 'Qu'un long regard sur le calme des dieux!' Perhaps Valéry, in whatever afterworld poets go to, has found the calm of the gods. The other celebrated son of Sète is the singer-songwriter Georges Brassens, the gentle voice of the 60s and 70s. He is buried on the other side of Mont de Sète. Above the Cimetière Marin is the Musée Valéry with not only the works and artifacts of Valéry, but a room devoted to George Brassens and a room with a number of 19th and 20th century drawings and paintings. It is also a wonderful place just to sit and watch the sea as there is often a cooling breeze here to temper the summer heat.

Provisions Good shopping for all provisions in the town. Excellent fresh fish of all types from the fish market near the Vieux Port or from wet fish shops. Ice from the fish market.

Eating out Numerous restaurants, mostly along the W side of the Canal du Sète. Excellent *coquillage* restaurants around the W end of the Vieux Port.

Other Post office. Banks. Hire cars. Bus and train service along the coast. Ferries to Morocco and the Balearics.

General

Sète, formerly known as Cette and Settin, was colonised by the Greeks and later the Romans, though it was a minor colony compared to Agde along the coast. Not until Paul Riquet decided to make Sète the eastern terminal of the Canal du Midi did it become anything more than a small fishing village, and indeed Riquet's original port with canals bisecting the town still determines the character of the place. The old town is built around the Canal de Sète and everywhere you walk there are watery vistas, from the old harbour, to the canals, to the Etang de Thau. Fishing boats moor along the sides of the canal and add colour and noise to the cheerful confusion on the streets. Though it is tempting to make comparisons, Sète is not a little Venice – it is less formal, more work-a-day, less ostentatious.

Sète is very much a working harbour in stark contrast to the purpose-built marinas dotted around the coast to the west and east. Most of the fish for the

FRONTIGNAN

Approach

A marina dredged out of the thin sand spit between the Etang d'Ingril and the sea some 3 miles NE of Sète.

Conspicuous Just E and NE of Frontignan is a large oil refinery with two tall chimneys and a number of shorter chimneys conspicuous. The storage tanks and buildings attached to the refinery are also easily recognised. Closer in the breakwaters sheltering the Avant Port and the light structures on the ends will be seen.

By night The flares at the refinery show up well. The harbour entrance is lit: Fl(2)R.6s7M and Fl.G.4s7M.

Dangers With strong southerlies there is a confused swell at the entrance and in southerly gales entry could be dangerous.

Mooring

Details 600 berths with 60 berths for visitors. Maximum LOA 18 metres.

Berth at or close to the fuel quay and report to the *capitainerie* for a berth. There are finger pontoons at most berths.

Shelter Good all-round shelter.

Authorities Port captain and marina staff. A charge is made.

Sète. The Nouveau Bassin.

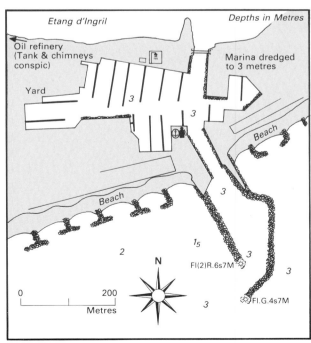

FRONTIGNAN 43°25'·8N 3°46'·3E

Facilities
Services Water and electricity at every berth. A shower and toilet block.

Fuel On the quay at the entrance to the basin.

Repairs A 16-ton travel-hoist. Mechanical repairs. GRP repairs. Electrical and electronic repairs. Sailmakers. Chandlers.

Provisions Limited provisions. Ice available.

Eating out Several restaurants open in the summer.

Other Taxi to Sète.

General
Frontignan has good shelter from the elements and good repair facilities, but apart from that it really doesn't have a lot going for it. There is little to see and do ashore with Frontignan village some 2½ kilometres away and Sète *centre ville* about 7 kilometres away. But the real blot on the harbour's landscape is the oil refinery adjacent to it – if the wind has an easterly component to it the harbour is permeated by the dank acrid smell of hydrocarbons being processed nearby.

Palavas-les-Flots. The canal leading to the Canal du Rhône à Sète.

Palavas-les-Flots looking NW. Note the conspicuous water tower.

PALAVAS-LES-FLOTS

Approach

Conspicuous The buildings of the town are easily recognised with a large round water tower in the town conspicuous. Closer in the outer breakwater and the light towers at the entrance will be seen.

By night The entrance is lit: Fl.R.4s8M and Oc.G.4s8M.

Dangers With strong southerlies there is a confused sea at the entrance and in southerly gales the entrance would be dangerous.

Mooring

Details 620 berths with 40 berths for visitors. Maximum LOA 13 metres.

Berth on the *quai d'accueil* just inside the entrance and report to the *capitainerie* for a berth. There are posts around which you must take a line.

Shelter Good shelter although SW winds can cause a surge.

Authorities Port captain and marina staff. A charge is made.

Facilities

Services Water and electricity at every berth. A shower and toilet block.

Fuel On the quay near the entrance.

Repairs A 12-ton travel-hoist and slipway. Mechanical repairs. Chandlers.

Provisions Good shopping for provisions in the town. Ice available.

Eating out Numerous restaurants along the canal and around the waterfront.

Other Post office. Bank. Hire cars. Buses to Sète and Montpellier. Internal and some international flights from Montpellier.

General

Palavas-les-Flots was at one time an important tunny fishing centre, but in recent years has turned towards the tourism that has transformed the coast. It has always been something of a seaside resort for the locals from Montpellier and retains some of the character of a 19th-century resort town. In 1890 Augustus Hare described it as having '... all the picturesqueness which red balconies and green shutters give, and possesses every kind of café, from the best to the humblest ...', and it remains much like that today. It has the added attraction of an aerial cable-car across the Rivière Lez which divides the town in two, a watery High Street, and like any older town close to the Camargue, it has an arena on the outskirts near the Etang du Grec.

THE RIVIERE LEZ

Just inside the breakwater on the NE side of the harbour the Rivière Lez runs into the sea. Local craft and fishing boats moor along the sides of the river and in a small basin about a kilometre upstream. The Lez has been dredged to just over one metre and craft with low topsides, not more than 2·4 metres, can proceed up to the basin or continue on to the Canal du Rhône à Sète at Palavas-les-Quatre-Canaux. (See Chapter I, page 45.)

CARNON-PLAGE (GRAU DE PEROIS)

Approach

Conspicuous The cluster of apartments just over 2 miles E of Palavas-les-Flots is easily identified. The breakwaters and entrance, at the western end of the apartment complex, are not easily identified until closer in.

By night The harbour entrance is lit: Fl(4)R.12s10M and Fl.G.4s3M.

Dangers With strong southerlies there is a confused swell at the entrance and in southerly gales entry could be dangerous.

Mooring

Details 700 berths with 50 berths for visitors.

Berth Go alongside the *quai d'accueil* at the entrance to the yacht basin and report to the *capitainerie* for a berth. There are posts around which you must take a line.

Shelter Good all-round shelter. The apartments block out the effects of northerly winds.

Authorities Port captain and marina staff. A charge is made.

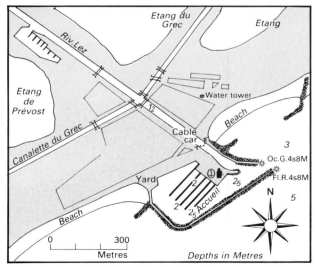

PALAVAS LES FLOTS 43°31'·6N 3°59'·9E

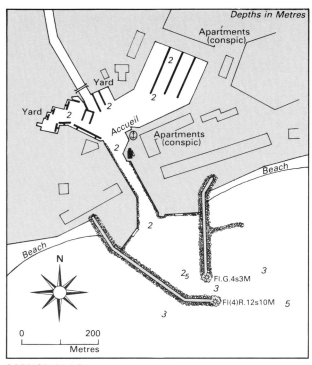

Depths in Metres

CARNON-PLAGE 43°32′·6N 3°58′·5E

Facilities

Services Water and electricity at every berth. Shower and toilet blocks around the marina.

Fuel On the quay near the *capitainerie*.

Repairs A 13-ton travel-hoist and a slipway. Covered storage ashore. Mechanical and engineering repairs can be made. GRP and wood repairs. Electrical and electronic repairs. Sailmakers. Chandlers.

Provisions Good shopping for provisions in the summer. Ice available.

Eating out Numerous restaurants and bars in the summer.

Other Post office. Bank. Hire cars. Taxi. Internal and some international flights from Montpellier.

General

Carnon-Plage used to be a tiny fishing village on the channel leading into the *étangs* until it was developed as part of the Languedoc-Roussillon scheme. Shallow draught craft drawing less than a metre can proceed up the Canal de Carnon to the Canal du Rhône à Sète though the lowest bridge before the canal has just 1·2 metres air height. (See Chapter I, page 45.)

Carnon-Plage. The channel leading to the yacht basins. The bridge in the background is over the Canal de Carnon leading to the Canal du Rhône à Sète.

La Grande Motte. Attempting to imitate the Pharaohs with La Grande Pyramide?

LA GRANDE MOTTE

Approach

The cluster of huge apartment blocks around the harbour can be identified from some distance off, being higher and denser than those at Port Camargue.

Conspicuous La Pyramide, the celebrated pyramidal apartment block at La Grande Motte, is conspicuous. Closer in the breakwaters and the masts of the yachts in the Avant Port will be seen. The sculpted light tower on the end of the outer breakwater is easily identified.

By night The entrance is lit: Fl(2)R.6s9M and Fl.G. 4s3M.

Dangers In strong southerlies and easterlies a swell piles up at the entrance which a yacht must turn side-on to when entering.

Mooring

Details 1364 berths with 15 berths for visitors. Maximum LOA 30 metres. Maximum draught 3·5 metres. In practice there are normally a greater number of berths for visitors when permanent berth holders are absent.

Berth Go alongside the *quai d'accueil* by the *capitainerie* and report for a berth. There is a mixture of finger pontoons, laid moorings tailed to the quay, or posts around which you must take a line, depending on where you are in the marina.

Shelter Excellent all-round shelter.

Authorities Customs. Port captain and marina staff. A charge is made.

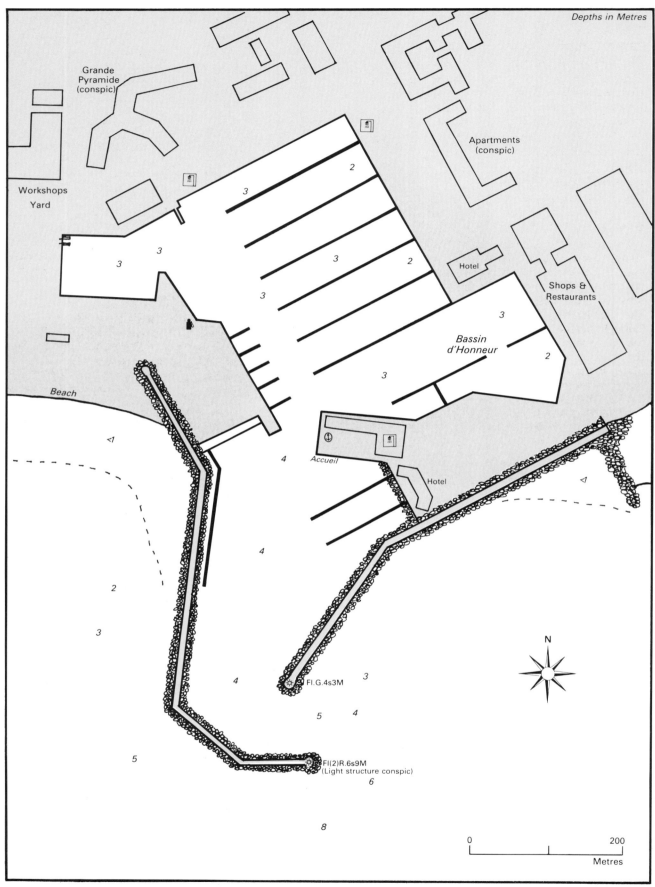

Depths in Metres

Grande
Pyramide
(conspic)

Apartments
(conspic)

Workshops
Yard

Hotel

Shops &
Restaurants

Bassin
d'Honneur

Beach

Accueil

Hotel

Fl.G.4s3M

Fl(2)R.6s9M
(Light structure conspic)

N

0   200

Metres

LA GRANDE MOTTE 43°33′·5N 4°05′E

Facilities

Services Water and electricity at every berth. Several shower and toilet blocks around the marina.

Fuel On the quay on the W side of the marina.

Repairs A 9 and 50-ton travel-hoist and a slipway. Covered storage ashore. Mechanical and engineering repairs. GRP and wood repairs. Electrical and electronic repairs. Sailmakers. Chandlers.

Provisions Good shopping for provisions in the summer. Ice available.

Eating out Numerous restaurants and bars around the waterfront in the summer.

Other Post office. Bank. Hire cars. Taxi.

General

La Grande Motte was one of the first of the Languedoc-Roussillon complexes to be constructed and hence is one of the best known. Its pyramidal apartment block features on many postcards and in most of the publications on the region. You either like it or hate it, to love the place would not be easy. Enough people obviously like it to have bought up the apartments as more have had to be built around the original complex. Whatever your feelings for the place, it has become something of a monument that 'has to be seen', even if only to say you dislike it. For me the place is more comfortable and amenable once berthed inside it, than it is from the distance when even La Pyramide does little to distinguish the reinforced concrete of La Grande Motte from many of the other complexes along the coast.

GRAU DU ROI

Approach

Conspicuous The old lighthouse, and the breakwaters and light towers on their ends are easily identified to the N of Port Camargue.

By night The entrance is lit: VQ(3)G.2s10M and Oc(2)R.6s7M.

Dangers
• With strong S–SW winds a heavy swell piles up at the entrance and can make entry dangerous with breaking waves and surf in the approaches and entrance. In these circumstances a yacht should not attempt to enter.

Note Care needs to be taken of boats entering and leaving through the narrow entrance and in the canal. The local fishing boats and tripper boats tend to exit at speed.

Mooring

Details 162 berths with 15 berths for visitors.

Canal Once into the canal ask permission to go alongside a fishing boat until the swing bridge opens. There are no berths available in the canal and a yacht should not be left unattended in case the fishing boat wants to leave.

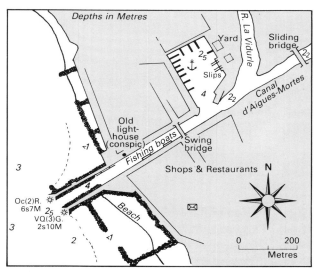

GRAU DU ROI 43°32′N 4°08′E

Swing bridge The bridge opens three times a day at 0800, 1315 and 1800 on weekdays, 0800, 1100, 1300 and 1700 on Saturdays, and 0830 and 2000 on Sundays. Check to confirm these times.

Berth Once past the bridge proceed into the Port de Pêche and find a vacant berth or berth where directed.

Shelter Excellent all-round shelter in Port de Pêche.

Authorities Customs. Port captain. A charge is made.

Facilities

Services Water on the quay.

Fuel In the town.

Repairs An 18-ton crane, and slipways. Mechanical and engineering repairs. GRP and wood repairs. Electrical and electronic repairs. Chandlers.

Provisions Good shopping for all provisions in the town. Ice available.

Eating out Numerous restaurants along the canal sides and in the town. Good fish restaurants.

Other Post office. Banks. Buses to Montpellier. Hire cars. Taxi.

General

Grau du Roi is like a poor Camargue peasant squeezed in between the well dressed newcomers nearby at La Grande Motte and Port Camargue. The fishing village has changed to accommodate the new tourism, but has not forgotten the local fishermen who occupy the canal and part of Port de Pêche. Originally Grau du Roi was the entrance to the port of Aigues-Mortes, hence the name which means 'channel of the king', referring to Louis IX who had the canal dug when he made Aigues-Mortes the base for his two crusades to the Holy Land. In fact in earlier times the port and channel were known as Le Grau Louis.

The port is well worth a visit though the difficulty of getting into Port de Pêche past the swing bridge and the few berths available may mean you have to

Grau du Roi. The approach looking NE. The old lighthouse is conspicuous.

Port Camargue. The distinctive *capitainerie* is conspicuous. The *quai d'accueil* is directly below it.

pay it a visit by land from La Grande Motte or Port Camargue – it is about a one mile walk around the beach from Port Camargue.

(See Chapter I for details on Aigues-Mortes and the Chenal Maritime leading to it from Grau du Roi.)

PORT CAMARGUE

Approach

The cluster of apartment blocks and holiday homes in the NE corner of Golfe d'Aigues-Mortes is easily identified from the distance, but until closer in the exact location of the harbour and entrance is difficult to determine.

Conspicuous From the W La Pyramide at La Grande Motte and the lighthouse at Grau du Roi are conspicuous. From the S the lighthouse and buoys off L'Espiguette are easily identified. Closer in it is difficult to see where the entrance is until the white light towers at the entrance to the Avant Port and the sculpted *capitainerie* tower inside can be identified.

By night Use the light on L'Espiguette, Fl(3)15s 24M, and the light at Port de l'Espiguette immediately S of Port Camargue, Q(9)15s8M. The entrance

to Port de l'Espiguette is lit, Oc.G.4s4M and Oc.R.4s4M. In the closer approach use the light off the breakwater at Port Camargue, VQ(9)10s9M. The entrance to Port Camargue is lit, Fl.G.4s9M and Fl.R.4s6M.

Dangers
● Keep well outside the buoys marking the sand-banks off Pointe de l'Espiguette.
● Do not cut in close to the breakwaters of Port Camargue, but approach the entrance on a south-easterly course to clear the shallows around the entrance.
● In strong southerlies there is a lumpy swell at the entrance making entry difficult. In gale-force southerlies the entrance could be dangerous.

Note In the summer, particularly at the weekends, there are large numbers of boats coming and going and care is needed when proceeding in or out of the comparatively narrow entrance.

Mooring

Details 1995 berths in the Port Public with 200 berths for visitors. Maximum draught 3 metres.

Berth on the *quai d'accueil* by the conspicuous sculpted *capitainerie* and report for a berth. There are laid moorings tailed to buoys or posts around which you must take a line.

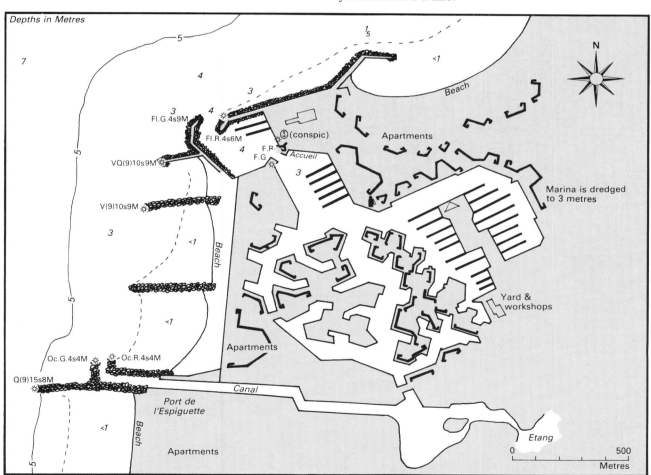

PORT CAMARGUE 43°31′N 4°08′E

Shelter Good all-round shelter although the *mistral* can make some berths, especially those in the Avant Port, uncomfortable.

Facilities

Services Water and electricity at every berth. Several shower and toilet blocks around the marina.

Fuel On the quay at the junction of the first and second basins.

Repairs A 45-ton travel-hoist and slipways. Covered storage ashore. Mechanical and engineering repairs. GRP and wood repairs. Electrical and electronic repairs. Sailmakers. Chandlers.

Provisions Good shopping for provisions in summer.

Eating out Numerous restaurants and bars scattered around the marina.

Other Post office. Bank. Taxi. Hire cars.

General

This vast marina and apartment complex, dredged and reclaimed from the salt marshes on the western edge of the Rhône delta, is one of the largest marinas in the world. There are nearly 2000 berths in the Port Public and another 2000 plus berths around the various 'island' apartment complexes, some 70 hectares of enclosed water in all. Along with La Grande Motte, Port Camargue was one of the first complexes to be constructed in the Languedoc-Roussillon scheme and although it is still under construction in places, it is basically complete and open for business. The sheer size of the place is impressive and without a plan you could easily lose your way whether on land or on the water, but already the architecture is looking dated and the paint is peeling off some of the earlier apartment blocks. Port Camargue is billed as 'la cité des hommes de la mer' and though it is not for this man of the sea, as a vast purpose-built complex to house boats and people, it succeeds in its purpose.

III. Provence

Provence, like the Côte d'Azur and the Riviera, is a region everyone knows about and which immediately conjures up images, but which no-one knows the exact location of. The only modern French *département* naming Provence, Alpes-de-Haute-Provence, does not include much of the vague region most people associate with the name. Most maps, including French ones, have the word 'Provence' in large spaced letters stretching across a region somewhere around Béziers or Montpellier to the pre-Alps around Grasse or Nice. Guidebooks are similarly vague about the geographical position of Provence.

The name is derived from the Roman *provincia* of Gaul which at the height of the Roman Empire included most of modern France. The Barbarian invasions constricted Roman *provincia* to the area between the Rhône, the Alps and the Mediterranean. Later *provincia*, corrupted to *Proenza*, came to mean virtually the whole of the south of France, the region where the Provençal language, *langue d'Oc*, was spoken. By the 9th century Arles emerged as the capital of the Kingdom of Provence. It passed to several sons of the nobility of Europe with René, King of Sicily, being the last Count of Provence and in 1481 the region was incorporated into the Kingdom of France.

I have placed Provence in the coastal strip from the western limits of the Rhône delta to La Ciotat in the east, not due to any departmental boundaries and for only a few historical reasons, because for me this coast encapsulates the essence of the elusive region. Happily it coincides with the coastal strip the Michelin *Green Guide* calls Provence.

The old Provençal capital of Arles and the region around it was Van Gogh's home for the period before his death and he, more than any other painter of Provence, has established those burning images, what Mervyn Peake called his 'quenchless canvases of twisted fire', that we associate with this area. For me the hard white limestone of Les Calanques, the cobalt blue sky that accompanies the *mistral*, the dull green of olive leaves, the earthiness and directness of the people that is not as evident in the more sophisticated resorts further east, are Provence. This is the region where the *mistral*, the scourge of Provence and of yachtsmen, tumbles into the Mediterranean with all its terrible violence.

Provence and things Provençal touch all of the other coasts I describe to the east and west of the region described here. It is a quintessential part of the south of France. The food, introduced to the north by Elizabeth David as Provençal cuisine, smells of thyme and rosemary even if you are just thumbing through her recipes. Provençal days by necessity include sitting in a shaded café sipping pastis or a glass of crisp white wine while watching the locals playing *pétanque*. Provence is as much an idea today as anything else and I have placed it within certain geographical limits somewhat arbitrarily. After all, the Côte d'Azur, likewise an idea and not really a region, has to fit somewhere and that somewhere sits more comfortably to the east of this chapter.

Weather

The wind everyone knows about, talks about and watches for with an eagle eye, is the *mistral*. It blows with the greatest force and highest frequency along this stretch of coast, and NW winds account for 50–60% of observations. The *mistral* blows down the Rhône Valley and off the delta from a northerly direction, but soon fans out to blow from the NW along the coast to the E of the Rhône. A full-blown *mistral* will blow from gale force up to force 9–10, and force 11–12 is sometimes recorded. Fortunately a full-blown *mistral* is rare in the summer, though a local *mistral* is common blowing at force 5–6 and occasionally 7. The local *mistral* is only felt off the Rhône delta and along the coast as far as Marseille and sometimes La Ciotat. When the local *mistral* blows care needs to be taken of gusts into the Golfe de Fos, Rade de Marseille, and Baie de La Ciotat.

The other common wind along the coast is the sea breeze, the *marin*, which blows from the S–SE though it can be much altered by the local topography. It generally gets up in the mid-morning, blows around force 3–4, although it can get up to force 6 sometimes, and dies down at night. Southerlies, including the *marin*, set heavy seas onto the coast, and in southerly gales care needs to be taken, especially off the Rhône delta.

Bouches du Rhône

From Port Camargue to the Golfe de Fos there is over 40 miles of low and featureless coast around the seaward end of the Rhône delta. The delta has built up over thousands of years to form the region, presently some 220 square miles of salt lakes, sand banks and low-lying land, known as the Camargue. Around the coastline of the delta the depths change as winter storms bite into the coast and the silt brought down by the Rhône is deposited in the sea. The Rhône is France's largest river and the mud and sand brought down in suspension is calculated to ex-

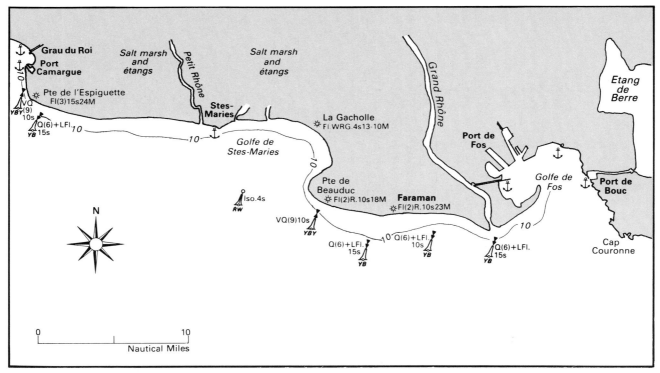

RHONE DELTA: PORT CAMARGUE TO CAP COURONNE

tend the coastline some 10–15 metres every year. This is not a straightforward dumping of silt at the mouth of the Rhône, as the easterly current flowing along the coast takes the silt and deposits it in an irregular fashion depending on the strength of the current, which in turn depends on the strength of congruent or opposing winds. And in the winter southerly gales can remove whole chunks of coast and deposit them elsewhere.

Stes-Maries de la Mer, now situated right on the sea, illustrates just how the delta has changed over the centuries. In 1696 a chronicler, Pierre-Louis of Arles, recorded that 'The town of Notre Dame de la Mer (the old name of Stes-Maries) was formerly situated at a greater distance from the sea, and, if it is possible to judge the past by the present, it must have been 4 or 5 leagues (1 league is approximately 3 miles) distant, for sixty years ago, or the number of years that I have been coming here, it was half-a-league further away than it is now.' (Quoted in Alain Albaric's *Camargue*.) Sometime in the 15th century it is supposed that the Rhône changed its course to the present-day channel, and Stes-Maries, built on the old alluvial deposits of the river, gradually got closer as the old coastline was washed away. In 1811 it was recorded as being 1200 metres from the sea, whereas today it sits right on the coast, protected by a series of sea walls and breakwaters to stop the sea washing it away completely. Other harbours such as Port St-Louis du Rhône suffered the opposite fate and it is now further from the sea than it ever was. Similarly the land bulging out to the east of Stes-Maries is of comparatively recent origin.

For a yacht on passage around the delta there are normally no problems that a little care and attention to coastal navigation will not solve. There is one harbour, Port Gardian at Stes-Maries de la Mer, between Port Camargue and the harbours in the Golfe de Fos. The problems along this stretch of coast are encountered in bad weather. The *mistral* blows with its greatest strength down the Rhône valley and off the delta. There may be a local *mistral* here, blowing at force 5–6, when there is no wind at Sète or east of Marseille. With a full-blown *mistral* the wind off the delta can be of great violence. With strong southerlies a heavy sea breaks in the shallow water fringing the delta and there can be breaking waves and surf as far out as the 20 metre line. Before proceeding along this coast a yacht should get a reliable forecast and on passage should constantly monitor the weather forecasts. The only harbour at Port Gardian can be difficult to enter in a *mistral* and dangerous to enter in a southerly gale.

The shoal water off the delta is well marked by buoys and there are a number of conspicuous objects around the coast. However in bad visibility it can be difficult to identify the buoys and conspicuous objects from the distance, and care must be taken with your dead-reckoning course and every opportunity taken to update it with position fixes, visual or electronic. Constant use of the depth sounder will also give you some indication of your position and warn you should you stray into shallower water.

The outer buoy marking the shoal water off Pte de l'Espiguette
and l'Espiguette lighthouse in the background.

Buoys and conspicuous objects from west to east

● *Pte de l'Espiguette* A squat square lighthouse with
a white base and black top. Fl(3)15s24M light.

● *L'Espiguette buoys* There are two buoys off the
point: a YBY conical buoy with a ⟨topmark⟩ topmark. It has a
high-pitched whistle, VQ(9)10s light; a YB conical
buoy with a ⟨topmark⟩ topmark, Q(6)+LFl.15s light. Local
yachts cut inside the buoys, though not by very
much, and I noted that the local trawlers did not.

● *Stes-Maries de la Mer* The cluster of buildings and
particularly the fortress-like church stand out well.

● *Stes-Maries buoy* A RW conical buoy with a ⊚ topmark situated 4 miles S of Port Gardian, Iso.4s light.

● *Beauduc lighthouse* A tall white tower with a large
white building next to it on Pte de Beauduc. Fl(2)R.
10s18M Siren Mo(N)60s.

● *Beauduc buoy* A YBY conical buoy with a ⟨topmark⟩ topmark, VQ(9)10s light.

● *Faraman lighthouse* A tall lighthouse (41 metres
high) with black and white bands that stands out
well. There are white dwellings next to it. Fl(2)10s
23M light.

Note The present Faraman lighthouse dates from
1917. The old Faraman lighthouse was swept away in
a fierce southerly gale in 1917 that 'ate' away the bit
of coast the old lighthouse was on.

● *Faraman buoys* Two buoys off Faraman lighthouse, approximately 3 miles SW and SE respective-
ly: SW buoy; a YB conical buoy with a ⟨topmark⟩ topmark,
Q(6)+LFl.15s light, whistle. SE buoy; a YB conical
buoy with a ⟨topmark⟩ topmark. VQ(6)+LFl.10s light.

● *Grand Rhône beacons* On either side of the mouth
of the Rhône are several beacons. There is a Racon
transmitter on one of the E beacons.

● *Grand Rhône buoys* Approximately 1 mile off the
mouth of the Grand Rhône there is a YB conical
buoy with a ⟨topmark⟩ topmark, Q(6)+LFl.15s; and a YB pillar buoy with a ⟨topmark⟩ topmark and a bell.

● *They de la Gracieuse* The long low sandbank running in a NE direction from the mouth of the Rhône.
There are numerous beacons near the NE tip of the
sandbank. There are three buoys: *Balancelle*, a BYB
conical buoy with a ⟨topmark⟩ topmark, VQ(3)5s. *Annibal
Est*, a BYB conical buoy with a ⟨topmark⟩ topmark, Q(3)10s.
GE, a BYB conical buoy with a ⟨topmark⟩ topmark, VQ(3)5s.

● *Les Laurons power station* Although on the E side
of the Golfe de Fos, the four chimneys and large
building of the power station are the most conspicuous objects in the gulf and are a useful reference
point.

Notes

● Local yachts often cut inside the buoys and follow
the coast closely. In the Golfe des Stes-Maries a yacht
can follow the coast more closely, though not as close
as some local yachts and not inside the 10 metre line.
Otherwise I do not recommend cutting inside the
buoys, and having seen a local yacht go aground cutting the corner at L'Espiguette, do not assume that
local knowledge necessarily has a large component of
'knowledge' in it.

● With light offshore winds or in calm weather a
yacht can anchor almost anywhere along the coast,
creeping slowly inshore until suitable depths for anchoring are reached. Some shelter from easterlies can
be obtained on the eastern side of Golfe des Stes-
Maries. The bottom everywhere slopes gradually to
the shore and the holding on sand and mud is good.
In the event of moderate or strong winds from any
direction a yacht should proceed to a safe harbour.
The seas off the delta in a *mistral* are best seen from
somewhere like Port Gardian when you can stand on
the breakwater and watch, glad that you are berthed
securely inside.

PETIT RHONE

Small and some not-so-small yachts enter the Petit Rhône and proceed up it to moor along the banks or at Port Dromar. There are leading beacons and lights showing the entrance into the river (Q.G.14M), but because the sandbanks at the entrance shift, it is unwise and possibly dangerous for visiting yachts to attempt to enter. There are said to be 1·5 metre depths into and in the river, but I have not tested the local knowledge and recommend any yacht wishing to proceed up the river to obtain information locally at Port Gardian.

Caution A yacht on passage along the coast should keep well off the entrance to the Petit Rhône where a sandbank forms extending up to just under half a mile off. The position of the bank and the depths over it are constantly changing and chart details cannot always be relied upon.

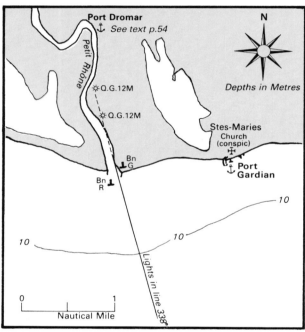

PETIT RHONE AND STES-MARIES

PORT GARDIAN (STES-MARIES DE LA MER)

Approach

The recommended safe approach is to proceed to Stes-Maries buoy (RW with a ○ topmark) and from there turn onto a course of due N towards the prominent church in the town.

Conspicuous The cluster of buildings and particularly the fortress-like church in the town are conspicuous from some distance off. Set a course for the church until the harbour breakwater and the light tower on the end can be identified, although initially it is hard to distinguish the breakwater of the harbour from the breakwaters protecting the coast and beach.

By night Use the leading lights for the Petit Rhône (Q.G.14M) and the light on Stes-Maries buoy (Iso.4s). The harbour entrance is lit: Fl.R.4s7M and Fl.G.2·5s2M.

Dangers
● See the caution above on the sandbank off the mouth of the Petit Rhône. A yacht should not cut across the mouth of the Petit Rhône in the approach from the W.
● Approximately 50 metres W of the outer breakwater are the sunken remains of an old breakwater.
● With southerly gales there are breaking waves at the entrance and entry is dangerous. With the *mistral* the approach is difficult and possibly dangerous with a confused sea in Golfe des Stes-Maries.

Note
● A line of yellow buoys on the N side of the entrance marks the bathing area off the beach. A good lookout should be kept for bathers and sail-boards.
● The entrance is quite narrow and care needs to be taken of other craft entering and leaving.

Mooring

Details 350 berths with 60 berths for visitors. Maximum LOA 14 metres.

Berth where directed at visitors' berths in the outer part of the harbour or go onto the *quai d'accueil* and report to the *capitainerie* for a berth. There are laid moorings tailed to the quay, or posts around which you must take a line. The laid mooring lines have large-link chain on the end through which a line should be taken. The bottom of the harbour is glutinous black mud and it gets everywhere making a horrible mess.

Note There is little room for manoeuvring between the visitors' pontoons, and with the *mistral* blowing, boats get into all sorts of problems when berthing.

Shelter Good shelter although a strong *mistral* can cause problems. Most of the berths exposed to the *mistral* have posts.

Authorities Port captain and marina staff. A charge is made.

Facilities

Services Water and electricity at every berth. A shower and toilet block at the *capitainerie*.

Fuel On the quay near the yard.

Repairs A 14-ton travel-hoist. Mechanical repairs. Chandlers.

Provisions Good shopping for provisions in the town. Ice available.

Eating out Numerous restaurants and bars in the town.

Other Post office. Bank. Hire cars. Buses to Arles.

General

The fortified church, so prominent from seaward, houses the mythopoeic origins of the town and provides for much of its current prosperity from the pilgrims and tourists who travel here to see it. The pres-

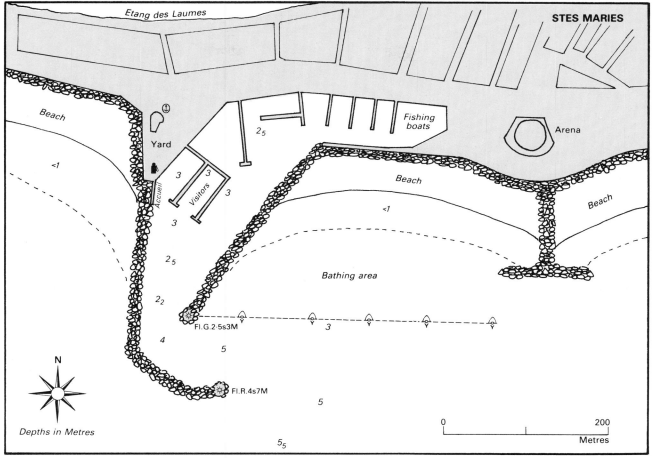

Etang des Laumes

STES MARIES

Beach

Yard

2₅

Fishing boats

Arena

Accueil

Visitors

3 3 3

3

3

2₅

Beach

<1

Bathing area

2₂

FI.G.2·5s3M

3

4

5

N

FI.R.4s7M

5

Depths in Metres

5₅

0   200

Metres

Beach

PORT GARDIAN (STES-MARIES) 43°23'·4N 4°51'·1E

ent church was mostly constructed in the 12th century, replacing an earlier structure. It's appearance with crenellated walls, lancet windows and the keep-like tower, leaves one in no doubt as to its dual role as a place of refuge from the Saracen corsairs who frequently raided along this stretch of coast. Inside the dark church there are the remains of the two Marys, the Saintes-Maries, after whom the church and the town are named.

The origins of the town are contained in a Provençal legend in which a boat, without sails or oars, was cast up here around 40 AD. Its cargo was a saintly one consisting of Mary Magdalene; Mary Jacobé, sister of the Virgin Mary; Mary Salomé, mother of the disciples James and John; Lazarus, the same Lazarus who rose from the dead; Martha, sister of Lazarus; Maximin; Sidonius, the blind man who later could see; and Sarah, the black servant of the Marys. This saintly cargo had been cast out in a cockleshell boat by the Jews of Jerusalem and had drifted until touching land on this remote coast. Sarah, the black servant, was initially left behind in the Levant, but wailed so loudly that Mary Salomé threw her cloak on the water and Sarah was able to walk across it to the boat. From the coast they separated to spread the gospel; Mary Magdalene to Ste-Baume, Lazarus to Marseille, Maximin and Sidonius to Aix-en-Provence, and Martha to Tarascon. Mary Jacobé and Mary Salomé remained with Sarah in the

wild region where they had landed and when they died were buried in a small church.

At some time pilgrims began to make the arduous journey to this isolated place to worship at the church and at some time the gypsies adopted Sarah as their patroness, despite the fact she was not a saint. Her dark lowly status must have aroused feelings congruent with their own position in society and the remoteness of Stes-Maries, away from the prying eyes of the outside world, provided the perfect place for an annual gathering of the *Romanichel*.

Today the town, though crowded in the summer, is a lively interesting place. There are few gypsies to be seen in the summer months; sensibly they depart to quieter places, though large numbers of the younger generation with the wanderlust inhabit the town and provide entertainment with impromptu busking in the square by the church. From Stes-Maries trips can be organised to other places of interest in the Camargue. The tourist office on the road into the town from the harbour can provide details.

THE GYPSY FESTIVAL

On the 24th and 25th of May, a festival takes place at Stes-Maries de la Mer which draws gypsies from all over the country to venerate the two Marys and the gypsies' own patroness, Sarah. A week before the festival the gypsies start arriving and the roads are soon choked by motorised caravans and mobile

Approach to Stes-Maries de la Mer looking N. Note the conspicuous fortified church.

homes, the chrome glinting in the sun, and the cars of tourists and the devout arriving to see the festival and procession. The streets are full of dark faces and bright skirts and innumerable opportunities to have your palm read. Occasionally, as one writer dryly observed, a hand must be gently helped from within *gadjo* pockets and bags.

The religious festival begins on the afternoon of the first day when the shrine with the two Marys is lowered from the upper chapel to an altar in the chancel. An all-night vigil and mass keeps the relics company. The next day a procession carries the wooden votary of the two Marys in their boat down to the sea. It is quite unlike most religious processions with the *gardians* on their horses accompanying the crowd, voluble gypsies running and scrambling about the beach, and crowds of sightseers all trying to get a look at the two mournful Marys. At the waters edge the *gardians* ride their horses into the sea, the bishop blesses the sea, and then everyone returns to the church. There is a further ceremony in the afternoon, but by then the festivities are well underway.

Nobody really knows why the gypsies were drawn to Stes-Maries or when they first began to gather here. Their veneration of Sarah is also mysterious since she is not a saint. She is normally described as the black maid servant of the two Marys, but other traditions variously describe her as the repudiated wife of Pontius Pilate or, in gypsy legend, as Sarah, the gypsy queen of the Camargue who welcomed the boat load of saints and gave them shelter. One of the

earliest records of Sarah being worshipped dates back to 1686 and I wonder if it is coincidence that a few years before, in 1682, Louis XIV imposed severe new edicts on the gypsies in France – that '... the men be attached to the chains of convicts to be led to the galleys and there to serve out a life sentence' and the women '... to be thrashed and banished from the kingdom'. (Quoted in A. Albaric *The Camargue*.) After these edicts the gypsies split up into smaller, less obtrusive groups and moved to more remote areas, one of them being the Camargue. Surprisingly Sarah has only been included in the procession since 1935 when the local marquis obtained permission from the church for the uncanonised Sarah to go along with the two Marys.

Stes-Maries de la Mer looking N. The end of the outer breakwater of Port Gardian is in the foreground and the conspicuous fortified church in the background.

Golfe de Fos

The Golfe de Fos opens northwards between the mouth of the Rhône and Cap Couronne to the E. Around the shores of the gulf are the biggest petrochemical installations on the French Mediterranean coast, if not the largest in France. There are buoyed deep-water channels for large tankers into Port de Fos and Port de Bouc and consequently the northern half of the gulf is peppered with buoys. From Port de Bouc a canal runs east to Martigues and the Etang de Berre.

Despite the extensive petrochemical installations around the shores of the gulf, there are a number of yacht harbours and anchorages that are both useful and attractive. Don't be put off totally by the industrial approaches as the feel and appearance of some of the harbours, once inside, is quite different from what it looks like from seawards.

Note

• In windless conditions the smoke and fumes from the petrochemical installations can reduce visibility considerably in the gulf.

• With the *mistral* or strong southerlies there are confused and steep seas in the gulf, out of all proportion to the wind, and it can be a very uncomfortable place to be.

• Ships underway in the gulf have right of way over pleasure craft and you should keep well out of their way.

Fos. The nightmare industrial complex at the head of the Golfe de Fos.

They de la Gracieuse

The low sandbank extending out from the western side of the gulf has a useful anchorage with good shelter from southerlies behind it. Care needs to be taken as the depths come up quickly from 4–5 metres to less than a metre some distance off it. Anchor where convenient in 5–8 metres on mud.

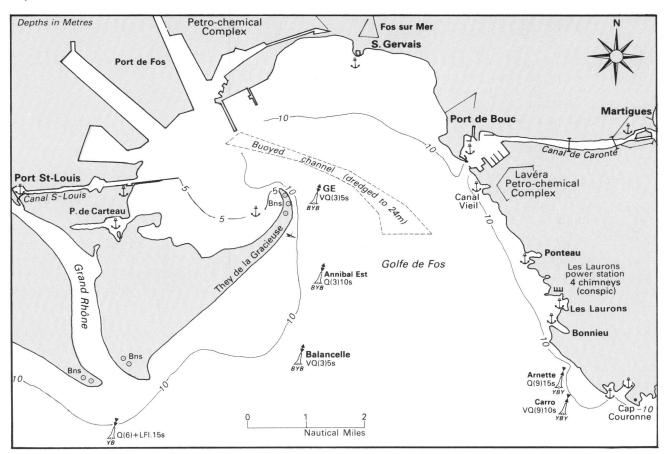

GOLFE DE FOS

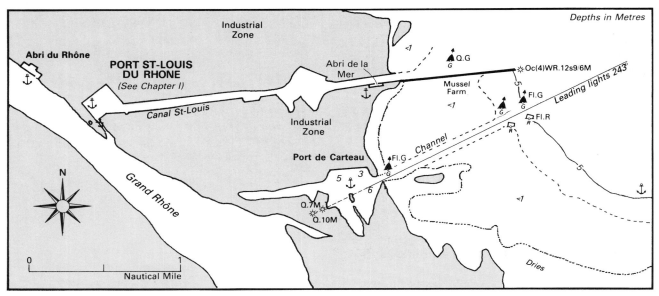

CANAL ST-LOUIS AND PORT CARTEAU

PORT DE CARTEAU

Approach
A large basin on the W side of the gulf approached by a buoyed channel with 1·9 metres least depth in it.

Conspicuous Around They de la Gracieuse the light tower at the entrance to Canal St-Louis will be seen. Closer in the buoys marking the channel can be identified close S of the breakwater protecting the canal entrance.

By night Though there are leading lights and the channel buoys are lit, a night approach is not recommended. Use the light at the entrance to Canal St-Louis Oc(4)WR.12s9/6M and the lights of the outer pair of buoys; Fl.G and Fl.R. The leading lights into the harbour are Q.8M on 243°.

Note The channel has been dredged to 1·9 metres, but is liable to silting.

Mooring
Berth on the quay where convenient. The harbour is used by fishing boats and local yachts. It is likely that there will be further development here in the future.

Facilities
Water and electricity. Provisions and restaurants at Port St-Louis du Rhône about 2 miles away.

General
The harbour and land around here, just south of the industrial zone of St-Louis du Rhône, will most likely be developed as an industrial port to supplement the facilities at Port de Fos and Port de Bouc.

PORT ABRI DE LA MER

A yacht basin at the eastern end of the Canal St-Louis. The harbour is crowded with local yachts and the club here actively encourages you to go to Port St-Louis du Rhône.

PORT ST-LOUIS DU RHONE

A basin at the western end of the Canal St-Louis connected to the River Rhône by a lock. Port St-Louis is the place where yachts normally enter or exit from the Rhône. (See Chapter I for details on the harbour and on getting to and from the Rhône.)

PORT DE FOS

The huge commercial port for the petrochemical installations and other heavy industry so conspicuous around the NW corner of the gulf. A yacht should not attempt to enter the port, which is exclusively for commercial traffic. The port handles a staggering 60 million tons of cargo every year making it one of the largest ports in France. With its sister port Marseille which handles 30 million tons annually, the Fos-Marseille complex is second only to Rotterdam in Europe.

FOS-SUR-MER (ST-GERVAIS)

Approach
Conspicuous The old walled village of Fos-sur-Mer on a rocky bluff is easily identified. A church on the summit is conspicuous. Closer in the tall thin tower (45 metres) of St-Gervais lighthouse and the sculpted *capitainerie* in the harbour are conspicuous. The har-

Fos-sur-Mer (Port Gervais) at the head of the Golfe de Fos. Note the conspicuous lighthouse and *capitainerie*.

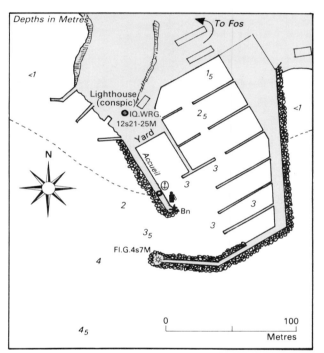

ST-GERVAIS 43°25'·6N 4°56'·5E

Shelter Good all-round shelter although strong southerlies may cause a surge.

Authorities Port captain and marina staff.

Facilities

Services Water and electricity at every berth. A shower and toilet block.

Fuel On the quay by the *capitainerie*.

Repairs A 15-ton crane. Mechanical repairs. Electrical and electronic repairs. Chandlers.

Provisions Some provisions available nearby. Better shopping in the village about 30 minutes walk away.

Eating out Several restaurants and bars nearby.

Other Post office and bank in the village. Buses to Port de Bouc and Martigues.

General

St-Gervais, sitting under the shadow of heavy industry and with the acrid tang of refined hydrocarbons in the air, struggles to be a resort for locals. The old village of Fos-sur-Mer on the rocky knoll inland is a gem hemmed in by a nightmare complex of grimy tanks and lattices and chimneys.

Fos and Fos-sur-Mer are named after the Fossés Mariennes, (*fossé*, a hole or canal), the canal dug from here to the Rhône near Arles by Marius' legionnaires in 102 BC to enable his galleys to supply the garrisons on the river. Little remains of the Roman period, but the walled village of Fos-sur-Mer has numerous medieval buildings and is a surprisingly quiet and leafy place in the midst of the industry around it.

PORT DE BOUC

Approach

The commercial port for the refinery at Lavéra with two yacht basins inside. It is also the entrance to the Canal de Caronte leading to Martigues and the Etang de Berre.

Conspicuous The four chimneys and large building of Les Laurons power station and the oil storage tanks, chimneys and flares at Lavéra oil refinery SE of Port de Bouc are conspicuous from some distance off. Closer in the apartment blocks of Port de Bouc and Fort de Bouc on opposite sides of the entrance to the harbour are easily identified. The pilots' tower, a tall tower with a 'golf-ball' top is conspicuous on the N side of the entrance.

By night Use St-Gervais light IQ(7)WRG.12s25-21M, until the lights for Port de Bouc are picked up. Use the light on Fort de Bouc, Oc(2)WRG.6s12-9M and the lights at the entrance, Fl(4)R.12s6M and Fl.Vi.5s9M. There are leading lights into the harbour: Q.R.15M on 037° and F.R.11M on 031°.

Note Commercial traffic has right of way over pleasure craft in the approaches and in the harbour. Pilot launches and tugs also charge in and out of the entrance at speed and a good lookout should be kept for them.

bour breakwater and light tower at the entrance are easily recognised.

By night Use the St-Gervais lighthouse, IQ(7)WRG.12s25-21M. The white sector shows the safe approach into the Golfe de Fos on 340°–348°. The harbour entrance is lit, Fl.G.4s7M.

Dangers With the *mistral* and strong southerlies there is a confused sea in the approach and entrance.

Mooring

Details 600 berths with 25 berths for visitors.

Berth on the *quai d'accueil* just inside the entrance by the sculpted *capitainerie* and report for a berth. There are laid moorings tailed to the quay.

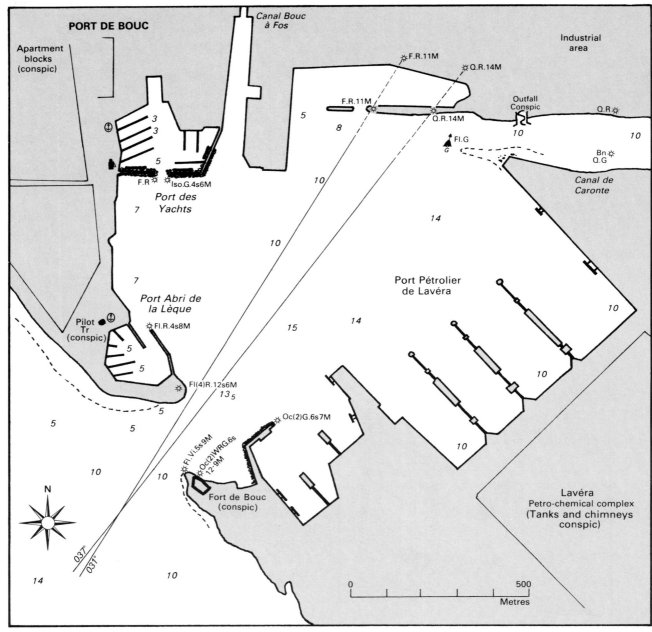

PORT DE BOUC 43°24′N 4°59′E

Mooring

There are two pleasure-craft basins on the W side of Port de Bouc: Port Abri de la Lècque and Port des Yachts. It is prohibited to anchor in the harbour.

Port Abri de la Lècque A yacht basin tucked under the northern entrance of Port de Bouc. It is used by the pilot launches and fishing boats as well as local yachts. Berth where convenient amongst the local yachts and report for a berth. The harbour is uncomfortable from the wash of the pilot launches coming and going at speed and a visiting yacht is better off going to Port des Yachts off the town.

Port des Yachts A yacht basin in the NW corner of Port de Bouc.

Details 450 berths with 80 berths for visitors. Maximum LOA 16 metres.

Berth where directed or on the first pontoon and report to the *capitainerie*. There are laid moorings tailed to buoys or to the quay.

Shelter Good all-round shelter.

Authorities Customs. Immigration. Port captain and marina staff. A charge is made.

Facilities

Port des Yachts

Services Water and electricity at every berth. A shower and toilet block.

Fuel On the quay inside the entrance.

Repairs A 16-ton hoist. Mechanical repairs. Chandlers.

Provisions Good shopping for provisions in the town.

Eating out Restaurants and bars in the town.

The entrance to Port de Bouc and the yacht harbour just inside the entrance, looking NW.

Other Post office. Bank. Buses and trains to Marseille.

General

Port de Bouc is not really the sort of place you would go out of your way to visit. It exists as a dormitory suburb for the petrochemical installations nearby and its attractions go little beyond that.

Note There are plans to build a 600-berth marina at Port de Bouc, either extending Port Abri de la Lècque, or building a marina on the W side of Les Lècques. Work has not begun at the time of writing.

Canal Port de Bouc a Fos

A canal linking Port de Bouc and Port de Fos that follows the coastline just inland of it. It is prohibited to pleasure craft.

Canal de Caronte

The canal that runs from the NE corner of Port de Bouc to Martigues and the Etang de Berre. The entrance to the canal is difficult to make out with certainty until close to it when the green buoy marking the shallow area at the corner of the canal will be seen. A factory on the N bank near the entrance discharges large amounts of water and effluent.

There is always a substantial W-going current in the canal that can reach 2–3 knots on occasion, though normally it is less than 1 knot. The canal is well marked along its length by buoys or beacons showing the channel. The buoys and beacons are lit making a night transit possible.

Approximately halfway along the canal there is a railway bridge. The navigable channel is under the northern and highest (21 metres air height) arch. Do not attempt to pass under the other arches, where there are obstructions. Closer towards Martigues there is a high modern road bridge (44·5 metres air height) and the buildings of Martigues will be seen beyond it. A lifting bridge connects the canal with the Etang de Berre.

Small commercial ships and large *péniches* use the canal to get to the commercial ports on the E side of the Etang de Berre. Commercial ships have right of way in the canal and a yacht should keep well out of the way.

MARTIGUES

Approach

Proceeding up the Canal de Caronte you come to Martigues. Some 500 metres past the high road bridge the entrance to Bassin de Ferrières will be seen on the N side of the canal. The town hall, a ghastly modern affair that looks like a pile of children's pastel-coloured building blocks, will be seen at the entrance to the yacht basin.

Mooring

Details 320 berths with 15 berths for visitors. Maximum LOA 12 metres though larger yachts come here.

Berth in a vacant spot and report to the club office on the N side of the basin. There are laid moorings tailed to the pontoons or to buoys.

Shelter Good all-round shelter.

Authorities Port captain and marina staff. A charge is made.

Note The berths on the S side of Bassin de Ferrières are for fishing boats and you are likely to find an irate trawler skipper requesting you to leave if you

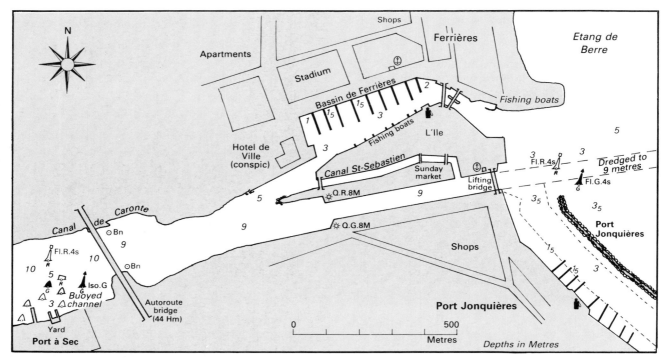

MARTIGUES 43°24′·5N 5°03′·2E

Martigues looking from the road bridge to Bassin de Ferrières.
Note the awful Hôtel de Ville on the left of the photo.

berth here. A yacht can also berth alongside on the N side of Passe de Jonquières though it is very uncomfortable here and your topsides are likely to suffer against the wall when commercial craft pass. The berths in the Canal de St-Sebastien are all private and yachts should not attempt to enter it.

Facilities

Services Water and electricity at every berth.

Fuel On the quay in the SE corner of Ferrières.

Repairs For hauling, yachts usually go to Port à Sec on the canal. Chandlers and sailmaker at Port à Sec.

Provisions Good shopping for provisions in the town. Sunday morning market on L'Ile. Ice available.

Eating out Several restaurants in Ferrières, L'Ile, and Jonquières.

Other Post office. Banks. Buses and trains to Marseille. Internal and international flights from Marignane airport nearby.

General

If you can ignore the industrial outskirts and the outlying apartment blocks on a similar architectural theme to the town hall, the old core of Martigues lives up to its 19th-century epithet of a 'little Venice'. The town has an ancient pedigree, but only acquired its name in 1581 when the three fishing villages of Ferrières, L'Ile and Jonquières amalgamated to become Martigues, though the three quarters are still known by their original names.

It has had a long history as a fishing and trading port and it still retains the feeling of one. Alexandre Dumas visited it on his travels and gave this description of the 19th-century village:

'The most striking feature about Martigues, is its joyous appearance, its streets intersected with canals and strewn with cyanthas and the pungent seaweed; its crossways, where boats ply, like coaches in ordinary streets. Then at every step, dwarfs of ships rise into view, with their tarred bottoms and dried nets. It is a vast boat, in which everyone is engaged in fishing; men with nets, women with lines, children with their hands; they fish in the streets, they fish under the bridges, they fish from windows; and the fish, always plentiful and always stupid, thus allow themselves to be captured in the same spot, and by the same means, for the last two thousand years.' (Alexandre Dumas *Voyage dans le Midi de la France* quoted in Raison *The South of France*.) Dumas goes on to say the Martegao are considered in Provence to be somewhat dull-witted, the butt of jokes in the way the Irish are in England, a reputation I am informed they retained until not so long ago in the eyes of the Marseillais.

The town became fashionable in the late 19th century with a number of painters, most notably Felix Ziem. The Ziem museum in the town houses a number of his paintings as well as paintings by other Provençal artists. You can see what charmed Ziem, and the other artists and poets who came here, in a brief wander around L'Ile. From the bridge across

Martigues. Intersected by canals that cut the town into three parts, it has often been described as Provence's 'little Venice'.

the Canal St-Sebastien there is a famous view, the *Miroir aux Oiseaux*, which translates a little inadequately as the 'Bird's Looking Glass'. The Sunday market is held in the square nearby and there is nothing more pleasant to do on a Sunday than wander aimlessly around the market before settling down to a beer or *pastis* in Le Flash bar in Ferrières. I have visited Martigues whenever I have been on passage along this coast from as far back as 1977 and I still enjoy coming here – it has a sort of careless intimacy that grows on you.

PORT A SEC – MARTIGUES

On the S side of Canal de Caronte just W of the high road bridge is the huge Port à Sec with hard standing ashore for over a 1000 yachts. The access channel to the yard is well buoyed and has a least depth of 3 metres. There is a pontoon to go alongside, close to the travel-hoist bay. A 16-ton travel-hoist is used. Water and electricity (220 and 380v) are included and there are toilets and showers at the yard. There is a chandlers, several hardware and tool shops, and a huge DIY superstore nearby. All mechanical and engineering repairs, GRP and wood repairs can be carried out. Electrical and electronic repairs. Sail-makers. The only disadvantage of the yard is that it is some distance from the town.

Martigues Bridge

The lifting bridge connecting the Canal de Caronte with the Etang de Berre. The bridge opens in the morning and evening and on demand for commercial vessels. Enquire at the bridge office on L'Ile close to the bridge for the exact opening times.

Traffic signals on either side of the bridge operate:
F.R Bridge closed.
F.Y Bridge about to open.
Fl.G/F.G Bridge open and passage permitted.

Once through the bridge a series of conical red and green buoys shows the deep-water passage (dredged to 9 metres) into the Etang de Berre.

Etang de Berre

A large salt inland lake with a number of small yacht harbours around it. The *étang* is approximately 9 miles long by 8 miles wide and the depths in it vary from 5 to 9 metres for the most part, except for some shoal patches in the N and E. On the E side there is a large petrochemical installation at Berre l'Etang

and the airport of Marignane serving Marseille. The S side also has some oil installations and industry. All this may make it sound a wholly unattractive place, but the W side and St-Chamas in the N are most attractive in contrast to the industrial E side.

The comparatively shallow water of the *étang* means that any strong winds quickly raise a steep and vicious sea. The *mistral* is funnelled by the hills so it comes from the N and NNE and when it blows the Etang de Berre is no place to be. With strong southerlies the wind is stopped to some extent by the high land to the S, but vicious seas will still be encountered at the N end of the *étang*.

PORT DE JONQUIERES

Approach

A small marina situated at the Martigues end of the now disused Canal de Marseille au Rhône. Until 1963 when a section of the roof caved in in the long tunnel to Marseille, *péniches* could get from the Rhône to Marseille along this canal. Since 1963 and the cave-in the canal has not been used though recently there has been talk in the local paper about re-opening it.

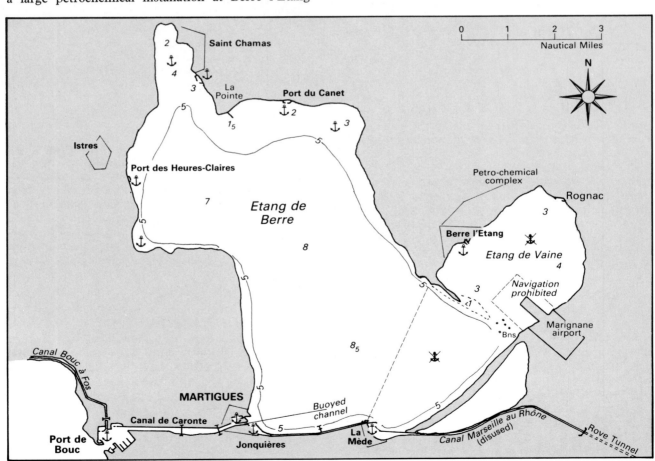

ETANG DE BERRE

Mooring

Berth in a vacant berth towards the end of one of the pontoons (depths decrease towards the shore) and report to the club office for a berth. There are 3·5 metre depths in the outer part of the old canal decreasing to 1 metre and less close to the shore. Shelter is better than it looks although a strong *mistral* makes the outer berths uncomfortable. A charge is made.

Facilities

Services Water at every berth and electricity can be connected.

Fuel On the end of one of the pontoons.

Repairs There is a small crane, but hard standing is limited. Most yachts go to Port à Sec.

Provisions Good shopping for provisions nearby.

Eating out Several restaurants and bars nearby.

General

Jonquières is not really set up for visitors and most yachts go to Bassin de Ferrières.

PORT DES HEURES-CLAIRES

Approach

A small yacht harbour on the W side of the Etang de Berre.

Conspicuous The harbour breakwater and the masts of the yachts inside are easily seen under the steep slopes around it.

Mooring

Details 280 berths with 20 berths for visitors.

Berth where directed or in a vacant spot and report to the office. Good all-round shelter inside. A charge is made.

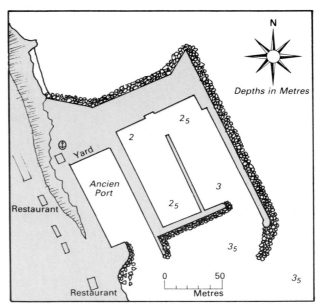

PORT DES HEURES-CLAIRES

Facilities

Water and electricity at all berths. There are few facilities at the harbour itself, several restaurants and a bar ashore, but for provisions and fuel you must go to Istres about 4 kilometres away.

General

The harbour, situated under steep pine-clad slopes, is an unexpected and peaceful place. It is popular in the summer with the locals who flock here choking the narrow road down to the harbour.

ST-CHAMAS

A small village at the N end of the *étang*. Miramas, a medieval village on a rocky hummock just W of St-Chamas is conspicuous. Closer in the limestone cliffs behind St-Chamas stand out well and the village, with a conspicuous clock tower, will be seen.

Vieux Port A miniature basin at the town itself. The approaches to it have silted and craft drawing more than a metre should not attempt to enter. Two abandoned ferrocement yachts on the N side of the entrance are conspicuous.

Nouveau Port A new harbour just SE of the town. The breakwater, a piled and timbered affair, and the masts of the yachts inside, are easily identified. In the approach there are 1·5–2 metre depths and in the harbour there are 2 metre depths in the outer part decreasing to 1 metre near the quay. Berth in a vacant spot or where directed.

There is good shopping for provisions, and restaurants in St-Chamas.

Port des Heures-Claires on the W side of the Etang de Berre.

St-Chamas. The old fishing harbour.

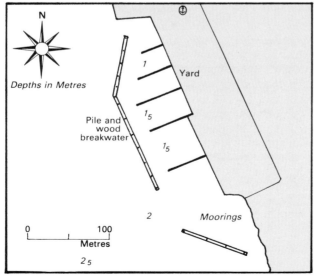

ST-CHAMAS MARINA

(map labels: N, Depths in Metres, 1, 1₅, Yard, Pile and wood breakwater, 1₅, 1₅, 2, Moorings, 0, 100, Metres, 2₅)

PORT DU CANET

A small harbour just E of the hydroelectric station where the river Durance enters the *étang*. The buildings of the hydroelectric station, particularly a tall tower, are conspicuous. There are 2 metre depths in the entrance to the harbour and 1–1·8 metre depths inside. There is water and electricity at the harbour and a petrol station and restaurant nearby on the coast road behind the harbour, but otherwise there are no facilities.

Etang de Vaïne

The eastern arm of the Etang de Berre. A shoal extends from La Pointe nearly across to Marignane on the other side. A series of beacons show the deep-water passage (3–5 metres) close to the southern side. It is prohibited to anchor in the Etang de Vaïne because of pipelines and there is an area where it is prohibited to enter because the flight path into and out of Marignane airport crosses it. Around the Etang de Vaïne there are two small harbours, at Berre l'Etang and Rognac, which craft drawing 1 metre or less could use with caution.

BERRE L'ETANG

The small harbour here on the NW side of Etang de Vaïne has 1–1·5 metre depths inside. The approaches to it were being dredged at the time of writing. Although right next to a large petrochemical installation, the little harbour and village is quite convivial.

ROGNAC

The small harbour here has mostly less than 1 metre depths.

The large petrochemical installation at Berre l'Etang and the noise of aircraft taking off and landing at Marignane greatly diminish any charm the place has though incredibly at Rognac, a watersports centre somehow survives.

LA MEDE

On the S side of the Etang de Berre a group of rugged rocks, Les Trois Frères, are conspicuous close to the coast. Just to the E of the rocks there is a disused harbour on the old Canal de Marseille au Rhône. A few local yachts are berthed here and there is a slipway and a small yard. However the area is run-down and somewhat depressing.

La Côte Bleue

Between Martigues and Marseille, the hard limestone hills of Chaîne de l'Estaque border the sea, and this hilly coast, cut by *calanques* and rocky coves, has been christened La Côte Bleue. The *calanques* have been formed over time by streams and creeks, many of them dry in the summer, cutting through the limestone over thousands of years to form the steep-sided fjord-like coves. This area is a taste of the steeper and more spectacular coast to come between Marseille and La Ciotat. For train enthusiasts the line that runs around the coast, teetering on the edge of cliffs and boring through the hills, is a must.

ANCHORAGES BETWEEN PORT DE BOUC AND PORT CARRO

Most of the anchorages on the E side of the Golfe de Fos to Port Carro offer shelter from easterlies, but are open to westerlies and to the *mistral*.

Canal-Vieil

A cove just S of Port de Bouc. It is close to the petrochemical installation at Lavéra and has a power station on the S side – enough said unless you relish those sort of surroundings.

Ponteau

An inlet about 1½ miles S of Canal-Vieil. It is mostly shallow and in any case industrial.

Anse des Laurons

The four tall chimneys of the Les Laurons power station are the most conspicuous objects in the gulf. On the N side of this bay there is a small harbour for supplying the power station. The cove on the SE side of the bay has permanent moorings for local yachts kept here in the summer. Anchor in 2–6 metres where convenient. There are a number of houses around the bay and a restaurant-bar opens in the summer.

Anse de Bonnieu

A small cove just S of Les Laurons. It is a naturist colony.

Rague d'Arnette and Rague de Carro

Two shoal patches off the coast of Carro with least depths of 2·5 and 2·7 metres. Two buoys mark the extremity of the shoal water: *Arnette*, A YBY conical buoy with a ⅄ topmark, Q(9)15s; and *Carro* a YBY conical buoy with a ⅄ topmark, VQ(9)10s.

In calm weather local yachts cut inside the buoys, but with any swell running there is a confused sea for some distance off this corner and even local yachts keep well off.

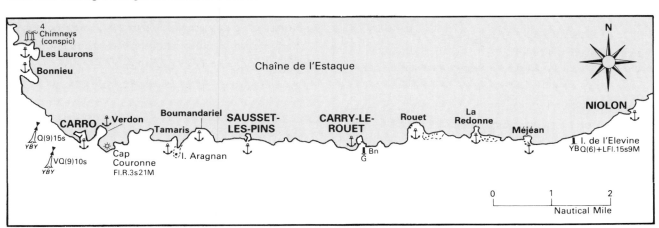

LA COTE BLEUE: PORT CARRO TO NIOLON

PORT DE CARRO

Approach

Conspicuous From the W and E the lighthouse on
Cap Couronne, a white tower with a red top, is conspicuous. The two buoys marking the shoal water off
the SW side of Pte Carro are easily identified. Closer
in a white signal station on Cap Couronne will be
seen. The small beacon on Pte de Carro and the harbour breakwater will not be seen until close to.

By night Use the light on Cap Couronne: Fl.3s21M.
The harbour entrance is lit: Oc(2)WR.6s9/6M. The
white sector covers the safe approach to the harbour
on 322°–355°.

Dangers
● Care must be taken of Ragues d'Arnette and
Ragues de Carro mentioned above.
● With strong southerlies there are confused seas at
the entrance making entry difficult.

Mooring

Details 200 berths with 20 berths for visitors. Maximum LOA 11 metres.

Berth where directed or in a vacant spot and report to
the *capitainerie* for a berth.

Shelter Good all-round shelter.

Authorities Port captain. A charge is made.

Anchorage In Anse de Carroussel there are several
mooring buoys. If these are in use anchor in 3–6
metres where convenient.

Facilities

Services Water points on the quay and electricity can
be connected on the S side.

Fuel Close to the quay on the S side.

Repairs A 50-ton slipway and a 6-ton crane. Most
mechanical and engineering repairs. GRP and wood
repairs. Chandlers. The area on the S side is being
developed as a large yacht yard.

Provisions Most provisions can be found.

Eating out Several restaurants and bars open in the
summer.

Other Post office. Train to Martigues and Marseille
from La Couronne about half a mile away.

General

Carro is an unadorned fishing harbour that has a raw
appeal to it, smelling of fish and littered with nets
and trawl-boards. In recent years an aquatic resident,
Fanny the dolphin, has made the waters off Pte
de Carro her home, and was a great attraction for
summer visitors who tried to get a glimpse of her
from an observation platform on the beach. In the
winter of 1988–89 Fanny was joined by a mate much
to the delight of the local mass media which in typically Gallic fashion had been worried by her solitary
existence. Recently she has left the area though the
locals believe she will return.

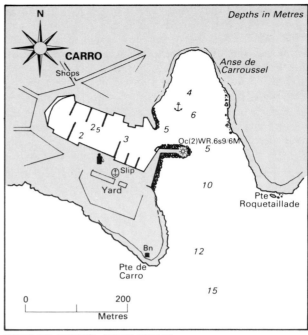

PORT DE CARRO 43°20'N 5°02'·6E

ANCHORAGES BETWEEN CARRO AND SAUSSET-LES-PINS

Anse du Verdon A large cove immediately E of Port
de Carro with Cap Couronne forming its eastern side.
It provides good shelter from northerlies, but is open
to the SW–S. With a strong *mistral* a swell is pushed
in here. Anchor in 4–8 metres on sand and mud,
good holding. A restaurant-bar opens in the summer.

Port de Ste Croix A fairly open bay about ¾ of a mile
NE of Cap Couronne. In calm weather anchor in 2–5
metres on sand and rock.

The chapel of Ste Croix is dedicated to the Marys
of Stes-Maries who are said to have landed here before going on to the Rhône delta. On the beach they
found a dumb child who miraculously gained the
power of speech from the saintly Marys.

Anse des Tamaris A tiny cove immediately E of Ste-
Croix. Care needs to be taken of Ile Aragnon, connected to the coast by a reef, off the eastern entrance
to the cove. The cove is home a number of local
boats kept here in the summer on laid moorings. Anchor in 3–5 metres in the entrance.

Anse de Bourmandariel A bay suitable in calm
weather or light northerlies just E of Ile Aragnon.
Villas have been built around the slopes to the E.
Anchor in 4–6 metres on sand.

SAUSSET-LES-PINS

Approach

Conspicuous A château on a wooded hummock stands out well from the much built-upon slopes around the harbour. Closer in, the harbour breakwater and the light tower at the entrance will be seen.

By night The entrance is lit, Oc(3)R.12s9M.

Mooring

Details 370 berths. Maximum LOA 12 metres.

Berth where directed or at the fuel quay and report to the *capitainerie* for a berth. There are laid moorings tailed to the quay.

Shelter Good shelter except from strong southerlies which can make some berths very uncomfortable.

Authorities Port captain. A charge is made.

Note There are plans to increase the number of berths in the harbour by utilising the space in the N. Work is to begin soon.

Facilities

Services Water and electricity at every berth. A small shower and toilet block.

Fuel On the quay.

Repairs A 5-ton crane, but there is limited hard standing on the quayside. Some mechanical repairs. Chandlers.

Provisions Good shopping for all provisions nearby.

Eating out Numerous restaurants and bars on the waterfront.

Other Post office. Train to Martigues and Marseille.

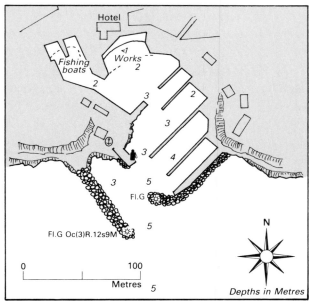

SAUSSET LES PINS 43°20′N 5°06′·5E

General

Sausset-les-Pins has become a fashionable very outer suburb for Martigues and Marseille with large villas around the coast and nearby slopes.

CARRY-LE-ROUET

Approach

Conspicuous A tall apartment block behind the harbour stands out well from the distance. Closer in, the breakwater, the small beacon on Pain de Sucre, and *L'Estéo* beacon will be seen. The entrance is difficult to make out though the light tower at the entrance can be seen.

By night Use the light on Pain de Sucre, Fl.R.2·5s3M, and the light at the entrance, Fl.G.4s11M. Care is needed as *L'Estéo* beacon is not lit.

Dangers
- Care needs to be taken of *L'Estéo* beacon, G with a ▲ topmark, marking the reef and shoal water to the E of it.
- With strong southerlies there is a confused swell at the entrance.

Mooring

Details 490 berths with 10 berths for visitors. Maximum LOA 15 metres.

Berth at the *quai d'accueil* just inside the entrance and report to the *capitainerie* for a berth. There are laid moorings tailed to the quay.

Shelter Good all-round shelter although strong southerlies cause a surge.

Authorities Port captain and marina staff. A charge is made.

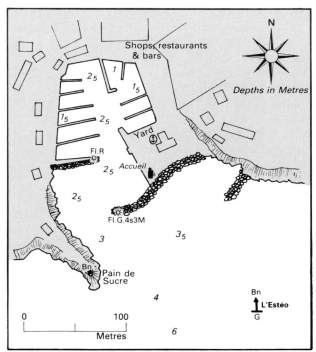

CARRY LE ROUET 43°19′·7N 5°09′·3E

Facilities

Services Water and electricity at every berth. A shower and toilet block.

Fuel On the quay at the entrance.

Repairs A 10-ton crane, but there is limited hard standing. Some mechanical repairs. Chandlers.

Provisions Good shopping for provisions ashore.

Eating out Numerous restaurants and bars open in the summer.

Other Post office. Bank. Train to Martigues and Marseille.

General

Carry is the more up-market resort along La Côte Bleue with a new development around the harbour and expensive villas fringing the coast. Like Sausset-les-Pins it has become something of an outer commuter suburb for Martigues and Marseille. The famous and much-loved comic actor Fernandel lived here off and on until his death a few years ago.

PORT DU ROUET

A bay approximately 1 mile E of Carry. Care needs to be taken of shallows off the coast and of the above and below-water rocks E of Rouet. There is a small harbour on the NW side of the bay, with 0·5–1·5 metre depths, but it is usually full of local boats. Anchor in 3–6 metres in the middle of the bay. Open to the S and E.

LA REDONNE AND PORT MADRAGUE

Approach

These two small harbours lie approximately 1 mile E of Rouet. A railway viaduct behind La Redonne is conspicuous. Port Madrague is tucked in behind the western entrance point and La Redonne lies at the head of the cove. There are no lights for a night entry.

Mooring

Both harbours are crowded in the summer and no provision is made for visitors. A small yacht (8–9 metres LOA) can try to find a berth in Port Madrague. La Redonne is usually crowded with local boats on the quay and on moorings behind the breakwater.

Berth wherever a space can be negotiated, taking care of uneven depths and underwater rubble off the quay. Larger yachts can anchor off between La Redonne and Port Madrague.

Good shelter in Port Madrague except from SE–E. Good shelter in La Redonne except from strong southerlies which cause a surge.

Facilities

Some provisions can be obtained and several restaurants and bars open in the summer.

La Redonne looking down from the steep slopes behind.

Left Vallon des Auffes near Marseille. *Above*
L'Estaque coast on the NW side of Rade de
Marseille. *Below* Marseille. Vieux Port looking out
to the entrance and Fort St-Jean.

Niolon. For very small boats the perfect harbour along this coast. *Left* Seaside monument or seaside slum? La Grande Motte in Roussillon. *Below* Château d'If, for centuries a political prison and also the setting for Dumas' *The Count of Monte Cristo*. Dumas knew these waters well, sailing around them in his yacht for a number of years until ill health forced him ashore.

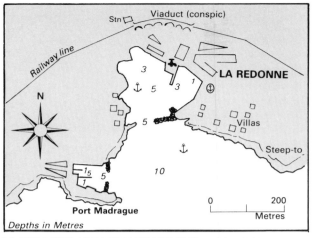

LA REDONNE AND PORT MADRAGUE 43°20'N 5°12'E

General

The small village lying under steep pine-clad slopes is an attractive place and although popular in the summer, it has not been extensively developed and built-up. Unfortunately it is very popular with local yachts and the chances of finding a berth are slim, but if you can find somewhere to squeeze in, don't hesitate.

PORT DE MEJEAN

A tiny harbour approximately 1 mile E of La Redonne. There are 1·5–3 metre depths inside, but there are few berths available for visitors. Several restaurants and bars open in the summer.

Just W of Méjean is Calanque de Figuières, a small cove with a slipway and quay, but it is crowded in the summer and only the smallest craft will be able to find a space here.

Ile de l'Elevine

A small islet about ¾ of a mile E of Cap Méjean. It is marked by a beacon, YB with a ▼ topmark. It is lit, Q(6)+LFl.15s9M.

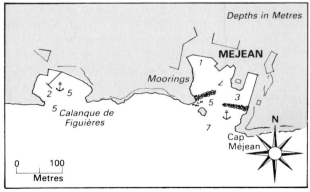

FIGUIERES AND MEJEAN

NIOLON

A tiny harbour just over 2 miles NE of Ile de l'Elevine. There are 3 metre depths in the entrance and 1–2 metre depths inside. In the summer it is crowded with local boats and even very small craft will have difficulty finding a berth. This is a pity as the harbour and village are enchanting. Several restaurants open in the summer.

Rade de Marseille

Rade de Marseille is entered between Cap Méjean and Ile de l'Elevine on the N and Ile Maire and Cap Croisette on the SE side. Iles du Frioul, two large islands with ragged coasts, lie off the eastern side of the *rade*. Marseille itself spreads around the coast in either direction with most of its industry and the commercial port on the NE side.

A number of objects are conspicuous in the approaches to the *rade*.

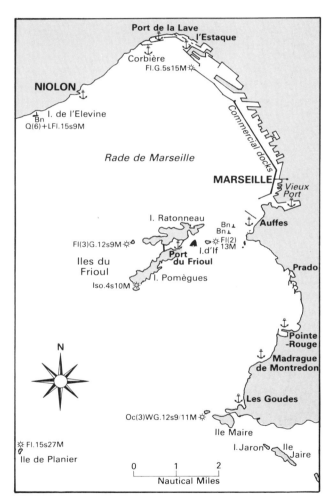

RADE DE MARSEILLE

Ile de Planier A low islet lying approximately 4½ miles WSW of Ile Maire. The tall white lighthouse (68m/223ft) on the islet is conspicuous from some distance off; Fl.5s27M light. The islet has shoal

121

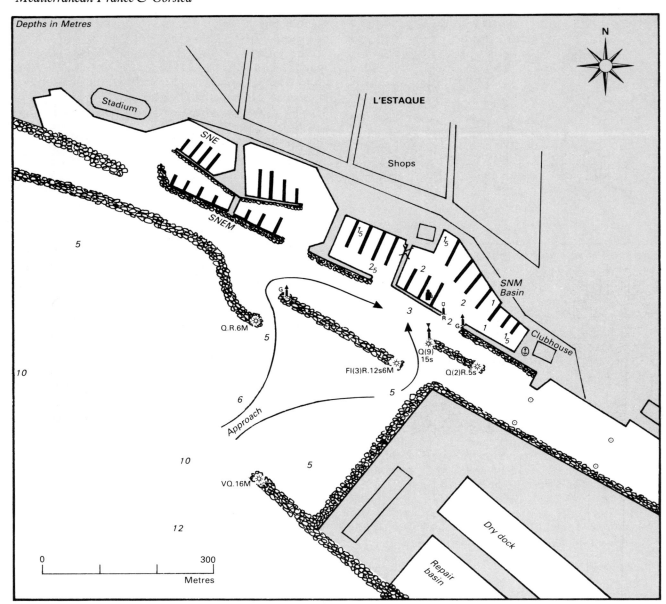

L'ESTAQUE 43°21'·5N 5°19'E

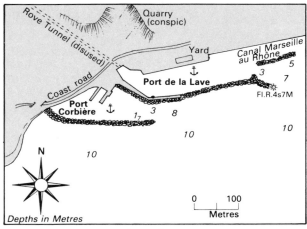

PORT CORBIERE AND PORT DE LA LAVE 43°21'·5N 5°18'E

water close off it with an underwater rock, La Pierre-à-la-Bague, on the SW, marked by a conical buoy, YBY with a ⅄ topmark. One mile NE there is a shoal bank, Le Veyron, with least depths of 13·2 metres over it.

Iles du Frioul The high jagged outline of the islands is easily identified. From the W the lighthouse on Ilot Tiboulen, a white tower, is conspicuous; Fl(3)G.12s9M light. From the W and SE the signal station on the southern end of Ile Pomègues is conspicuous.

Ile Riou A high jagged island (190m/623ft) that is easily identified in the eastern approaches to the rade.

PORT DE LA CORBIERE

A disused commercial harbour close to the entrance of the now disused Rove tunnel and canal that formerly led to the Etang de Berre. There are 5–8 metre depths in the entrance, but these rapidly decrease inside. The harbour has silted and care must be taken of the uneven depths inside. Anchor off or go bows-to the quay. Good shelter from northerlies, but SE winds make it uncomfortable.

PORT DE LA LAVE

The disused entrance to the Rove tunnel and canal. Local yachts are kept here on the quay and there is a crane and covered workshop ashore. It is gradually being developed as a yacht harbour and boatyard. Care needs to be taken as the depths inside are uneven.

Port de la Corbière looking E across to Ports de l'Estaque.

PORTS DE L'ESTAQUE

Four yacht basins at the NW end of the commercial harbour which stretches from Marseille Vieux Port for some 4 miles to the yacht harbour at L'Estaque.

Approach

Conspicuous The cargo ships and cranes and gantries of the commercial harbour will be seen from some distance off. A large quarry and crusher plant above Port de la Lave is conspicuous. Closer in, where the commercial port ends, the masts of the yachts in the basins at L'Estaque will be seen. Either of the two entrances, Passe de l'Estaque or Passe des Chalutiers, can be used.

By night The approach and entrances to the basins are lit. Use the light at the NW end of Digue de Saumaty, VQ.16M. Passe de l'Estaque is lit, Q.R.6M. Passe des Chalutiers is lit, Fl(3)R.12s6M and Fl.G.4s6M. The inner breakwater of Passe des Chalutiers is lit at the W end, Q(9)15s, and the E end, Q(2)R.5s.

Dangers In strong southerlies there is a reflected swell off the breakwaters causing a confused sea and care is needed. With strong SE–E winds use Passe des Chalutiers.

Mooring

Details There are five yacht clubs administering the berths in the various basins. There is a total of 1540 berths with 50 berths for visitors at the Société Nautique de Mourepiane (SNM) in the SW basin.

Berth Make for the SW basin and berth where directed or go onto the fuel quay and report to the club office for a berth. There are laid moorings tailed to the quay or to a buoy.

Shelter Good all-round shelter

Authorities Club officers and helpers. A charge is made.

Facilities
(SNM)

Services Water and electricity at every berth. A shower and toilet block at the club.

Fuel On the quay near the entrance to the SW basin.

Repairs Two slipways up to 12 tons and a 6-ton crane. Most mechanical and engineering repairs. Chandlers. All other repairs can be arranged from Marseille.

Provisions Most provisions can be found nearby. Ice available.

Eating out Numerous restaurants on the waterfront nearby.

Other Post office. Buses and trains to Marseille.

General

Despite being so close to the commercial port, the yacht basin is a surprisingly pleasant spot. The Rove tunnel and canal nearby at Port de la Lave, part of the old Canal de Marseille au Rhône, was built in the 1920s to link the Etang de Berre and Marseille. It is some 4 miles long, a dead straight tunnel bored through the limestone of the L'Estaque hills, and until a cave-in closed it in 1963, it was an important commercial link between Marseille and the Etang de Berre, and via the canal to Arles on the Rhône, to the interior. It was decided not to re-open it and has been disused since 1963.

MARSEILLE VIEUX PORT

Approach

Conspicuous Once up to Iles du Frioul the most conspicuous object in the vicinity of Marseille is the church of Notre Dame de la Garde on a peak S of the Vieux Port. Ile d'If with its conspicuous château and the two beacons, *Sourdaras* and *Canoubier* to the SW of the port, are easily identified closer in. The entrance to the Vieux Port is difficult to identify, but the cathedral with a large cupola and several smaller cupolas to the NE of the entrance will be seen, and a yacht should head for it until the entrance can be seen. The light structures on Pte de la Désirade and Digue Ste-Marie are easily identified.

Marseille. Approach to the Vieux Port. Note the conspicuous cathedral.

Marseille. The entrance to the Vieux Port.

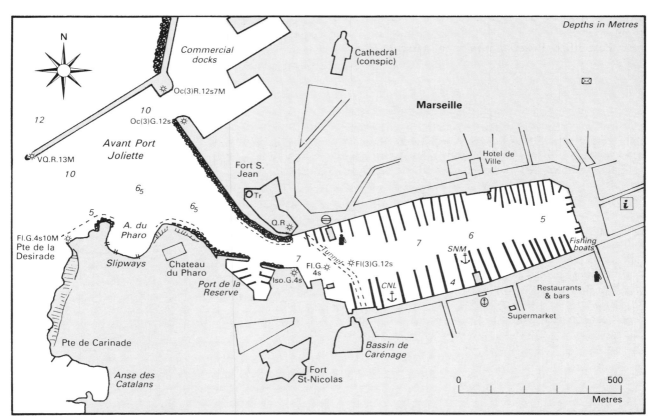

MARSEILLE: VIEUX PORT 43°17'·7N 5°22'E

By night Ile d'If is lit on the E side, Fl(2)6s13M. Sourdaras beacon is lit, Q(9)15s8M. In the closer approach use the lights on the end of Digue des Catalans, Fl(3)G.12s5M; Pte de la Désirade, Fl.G.4s 10M; and on the end of Digue Ste-Marie, VQ.R. 13M. The inner entrance to the Vieux Port is lit, Iso.G.4s, Fl(3)G.12s, Q.R and Fl.G.4s.

Note Care must be taken of the numerous craft coming and going from the Vieux Port, especially the ferries running to Frioul which charge in and out at speed.

Mooring

The pontoons crammed in around the Vieux Port are administered by various clubs. Two clubs, the Centre Nautique du Lacidon (CNL) and the Société Nautique de Marseille (SNM) have visitors' berths available. The CNL berths are on the S side just inside the entrance and the SNM pontoons are further along near the middle of the harbour. Most yachts make for the SNM pontoons where a yacht should go alongside the floating clubhouse to be allotted a berth. There are laid moorings tailed to buoys through which a line should be taken or in the case of the smaller buoys hauled aboard.

Shelter Good all-round shelter.

Authorities Customs. Immigration. Port captain. Club officers and staff. A charge is made.

Note Very large yachts should call up on VHF in advance to check if there is a suitable berth free.

For some time there have been plans to build a marina in the Avant Port Joliette just before the entrance to the Vieux Port. As yet permission has to be obtained and plans finalised. It could be another tall Marseillais tale!

Facilities

Services Water and electricity at every berth. A shower and toilet block at the SNM clubhouse.

Fuel On the quay on the N side near the entrance.

Repairs There are several small cranes and slipways around the Vieux Port, but these are mostly for small local craft and there is limited hard standing. Slipways in Anse du Pharo near the entrance to the Vieux Port can haul larger craft. Virtually all repairs can be carried out in Marseille and most spares can be obtained here. All mechanical and engineering repairs. GRP and wood repairs. Electrical and electronic repairs. Sailmakers. Chandlers.

Provisions Good shopping for all provisions nearby. Market in the old town behind the harbour. Ice available.

Eating out Any number of restaurants of every category nearby. In the streets immediately behind the SNM pontoons are numerous excellent restaurants in a convivial pedestrian precinct.

Other Post office. Banks. Hire cars. Buses and trains along the coast. Internal and international flights from Marignane Airport nearby.

General

More than any other town along the coast, Marseille is a traveller's town rather than a tourist town. It is noisy, frenetic, dirty, crowded, bustling and busy. The traffic chokes the old streets, yachts and fishing boats choke the old harbour, it fairly hums with life and that life is uniquely coloured by the Marseillais themselves. What other people could lead the Revolution, give France its national anthem, and then rebel against the Revolution they were amongst the first to fight for? The local rebellion was cruelly crushed by the Republicans who had a guillotine permanently set up on the Canebière to deal with the rebels. The Marseillais are paradox to themselves let alone to others.

The city was founded by the Phocaeans from Asia Minor around 600 BC. These early Greek colonists, not to be confused with the Phoenicians, established a whole string of colonies around the coasts of France, Italy and Corsica. By the Vieux Port they built a town they called Massalia and over the centuries it grew into the most prosperous trading town on the coast. The Massalians were constantly troubled by the native Ligurians and eventually asked Rome for help. In 122 BC Massalia was made an autonomous province under Roman jurisdiction. Things continued happily until Massalia sided with Pompey against Caesar in the struggle for the control of the Empire. Caesar won and after his victory stripped Massalia of its riches and power. Thereafter its fortunes continued to decline through the Barbarian invasions and attacks by Saracen corsairs until the 11th century when its fortunes revived trading in human cargo, shipping the Crusaders to the Holy Land. Little by little its prosperity returned until the volatile Marseillais, after fighting for the French Revolution, decided after all that it was not such a good idea and rebelled. The Canebière ran with blood from the daily guillotining and Marseille was called 'the city with no name'.

Marseille quays around the turn of the century.

In the 19th century its fortunes revived with the development of the railways and the opening of the Suez Canal. The Vieux Port was too small to accommodate the increasing numbers of merchant ships and so construction began on the new docks to the north. In World War II much of the commercial harbour and much of Marseille was destroyed. What little that was not flattened by Allied bombers was blown up by the Germans shortly before they left. The discovery of oil in North Africa in the post-war years again put Marseille on the map and it is now the second largest port in France.

In the Vieux Port you are right in the heart of old Marseille, in fact in one of the quietest places in the city if you are near the middle of the harbour, though 'quiet' is a relative term in this noisy bustling place. Marseille is not a place where you have to go and look at museums, though it has plenty of those and good ones to; rather it is a memorial to itself, to a 19th-century harbour town and to the spirit of the Marseillais themselves. The inhabitants have always had a reputation for a droll and relaxed outlook on life and for a special sort of jocularity renowned throughout France. It goes a long way back. In 1650 when the unpopular Duke de Joyeuse was resident in Marseille, the locals worked out a way to get rid of him:

'The townspeople, tired of the nobleman's presence, spread a rumour that the plague had broken out in the city. For several days all funeral processions were routed under the Duke's windows. He was so terrified that he promptly left and by this stratagem the people of Marseille rid themselves of an irksome authority.' (Berenger-Feraud quoted in Raison's *The South of France*.) Edmund Swinglehurst in his readable book on *The Midi* describes the sort of scene you see often in Marseille which encapsulates the energetic and eccentric character of the Marseillais:

'The Marseillais are quite unlike any other Frenchmen or women. I recently witnessed a typical Marseillais scene while sitting in a café on Quai du Port. A tall man in a sports jacket with the air of a university professor – glasses, long lank hair – was standing on the pavement talking to a businessman – smartly dressed, cropped grey hair, briefcase under his arm. The tall man was waving his arms about like a windmill. Evidently there was an argument in progress. Suddenly he strode into the street and lay down before the oncoming traffic, which passed on each side of him with no more than a passing curse from the drivers. The businessman shrugged and walked away. A few moments later the prostrate man stood up, dusted himself and returned to the pavement where he was soon rejoined by his friend. The argument continued.'

For many people Marseille is the home of the French Mafia, the centre of drug smuggling along the coast, the place where it all happened in the film *The French Connection*. The Marseille Mafia still exists, though much reduced in its effectiveness by its very notoriety, but the traveller sees nothing of this. The city has been cleaned up and much restoration work is going on in the old quarters. There is a fresh lively spirit here that is fast making Marseille the new cultural capital of the south, supplanting its age-old rival, Aix-en-Provence. Though the red-light area should be avoided late at night, Marseille is as safe as any other city to walk around, and for the traveller looking for the everyday sights and sounds of the south of France, much of it will be found here.

The Vieux Port c. 1900.

BOUILLABAISSE

It is nearly impossible to move around the head of the quay of the Vieux Port when the fishing boats return with their catch. Half of Marseille seems to be there. Old women with string bags poke the fish with horny fingers. Cars stop in the middle of the road causing traffic jams as drivers leap out to buy something from the catch. Stall-holders accost the passers-by with a sales pitch – *Achetez mon poisson...Poissons de roche pour la soupe... Bouillabaisse, bouillabaisse. Attendez monsieur, madame, achetez mon beau poisson! Tout frais de ce matin* – designed to get you to buy a bagful of slithering fish at all costs. In the restaurants around the waterfront and just about everywhere you will see *bouillabaisse*, always described as a 'genuine Marseillais *bouillabaisse*', featured prominently on the menus along with other fish dishes. Marseille is seafood mad and lays claim to being the home of *bouillabaisse*, that messy mixture of soup and fish that as much as any other dish, typifies Mediterranean food.

The mythopoeic origins of *bouillabaisse* are as tall as any Marseillais tale. Fish soup with saffron is said to be soporific and the tale goes that Aphrodite invented *bouillabaisse* to put her husband Hephaestus to sleep when she had an amorous appointment with Ares. It is likely that *bouillabaisse* did have Greek origins since fish soup was and is now a common dish in the Mediterranean countries and *bouillabaisse* is only the best known variation on a common culinary theme. The name *bouillabaisse* comes from the Provençal *bui-abaisso*, because when the soup boils (*boui*) you must reduce the heat (*abaisso*); this ensures that the olive oil and water bind together, but that the fish is not overcooked.

Unfortunately you are unlikely to come across good *bouillabaisse* in all but a few restaurants. Having tasted the *bouillabaisse* of Odile's favourite aunt in Marseille, the thin gruel, smelling vaguely of fish, that I have sampled in several restaurants in Marseille bears little resemblance to the real thing. As Leslie Forbes acidly comments in her *A Table in Provence*, there are only a few restaurants in Marseille that cook the real thing:

'Marseille is a city where every fishstall with more than one chair claims to serve authentic *bouillabaisse*, and the recipe has been so debased that a group of Marseillais fishermen, restaurateurs and journalists finally wrote a chart to establish the soup's essential ingredients once and for all. But of all the cafés and restaurants in Marseille only 13 have kept to the relatively simple guidelines set down in this chart. Understandably. Any Claude, Marc or Henri can wave a watery broth over some seaweed and call it '*la vraie Bouillabaisse*', but it takes time and care to make a real one.'

If you don't have a friend with an aunty in Marseille, you can always attempt to make your own *bouillabaisse*. I have adapted and simplified the various recipes so that it can be more easily produced on a yacht, though I hope the essential ingredients remain.

Bouillabaisse *(for four)*

500gm of fish, any of racasse, wrasse, red mullet, bream, conger eel, John Dory and bass. The fisherman on the waterfront will know what you need once you point a few out and usually have an assorted selection of ugly small fish just for *bouillabaisse*.

A *bouillabaisse* normally includes the weeverfish, but as its dorsal spines can inject a dangerous venom, it is best excluded or you may have to rush the cook to hospital! When the weeverfish is cooked its venom breaks down.

1 medium onion, sliced
250gm of tomatoes, skinned and chopped
250gm of potatoes, peeled and sliced
2 cloves of garlic, chopped
Some parsley, chopped
1 or 2 bay leaves
Thyme and fennel
Salt and pepper
100ml of olive oil
A heaped teaspoon of saffron threads
Rouille (it is best to buy this as it is messy to make on board)
A slightly stale *baguette*

Heat the olive oil in a large pot or a pressure cooker and add the sliced onions, chopped tomatoes, garlic, parsley, bay leaves, thyme and fennel, and salt and pepper to taste. To this add two of the small cleaned and gutted fish, a little water, and simmer it for an hour or half an hour in the pressure cooker until it has a thin purée-like consistency. Sieve this mixture, add a little water and a tablespoon of *rouille*, and then add the other cleaned and gutted fish, the sliced potatoes, and the saffron. Put it on a high flame and cook fast for 10–15 minutes, until the fish and potatoes are cooked. The fish and potatoes should now be removed and put on the serving plates.

The soup is normally eaten separately from the fish, though you can pour it over the fish if you want to. It is better not to as you simply end up with a lot of fish bones and bits in the soup. The soup is eaten with *rouille* and toasted slices or half slices of the *baguette*.

There is a ritual order to preparing the soup for eating. Usually a clove of garlic accompanies the toasted bits of *baguette* and it is rubbed over the bits to make a sort of garlic bread according to your taste. The slices are then assembled in the soup plate, *rouille* dotted on each slice according to taste, grated cheese may then be heaped on the *rouille*, and only then is the soup ladled into the plate.

Iles du Frioul

Iles du Frioul are the two large islands, Ile Raton-neau and Ile de Pomègues, joined by a causeway, and Ilot Tiboulen off the western end of Ratonneau. The two large islands are much indented with bays and coves and are a popular destination for local yachts. There is a large marina at the former naval harbour between the two islands and much development of both the marina and general facilities on the islands is going on.

ILE RATONNEAU

The northern island. The old quarantine hospital, now disused, on the eastern end is conspicuous. Anchorages around the island are as follows.

Calanque de St-Estève A narrow *calanque* due W of Ile d'If. Basse St-Estève, an underwater rock with 2·5 metre least depth over it lies SE of the entrance. The rock is marked by a buoy, YB with a Ŧ topmark and is lit, Q(6)+LFl.15s. The old quarantine hospital is on the slopes N of the *calanque*. The anchorage is open SE and is uncomfortable in even moderate southerlies.

Calanque de Ratonneau A *calanque* immediately NE of St- Estève. Anchor in 3–6 metres. Like St-Estève it is uncomfortable in southerlies.

Port de Banc A bay on the N side of the island, directly across from Calanque de St- Estève. Anchor in 5–10 metres on sand and weed. Good shelter from southerlies, but open to the *mistral*.

Havre de Morgiret A bay SW of Port de Banc with an islet, Ile des Eyglaudes, off its southern entrance point. Anchor in 5–10 metres on sand and weed. Good shelter from southerlies and easterlies, but open to the *mistral*.

Baie du Grand Soufre The anchorage on the western side of the causeway. The bay itself is too deep for most yachts to anchor in, but a cove on the N side provides good shelter from all but W-SW winds. Anchor in 3–10 metres on sand and weed.

Ilot Tiboulen

The small island lying off the W end of Ile Raton-neau. The lighthouse on it is conspicuous, Fl(3)G. 12s9M light.

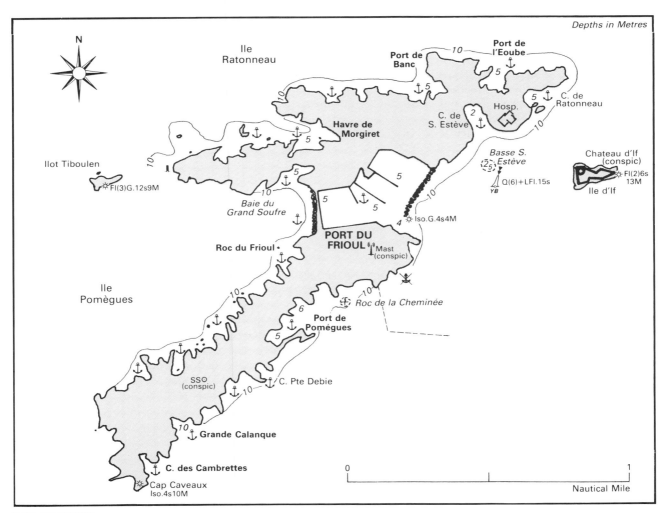

ILES DE FRIOUL

PORT DU FRIOUL

A new marina created behind the causeway joining the two islands.

Approach

Conspicuous Ile d'If is easily identified by the fortified château on it. A transmitter tower on the N end of Ile Pomègues is conspicuous. Closer in the breakwater and the masts of the yachts inside will be seen.

By night Use the light on Ile d'If, Fl(2)6s13M. The harbour entrance is lit, Iso.G.4s4M.

Dangers
• A conical light buoy, Q(6)+LFl.15s marks Basse St-Estève, an underwater rock with 2·5 metres over it, NE of the harbour entrance.
• With strong SE winds a swell piles up at the entrance.

Note Ferries and tripper boats from Marseille charge in and out of the entrance at speed and a good lookout should be kept for them.

Mooring

Details 1500 berths with 150 berths for visitors.

Berth where directed on the outside pier and report to the *capitainerie* for a berth. There are laid moorings tailed to the quay or to buoys.

Shelter Good all-round shelter except in strong easterlies which make the outer berths uncomfortable.

Authorities Port captain and marina staff. A charge is made.

Facilities

Services Water and electricity at or near every berth. A shower and toilet block.

Fuel On the quay on the NE side of the harbour.

Repairs A 30-ton travel-hoist. Chandlers. All repair facilities can be found in Marseille.

Provisions Most provisions can be found. Ice available.

Eating out Restaurants and bars nearby.

Other Regular ferries to Marseille.

General

The islands were only recently bought from the military by the Municipalité de Marseille and the yacht marina is the first stage of a large leisure complex planned over the next few years. At the moment development is concentrated on and around Port du Frioul and while most of the local yachtsmen would like to keep it that way, it is likely development will begin in other parts of the islands in future years.

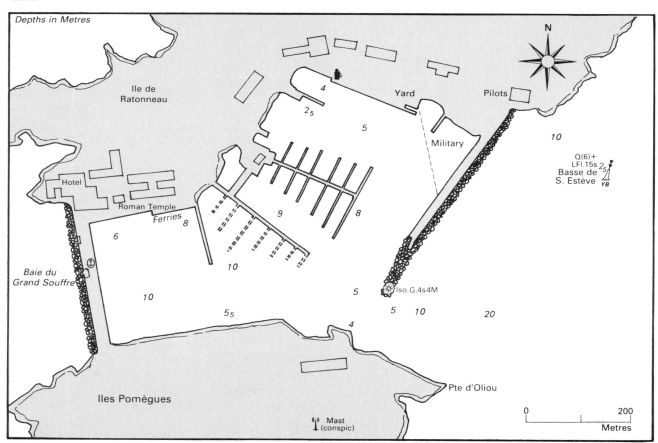

PORT DU FRIOUL 43°16'·8N 5°18'·6E

Frioul. Visitors' berths on the long central quay. There will eventually be pontoons off here.

ILE POMEGUES

The southern island of Iles du Frioul. A signal station on the summit of the island and the lighthouse, Iso.4s10M, at the southern end on Cap Caveaux are conspicuous. Anchorages around the island are as follows:

Port de Pomègues A bay on the eastern side affording all-round protection. Anchor in 5–8 metres on sand and weed. The anchorage is popular in the summer and yachts anchor all around the coast between Port Pomègues and Pte Courille. Care needs to be taken of Roc de la Cheminée, an underwater rock with 1·8 metres over it about 200 metres SW of Pte Courille.

Calanque Pte Debie A small cove immediately N of Pte Debie. Anchor in 5–8 metres. Open S-SE.

Grande Calanque A calanque about 500 metres NE of Cap Caveaux. Anchor in 5–10 metres. Open S-E.

On the NW side of Ile Pomègues there are numerous coves dotted along the coast that are suitable in light southerlies or easterlies, but are open to the *mistral*.

ILE D'IF

The island lying off the eastern side of Iles du Frioul. The fortified château on it is conspicuous and tripper boats regularly ply backwards and forwards between Marseille and Ile d'If bringing visitors.

The medieval château has been used as a prison for centuries. Protestants and other declared heretics were quartered here before serving their terms as galley slaves. Mirabeau was prisoner here in the 18th century for non-payment of his debts. In the 19th century opponents of Napoléon III were imprisoned here. But the most well known prisoner of the Château d'If was fictional, Alexandre Dumas' *Count of Monte Cristo*. The story is taken from the real-life prisoner kept in Fort Royal on Ile Ste-Marguerite off Cannes and transposed to the Château d'If, but that won't stop the guide showing you the cell where Edmond Dantès is supposed to have languished.

Marseille to Cap Croisette

Between Marseille and Cap Croisette there are a number of small fishing harbours and coves that in theory could be used by yachts, but in practice are so crowded with fishing boats and local craft kept there permanently for the summer that a berth is next to impossible to find. The only place you can rely on getting a berth at is the large marina at Pointe-Rouge.

Port des Auffes A small fishing harbour just over half a mile S of Pte de la Désirade. It is entered under a road bridge with an air height of approximately 10–12 metres. It is packed with local fishing boats and the chances of obtaining a berth are remote.

Port d'Endoume A small and mostly shallow fishing harbour immediately N of Pte d'Endoume. The entrance is rock bound and in any case there are mostly depths of less than 1 metre inside.

Port du Prado A harbour under Pte du Roucas-Blanc. It is reserved for board and dinghy sailors and a yacht should not attempt to enter.

PORT DE LA POINTE-ROUGE

The only harbour with good shelter and room for visiting yachts between Marseille and Cap Croisette.

Approach

Conspicuous The disused factory at l'Escalette and the transmitter tower on Mont Rose are conspicuous. At La Pointe-Rouge a white apartment block in front of a low wooded hummock can be identified amongst the rest of the apartment blocks and buildings. Closer in the harbour breakwater and the masts of the yachts inside will be seen. The entrance is difficult to see until close to it.

By night The entrance is lit, Oc(2)G.6s6M.

Dangers With the *mistral* blowing there are heavy seas at the entrance and entry can be difficult.

Note Numerous sailboards will be encountered in the area immediately NE of the entrance and a good lookout should be kept for them.

Mooring

Details 1200 berths with 10 berths for visitors. Maximum LOA 25 metres. In practice there are more berths available to visitors in the summer.

Berth at the fuel quay at the entrance or the *quai d'accueil* in the SE corner and report to the *capitainerie* for a berth. There are laid moorings tailed to the quay.

Shelter Good all-round shelter. Although the *mistral* makes entry difficult, there is good shelter from it inside.

Authorities Port captain and marina staff. A charge is made.

Note There are plans to increase the capacity of the harbour by 800 berths by constructing a new basin E of the present one. Work has yet to begin.

Facilities

Services Water and electricity at every berth. A shower and toilet block.

Fuel On the quay at the entrance.

Repairs A 30-ton travel-hoist and slipways. Mechanical and engineering repairs. GRP and wood repairs. Electrical and electronic repairs. Sailmakers. Chandlers.

Provisions Good shopping for provisions nearby. Ice available.

Eating out Numerous restaurants nearby including some good fish restaurants.

Other Post office. Buses to Marseille.

General

La Pointe-Rouge provides some escape from the hustle and bustle of Marseille, though I for one, miss

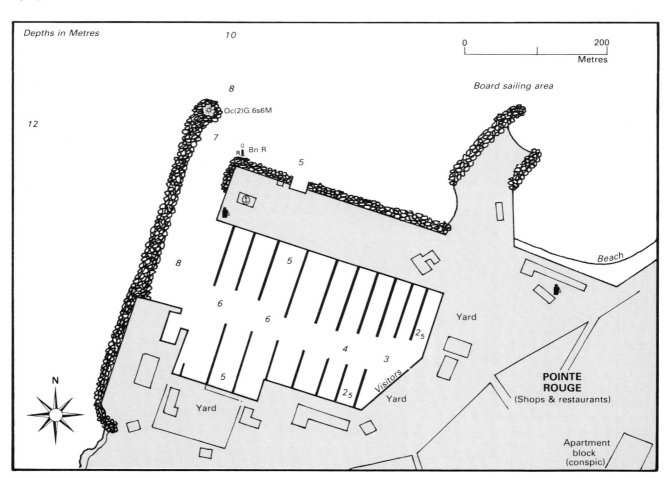

PORT DE LA POINTE ROUGE 43°14′N 5°21′·2E

that. For hauling, this is the logical place to make for from Marseille with several large yards adjacent to the marina and good facilities for the care and repair of boats.

MADRAGUE DE MONTREDON

A small fishing harbour under Mont Rose. The breakwater shows up well. It is crowded with fishing boats and local yachts permanently based here and there is little room for visiting yachts, even small ones. There are shops and restaurants nearby.

Between Madrague de Montredon and Port des Goudes on the N side of Cap Croisette there are a number of small coves suitable in settled weather.

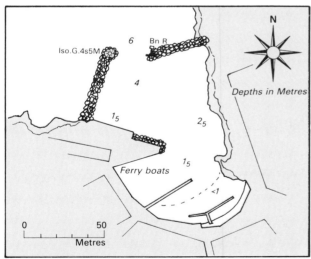

MADRAGUE DE MONTREDON 43°14′N 5°21′·3E

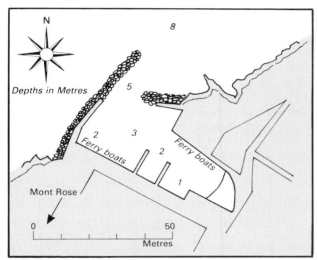

LES GOUDES 43°13′N 5°20′·8E

PORT DES GOUDES

A small harbour tucked into the N side of Cap Croisette. The blank concrete buildings of Les Goudes stand out against the barren rock and the harbour breakwaters are easily identified closer in. The entrance is lit, Iso.G.4s5M. The harbour is crowded with local craft, but a small yacht may find

Ile Maire and Cap Croisette looking NW.

a berth here. It is dangerous to enter and can be dangerous in the Avant Port in a *mistral*. There are restaurants and bars ashore.

Ile Maire

The jagged rocky island sitting under Cap Croisette. Off its western end is an islet, Ilot Tiboulen de Maire, with a light on its summit, Oc(3)WG.12s 11/9M. Both Ile Maire and Ilot Tiboulen are easily identified in the closer approaches. Between Ile Maire and Ilot Tiboulen there is a passage with good depths in the fairway except for a 3·3 metre patch off Ile Maire. Between Ile Maire and Cap Croisette there is a passage used by local yachts with reported depths of 2 metres. I have not attempted it and would advise that only shallow-draught craft try it and then only in calm weather with a lookout forward. Off the SE tip of Ile Maire there are two above-water rocks, Les Pharillons, which are easily identified.

In calm weather it is possible to anchor at the eastern end of the passage between Ile Maire and Cap Croisette in 5–10 metres. With any kind of wind at all there is a swell in here.

Calanque de Callelongue

A very small *calanque* half a mile E of Ile Maire. The entrance is difficult to pick out from seaward until close in. It is crowded with local boats and in any case too narrow for all but the smallest yachts.

Ile Jaron, Ile Jaïre, Ile Calseraigne and Ile Riou

A group of islands lying half a mile to 2 miles off the coast SE of Ile Maire and Cap Croisette. They are connected to the coast by shoal water, the Plateau des Chèvres, with a passage with least depths of 7–10 metres between Ile Jaïre and the coast. The islands, like the coast, are hard white limestone which has weathered into jagged shapes. There are numerous anchorages around the islands depending on the wind and the sea. Anchoring and fishing is prohibited in a triangular area E of Ile Calseraigne and Ile Riou.

Ile Jaron

A small island off the NW end of Ile Jaïre, from which it is separated by a small gap. In calm weather local boats anchor off the N and NE side.

Ile Jaïre

The large island just E of Ile Jaron. It lies in a NW-SE direction and is connected by shoal water to the coast at the NW end.

Plateau des Chèvres

A yacht should keep approximately 200–300 metres off the coast of Ile Jaïre where there are least depths of 7–8 metres. Although it is a little frightening to watch the bottom gliding by under you when crossing the plateau, there are no problems using the passage and it is a useful short cut even in brisk winds. A current runs in the channel between Ile Jaïre and the coast, according to the wind direction, and can reach 2 knots or so at times.

In calm weather local yachts anchor off along the N and NE side of Ile Jaïre.

Ile Calseraigne

The island lying SE of Ile Jaïre. Between it and Ile Jaïre there is an underwater rock, Ecueil de Miet, with 2·5 metres least depth over it. Between the SE tip of the island and Ile Riou to the S, there is an isolated above-water rock, Ecueil du Milieu, marked by a beacon with 2 vertical balls as topmark.

On the NE side of Ile Calseraigne there is a cove, Calanque de Pouars, sheltered from the W–S.

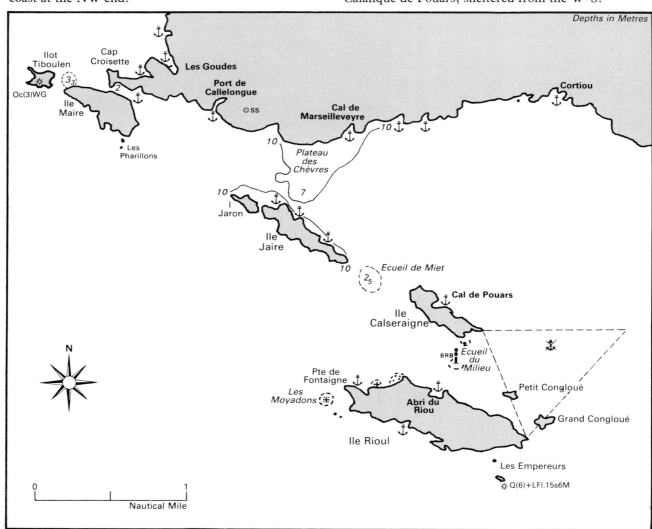

ILE MAIRE TO ILE RIOU

Ile Riou

The southernmost and largest of this group of islands. Off the NE end are two islets, Grand and Petit Congloué. Off the SE end of Ile Riou are two small islets, Les Empereurs. There is a conical buoy, YB with a ▼ topmark, Q(6)+LFl.15s light, off the outermost rock. Off the W end of Ile Riou there is a rock just awash, Les Moyadons, and a group of above-water rocks, I. Moyade.

On the N side of the island there is the only good anchorage, Abri de Riou, sheltered from southerlies only. There are several other anchorages on the NW side which can be explored in calm weather.

Les Calanques

The stretch of coast between Cap Croisette and Cassis, where the steep limestone ranges of the Marseilleveyre and the Puget meet the sea, is known as Les Calanques. Although *calanque* is a general term for the steep-sided fjord-like inlets that have been carved out by streams and winter torrents, and although there are *calanques* elsewhere, notably around La Côte Bleue and in Corsica, the term is used specifically for this coast because some of the most spectacular *calanques* are to be found here. In places the *calanques* are hemmed in by cliffs up to a 100 metres (330 feet) and more high. The limestone is often weathered into pinnacles and fantastic shapes peppered over with pine growing out at what seem impossible angles for trees to survive.

Calanque de Marseilleveyre A *calanque* at the eastern end of Plateau des Chèvres. Care needs to be taken of the shallow water extending off the eastern entrance point. Only shallow-draught craft can use it as the bottom comes up quickly some distance out. A restaurant opens in the summer.

Between Marseilleveyre and Sormiou, some 2½ miles to the E, there are several small coves and bights that can be used in calm weather.

Calanque de Sormiou A steep-sided and deep *calanque* under Bec Sormiou, a craggy steep headland. Once around Bec Sormiou the buildings at the head of the *calanque* will be seen. There is good shelter in here from the N and W, but it is open to the S and E. Anchor where convenient in 10–20 metres. With the *mistral* there are severe gusts down into the *calanque* so ensure the anchor is well in. The bottom is sand and weed, patchy holding in places.

The cove on the N side at the head of Sormiou is cluttered with laid moorings and local boats. Ashore there are several restaurants and bars.

Calanque de Morgiou A steep-sided *calanque* under Cap Morgiou. La Grande Chandelle is a conspicuous fort-like peak (464m/1520ft) immediately E of Morgiou. Cap Morgiou is a low flat headland that is difficult to identify from the distance. Once around Cap Morgiou a few buildings will be seen against the barren land at the head of the *calanque*.

Two breakwaters shelter the head of the *calanque*, but most of the space is taken up by fishing boats and local craft. Yachts usually anchor outside the breakwaters in 5–15 metres on sand and weed. The holding is patchy and with the *mistral* there are strong gusts down into the *calanque*, so ensure your anchor is well in. If there is room you can anchor off one of the breakwaters and take a long line to it from

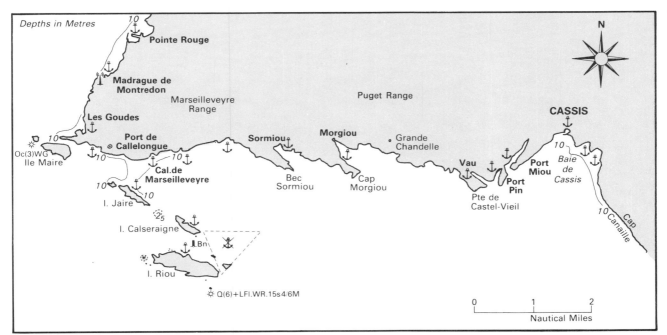

LES CALANQUES PORT DE LA POINTE ROUGE TO CASSIS

Calanque de Sormiou.

Calanque de Morgiou.

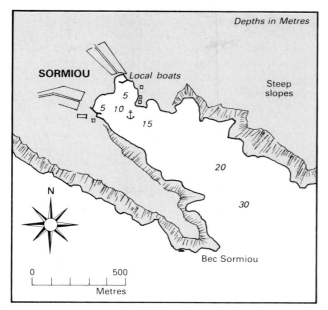

CALANQUE DE SORMIOU 43°12'·5N 5°25'·5E

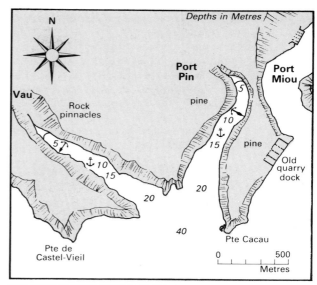

CALANQUE D'EN VAU AND PORT PIN 43°12'N 5°30'·5E

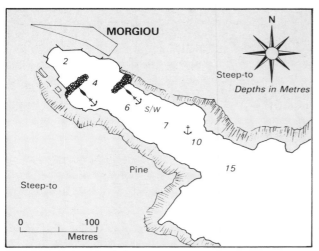

CALANQUE DE MORGIOU 43°12'·5N 5°27'E

Calanque d'en Vau. The entrance looking NW.

the stern. The *calanque* is only open to the S although in light SW-S winds it is tenable.

Ashore restaurants open in the summer. The surroundings are most attractive with pine scattered over the precipitous white limestone slopes. Immediately E of Morgiou there are several tiny idyllic coves that can be used with care in calm weather.

Calanque d'En Vau and Port Pin Two deep narrow *calanques* immediately E of Pte de Castel-Vieil. A staircase of rocky spikes will be seen on the coast near the point, but otherwise the entrance is difficult to make out. In the entrance you can choose to anchor in either Calanque d'En Vau or Port Pin depending on the wind and sea and on where there is room as the *calanques* are popular anchorages in the summer.

In Calanque d'En Vau anchor where possible and take a long line ashore to the S side. In Port Pin anchor as far in as possible and take a long line ashore

137

to the E side. There is not room to swing to an anchor. The two *calanques* are only open to the S and are generally tenable in light southerlies.

The surroundings are spectacular. In Calanque d'En Vau there are tall rocky spikes and columns lodged around the steep sides like some giant's ruined castle. In Port Pin, as the name suggests, the steep sides are covered in pine. The only thing disturbing the surroundings is the constant coming and going of the tripper boats from Cassis.

PORT MIOU

A long *calanque* immediately E of Port Pin affording all-round shelter in wonderful surroundings.

Approach

From the E the white scar of the old quarry workings around Port Miou shows up well, but the entrance will not be seen until close-to from both the E and W. The constant coming and going of tripper boats in the summer provides a clue to the whereabouts of the entrance – they appear to vanish from sight into the cliffs or appear out of nowhere.

Mooring

The inner half of the *calanque* has a catwalk around either side and is administered by two clubs, the Yachting Club des Calanques on the NW side and the Club Nautique de Port Miou on the SE side. There may be a berth free in here, but most yachts choose to anchor in the outer half of the *calanque*.

In the outer part drop your anchor well out and take a long line ashore to the eastern side where there are numerous mooring rings let into the rock. The holding is not the best, on thick weed, so ensure your anchor is well in or row out a second one if in doubt. Shelter here is all-round although easterlies cause a light surge, slightly uncomfortable rather than dangerous. The wash from the tripper boats doing a circuit around the *calanques* causes more discomfort than any swell outside.

Facilities

There is water and a small slip in the inner part of the *calanque*. On the slopes above the SE side there is a bar and further along a restaurant.

General

Although it is crowded in the summer, you can always find somewhere to squeeze in at Port Miou, and it remains one of my favourite anchorages along the coast. The tripper boats are disturbing at first, but you get used to them and they don't start running until mid-morning and stop early in the evening. The water in Port Miou is cooled by a freshwater spring flowing into it and is deliciously cool even on the hottest days. Cassis and all its facilities is about 25 minutes hot and sweaty walk away, though the municipal motorised 'train' can be stopped on the road above or you can catch it back from Cassis. If returning at night be sure to take a torch with you as there is a very real chance of falling over the edge of the cliffs around the *calanque*, especially if you have been sampling a glass or two of the excellent Cassis white.

The quarry at Port Miou is not worked anymore, at least not in the summer. Formerly it provided a hard white stone that was exported all over the Mediterranean as far afield as Egypt where it was used in the construction of the Suez Canal. Many of the buildings in Marseille were built from the convenient supply of white stone at Port Miou and some idea of the scale of activity here can be gauged from the extensive chutes and quays for filling barges. The chutes are now used by daredevil teenagers to high dive some 20 or 30 metres into the water.

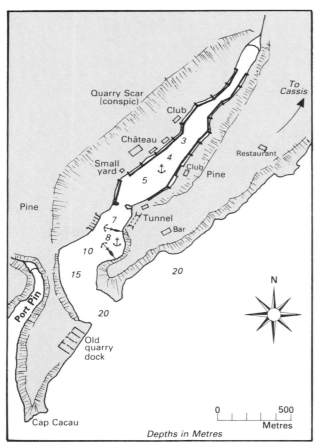

PORT MIOU 43°12'·4N 5°31'·E

Pte de Castel-Vieil on the SW side of the entrance to Calanque d'en Vau. From the distance it looks like a man-made castle – hence its name.

CASSIS

Approach

Conspicuous From the W and E, Bec de l'Aigle is unmistakable. The high red cliffs of Cap Canaille to the E of Cassis, at 399 metres (1310 feet), are among the highest cliffs in France and stand out well. Once into Baie de Cassis, the cluster of buildings of the town in the NW corner of the bay will be seen and closer in the harbour breakwater and the solid light tower at the entrance are easily identified.

By night The harbour entrance is lit, Oc(2)G.6s6M and Fl.R.4s6M.

Dangers In strong southerlies there is a confused swell at the entrance making entry difficult, and in southerly gales entry could be dangerous.

Note The outer and inner entrances are narrow and with tripper boats charging in and out considerable care is needed.

Mooring

Details 450 berths. Maximum LOA 14–15 metres.

Berth at the *quai d'accueil*, also the fuel quay, just inside the entrance, and report to the club office for a berth. The harbour is very crowded in the summer and berths are not always available. There are laid moorings tailed to the quay.

Shelter Good all-round shelter.

Authorities Customs. Port captain and club staff. A charge is made.

Facilities

Services Water and electricity at or near every berth. A small shower and toilet block.

Fuel On the quay near the entrance.

Repairs A 6-ton crane and a 30-ton slipway, but there is limited hard standing. Most mechanical repairs. Chandlers.

Provisions Good shopping for all provisions. Ice available.

Eating out Numerous restaurants of all types on the waterfront and in the town.

Other Post office. Banks. Hire cars. Buses to Marseille.

General

The small town is a gem with buff and rose coloured houses crammed onto the waterfront overlooking the harbour and a restored 14th-century castle on a rocky bluff overlooking the town. In the summer it is un-

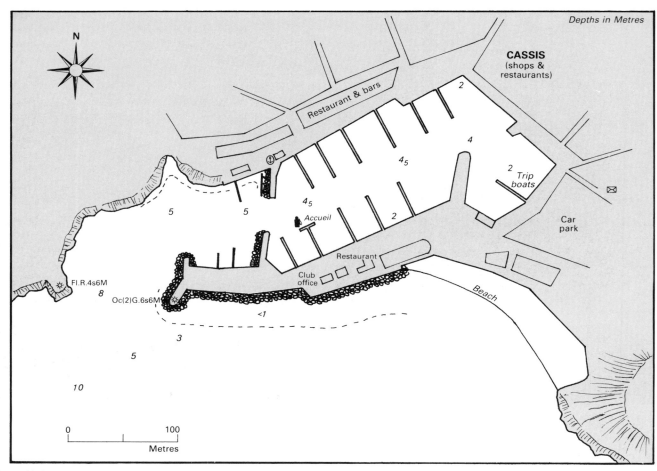

CASSIS 43°13′N 5°32′E

derstandably popular and its streets are thronged with tourists. Thankfully some of the streets are pedestrian zones. Buskers move from restaurant to bar to restaurant, stalls selling paintings or sculpture or just knick-knacks are set up by the harbour, and everyone seems set on enjoying themselves. The town vibrates with the babble of conversations mingled with music from the buskers. By day the tiny town beach has every square inch occupied by oiled bodies and the stratified rocky coast of Presqu'île between Cassis and Port Miou is dotted with the colourful towels and bare bodies of the overflow from the beach.

Cassis has long enjoyed a tourism of sorts. At the turn of the century a number of artists, among them names like Derain, Vlaminck, Matisse and Dufy, came here for the summer. Virginia Woolf, the novelist whose own unhappiness casts such dark shadows over her work, spent some of the happiest moments of her travels in Cassis: 'Even I myself, stirring occasionally in the pool of content, could only say But this is all I want; could not think of anything better; and had only my half superstitious feeling at the Gods who must when they have created happiness, grudge it.' (From *A Writer's Diary* describing her stay in Cassis.)

For a while Cassis had a reputation for being the place where the drugs smuggled by the Marseillaise Mafia came ashore and it is said that many of the large villas around the coast are owned by the 'Mr Bigs' of the business. I suspect now it is only the punters off the tripper boats who come ashore at Cassis.

Baie de Cassis

A yacht can anchor off in the double-headed NE corner of Baie de Cassis. With southerlies, SW-SE, and with the *mistral*, a swell rolls in here.

La Cassidaigne

A reef lying just under 3 miles WSW of Bec de l'Aigle. It has a lighthouse on it, BRB, some 25 metres (82 feet) high, that is conspicuous from some distance off; Fl(2)6s8M light.

Cassis. One of the most agreeable harbours along this coast.

Cassis. The harbour c. 1900.

Bec de l'Aigle

The conspicuous eroded cape that is easily recognised from the distance. It is 155 metres (492 feet) high, but it is its distinctive shape not unlike the head and beak of an eagle more than its overall height, that makes it readily identifiable from afar.

CALANQUE DE FIGUEROLLES

A spectacular anchorage half a mile NW of the conspicuous Bec de l'Aigle. A signal station is perched on the edge of the cliffs NW of the *calanque* is conspicuous. The anchorage is only open to the S and is untenable even in moderate southerlies when a swell rolls in. Anchor in 5–12 metres where convenient. The small islet, Isle du Lion, on the E side of the *calanque* has a mooring ring on its N end that a yacht can take a long line to. Ashore there is a hotel, restaurant and bar. La Ciotat is about 20 minutes walk away.

The much eroded and pitted rocks around the *calanque* are spectacular. The knobbly statue-like rock on the W side is known as the 'Capucin Friar'.

ILE VERTE

An island lying just over a quarter of a mile E of Cap de l'Aigle. The channel between the island and the cape is a useful and spectacular short cut under the beak of the eagle. A green beacon, with a ▲ topmark, in the passage marks an underwater rock known as Canonnier du Sud. To the N of it is an unmarked underwater rock with 4 metres least depth over it known as Canonnier du Nord. In the fairway of the channel to the W of the beacon there are considerable depths and no further dangers.

On the N side of Ile Verte there is a small cove, Calanque St-Pierre, open only to the N–E. It is popular with day-trippers from La Ciotat.

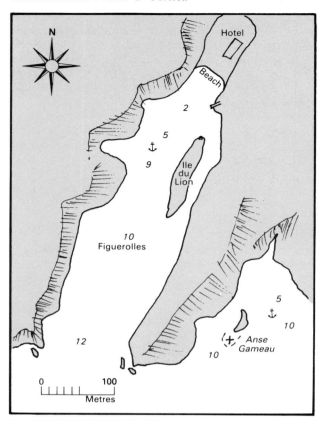

CALANQUE DE FIGUEROLLES 43°10'N 5°35'·8E

LA CIOTAT

Approach

Conspicuous Bec de l'Aigle is unmistakable from the W and E. Once into Baie de La Ciotat the huge cranes and gantries in the shipyard S of the yacht harbour are conspicuous. Closer in the harbour breakwaters and the masts of the yachts inside will be seen.

By night Use the lights at the commercial harbour, Oc(2)R.6s13M and Fl.R.4s9M; the Vieux Port, Iso.G.4s12M and Iso.4s3M; and the yacht harbour, S end Oc(2)G.6s5M and N end Fl(2)R.6s9M.

Mooring

Details 600 berths with 20 berths for visitors. Maximum LOA 15 metres.

Berth Head for the Bassin Bérouard, the southern of the two yacht basins, and berth where directed or in a vacant spot on the outermost pontoon and report to the *capitainerie*. There are laid moorings tailed to the quay or to buoys.

APPROACHES TO LA CIOTAT

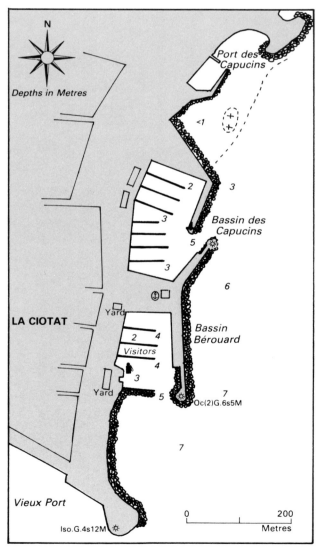

LA CIOTAT YACHT HARBOURS 43°10'·7N 5°36'·8E

Shelter Good all-round shelter.

Authorities Customs. Port captain and marina staff. A charge is made.

Note The Vieux Port is reserved for fishing boats.

Facilities

Services Water and electricity at or near every berth. A shower and toilet block.

Fuel On the quay in Bassin Bérouard.

Repairs A 10-ton crane and a 1½-ton fork-lift affair used to pull out and put in small powerboats stored in 'racks' on the quay. Most mechanical and engineering repairs. Chandlers.

Provisions Good shopping for provisions in the town. Ice available.

Eating out Numerous restaurants around the waterfront and in the town.

Other Post office. Banks. Buses to Marseille and Toulon.

General

At first sight you could be forgiven for wondering why anyone would come here with the giant dockyards dominating the waterfront. You soon get used to them and in the old town the dockyards could be a hundred miles away apart from the odd sighting of a crane gantry through the houses. The old town, built in tiers on the slopes above the bay, with streets running off at all angles, is a thoroughly likable place.

It has an ancient pedigree. The Phocaean Greeks from Marseille founded a colony, Citharista, here, which was in turn settled by the Romans. There has been a dockyard and shipbuilding going on here since the 16th century and today the yard builds supertankers. Its docks can accommodate ships up to 300,000 tons and since the largest of the dry-docks has 7–8 metre depths, I assume this sort of leviathan draws just less than this when unladen.

PORT DE ST-JEAN

A small boat harbour approximately 1 mile NE of La Ciotat. It has mostly 1 metre depths and is usually full in the summer with local craft kept here.

PORT LIOUQUET

It is proposed to build an 800-berth marina approximately 1km E of St-Jean. Work has yet to begin.

Ile Verte and Bec de l'Aigle looking SW.

IV. Côte d'Azur

i. West – Les Lecques to Cavalaire-sur-Mer

Nobody reads the obscure 19th-century poet Stephen Liégard today, but a phrase he coined in one of his poems somehow stuck after the poet and his poems faded into obscurity. The Côte d'Azur, the 'azure coast' neatly summed up the interplay of light between the sky and the sea that attracted painters and writers and those just generally tired of grey northern skies to villages and resorts along this coast. It is not surprising that modern travel-brochure writers have picked up the phrase and attempted to describe whichever resort they are selling as being on the Côte d'Azur with the result that the boundaries of the coast have been extended, at least in the glossy literature of tour operators, to include anything between the Rhône delta and the Italian border.

In reality there is no such place as the Côte d'Azur. The coast described in this chapter comes under the French *départements* of Var and Alpes-Maritimes.

The Michelin *Green Guide* for this coast is called the *French Riviera* with *Côte d'Azur* as a subtitle. Without being pedantic, I have taken the Côte d'Azur as starting at Les Lecques and extending as far as the River Var just west of Nice. To me the coastal region described as Provence in Chapter III has a different feel and character to the resort coast described here, though I'm not sure whether this is just wishful thinking as I divide up the chapters into convenient chunks of information. Certainly when most people think of the Côte d'Azur, it includes Hyères, St-Tropez, Cannes, Antibes and other well known resorts. It's a little more difficult to fit somewhere like Toulon into the popular picture of the Côte d'Azur, though the city's tourist office does its best with phrases like 'the most beautiful *rade* in the Côte d'Azur'.

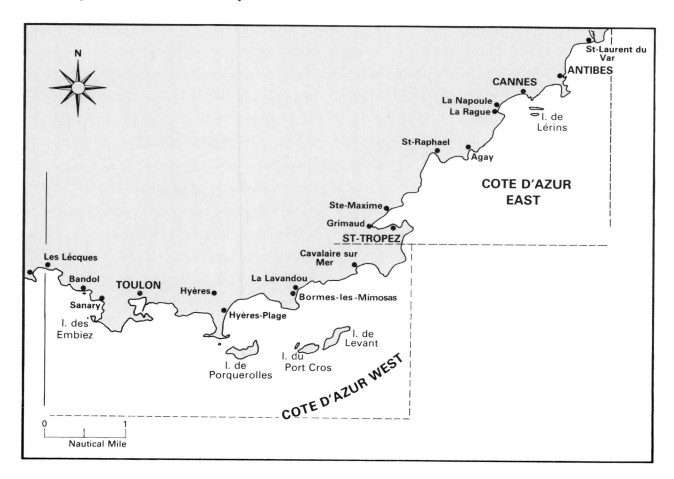

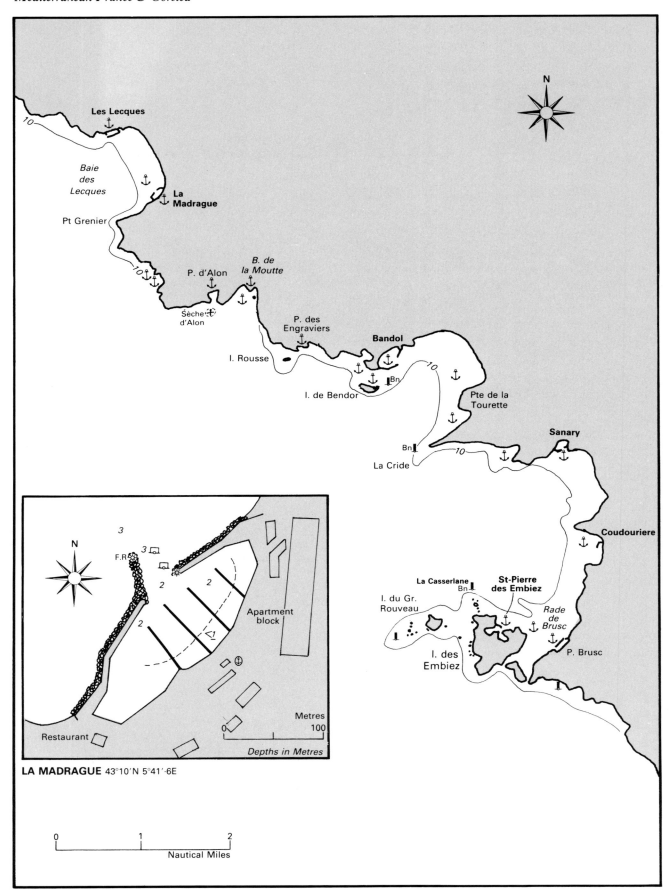

Les Lecques

N

*Baie
des
Lecques*

Pt Grenier

La
Madrague

*B. de
la Moutte*

P. d'Alon

Sèche
d'Alon

P. des
Engraviers

Bandol

I. Rousse

Bn

I. de Bendor

Pte de la
Tourette

10

Bn

La Cride

10

Sanary

Coudouriere

3

F.R

3

2

2

2

2

1

Apartment
block

Metres
0   100

Restaurant

Depths in Metres

LA MADRAGUE 43°10′N 5°41′·6E

La Casserlane

Bn

**St-Pierre
des Embiez**

I. du Gr.
Rouveau

*Rade
de
Brusc*

I. des
Embiez

P. Brusc

0   1   2
Nautical Miles

LES LECQUES TO ILE DES EMBIEZ

This chapter is divided up into two parts:

i. Côte d'Azur West covers the coast from Les Lecques to Cavalaire-sur-Mer and the southern approach to Golfe de St-Tropez.

ii. Côte d'Azur East covers the coast from St-Tropez to St-Laurent du Var on the banks of the Rivière Var just west of Nice.

Weather

The prevailing wind in the summer is the sea breeze blowing onto the coast from the SE–E. It normally gets up before midday and typically blows force 3–4 before dying down in the evening. However this prevailing wind is often interrupted by other winds. Moderate NW winds blow off and along the coast. These are not full-blown *mistrals*, usually the *ponant*, and generally die down in the evening.

Gale force winds usually come from the NW–W (the *mistral*), the NE or the S. The *mistral* produces the strongest winds although southerly gales send heavy seas onto the coast and can be just as bothersome in their effects even though the wind force is less than that of a strong *mistral*. From Cannes to the E the *mistral* is much reduced in force compared to the area around Toulon.

LES LECQUES (St-Cyr les Lecques)

Approach

The marina lies in the NE corner of Baie de La Ciotat.

Conspicuous Bec de l'Aigle is conspicuous from the W and E. Once into Baie de La Ciotat the cluster of buildings on the coast to the E of the marina will be seen, but until the harbour breakwater and the masts of the yachts inside are seen there is little else to locate the marina.

By night The harbour entrance is lit, Iso.G.4s9M and Q.R.7M. The shallow northern harbour is also lit, Fl(2)R.6s7M.

Dangers With strong southerlies there can be a dangerous breaking sea at the entrance.

Note In Baie de La Ciotat off Les Lecques there is a triangular area marked by three conical yellow buoys where anchoring and fishing is prohibited.

Mooring

Details 430 berths. Maximum LOA 15 metres.

Berth where directed or in a vacant spot and report to the *capitainerie* for a berth. There are laid moorings tailed to the quay or to buoys.

Shelter Good shelter although strong southerlies can cause a surge.

Authorities Port captain and marina staff. A charge is made.

Facilities

Services Water and electricity at every berth. A shower and toilet block.

Fuel On the quay at the entrance.

Repairs A 10-ton crane. Most mechanical and engineering repairs. Chandlers. For other repairs go to La Ciotat.

Provisions Limited shopping in the marina. Ice can be ordered.

Eating out Several restaurants and bars in the marina.

General

The marina is set under gentle wooded slopes, a sharp contrast to the rugged limestone to the west. It is a quiet place, popular with locals who drive here for an evening promenade and to watch the local yachts.

Apollodorus, the Greek historian relates how a Phocaean ship, en route to what is now Marseille, foundered off Les Lecques. The crew who managed to get ashore established a trading post here and called it Tauroëis from the bull's head that was carved as a figurehead on the ship. In Roman times the settlement was known as Tauroentum. Little remains of the settlement as apparently, Atlantis-like, it disappeared under the sea as the coastline sank over the years. Interestingly a number of bull figurines have been found in the area. Towards La Madrague there is the Tauroentum Museum, built on the foundations of a Roman villa, that houses Greek and Roman artifacts found locally.

Ancien Port Adjacent to the marina at Les Lecques is the old fishing harbour which is now used mostly by pleasure craft. There are 2·5 metre depths at the entrance, but only 0·5–1·5 metre depths inside. The depths inside vary as the harbour silts in the winter with southerly gales and is periodically dredged. Shallow-draught craft drawing 1 metre or less could use it with caution.

LA MADRAGUE

A small and mostly shallow harbour tucked into the E side of Baie des Lecques. There are 3 metre depths in the entrance, but only 1–2 metre depths inside. A small yacht should feel its way carefully into the harbour and berth on the S breakwater where there are mostly 2 metre depths at the end. Care is needed as the bottom is uneven. There is reasonable shelter inside except from the *mistral* which blows directly into the harbour. Ashore there are restaurants and bars.

Anchorage In calm weather or moderate easterlies a yacht can anchor off to the N of La Madrague harbour in 3–5 metres. The bottom is sand and weed, good holding once through the weed. A swell rolls around the corner into the bay with moderate SE winds, more uncomfortable than dangerous. The anchorage is open to westerlies.

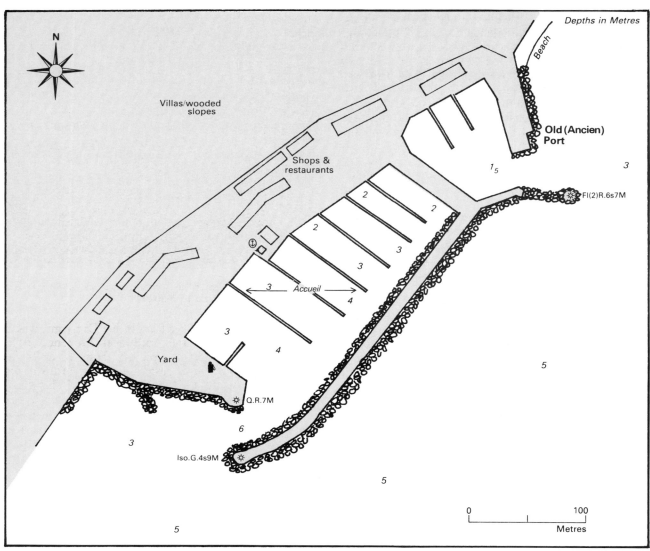

ST-CYR LES LECQUES 43°10′·8N 5°41′E

La Madrague to Bandol

From La Madrague the coast is rocky and wooded with a number of coves and bays that can be used depending on the wind and sea.

Pte des Trois Fours A jagged rocky headland just SE of Pte Fauconnière. In settled weather a yacht can anchor to the N or S of the point taking care of rocks off the coast. The anchorages are open S and usually have an uncomfortable swell rolling in even if the sea appears flat calm outside.

Port d'Alon A cove just over half a mile E of the bluff Pte du Défens which has a few villas built on it. Care must be taken of Sèche d'Alons, a reef with 0·6 metre over it lying directly in the entrance to Port d'Alon. It is difficult to see even in calm weather though any swell tends to break on it. Care should be taken in the approach until the reef has been positively identified.

Port d'Alon affords good shelter from northerlies, but is open to the S, and with the prevailing SE sea breeze is very uncomfortable and not really tenable. Anchor in 5–12 metres in the cove which is crowded with local boats in settled weather. The surroundings are attractive with pine around the rocky coast. A restaurant and bar opens in the summer.

Baie de la Moutte A bay immediately E of Port d'Alon. In the approach from the W care needs to be taken of Sèche d'Alon, but otherwise the approach is free from dangers. Anchor in one of the two coves at the head, the E cove off the small beach being most popular. The bay affords good shelter from northerlies, but like Port d'Alon, is open to southerlies.

Ile Rousse A small islet off the coast, easily identified from the W and E. As its name suggests, it is composed of reddish coloured rock. The passage between

Ile Rousse and the coast is mostly shallow and the prudent course is to go outside the islet. The passage close to the mainland coast, approximately 80 to a 100 metres off, is reported to have 2·5 metres least depth, but I would advise that it be used with caution, in calm weather only.

In calm weather the local boats anchor in the shoal water between Ile Rousse and the coast and from the number of boats and fishing lines dangling over the side, the fishing in the vicinity is presumably good. Just N of Ile Rousse is Pte des Engraviers and just under the point is a small cove affording some shelter from northerlies, but open to the S.

Port d'Athéna A small private harbour, part of a holiday apartment complex ashore. The unimaginative rectangular apartment block is conspicuous from the S and E, but will not be seen from the W until close to it.

Creux de Bandol A cove immediately W of Bandol harbour. In the summer much of the cove is pegged out with buoys marking the bathing area and there is little room for a yacht to anchor. In calm weather a yacht can anchor off outside the entrance in the bight partially sheltered by Ile de Bendor.

Ile de Bendor

A small island off Bandol with shoal water in the passage between it and the coast. The island is privately owned by M. Paul Ricard, the same Ricard whose name appears on *pastis* bottles all over France. He has developed the island into a sort of French Provençal village-cum-conference-centre-cum-tourist attraction. It is all done tastefully, and naturally enough is popular in the summer when tripper boats run frequently across to the island.

One of the exhibitions on the island is the *Universal Wines and Spirits Exhibition* – a not totally unexpected interest of the man who has made millions from the French passion for his aniseed apéritif. Aniseed is the preferred taste with alcohol in the Mediterranean: the Turks call it *raki*, the Greeks *ouzo*, the Italians *sambucca*, and the French *pastis*. In the early 20th century, *absinthe*, the then preferred *anis* drink, was considered to have devastated the French and reduced them to a nation of alcoholics, the theory being that the *anis* was toxic as well as the alcohol, and in 1915 *absinthe* was banned. Not until 1932 was it possible to commercially produce *anis* flavoured alcohol again, and this is where M. Paul Ricard comes into the picture. At the time, he was happily painting pictures in Marseille, but his father considered this occupation to be beneath the son of a wine dealer and told him to get a real job. The 23-year-old Ricard blended Provençal herbs, *anis*, and alcohol to produce what is now the most popular apéritif in France.

He evidently has a great love of the countryside of his youth. Apart from Ile de Bendor, he owns a part of Ile des Embiez and sponsors oceanographic re-

Port d'Athéna (with the ugly apartment block) and Ile Rousse with Bec de l'Aigle in the background.

search there, and a large farm in the Camargue where he raises bulls for the traditional Provençal bullfights. One interesting spin-off from Ricard's increasing production of *pastis* was a new industry for the Camargue. In 1974 it was discovered that *pastis* tasted just as good when home-grown Camargue fennel was used instead of the costly Chinese star *anis* which had always been used until then. The Camargue farmers were persuaded to grow fennel for the *pastis* and the region now has a thriving new industry.

PORT DE BENDOR

The tiny harbour on the NE corner of the island is largely reserved for the use of the tripper boats running across from Bandol. There is some room for visitors, though the harbour is noisy and uncomfortable from the wash of the tripper boats constantly coming and going. If you wish to visit the island the best thing to do is leave your yacht in Bandol and catch a tripper boat across.

PASSAGE BETWEEN ILE DE BENDOR AND THE COAST

Small local yachts use the passage between the island and the coast, but I noted that most local boats of any size opted to go around the island. There are reported to be 1·8 metres least depth in mid-channel. I opted out of traversing it after having a look at the depths, which are irregular, and I advise visiting yachts to take the safe route around the outside of Ile de Bendor. Anchoring in the channel is prohibited because of submarine cables running across to Ile de Bendor from Bandol.

La Fourmigue beacon in the approaches to Bandol harbour.

BANDOL

Approach

Conspicuous From the W, Ile de Bendor is easily identified. From the S and E a large apartment complex on the slopes above Bandol, looking something like the radiator grill of a large American car, and a viaduct on the N side of Baie de Bandol, are conspicuous. Closer in *La Cride* and *La Fourmigue* beacons are easily identified and the harbour breakwater and entrance will be seen.

By night The harbour entrance is lit, Oc(4)WR.12s 13/10M and Fl.G.4s6M. The sectored entrance light shows the safe approach between *La Cride* and *La Fourmigue* in the white sector on 351°–003°. The entrance to Port de Bendor is also lit, Oc.R.4s7M and Fl(2)G.6s5M.

Dangers
• *La Cride* beacon, YBY with a ⵣ topmark, just off Pte de la Cride marks a rock and shoal water. There are least depths of 3·5 metres in the fairway between the point and the beacon.
• *La Fourmigue* beacon, BR with 2 vertical balls as topmark, just E of Ile de Bendor marks a rock and shoal water. It should be left to port in the approach to Bandol.
• With strong southerlies there is a confused swell at the harbour entrance making entry difficult.

Mooring

Details 1290 berths with 70 berths for visitors.

Berth on the N quay just inside the entrance and report to the *capitainerie* for a berth. There are laid moorings tailed to the quay or to buoys.

Shelter Good all-round shelter.

Authorities Customs. Port captain and marina staff. A charge is made.

Facilities

Services Water and electricity at all berths. A shower and toilet block.

Fuel On the N quay by the entrance.

Repairs A 30-ton travel-hoist and several slipways. Mechanical and engineering repairs. GRP and wood repairs. Electrical and electronic repairs. Sailmakers. Chandlers.

Provisions Good shopping for all provisions in the town. Ice available.

Eating out A wide choice of restaurants around the waterfront and in the town.

Other Post office. Banks. Hire cars. Trains and buses along the coast.

General

Bandol is a busy resort, more of a local tourist spot than an international resort. The harbour front is lined with palms behind which is the old town, an attractive amalgam of buildings from several centuries. Fortunately the newer apartment blocks on the slopes above do not intrude on the view from the harbour. In the hinterland around Bandol the slopes are much cultivated with the vine and some of the best known rosés and reds of the Côtes de Provence wines come from this area.

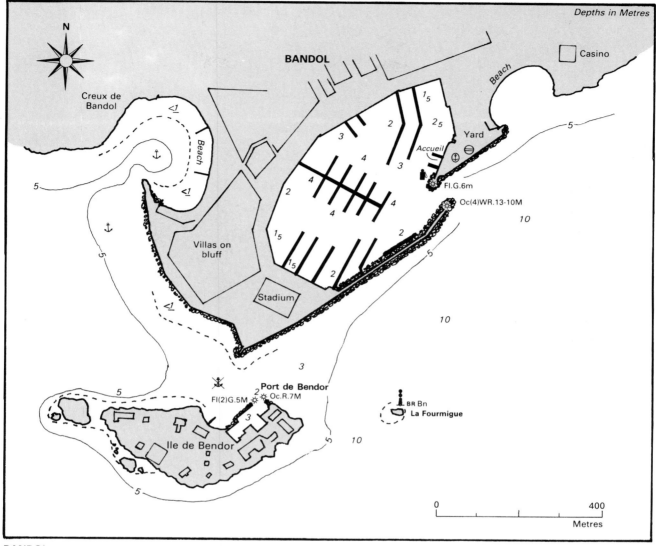

BANDOL 43°08′N 5°45′·5E

BAIE DE BANDOL

On the E side of the Baie de Bandol there are two pleasant anchorages on either side of Pte de la Tourette. On the N side anchor in 2–5 metres on sand and weed. On the S side anchor in 2–4 metres on sand, rock and weed. Holding in both anchorages is good. With southerlies, including SE winds, a swell rolls in. With the prevailing SE sea breeze the bays are tenable, though uncomfortable if staying for more than lunch and a swim.

SANARY-SUR-MER

Approach

Conspicuous Pte de Bau Rouge, which as its name suggests, has a red or maroon tip, is easily identified to the E of the tapering Pte de la Cride. An apartment block on the coast immediately W of the harbour and a belfry in the town are conspicuous. Closer in the harbour breakwater and the light tower at the entrance can be seen.

By night The entrance is lit, Fl.R.4s10M. The green buoy marking the entrance channel is lit, Fl.G, though it should not be relied upon.

Dangers
● The channel into the port is marked by a green conical buoy. The approach should be made on 045°–090° towards the light structure, then leaving the buoy to starboard.
● With strong southerlies there is a confused swell at the entrance and caution is advised.

Mooring

Details 520 berths with 100 berths for visitors.

Berth where directed or at a vacant spot and report to the *capitainerie* for a berth. There are laid moorings tailed to the quay.

Shelter Good all-round shelter.

Authorities Customs. Port captain and marina staff. A charge is made.

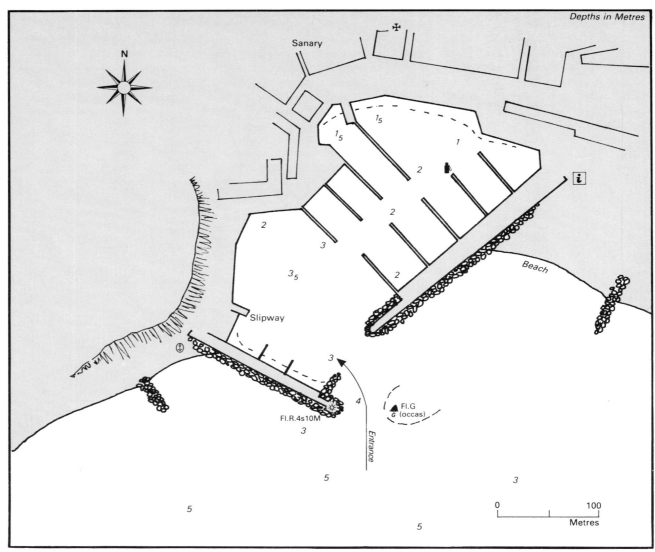

Depths in Metres

Sanary

N

Beach

Slipway

Fl.R.4s10M

Fl.G
(occas)

Entrance

0   100
Metres

SANARY 43°07′N 5°48′·2E

Sanary-sur-Mer.

Facilities

Services Water and electricity at or near most berths.
Fuel On the end of a pier in the inner harbour.

Repairs A 7-ton crane and slipways up to 100 tons. Mechanical and engineering repairs. GRP and wood repairs. Electrical and electronic repairs. Sailmakers. Chandlers.

Provisions Good shopping for all provisions in the town. Ice available.

Other Post office. Banks. Buses along the coast.

General

The resort, fringed by pink and white houses and palm trees, and the harbour which attracts a mixture of craft rather than serried rows of plastic look-alikes, is a delightful place. The discriminating Aldous Huxley came here to rest up and must have mourned the time when his failing sight denied him the pleasures of Sanary. Understandably Sanary attracts its fair share of visitors in the summer, yet it retains the cohesion, the feel of an old Côte d'Azur resort, despite the burgeoning development around

Above Getting to grips with the folk culture. *Below* Old fashioned carousel at Stes-Maries de la Mer, finely detailed and still earning a good living.

Above Palm-fringed waterfront of Banyuls-sur-Mer with the foothills of the Pyrénées behind. *Below* Typical Catalan-type fishing boat permanently on the hard at Canet-en-Roussillon.

Left Port de Santa Lucia. The Grand Canal. *Above* Port Miou. The anchorage in the outer part of the *calanque*. *Below* Port des Auffes. Picturesque, but not really a practical harbour for even small pleasure boats.

the coast from it. Perhaps its patron saint, St-Nazaire, from whom the town takes its name in the Provençal dialect, exercises some special power over it.

Rade du Brusc

Port de la Coudourière

A small harbour under Pte Nègre on the eastern side of Rade du Brusc. It is full of local boats and there is little if any room for visitors. There are 2·5 metre depths in the entrance and 1–2 metre depths inside. In easterlies a yacht can anchor off to the SW of the harbour in 2–5 metres on sand, mud and thick weed, good holding once through the weed.

Note The harbour entrance is lit, Fl(3)R.12s6M.

Port du Brusc A mostly shallow harbour in the SE corner of Rade du Brusc. The harbour is really more of a bight protected by a detached breakwater. There are 2 metre depths at the NE entrance, but mostly 0·5–1 metre depths inside. The central jetty inside is exclusively for the local ferries to and from Ile des Embiez which run constantly through the summer.

Other anchorages There are a number of anchorages around Rade du Brusc which afford good protection from easterlies and southerlies, including the prevailing SE sea breeze. Around the edge of the *rade*, particularly on the S in the channel between Ile des Embiez and the coast, the bottom comes up quickly from 2·5–2 metres to less than a metre. Judging by the numbers of local yachts going hard aground, this is not common knowledge. The best anchorage is NE–E of Pte du Canoubié on Ile des Embiez. The point is easily recognised by the white light tower on it. Anchor in 2·5–3·5 metres. The bottom is mud and thick weed, good holding once through the weed, though getting through the weed may take several attempts. In the daylight hours there are lots of small local boats buzzing around, but by dusk they have all gone home.

Ile des Embiez

A comparatively low-lying island on the W side of Cap Sicié. It is surrounded by islets, rocks, reefs and shoal water, and some care is needed in the approaches to the island. The most conspicuous objects in the approach from the W are the lighthouse on Ile du Grand Rouveau, the tower on Ile des Embiez, and *La Casserlane* beacon. From the SE the lighthouse on Ile du Grand Rouveau, the tower on Ile des Embiez, and a water tower close to the tower on Ile des Embiez are conspicuous. Closer in the stumpy beacon on Sèche des Magnons will be seen.

The beacon on Sèche des Magnons, YBY but in need of paint (topmark ✗ when repaired), marks the SW extremity of the rocks and reefs. The beacon on La Casserlane, BY with a ♦ topmark, marks the northern extremity of the rocks and reefs.

Ile du Grande Rouveau. Note the conspicuous lighthouse.

PASSAGE BETWEEN ILE DU GRAND ROUVEAU AND ILE DES EMBIEZ

In calm weather local yachts use a short-cut between Ile du Grand Rouveau and Ile des Embiez. There are least depths of 3·3–5 metres in the channel. It should only be attempted the first time with due care and a lookout forward, or follow a local boat through that you know draws as much or more than you – at a discreet distance.

From the S head on a course of 020° for *La Casserlane* beacon, then leave it to starboard. From the N head on a course of 200° from *La Casserlane* beacon, taking back-bearings on it to stay in the fairway. The channel is closer to the above-water rocks off Ile du Grand Rouveau than to La Cauvelle islet.

In calm weather or with moderate SE winds, yachts anchor under Ile du Petit Rouveau. Anchor in 4–10 metres on sand, rock and weed. Local yachts stay here overnight though care is needed should the wind change in the night.

ST-PIERRE DES EMBIEZ

Approach

The marina on the N side of Ile des Embiez is approached by a buoyed channel.

Conspicuous The lighthouse on Ile du Grand Rouveau and *La Casserlane* beacon are conspicuous. Closer in the buildings around the marina and the harbour breakwater and the masts of the yachts inside will be seen. The buoys marking the channel into the marina are very small and will not be seen until close to.

By night Use the light on Ile du Grand Rouveau, Oc(2)W.6s15M and the light on Pte du Canoubié Fl(4)W.15s8M. The entrance is lit, Fl.WG.4s.

Dangers The *mistral* blows straight into the entrance and in a strong *mistral* entry could be dangerous.

Note In the summer the ferries from Port du Brusc are constantly coming and going and a good lookout should be kept for them.

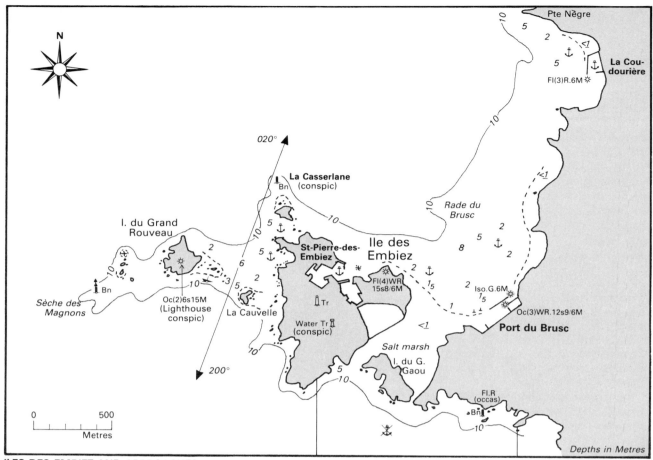

ILES DES EMBIEZ AND APPROACHES

Mooring

Details 600 berths with 20 berths for visitors. Maximum LOA 35 metres.

Berth Go onto the *quai d'accueil* just inside the entrance and report to the *capitainerie* for a berth. There are laid moorings tailed to the quay.

Shelter Good all-round shelter.

Authorities Port captain and marina staff. A charge is made.

Note Dogs and cats are not allowed on the island which is a nature reserve.

Facilities

Services Water and electricity at every berth. A shower and toilet block.

Fuel On the quay by the *capitainerie.*

Repairs A 15-ton crane and a 60-ton slipway. Most mechanical repairs. GRP and wood repairs. Electrical and electronic repairs. Chandlers.

Provisions Most provisions available in the marina in the summer. Ice available.

Eating out Several restaurants and bars around the marina.

Other Exchange office. Regular ferries across to Le Brusc and the mainland in the summer.

General

The island and the anchorage behind it must have been a much-used natural harbour from the Greek and Roman period, though little remains to tell us whether it was so. Port du Brusc is sometimes mentioned as the Roman port of Tauroentum though the location at Les Lecques seems more likely. There are the remains of an aqueduct near Six-Fours. The fort on Ile des Embiez was built in the Middle Ages to defend the approaches to Toulon.

Ile des Embiez owes much of its prosperity today to the munificence of M. Paul Ricard who has developed the island not just for the commercial gains to be had from the marina and adjoining apartment complex, but as a nature reserve and a centre for marine research. The old naval gun site on the north of the island houses the Ricard Oceanographic Foundation which is divided up between the museum and aquarium and research laboratories whose special field is fish farming and marine pollution. The shallow lagoon to the east of Port des Jeunes is an experimental basin for fish farming and the sea around Ile des Embiez is monitored for pollutants. The museum and aquarium are open to the public, but not the research laboratories.

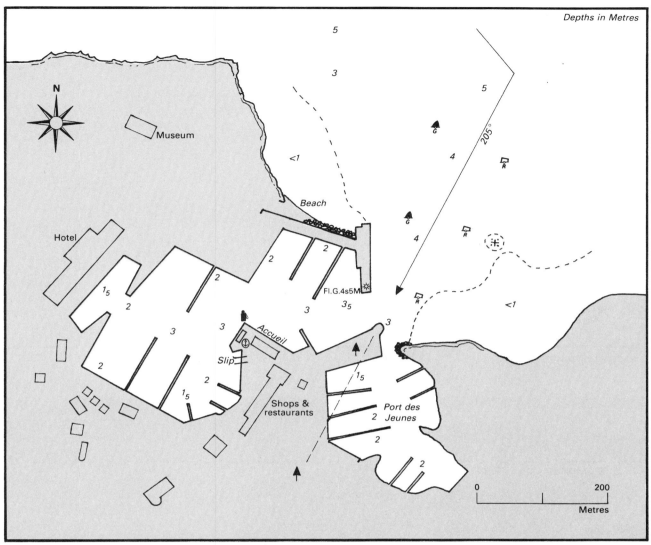

ST- PIERRE-DES-EMBIEZ (AND PORT DES JEUNES) 43°04′·8N 5°47′E

Cap Sicié

This high cape drops abruptly down to the sea from some 360 metres (1180 feet). There are mostly good depths right up to the bottom of the cliffs. There is a light structure on the cape proper, but it is not conspicuous. On the summit of the cape the most conspicuous objects are a transmitter pylon, the chapel of Notre Dame du Mai, and an old signal station. To the E of the cape two detached rocks, Les Deux-Frères, are easily identified.

Off the cape there is a reef with 4·5 metres least depth over it. While a yacht can follow the coast close-to in calm weather, like most capes there is a confused sea off it in strong winds. In anything over force 6 it pays to keep a good mile off as there are wicked cross seas set up from the reflected swell off the cape.

The chapel of Notre Dame du Mai, really more of a large church, is a place of pilgrimage. It is known as *Our Lady of the May Tree* and also as *Our Lady of the Good Protection*. The chapel contains many votive offerings and I should imagine the view from the top of the high cliffs is magnificent.

BAIE DE ST-ELME

A bay under the isthmus connecting Presqu'île de St-Mandrier to the coast. In calm weather or light northerlies a yacht can anchor in 3–8 metres where convenient. The small harbour on the E side is shallow with depths of less than a metre inside and is used by small local craft and fishing boats.

Rade de Toulon

The natural harbour and anchorage of Toulon has long been a naval base with its huge *rade* for a fleet anchorage and extensive dockyard facilities ashore. It is presently the second naval base of France and the principal naval base in the Mediterranean.

Rade de Toulon is made up of Grande Rade entered between Presqu'île de St-Mandrier and Pte de Carqueiranne on the E; and Petite Rade enclosed by a long breakwater on the W side of Grande Rade.

155

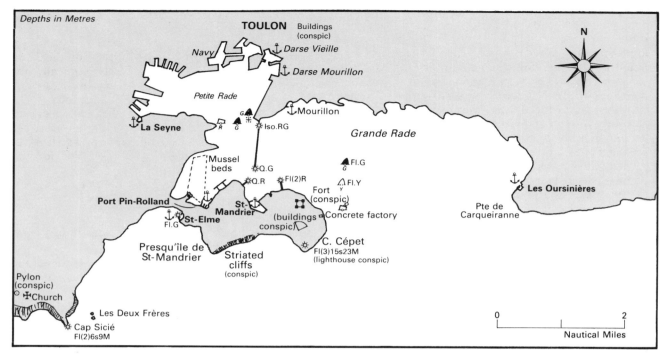

TOULON AND APPROACHES

Presqu'île de St-Mandrier. The lighthouse and communication
towers conspicuous on Cap Cépet.

Conspicuous From Cap Sicié and the S, the striated cliffs on the S side of Presqu'île de St-Mandrier stand out from some distance off. A number of multi-storeyed buildings on the E end of St-Mandrier, the lighthouse and a number of communication aerials on Cap Cépet, and a cement factory by the shore on the NE corner of St-Mandrier are conspicuous. From the E Les Fourmigues in the Golfe de Giens, the fort and signal station on the summit of St-Mandrier, and the concentration of buildings around Toulon are conspicuous.

Once into Grande Rade, the breakwater protecting Petite Rade is easily identified. A white building at the N end of the breakwater at Passage de Pipady and the large light towers on the S end of the breakwater and on the extremity of the breakwater running out from St-Mandrier are all conspicuous.

Night approach

Use the light on Cap Cépet, Fl(3)15s23M. The deepwater channel into Petite Rade is lit by two buoys, Fl.R.2·5s and Fl(2)G.6s with a yellow buoy marking the centre of the channel Fl(3)Y.12s. Grande Passe is lit, Fl(2)R.10s10M, Q.R.7M and Q.G.11M. Passe de Pipady is lit, Iso.RG.4s10M.

Note There are numerous unlit mooring buoys in Grande Rade. Most of these are clustered off the cement factory on the E end of Presqu'île de St-Mandrier with others to the N of the deep-water channel.

Entry into Petite Rade

Grande Passe at the S end of the breakwater is straightforward with good depths everywhere. Passe de Pipady has least depths of 4·5 metres and should be traversed due W or E. With strong SE winds a swell piles up at Passe de Pipady, and Grande Passe should be used.

Harbours around Grande and Petite Rade

St-Mandrier-sur-Mer On Presqu'île de St-Mandrier immediately S of Grande Passe. 600 berths with 20+ berths for visitors.

Port Pin-Rolland At the S end of Petite Rade. 400 berths.

Port de la Seyne On the western side of Petite Rade. 335 berths with 5 berths for visitors.

Toulon Darse Vieille and Darse du Mourillon At the N end of Petite Rade. 1300 berths. Numerous visitors' berths.

St-Louis du Mourillon On the NE of Passe de Pipady. Small and mostly private.

Les Oursinières A very small private harbour.

ST-MANDRIER-SUR-MER

Approach

Conspicuous The large white light tower on the S end of the breakwater protecting Petite Rade and the light tower on the end of the breakwater extending out from St-Mandrier are conspicuous. The numerous cranes and gantries in the naval dockyard on the E side of the harbour and the hulks of old naval ships moored nearby will be seen. The harbour breakwater and the masts of yachts inside identify the yacht harbour.

By night The harbour entrance is lit, Fl.G.4s5M.

Mooring

Details 600 berths with 20+ berths for visitors. Maximum LOA 14 metres.

Berth at the *quai d'accueil* just inside the entrance and report to the *capitainerie* for a berth. There are laid moorings tailed to the quay or to buoys.

Shelter Good shelter although a strong *mistral* kicks up a chop in the harbour.

Authorities Customs. Port captain and marina staff. A charge is made.

Anchorage In the season yachts anchor off to the N of the breakwater in 3–6 metres. The bottom is mud and weed. The anchorage is open to northerlies and is untenable in a strong *mistral*.

Facilities

Services Water and electricity at or near every berth. A shower and toilet block.

Fuel On the end of a pier in the middle of the harbour.

Repairs An 8-ton crane and a 15-ton slipway. Most mechanical and engineering repairs. Electrical and electronic repairs. Sailmakers. Chandlers.

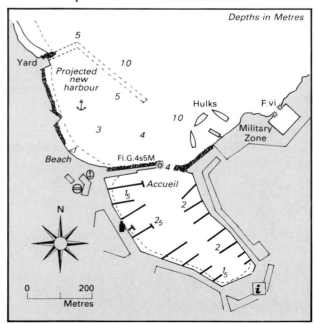

PORT ST-MANDRIER 43°05′N 5°56′·5E

Provisions Good shopping for provisions. Ice available.

Eating out Numerous restaurants and bars around the waterfront.

Other Post office. Bank. Ferries run to Toulon in the summer.

General

St-Mandrier-sur-Mer was originally a small fishing village that became a popular local resort in the 19th century. The houses around the waterfront give it a pleasant aspect and the naval dockyards on the eastern side don't intrude overly on the place.

PORT PIN-ROLLAND

Approach

Once through Grande Passe turn to the SW and follow the breakwater off the Lazaret Oil Depot until the masts of the yachts in the harbour are seen. The mussel beds to the NW of the port are easily seen. The harbour approaches are not lit and a night approach is not recommended.

Mooring

Details 400 berths.

Berth where directed. There are laid moorings tailed to the quay or to buoys.

Shelter Good shelter from all but strong northerlies. With a *mistral* the harbour is uncomfortable although the mussel beds stop the worst of the swell.

Authorities Port captain. A charge is made.

Facilities

Services Water and electricity at or near every berth. A shower and toilet block.

Repairs 80 and 20-ton travel-hoists. Covered storage ashore. Mechanical and engineering repairs. GRP and wood repairs. Electrical and electronic repairs. Sailmakers. Chandlers.

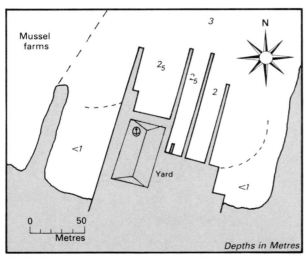

PORT PIN-ROLLAND 43°04'·8N 5°54'·5E

General

Port Pin-Rolland is not really a harbour to visit, more a harbour to base a yacht in or leave it for the winter with good facilities ashore for the care and repair of yachts.

PORT DE LA SEYNE

A small yacht basin on the far western side of Petite Rade. There is a lifting bridge across the entrance to the basin. Inside go on the *quai d'accueil* on the N side and report to the *capitainerie*. There are only a few places for visitors. Nearby there is a yard with a massive travel-hoist and slipways where very large yachts can be hauled.

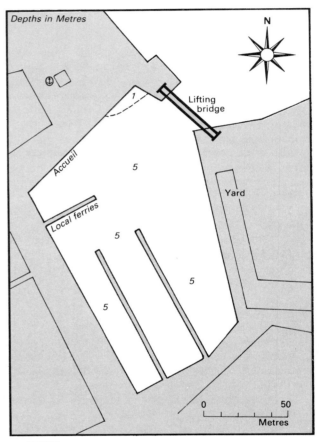

LA SEYNE 43°06'·1N 5°53'E

TOULON
Darse Vieille and Darse du Mourillon

Approach

Conspicuous Once into Petite Rade head for the cluster of tall buildings concentrated behind Darse Vieille. The red and green buoys marking the deep-water channel in Petite Rade are easily identified as is the green buoy off Fort de la Grosse Tour marking an underwater obstruction. Closer in the entrance to Darse du Mourillon and to Darse Vieille will be seen.

By night The buoys marking the deep-water channel in Petite Rade are lit, Fl(2)R.6s and Oc(2)G.6s as is the green buoy marking the obstruction, Fl.G.2s. The entrance to Darse du Mourillon is lit, Iso.G.4s 7M and Oc(2)R.6s6M. The entrance to Darse Vieille is lit, Q.G and Q.R.

Note
● The ferries running to St-Mandrier and other places operate from the Darse Vieille and charge in and out of the narrow entrance at speed, despite a speed restriction of 3 knots. Keep a good lookout for ferries coming and going.
● Sailing yachts do not automatically have right of way over powered vessels in Petite Rade.
● The naval basins to the W of Darse Vieille are restricted areas and entry is prohibited.

Toulon. The approach to Darse Vieille looking N.

Mooring

Details 1300 berths. Maximum LOA 60 metres.
Berth In the Darse Vieille berth on the *quai d'accueil* and report to the *capitainerie*. In Darse du Mourillon berth close to the *péniche* on the E side of the basin and report to the *capitainerie* for a berth. Most yachts tend to head for Darse Vieille where there are numerous visitors' berths available and you are closer to town. There are laid moorings tailed to the quay or to buoys in both basins.
Shelter Good all-round shelter in both basins. The wash from ferries coming and going in Darse Vieille is more bothersome than anything the wind can do.
Authorities Customs. Immigration. Port captain and marina staff. A charge is made.

Facilities

Services Water and electricity at or near every berth. A shower and toilet block.
Fuel On the quay just inside the entrance to Darse Vieille.
Repairs A 10-ton crane in Darse Vieille and a 27-ton travel-hoist in Darse du Mourillon. There is only limited hard standing in Darse Vieille. Larger yachts

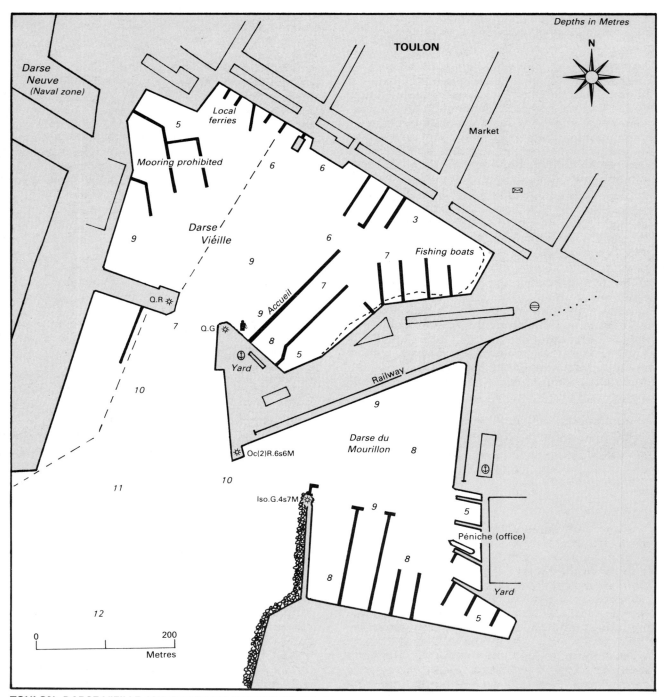

Depths in Metres

TOULON

N

Darse
Neuve
(Naval zone)

Local
ferries

Market

Mooring prohibited

5

6

6

3

Darse
Viéille

9

6

7

Fishing boats

9

9

7

Accueil

Q.R

8

5

Q.G

Yard

7

Railway

10

9

Oc(2)R.6s6M

Darse du
Mourillon

8

10

11

Iso.G.4s7M

9

Péniche (office)

5

8

8

Yard

12

5

0

200

Metres

TOULON: DARSE VIEILLE AND DARSE DU MOURILLON 43°07′N 5°55′·8E

should go to Port Pin-Rolland and very large yachts over 80 tons to La Seyne. All mechanical and engineering repairs. GRP and wood repairs. Electrical and electronic repairs. Sailmakers. Chandlers all around the waterfront of Darse Vieille.

Provisions Excellent shopping for all provisions. A daily street market close to the NE corner of Darse Vieille. Ice available.

Restaurants Numerous restaurants on the waterfront and in the town.

Other Post office. Banks. Hire cars. Buses and trains along the coast. Ferries to Corsica.

General

The approach from seawards is Toulon's principal asset. The Grande Rade is a wonderful place to sail into, but as you get closer to Petite Rade and Toulon itself, the sea has that rainbow translucency betraying diesel on it and the surroundings are tawdry; the final approach framed by gantries and cranes and the high apartment blocks of the inner suburbs of Toulon. Most of Toulon was flattened in 1944 by Allied bombers. What was left was blown up by the Germans before they left and consequently most of Toulon had to be rebuilt after the war.

Toulon. Darse Vieille.

If I give the impression I don't like Toulon very much, that is not so. The seedy atmosphere that all naval towns seem to have conceals a vitality and real devotion to the sea and things maritime that other prettier towns along the coast do not have. On the waterfront along Quai Stalingrad are numerous chandlers and specialist marine shops. Several of the big racing multihulls on the international circuit are based at Toulon along with a modest IOR fleet. When I was there a 15-metre steel yacht was being strengthened and fitted out for a research voyage to the Antarctic. And around Darse Vieille and Darse du Mourillon old wooden boats are being lovingly restored and plastic ones get their bottoms cleaned. If you need to do a refit Toulon is as good a place as any to head for.

Away from the waterfront things get smarter as you get into the city centre with fashionable boutiques and chic cafés. There is a naval museum, a museum of art and archaeology, and the cathedral, though none of it is essential to your education. Toulon is more of a place to wander around looking in shop windows, and for sitting in a waterfront café watching the boats churn in and out of Darse Vieille; '– a port, all sailors, cats and queer people – a blue sea, bright sun, but a cold little tiny wind –' the ailing D. H. Lawrence called it in 1929.

THE FRENCH NAVY

The all-round protected anchorage at Toulon has long been a naval harbour though little remains of the Greek and Roman presence. Its importance for the French began in 1589 when the Governor of Provence ordered the Darse Vieille to be built. To finance it a 25% tax on olive oil was imposed and the harbour was completed in 1610. Originally it had a chain slung across the entrance to prevent an enemy attack. The king did not have a royal fleet at this time and hired ships and mercenaries from seafaring lords and captains when he needed them. It was Richelieu and Louis XIV who saw the need for a royal navy and Toulon was the obvious place to base it. Richelieu established a military arsenal and in 1680 Darse Neuve, immediately west of Darse Vieille, was constructed to take the rapidly growing naval fleet. Darse Vieille now became the commercial port for the merchant fleet.

One of the bizarre tourist attractions for travellers of the time was to visit the galleys of the naval fleet. Galleys were manned by criminals condemned to service for their crimes and by political and religious prisoners. There were even volunteers! John Evelyn in his fascinating diary of his European travels between 1643 and 1647 left us this description of the galleys and their occupants.

161

'The Captaine of the Gally royal gave us most courteous entertainment in his Cabine, the Slaves in the interim playing both on loud and soft musique very rarely: Then he shew'd us how he commanded their motions with a nod, and his Wistle, making them row out; which was to me the newest spectacle I could imagine, beholding so many hundreds of miserby naked Persons, having their heads shaven cloose, and onely red high bonnets, a payre of Course canvas drawers, their whole backs and leggs starke naked, doubly chayned about their middle and leggs, in Cupples, and made fast to their seates: and all Commanded in a trise, by an Imperious and cruell sea-man...

...Their rising forwards, and falling back at their Oare, is a miserable spectacle, and the noyse of their Chaines with the roaring of the beaten Waters has something of strange and fearfull in it to one in-accostom'd. They are ruld, and chastiz'd with a bulls-pizle dry'd upon their backs, and soles of their feete upon the least dissorder, and without the least humanity ...' From *The Diary of John Evelyn* ed. by John Bowle.

It is not surprising that Toulon and other galley ports were looked upon as perilous and rough places. Numbers of innocent travellers were swept up by the recruitment gangs and forced to work in the galleys. The galleys were eventually superseded by sailing ships and in 1748 galley service was abolished to be replaced by prisons and transportation to colonies overseas.

It was at Toulon that the young Napoléon Bonaparte distinguished himself in 1793. Toulon sided with the Royalists and on the 27th of April the port was handed over by the Royalists to an Anglo-Spanish force to protect it. The Republicans besieged the city, concentrating on a fort on the summit between La Seyne and Tamaris known as 'Little Gibraltar', because of its supposedly impregnable position. Napoléon manned an artillery battery that after terrible losses forced the British to give up the fort on the 19th of December. The British withdrew from Toulon, taking part of the local population with them, leaving the other unfortunates to face the bloody retribution of the Republicans. The young Napoléon was instantly made brigadier-general for his part in subduing Toulon and was on the first rung of his military career.

The harbour was gradually expanded in the 19th century as the French naval fleet grew. In 1836 Darse du Mourillon was built and in 1862 Napoléon III had Missiessy built. In 1942 during the Second World War over 60 French naval vessels were scuttled in the harbour by the Vichy Admiral Laborde to stop them falling into German hands. Not until the 13th of September 1944 was what was left of the French fleet to sail into Toulon again, the scuttled ships still on the bottom.

Today Toulon is France's second naval base after Brest. Naval dockyards are scattered around the perimeter. The basins to the west of Darse Vieille are prohibited to all but naval vessels and the blue-grey hulls of the navy are much in evidence. Surprisingly there is not an obvious naval presence in the town itself. Galley slaves used to be allowed into the town, chained together in pairs, and were much in demand as musicians at weddings and festivals. Today's naval ratings seem almost invisible by comparison and only in a few of the darker American bars in the back alleys are they obvious.

ST-LOUIS DU MOURILLON

A small harbour immediately NE of Passe du Pipady. There are only 1·5 metre depths in the entrance and mostly 0·5–1 metre depths inside. There are no berths for visiting yachts.

Note There are ambitious plans to build a large marina and apartment complex here. The initial stage, expected to begin soon, is to construct a breakwater to protect a basin for 400 yachts.

LES OURSINIERES

A small harbour on the W side of Pte de Carqueiranne. Most of the berths are occupied by local boats and there is rarely room for visiting yachts. There are 2 metre depths in the entrance and 0·5–1·5 metre depths inside.

Anchorage In settled weather a yacht can anchor immediately N of Les Oursinières harbour in 4–10 metres. Although there is protection from the prevailing SE sea breeze, a swell rolls around the point into the anchorage. It is open to the W and N.

Note Off Pte Ste-Marguerite to the W of Les Oursinières there is an area where entry is prohibited. The area is not buoyed and local yachts don't seem worried about the prohibition – nonetheless it should be kept in mind.

Golfe de Giens

The gulf immediately E of Grande Rade bound by the flat isthmus of Hyères and Presqu'île de Giens. Much of the gulf is a restricted area around the eastern coast and anchoring is prohibited on the N side of Presqu'île de Giens. In the NW corner of the gulf is Port de Carqueiranne.

CARQUEIRANNE

Approach

Conspicuous Les Fourmigues, the group of rocks off the W side of Presqu'île de Giens are conspicuous. Closer in the buildings around Les Salettes and the harbour breakwater and the light structure on the end will be seen.

By night The harbour entrance is lit, Oc(4)WR.12s 10/7M. The white sector covers the safe approach between Les Fourmigues and La Ratonnière on 356°–005°. The entrance proper is lit, Fl.G and Fl.R.

Dangers With strong southerlies there is a confused swell at the entrance.

Note There are only 1-metre depths in much of the harbour.

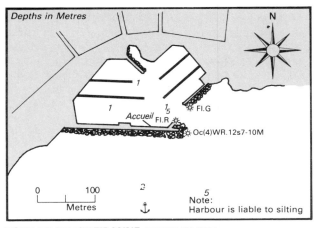

PORT DE CARQUEIRANNE 43°05′N 6°04′·7E

Mooring

Details 360 berths. Maximum LOA 9 metres.

Berth at the *quai d'accueil* just inside the entrance and report to the *capitainerie*. There are laid moorings tailed to the quay or to buoys.

Authorities Port captain. A charge is made.

Facilities

Services Water and electricity at or near every berth. A shower and toilet block.

Fuel On the quay near the *capitainerie*.

Repairs An 8-ton crane and a slipway. Most mechanical repairs. Chandlers.

Provisions Most provisions can be obtained in the village. Ice available.

Eating out Restaurants and bars nearby.

Other Post office. Bank. Buses to Hyères.

General

The resort is really an extension of the development surrounding Hyères and Mont des Oiseaux behind. It is a pleasant enough spot with a wooded foreshore and a sandy beach. There are plans to enlarge and dredge the harbour in the near future.

Presqu'île de Giens

The steep rocky end of the low isthmus dividing the Golfe de Giens and Rade d'Hyères. From the distance it looks like an island which it once was, the fifth member of the Iles d'Hyères. In 1811 after a ferocious southerly gale it became an island again for a brief time. The sandbank joining Presqu'île de Giens to the coast is itself divided into two by an *étang*, part of which is used for extracting salt. The eastern side of the sandbank is wider than the west and the resort and large marina of Hyères-Plage is sited on it.

Presqu'île de Giens has a number of small resorts and several tiny harbours around it. Much of the west side is a restricted military zone.

Presqu'île de Giens. Note the conspicuous dome on the western end.

Port du Niel

A small harbour tucked into the NW side of Baie du Niel just NNW of Ile du Grand Ribaud. There are 4–5 metre depths in the entrance, but the bottom comes up quickly to 1·5–2 metres inside. It is usually crowded in the summer and most places are occupied by local craft or are under dispute between local craft and visitors.

In settled weather a yacht can anchor off in Baie du Niel in 10–15 metres to the E of the harbour. The surroundings under the steep slopes are wonderful, but there is invariably a swell in the bay making it uncomfortable.

Ile du Grand Ribaud

A rocky island lying just off Presqu'île de Giens and connected to it by shoal water and above-water rocks. The lighthouse on the S point of Grand Gibaud, a white tower and dwelling, is conspicuous; Fl(4)15s15M light. A reef with least depths of 1·1 metres lies approximately 100 metres off the S end of Grand Ribaud. A yacht can pass between Grand Ribaud and Petit Ribaud on the N where there is a passage with mostly 8–10 metres in the fairway and 5·5 metre least depths. The passage is straightforward in all weather.

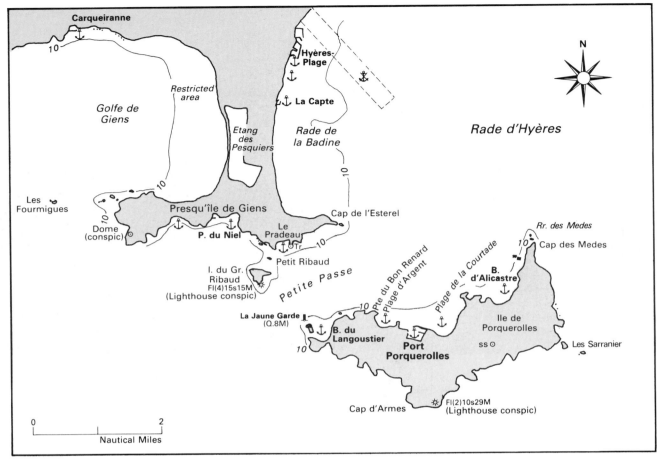

PRESQU'ILE DE GIENS AND ILE DE PORQUEROLLES

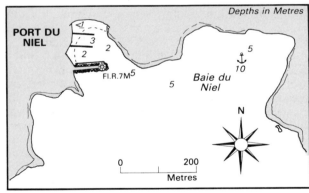

PORT DU NIEL 43°02'·2N 6°07'·7E

Port Auguier

A very small harbour on the W side of Pte de Terre Rouge. It has 1·5 metre depths in the entrance and 0·5–1·5 metre depths inside.

Le Pradeau

A small harbour on the W side of Pte de la Tour Fondue. The point is easily recognised by the fort on it, one of a number of defensive forts built by Richelieu. The harbour of Le Pradeau is used by the ferries running back and forth to the Iles d'Hyères

and there is nowhere for a visiting yacht to go. The wash from the ferries also makes anchoring nearby uncomfortable.

Iles d'Hyères

Iles d'Hyères includes four islands: Ile de Porquerolles, Ile de Bagaud, Ile de Port-Cros, and Ile du Levant. None of the islands are very large with Ile de Porquerolles, the largest of the group, measuring in at four miles long by just over a mile across. The islands are all quite high and their bold and steep-to coasts are easily recognised from the W and E.

In the summer the islands are popular destinations not only for yachts, local and foreign, cruising along the Côte d'Azur, but also for local yachts from Toulon to Cavalaire on day-trips or a weekend away.

The islands were colonised by the Greeks and later the Romans. In the 5th century they came under the sway of the powerful Abbot of Lérins on the small islands just off present-day Cannes. The Iles d'Hyères were difficult to defend and for most of the Middle Ages they were prey to pirates and corsairs and were left pretty much to themselves. In the 16th century under François I the islands were given the status of a marquisate on the condition that they were adequately protected from pirates.

Ile de Porquerolles. Pte du Langoustier and *La Jaune Garde* beacon. The anchorage under the point can be seen.

Despite attempts to foster agriculture and special tax exemptions for the marquisate, the islands did not prosper. In an attempt to attract manpower to the islands, a peculiar right was established whereby criminals could seek asylum and get immunity as long as they remained on the islands. The dispensation backfired as criminals flocked to the islands and while some became honest tillers of the soil, others organised and carried out pirate attacks. In the 17th century the right to asylum was abolished and the piracy cleaned up.

Today the islands are a popular destination for day-trips from the harbours between Toulon and Cavalaire-sur-Mer with ferries running frequently in the summer. The islands have been acquired by the French government and are designated as nature reserves. This means no camping, no fires, no shooting, and on Ile de Port-Cros, no smoking. The waters around the islands are a marine reserve and it is prohibited to fish, including spear-fishing, around much of the coast. It is also prohibited to anchor off Ile de Port-Cros and Ile de Bagaud for 600 metres off the coast, though in the summer local yachts do not pay much heed to this. The eastern end of Ile du Levant is a military area.

The attractions of the islands are the wonderful walks, all clearly sign-posted, and the clear turquoise water around them. There are mature stands of pine, including many umbrella pines, myrtle, cork and holm oaks, chestnuts, and that ubiquitous Australian species, the eucalyptus. There are specific botanical walks and you can buy guides to the flora and fauna of the islands. In the summer the prospective peace and quiet of the Iles d'Hyères is sought by thousands arriving on ferries or in yachts – so there is little of the elusive stuff to go around. On a weekday you may be lucky, or alternatively in the spring or autumn there are fewer visitors.

Ile de Porquerolles

The largest of the Iles d'Hyères. The southern coast is mostly high cliffs with the steep-to Cap d'Armes the southernmost extremity of the island. A lighthouse on Cap d'Armes, with a white square tower and dwelling is conspicuous, Fl(2)10s29M light.

From the W the lighthouse on Ile du Grand Ribaud, *La Jaune-Garde* beacon, BY with a ⬆ topmark, and the fort on Ile du Petit Langoustier, are conspicuous. The 1¼ mile channel between Ile du Grand Ribaud and *La Jaune-Garde* beacon is free of dangers in the fairway with least depths of 12 metres.

From the E the jagged Cap des Mèdes and the jagged group of rocks, Rocher des Mèdes, off it, stand out well from some distance off.

The N coast of the island is gentler than the S and there are several anchorages off it and the only harbour on the island, Port de Porquerolles.

PORT DE PORQUEROLLES

Approach

Conspicuous Once into Rade de Porquerolles, the old signal station, a building and tower on the summit of the island, and a fort, Ste-Agathe, on the slopes behind the harbour, are conspicuous. Closer in the buildings of Porquerolles village, a clock tower in the village and a large hotel immediately E, will be seen. The breakwater of the harbour and a light tower on the end are easily identified.

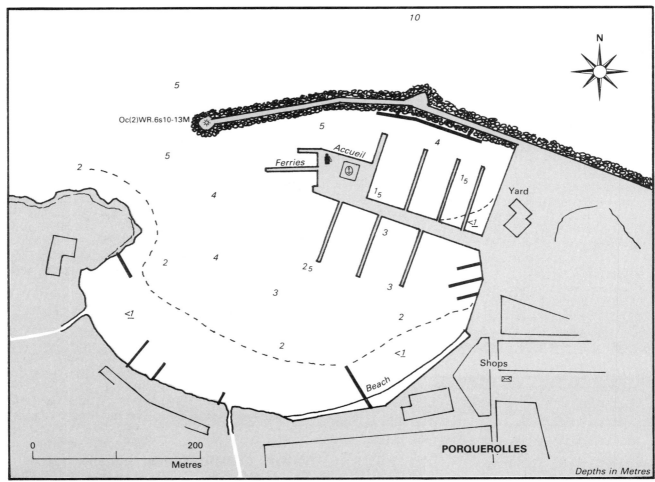

PORT DE PORQUEROLLES 43°00′N 6°12′E

By night The harbour entrance is lit, Oc(2)WR.6s 13/10M and Fl.G.2s. The white sector of the light shows the safe approach on 130°–230°.

Dangers With the *mistral* blowing, a lumpy swell piles up at the entrance.

Mooring

Details 500 berths with 200 berths for visitors. Maximum LOA 20 metres.

Berth at the *quai d'accueil* on the end of the central pier and report to the *capitainerie* for a berth. There are laid moorings tailed to the quay or to buoys.

Shelter Good shelter although the *mistral* can make some berths uncomfortable.

Authorities Port captain and marina staff. A charge is made.

Facilities

Services Water and electricity at every berth.

Fuel On the quay at the end of the central pier.

Repairs A 5-ton crane can haul onto the quay if necessary. Chandlers.

Provisions Most provisions available in the village. Ice available.

Eating out Numerous restaurants and bars in the village.

Other Post office. Exchange office. Ferries to Le Pradeau and Hyères-Plage.

General

The small village is a pleasant spot that in the winter must have a rather remote feel to it – though not in the summer. Porquerolles village was built comparatively recently, about 100 years ago by the military who used the island, and has given its name to the island.

Fort Ste-Agathe behind the village was captured in 1793 in a rather underhand fashion by the British. The British and Spanish fleet fleeing Toulon after its capture by the Republicans, anchored off in Rade de Porquerolles. The French commander at Fort Ste-Agathe had been forgotten by those on the mainland and had little idea of the tumultuous events happening there. The British admiral of the fleet invited him on board and while he was happily sampling the admiral's whisky, a force of British sailors captured the fort and blew it up. The fleet then sailed off taking the hapless French commander with them.

Anchorages

In the summer yachts anchor just about anywhere and everywhere along the N coast of Ile de Porquerolles. From the distance the forest of masts of the yachts at anchor is difficult to distinguish from the forest of masts of the yachts in the marina.

Baie du Langoustier The bay on the E side of Ile du Petit Langoustier. Anchor in 4–10 metres on sand, rock and weed. Good shelter from southerlies, but open to the N.

Plage d'Argent A bay immediately E of Pte du Bon-Renaud which has a beacon on the end. Anchor in 2·5–5 metres on sand and weed. Open to the N.

Plage de la Courtade The bay just E of Port de Porquerolles. Anchor off the beach in 2–5 metres. Open N and W.

Baie d'Alicastre The bay between Pte Lequin and Cap des Mèdes. Care needs to be taken of two dolphins off a wreck (3·7 metres least depth over) in the NE corner under Cap des Mèdes. Anchor in 2–8 metres on sand and weed. Open W and N.

ILE DE BAGAUD

The small island immediately W of Ile de Port-Cros. Landing on it and anchoring off it are prohibited, although in summer local yachts anchor off the E coast of the island. Unlike the other islands it is bare and rocky with just a patch or two of *maquis* in places.

Ile de Port-Cros

The highest island of the Iles d'Hyères at 207 metres (679 feet) though the steep-to and cliffy coast gives it the appearance of being higher. It is prohibited to anchor off around the coast except at Port-Cros and Port-Man, but in the summer local yachts anchor wherever they can along the N coast. It is also prohibited to fish around the island up to 600 metres off the coast. The passages on either side of Ile de Port-Cros are deep and free of dangers. In Passe des Grottes between Ile de Port-Cros and Ile du Levant there is an isolated rock close to Ile de Port-Cros, La Dame, marked by a beacon, BYB with a ♦ topmark.

Ile de Port-Cros takes its name from the cove on the W coast, Port-Cros or *Creux*, a 'hollow' or 'bowl'. The island was called *Mesé*, 'Middle Island', by the Greeks, for an obvious reason. It is densely wooded, being blessed with numerous freshwater springs, and like the other islands is a nature reserve.

PORT-CROS

Approach

This small cove, the only 'harbour' on the island, is on the W side of Ile de Port-Cros in the channel between it and Ile de Bagaud.

Conspicuous Ile de Bagaud is easily recognised and closer in the fort above the cove and the château built into the fortifications on the NE side will be seen. In the summer the numerous masts of the yachts in here identify it.

By night There are no lights.

Ile de Porquerolles. The jagged Rochers des Mèdes conspicuous off Cap Mèdes.

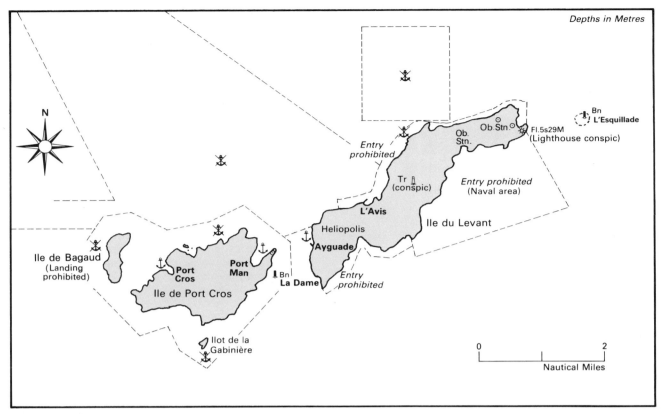

Depths in Metres

ILE DE PORT CROS AND ILE DU LEVANT

Note
• The channel into the jetties is marked off by red and green buoys. Yachts anchor to the S of this marked channel.
• The ferries to Port-Cros charge in and out at speed and a good lookout should be kept for them.

Mooring
Anchor to the S of the access channel in 2–15 metres. The anchorage is very crowded in the summer and you will have to anchor wherever you can. There are a few berths on the jetties in the NE corner, but it is rare to find a berth free in the summer. The anchorage is open to the W–NW.

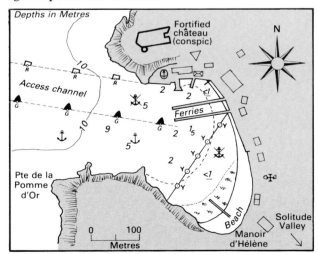

PORT CROS 43°00′·5N 6°23′E

Facilities
Several restaurants and bars open in the summer. Post office. Ferries to Hyères-Plage, Le Lavandou and Cavalaire-sur-Mer.

General
The small hamlet sits under the old fortifications running down a rocky ridge on the N side of the cove. Near the head of the cove is the *Manoir d'Hélène*, named after the heroine of Melchoir de Vogüé's novel, *Jean d'Agrève*, which is set on Ile de Port-Cros.

PORT-MAN
A cove on the NE tip of the island.

Approach
Conspicuous The villas of Heliopolis on Ile du Levant and closer in the tower on the eastern entrance point of Port-Man are conspicuous.

Mooring
Anchor wherever there is room. A line of small buoys at the head of the bay marks off an area where anchoring is prohibited. The bay is very deep with 25 metre depths at the entrance and 15–18 metre depths in the middle. The bottom is sand, rock, and thick weed. The cove is very crowded in the summer and many yachts anchor and take a long line ashore. Good shelter from southerlies, but northerlies send a swell into the bay.

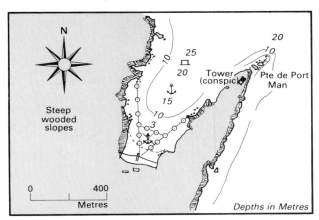

PORT MAN 43°00'·8N 6°25'E

Facilities

None.

General

On a fine August Saturday or Sunday afternoon this is obviously the place to be, judging by the numbers of boats jammed into the bay. For all that, it is a marvellous anchorage and ashore there are well marked walks around the island.

Ile du Levant

The easternmost of the Iles d'Hyères, just over half a mile E of Ile de Port-Cros. The island is easily identified with a number of conspicuous objects on it: the villas and buildings of Heliopolis on the western end; a tower in the middle of the island; the tower of the old observatory near the NE end; and the lighthouse, a white square tower and dwelling on Pte du Titan, Fl.5s29M light. Off the NE tip of the island there is a detached reef, L'Esquillade, with 1·4 metres least depth over it, marked by a beacon, BRB with 2 vertical balls as topmark. There are also numerous unlit mooring buoys around the island.

It is prohibited to anchor off the coast except at the western end. Off the S coast it is prohibited to enter a military zone which extends for up to 1½ miles off the coast (see plan). Since the navy employ their patch of Ile du Levant for rocket testing it is wise to stay well clear of the area. The island is divided between the military and the naturist colony at Heliopolis. The latter are serious sun-worshippers more akin to a religious sect than to their dilettante cousins on the resort beaches of the mainland. You can visit Heliopolis, but leave your camera behind as the naturists are not fond of visitors taking cheeky snaps of their bare anatomy.

There are two tiny harbours on the island, Port de l'Ayguade on the W coast and Port de l'Avis on the N coast.

Port de l'Ayguade

The harbour is tucked into a bight on the W coast directly across from Port-Man. The wreck of a coaster partly shelters the harbour from northerlies. A buoy, YB with a ■ topmark, marks the extremity of the wreck. Anchor off in 3–12 metres where convenient keeping well clear of the approach to the jetties where the ferries berth.

Port de l'Avis

A small harbour on the N coast also sheltered by the wreck of a coaster off it. The extremity of the wreck is marked by a buoy, YB with a ■ topmark. It is prohibited to anchor off and there is unlikely to be any space on the short jetties.

HYERES-PLAGE

Approach

Conspicuous The concentration of apartments on the flat isthmus stands out well from the distance. Closer in the harbour breakwaters and the light towers at the entrances can be identified.

By night The harbour entrances are lit. South basin: Fl.G.4s10M and Oc.R.4s8M. North basin: Iso.G.4s 10M and Q(6)+LFl.15s10M, and inner entrance Fl.R.4s5M.

Mooring

Details 1350 berths with 120 berths for visitors. A visiting yacht should head for the southern entrance and basins.

Berth at the *quai d'accueil* and report to the *capitainerie* for a berth. There are laid moorings tailed to the quay or to buoys.

Shelter Good all-round shelter.

Authorities Customs. Port captain and marina staff. A charge is made.

Anchorage A yacht can anchor off to the S of Hyères-Plage on sand and weed. It is prohibited to anchor off to the N of the harbour in the flight path of aircraft approaching Hyères-Palvestre airport.

Facilities

Services Water and fuel at every berth. A shower and toilet block.

Fuel On the quay at the end of the central pier.

Repairs A 50-ton travel-hoist, 10-ton crane, and slipways. All mechanical and engineering repairs. GRP and wood repairs. There are several boat-building and repair yards inland from the marina. Electrical and electronic repairs. Sailmakers. Chandlers.

Provisions Good shopping for provisions nearby. There is a market on the weekend in the street behind the north basin. Ice available.

Eating out Numerous restaurants and bars around the marina and along the waterfront.

Other Post office. Bank. Hire cars. Buses to Hyères.

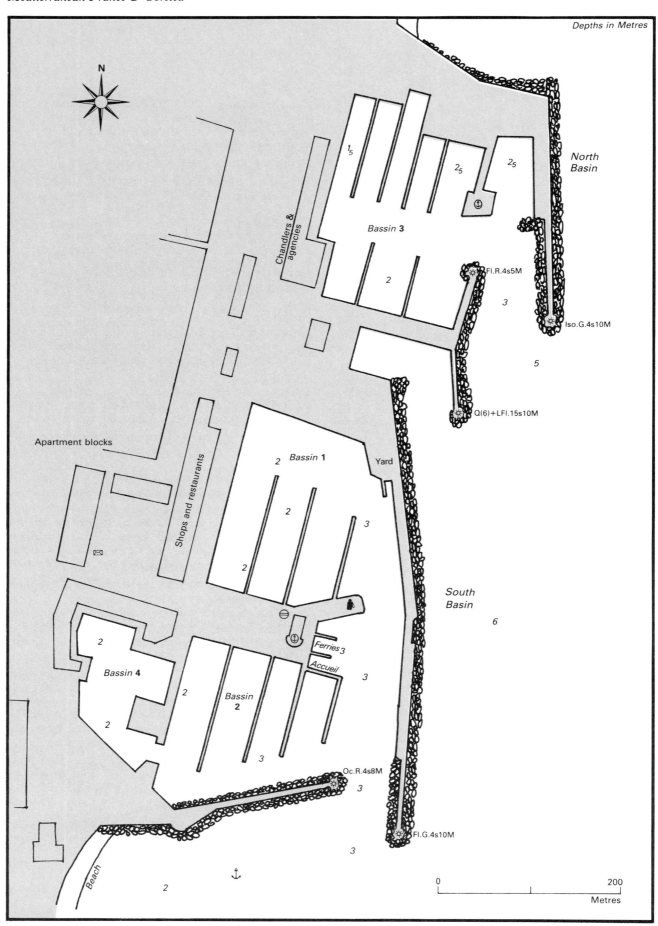

Depths in Metres

N

North
Basin

Chandlers &
agencies

Bassin **3**

1₅

2₅   2₅

2

Fl.R.4s5M

3

Iso.G.4s10M

5

Q(6)+LFl.15s10M

Apartment blocks

Shops and restaurants

Bassin **1**

Yard

2

2

2

3

South
Basin

6

2

Bassin **4**

2

Ferries 3

Accueil

3

3

Bassin
2

2

2

2

3

Oc.R.4s8M

3

Fl.G.4s10M

3

Beach

2

0   200

Metres

HYERES-PLAGE 43°05′N 6°10′E

General

The harbour and resort of Hyères-Plage is not to be confused with the older and more distinguished Hyères on the slopes inland. Hyères-Plage is the 20th-century extension of Hyères, built to accommodate those seeking sun, sea and sand; while Hyères is the old hill town that became a fashionable resort for the English in the 18th and 19th centuries.

The area was originally settled by the Phocaean Greeks from Marseille at L'Almanarre in the Golfe de Giens. The settlement was called Olbia and was succeeded by a Roman settlement called Pomponiana. In the Middle Ages the inhabitants, under threat from growing piracy in the area, moved inland to present-day Hyères. The port for medieval Hyères was switched to L'Ayguade just NE of Hyères-Plage. L'Ayguade was used by the crusaders to embark for the Holy Land and Hyères enjoyed some prosperity from the resulting trade. The port has subsequently silted although local craft drawing less than a metre still use it. Hyères itself declined in importance when Toulon was developed as a naval harbour by Louis XIV, though some prosperity returned with the beginnings of tourism in the late 18th century. Hyères attracted large numbers of invalids ordered to the mild winter climate of the south of France by their doctors and gained something of a reputation as one of the few healthy towns along the coast in the early 19th century, apparently, because of the pure water which had been piped to it.

Rade de la Badine

In westerlies or calm weather a yacht can anchor off the long beach running around the W side of Rade d'Hyères between Cap de l'Estérel and Hyères-Plage. The bottom comes up gradually from 5 metres to the beach. The holding on sand and weed is good once through the weed.

La Capte

A small harbour approximately 1 mile S of Hyères-Plage. Boats greater than 7 metres LOA should not attempt to enter as the entrance is very narrow and there is limited room for manoeuvring inside. There are 1·5 metre depths in the entrance and mostly less than 1 metre depths inside.

Port Pothau

A small fishing harbour off Les Salins. There are 4 metre depths in the entrance and 2–3 metre depths inside. However all of the berths on the S and NW are reserved for fishing boats and the quay on the E side is reserved for the navy.

Miramar-la-Londe

A small harbour immediately W of the River La Maravanne. The channel into the harbour is buoyed as the entrance silts and is periodically dredged. Only shallow-draught yachts should attempt to use it. There are 1·75–2 metre depths in the outer part of the harbour, but less than a metre off the quay and jetties. The harbour is presently being enlarged and dredged and there are plans to build a marina here.

La Maravanne

Local boats moor along the banks of the river, but great care is needed as the depths over the bar at the entrance vary and the depths inside are mostly less than 1 metre.

ILOTS DE LEOUBE

An islet close to the coast approximately 1¾ miles due E of Miramar-la-Londe. It is joined to the coast and in the bay under the islet on the E side there is shelter from northerlies. Anchor in 2–5 metres on sand and weed.

Batterie des Maures

An artificial islet with a square white tower on it lying approximately 200 metres offshore to the S of Ilots de Léoube. A fixed white light is exhibited on it.

Ilots de l'Estagnol

A small islet and above-water rocks close to the coast SE of Pte de Léoube. In the bay immediately NW of Ilots de l'Estagnol there is shelter from northerlies. Anchor in 4–6 metres on sand and weed.

CAP DE BREGANCON

A square bold cape which is actually an islet connected by a low isthmus to the coast. On the cape is a fort and both the islet and the fort are easily identified from the distance. There is an anchorage on the N side of the cape in 2–5 metres on sand and weed. Shelter from E–SE in attractive surroundings.

Port de la Reine-Jeanne

A miniature private harbour just E of Cap de Brégançon.

CAP BLANC AND CAP BENAT

These two capes on the western end of Rade de Bormes are easily identified. From Miramar-la-Londe to Cap Blanc and Cap Bénat the coast gets progressively higher and more rugged. This is the western end of the Maures *massif*. Cap Blanc, as its name suggests, is a light-coloured cape and has a conspicuous lighthouse on it, Fl.R.5s20M light. A signal station with a white tower and dwelling on the summit above the cape is conspicuous. Cap Bénat can be recognised by a jagged islet, Ilot Christaou, off it. The islet has a beacon on it with a ⁑ topmark.

Port du Pradet

A small private harbour tucked into the N side of Cap Bénat. A yacht can anchor off in the bay in 5–10

Cap Bénat. The conspicuous lighthouse and old signal station.

metres on hard sand, rock and thick weed. Good shelter from westerlies. With the prevailing SE sea breeze a swell rolls in, more uncomfortable than dangerous. The slopes around are part of a private estate with large villas discreetly built around the wooded slopes.

Anse du Gau

A bay immediately N of Pte de l'Esquillette. A yacht can anchor here in 3–6 metres on sand and weed. Good shelter from westerlies, but open to the E. With the prevailing SE sea breeze a swell rolls in.

La Fourmigue

A rocky islet in Rade de Bormes just over 1½ miles NE of Cap Bénat. It is marked by a solid beacon with a light, Fl(2)6s8M. In calm weather local boats anchor in the shoal water off the beacon to fish.

BORMES-LES-MIMOSAS

Approach

A large marina on the W side of Rade de Bormes.

Conspicuous La Fourmigue beacon stands out well and the concentration of apartment blocks beginning at Bormes-les-Mimosas and stretching around the coast to Le Lavandou is easily identified. Closer in the breakwater and the light tower on its end will be seen.

By night Use *La Fourmigue* Fl(2)6s8M and the lights at the entrance: Fl(2)R.6s10M on the breakwater and Fl.G on the green buoy marking the channel. The S end of the breakwater is lit by a F.Vi. The pier just inside the entrance is lit at the extremity by a Fl.R.

Note The channel into the harbour is marked by green conical buoys on the starboard side and red conical buoys on the port side.

Mooring

Details 950 berths with berths for visitors. Maximum LOA 20 metres.

Berth at the *quai d'accueil* just inside the entrance and report to the *capitainerie* for a berth. There are laid moorings tailed to the quay.

Shelter Good all-round shelter.

Authorities Port captain and marina staff. A charge is made.

Facilities

Services Water and electricity at every berth. Several shower and toilet blocks around the marina.

Fuel On the quay near the entrance.

Repairs A 45-ton travel-hoist and a slipway. Most mechanical repairs. Some GRP and wood repairs. Electrical and electronic repairs. Chandlers.

Provisions Most provisions can be obtained. Ice available.

Eating out Restaurants and bars open in the summer.

Other Exchange office.

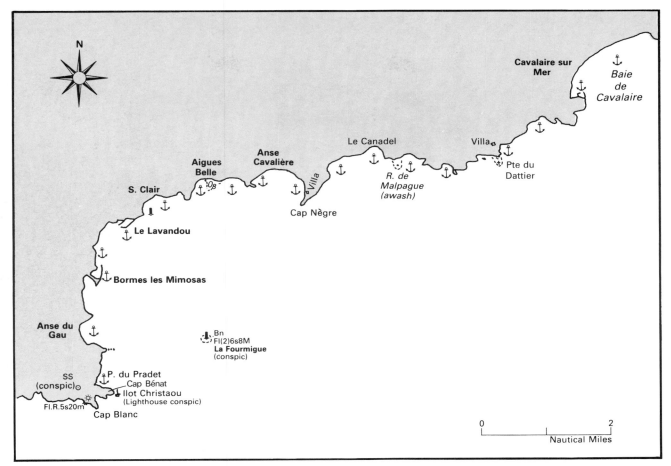

CAP BLANC TO BAIE DE CAVALAIRE

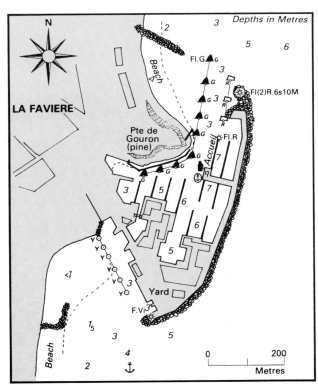

BORMES-LES-MIMOSAS 43°07′·4N 6°21′·9E

General

It all works: it has a fine beach on either side, it is conveniently sited close to the Iles d'Hyères, it has good facilities for yachtsmen, but it lacks that certain something. The hill village of Bormes-les-Mimosas behind Le Lavandou is, by contrast, a delightful Provençal village well worth a visit.

LE LAVANDOU

Approach

The marina is situated close N of Bormes-les-Mimosas and is virtually connected to it by a wall of apartment blocks around the coast.

Conspicuous The cluster of buildings around Bormes-les-Mimosas and Le Lavandou are readily identified and closer in the breakwater and the light tower on its end will be seen. The entrance is difficult to see until right up to it.

By night The entrance is lit, Iso.WG.4s13/10M and Fl(2)R.6s3M. The white sector of the sectored light shows the safe passages either side of La Fourmigue on 266°–317° and 332°–358°. The entrance to the old harbour is also lit, Q(9)15s7M.

Bormes-les-Mimosas. The approach to the entrance looking W.

Le Lavandou looking SW. The Vieux Port is just out of the picture on the right.

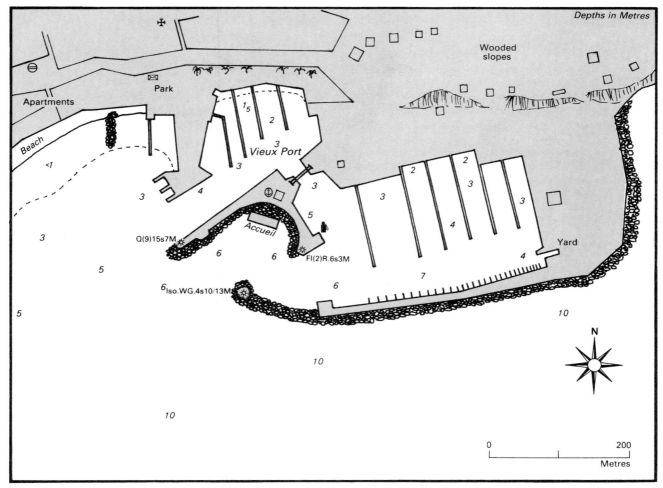

LE LAVANDOU 43°08'·2N 6°22'·3E

Mooring

Details 900 berths with 100 berths for visitors. Maximum LOA 24 metres.

Berth at the *quai d'accueil* at the entrance and report to the *capitainerie* for a berth. There are finger pontoons or laid moorings tailed to the quay.

Shelter Good all-round shelter.

Authorities Customs. Port captain and marina staff. A charge is made.

Facilities

Services Water and electricity at every berth. A shower and toilet block.

Fuel On the quay near the entrance.

Repairs A 50-ton travel-hoist and 25-ton crane. Covered storage ashore. Mechanical and engineering repairs. GRP and wood repairs. Electrical and electronic repairs. Sailmakers. Chandlers.

Provisions Good shopping for provisions in the town. Ice available.

Eating out A good choice of restaurants on the waterfront and in the town.

Other Post office. Banks. Hire cars. Buses around the coast. Ferries to Ile d'Hyères.

General

Le Lavandou rests more easily on the coast than Bormes-les-Mimosas. The old harbour next to the marina still has a fishing fleet, though the ferries running to the Iles d'Hyères now use part of the harbour. The town takes its name from the lavender fields around the slopes of the Maures *massif*. The old village of Bormes behind Le Lavandou apparently felt left out of the floral tributes along the coast and so rechristened itself Bormes-les-Mimosas after the abundant mimosa that grows around it. It is a pleasant Provençal village, all pastel shades of ochre, pink and cream, with steep lanes and alleys winding up the slopes.

Le Lavandou to Cavalaire-sur-Mer

Between Le Lavandou and the Baie de Cavalaire, the wooded hills of Les Maures rise up abruptly from the sea. There are small resorts tucked into the bays and coves where a yacht can anchor depending on the wind and sea.

Ste-Clair A bay immediately NE of Le Lavandou. A group of rocks extend out from the SW side of the bay and there is a beacon on the outermost rock, Pte du Nard-Viou. Anchor in 3–6 metres on sand and weed. Open to the S and E. There are restaurants and bars ashore.

Aigue Belle The bay immediately E of Ste-Clair. Care needs to be taken of a reef with 0·8 metre over it running out into the bay. A calm weather anchorage only.

Anse de Cavalière Not to be confused with Baie de Cavalaire. A thin beacon and a villa with two turret towers will be seen on Cap Nègre which forms the E side of the bay. There is some shelter in here from the N–E, but it is entirely open to the S. Anchor in 5–12 metres on the E side of the bay. Restaurants and bars ashore.

Le Canadel A large bay that can be used in calm weather. The coast to the E is steep-to and densely wooded with a number of coves and bights that can be used in calm weather.

Notes
• Care needs to be taken of a rock, Rocher de Malpague, just awash off the coast to the E of Le Canadel.
• A reef extends a short distance off Pte du Dattier which has a conspicuous large villa on it.

CAVALAIRE-SUR-MER

Approach

The marina sits tucked under Cap Cavalaire and cannot be seen when approaching from the W until you are right into the bay.

Conspicuous From the W the large villa standing alone on Pte du Dattier is conspicuous. The wooded slopes of Cap Cavalaire with a mast conspicuous on the summit can be identified and once into Baie de Cavalaire the harbour breakwater will be seen. From the E the concentration of apartment blocks around Cavalaire-sur-Mer is easily identified.

By night The harbour entrance is lit though the lights can be confusing. Outer breakwater Fl(2)R.6s 10M. Central pier Fl.R.2s1M. Spur jetty Q(3)R.6s 2M. The new breakwater is not yet lit.

Dangers With a strong *mistral* the wind is funnelled into the bay making the approach and entrance difficult. With strong southerlies a swell piles up at the entrance.

Mooring

Details 580 berths, soon to be expanded to approximately 1000 when the Nouveau Port is complete.

Berth off the end of the central pier and report to the *capitainerie* for a berth. There are laid moorings tailed to the quay or to small buoys.

Shelter Good shelter although the *mistral* can make some berths uncomfortable.

Authorities Port captain and marina staff. A charge is made.

Note The Nouveau Port adjacent to the marina will approximately double the capacity here.

Anchorage In settled weather a yacht can anchor off to the N of the harbour outside a buoyed area. Anchor in 5–10 metres on sand and weed.

Facilities

Services Water and electricity at every berth. A shower and toilet block.

Fuel On the end of the central pier at the entrance.

Repairs A 20-ton travel-hoist. Mechanical repairs. Some GRP and wood repairs. Chandlers.

Provisions Good shopping for provisions in the town about 10 minutes walk away. Market on Wednesdays. Ice available.

Eating out Restaurants in the town and around the waterfront.

Other Post office. Bank. Hire cars. Buses to St-Tropez and Le Lavandou.

General

Cavalaire-sur-Mer is a popular summer resort on the strength of the long sandy beach stretching for some 2½ miles around the bay. Out of season it virtually closes down and has a forlorn air to it. On the slopes inland up to La Croix-Valmer are extensive vineyards and the wine of the area is well known amongst Côtes de Provence labels.

Note The Nouveau Port, the new basin adjacent to the original basin of the marina, is virtually complete at the time of writing, with just the ancillary services to be installed.

CAP LARDIER

This rugged cape is the first on the stretch of coast between Baie de Cavalaire and the entrance to the Golfe de St-Tropez. Depending on the wind and sea a yacht can anchor on either side of the cape. Care needs to be taken of a reef with 1·1 metres over it just off the cape.

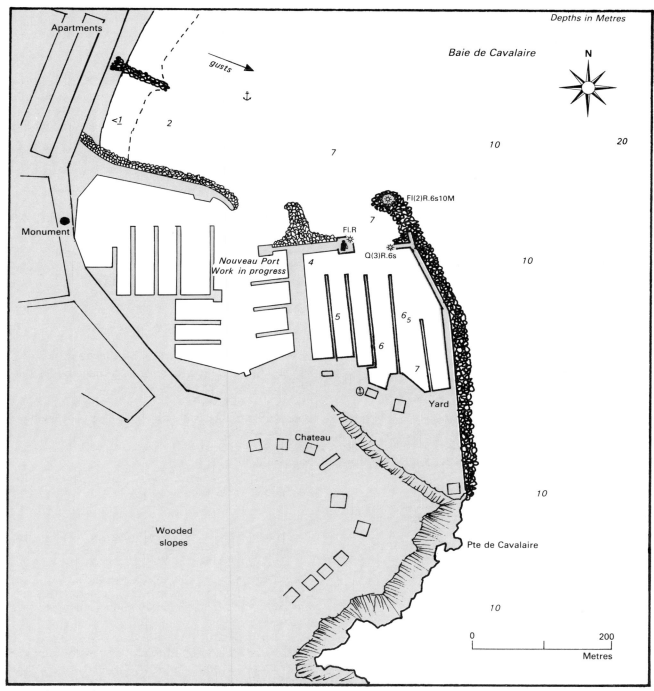

Depths in Metres

Baie de Cavalaire

N

Apartments

gusts

⚓

Monument

<1   2

7

10

20

Fl(2)R.6s10M

7

Fl.R

Q(3)R.6s

Nouveau Port
Work in progress

4

10

5

6 5

6

7

Yard

Chateau

10

Pte de Cavalaire

Wooded
slopes

10

0   200

Metres

CAVALAIRE SUR MER 43°10'·2N 6°32'·4E

BAIE DE BRIANDE

The large bay lying between Cap Lardier and Cap Taillat. Cap Taillat is easily recognised by the conspicuous girder tower on it. Anchor where convenient on sand, rock and weed. The favoured anchorage is on the N side of the bay.

BAIE DE BON PORTE

The large bay on the N side of Cap Taillat. Care needs to be taken of the group of rocks, L'Enfer, off the cap. The large bay is bordered by above and below water rocks and care is needed in the close ap-

Cavalaire-sur-Mer. Approach looking S.

177

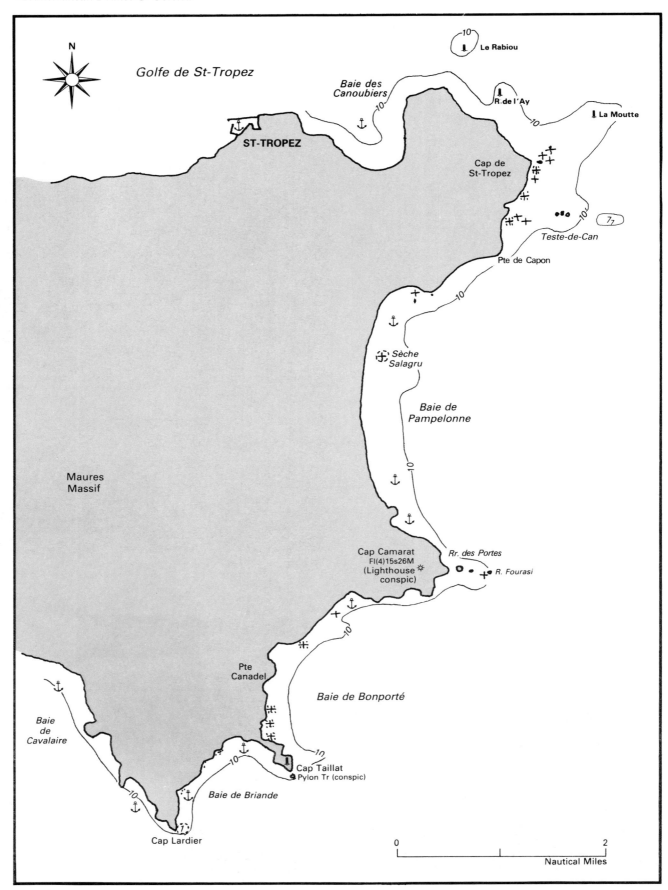

BAIE DE CAVALAIRE TO ST-TROPEZ

proaches to the coast. Anchor where convenient on sand and weed. The favoured anchorages are in the cove N of Pte Canadel and in a cove in the NW corner.

Cap Camarat

A bold wooded cape easily recognised by the lighthouse, a white tower and dwelling, and an old signal station, on it; Fl(4)15s26M light. A group of above-water rocks extending eastwards from the cape are easily identified. Roche des Portes is a large rock just off the cape and Roches Fouras are the outermost group of rocks. Local yachts cut inside the rocks through a passage outside the group of rocks off Roche des Portes, but the prudent course is to go outside Roches Fouras. On the N side of Cap Camarat is the large Baie de Pampelonne bordered by a long sandy beach.

BAIE DE PAMPELONNE

The large bay is mostly free of dangers except for Sèche Salagru with 0·4 metre over, just under 1½ miles N of Pte de Bonne Terrasse. In calm weather the yachts from the marinas around Golfe de St-Tropez charge around the corner to anchor off here until the afternoon sea breeze gets up.

Pampelonne beach itself has been divided up and renamed along its length so that the 'individual' beaches, mostly associated with restaurants and bars or camping grounds, reads like a list of tropical cocktails: Tropezina, Tahiti-Plage, Bora-Bora, Moorea, La Voile Rouge, Lagon Bleu, Sun 77, Le Liberty, Le Blouch, Force 7, Club 55, Niourlago, Les Palmiers, L'Aqua Club, Cabane Bambou, Tropicana .... Tahiti-Plage is probably the best known where, so I am informed, the most beautiful girls in France can be found not only topless, but bottomless as well.

Cap Camarat and its conspicuous lighthouse looking NW.

Bathing fashions from the age when you covered your top as well as your bottom.

ii. East – St-Tropez to St-Laurent du Var

The Côte d'Azur east of St-Tropez includes many of the place names commonly associated with the south of France. Names like St-Raphael, Cannes, Juan-les-Pins, Antibes, and St-Tropez itself trip off the tongue in a familiar recital of well known resorts. In the summer these and many other less well known resorts along this coast are crowded to overflowing; and you get the feeling in some places, like the Golfe de St-Tropez and Golfe de Napoule, that you are on a busy nautical motorway at rush hour. In other places there is still some peace and quiet to be found and outside of July and August the number of boats out and about diminishes substantially.

Along this coast the weather is more moderate than to the west. The *mistral* is less strong and not as frequent and the sea breeze blowing from the SE–E is the prevalent summer wind.

Golfe de St-Tropez

Cutting deep into the Maures massif, the Golfe de St-Tropez affords the first all-round shelter after rounding Cap Camarat.

Southern entrance

Off Cap de St-Tropez at the southern entrance point, shoal water peppered with above and below-water rocks extends for nearly a mile offshore over a large area. A bank, Basses de Can, with depths of less than 17 metres, extends for 2½ miles E of Pte de Capon. Basses de Can is not normally bothersome except in gale force winds when a confused swell heaps up over it with a vicious cross-swell and breaking waves.

The area of shoal water closer to the coast with the above and below-water rocks, is well marked by three beacons and a group of easily recognised above-water rocks.

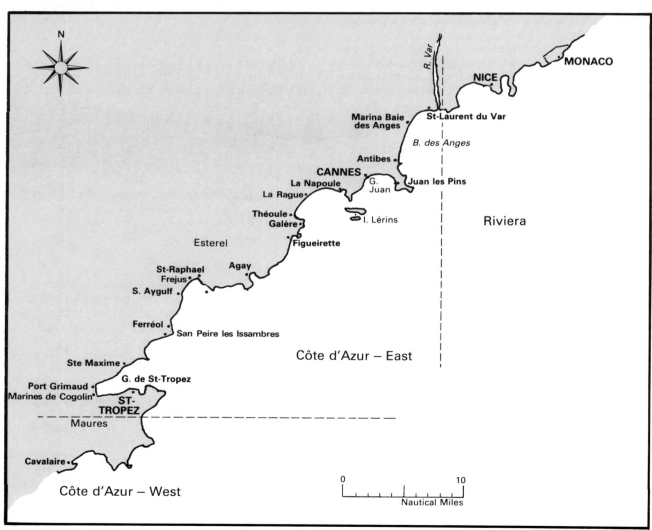

COTE D'AZUR – EAST

St-Tropez. Care is needed of the yachts charging in and out in the narrow entrance.

Teste de Can Three jagged rocks to the NE of Pte de Capon that are easily identified. Although there is a channel between Teste de Can and a reef running out from the coast, with 5 metres and greater depths in the fairway, the prudent course is to go to seaward of the rocks.

La Moutte A large beacon, BYB with a ♦ topmark and a wind generator on top, is easily identified from some distance off. It is lit, Q(3)WR.10s9/6M. The beacon marks the extremity of Basses de la Moutte, a rocky ledge extending NE from Cap de St-Tropez. There is an inshore passage close to the beacon with 2·2–2·8 metre depths in the fairway and though local yachts often use it, the prudent course is to go outside the beacon. There is a 4 metre patch close off the eastern side of the beacon, but otherwise there are 10 metre plus depths 500 metres to seawards of the beacon.

Roche de l'Ay A rock just awash, with a small beacon, BRB with 2 vertical balls as topmark, is easily identified. The beacon marks the extremity of a rocky ledge with depths of 5 metres over it. Local yachts go inshore of it, but the prudent course is to keep to seaward of it.

Roche de Rabiou An isolated rocky patch with 5·5 metres over it, marked by a beacon, BY with a ♠ topmark. Between the beacon and Pte de Rabiou there are 10–15 metre depths in the fairway. Local yachts use this channel and it is a straightforward short-cut with no dangers in the channel.

Northern entrance

Off Pte des Sardinaux a rocky ledge with above and below water rocks extends for ¾ of a mile eastwards. Near the extremity there are two beacons.

Les Sardinaux A rock at the NE extremity of the rocky ledge with a beacon, BYB with a ♦ topmark, on it. The beacon is conspicuous from some distance off. A reef extends a short distance to seawards of the beacon so it should be given a good offing.

Rocher de la Garde A group of above-water rocks between Les Sardinaux and Sèche à l'Huile: A reef with less than 2 metres over it with a beacon, YB with a ♦ topmark, on it. It is lit, Q(6)+LFl.WR.15s 9/6M.

Note Some of the beacons mentioned here could do with a lick of paint at the time of writing, but despite this are all easily located and identified.

BAIE DES CANOUBIERS

A large bay just inside the entrance on the S side of Golfe de St-Tropez. It is the only anchorage in the gulf offering nearly all-round shelter. Although open to the N, NE winds tend to get funnelled eastwards and NW winds are likewise deflected to the W. In gale force northerlies a yacht should make for one of the harbours around the gulf.

In the approach a line of yellow buoys across the entrance will sometimes be encountered. Anchor where convenient in 3–12 metres. The bottom is mud and weed, good holding once through the weed. Good protection from southerlies and reasonable shelter from northerlies, although a swell rolls in with NE winds, more uncomfortable than dangerous. Although a popular anchorage in the summer, most of the local boats will depart in the evening.

There are few facilities in the bay apart from several restaurants around the shore. In the summer a boat does the rounds taking orders for bread, crois-

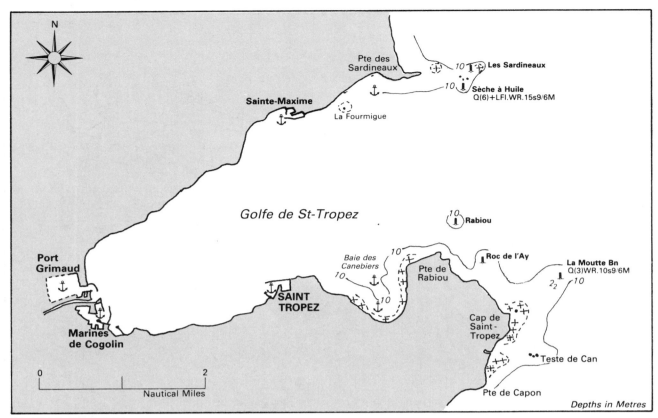

GOLFE DE ST-TROPEZ

sants and ice, all at prices considerably above shore-side prices, but after all, its not everywhere you can have fresh hot croissants delivered to your boat for breakfast.

ST-TROPEZ

Approach

Conspicuous Once past the beacon on Roche de Rabiou, the citadel above the town and the clustered buildings of St-Tropez are easily identified. A belfry in the town, a square tower at the root of the mole, and the old lighthouse at the elbow of the mole, are conspicuous. Closer in the harbour breakwater and the light tower at the entrance will be seen.

By night The entrance is lit, Oc(2)WR.6s13/10M and Fl.G.4s7M. The white sector of the sectored light shows the safe approach into the Golfe de St-Tropez on 228°–245°.

Dangers
● With a strong *mistral* blowing entry can be difficult.
● To the E of the entrance there is a large unlit mooring buoy.

Note The entrance to the harbour is quite narrow and care must be taken of the numerous yachts charging in and out of the entrance.

Mooring

Details 800 berths with 150 berths for visitors. Maximum LOA 20 metres.

Berth Go on the *quai d'accueil* at the entrance to the Vieux Port and report to the *capitainerie* for a berth. There are laid moorings tailed to the quay.

Shelter Good all-round shelter although the *mistral* can make some berths in the Nouveau Port uncomfortable.

Authorities Customs. Port captain and marina staff. A charge is made.

Anchorage In settled weather a yacht can anchor off to the W of the harbour in 5–15 metres. Make sure you are well clear of the entrance and approaches to the harbour. The bottom is mud and weed, good holding once through the weed. This anchorage is often a bit rolly, as much from the numerous boats charging up and down as from any swell entering the gulf.

Facilities

Services Water and electricity (220 and 380v) at every berth. Telephone and television connections at most berths. A shower and toilet block.

Fuel On the quay at the entrance.

Repairs A 20-ton crane and slipways up to 40 tons. Covered storage ashore, but overall there is limited hard standing. Mechanical and engineering repairs. GRP and wood repairs. Electrical and electronic repairs. Sailmakers. Chandlers.

Provisions Good shopping for provisions in the town. Ice available.

Eating out A wide choice of restaurants around the waterfront and in the town.

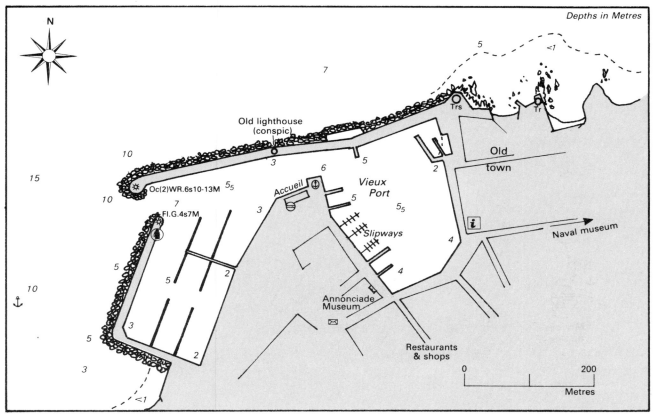

ST-TROPEZ 43°16'·4N 6°38'·4E

Other Post office. Banks. Hire cars. Buses along the coast.

General

St-Tropez is one of the best-known names along the coast, where the women are said to be more beautiful than anywhere else, and to reveal more; where the men are bronzed, handsome hunks; where the rich, the famous, the infamous, and hangers-on can be seen on their summer appearances; where the days are languorous and the nights debauched. It may have been true once, though no doubt the *paparazzi* and the media constructed much of it, but today you see little of the popular imagery of the place. St-Tropez is considered passé and if the rich and famous are around, they evidently prefer the privacy of a villa on the outskirts of town to the public gaze in the restaurants on the waterfront.

What you will find at St-Tropez is a compact town set under a wooded bluff that has retained its integrity and character. The harbour is surrounded by old houses (though on closer inspection you will find many of them are reconstructions, as the Germans blew up the harbour and waterfront before surrendering), with narrow and remarkably peaceful streets running up the hill behind to the citadel on the top. Around the harbour painters display examples of their particular talent for sale, and the rich display their yachts for approval. The crowds mill around the waterfront day and night.

St-Tropez was 'discovered' as a resort much later than many of the other places along the coast. One of

the reasons it was not fashionable early on is that the town faces into the *mistral* and so does not have the benign winter climate of other resorts sheltered from this cold vicious wind. Guy de Maupassant visited St-Tropez in his yacht *Le Bel-Ami* at the end of the 19th century and expounded on its charms to his friends. No doubt Paul Signac, the post-Impressionist disciple of Seurat, heard of it through the 'grapevine' and when he visited here on his yacht in 1892, he decided to stay. Over the years a celebrated group of artists came to join him including Matisse, Bonnard, Marquet and Dunoyer de Segonzac. We can thank M. Georges Grammont, a wealthy manufacturer of cables, for getting together a collection of the paintings of this group, and numerous other paintings and sculpture, which are housed in the deconsecrated chapel of L'Annonciade at the western end of the harbour. It is one of the best collections of early 20th-century French painters around and not to be missed.

After the First World War, St-Tropez became popular with what Archibald Lyall has described as 'Bohemians and cosmopolitans ... a sort of Montparnasse-on-Sea, full of artists, writers, hangers-on'. Colette moved to St-Tropez in 1926 and spent much of her time here in her villa behind Anse des Canoubiers. Her particular hedonistic approach to life is described in *La Naissance du Jour*, in which St-Tropez is described as a place where the visitors were motivated by *un caprice unanime*; as Patrick Howarth in *When The Riviera Was Ours* puts it: '...a place for idling, for siestas, for making love, perhaps for growing fat, as Colette herself did, a fact she duly recognised when she made a practice of asking for beef-steaks as thick as her own thighs.' Something of this languorous life remains today and though Colette and her lover are no longer here, the new breed of hedonists continue to worship sun, sand, and sea and the good life.

St-Tropez c. 1900. At the time it was visited by a few of the post impressionist painters, notably Signac; but not until much later did it attract the glitterati.

St-Tropez harbour looking down from the naval museum on the slopes above the town.

LA NIOULARGO

Nioulargo is the name of an underwater bank 5 miles SE of Cap de St-Tropez. It has 68 metres over it and is marked by a yellow buoy. All that is comparatively unimportant until the beginning of October when the buoy is the mark for a week of racing out of St-Tropez called Nioulargo Week. It all started in 1980 when a Swan 44 challenged a 12-metre to a race to *La Nioulargo* buoy and back. In the years since that first race between Dick Jayson's *Pride* and Jean Riddle's *Iskra*, Nioulargo Week has grown rapidly to become the closest thing to Antigua Race Week in Europe.

During the week there are a whole series of races, some of them around the original mark at La Nioulargo, for all classes of yachts from maxis to multi-hulls, IOR racers to cruising boats, 12-metres, 8-metres, and 6-metres, old gaffers to Formula-40 catamarans. On some days you will see all of these crashing their way through the Mediterranean chop.

As important as the racing are the social events ashore and the spontaneous parties afloat. On some mornings it's difficult to know how crews manage to survive on the water after the night's revelry, and perhaps in recognition of this the organisers slot a few days off through the week. If you happen to be in the vicinity at the time and feel like some relaxed racing and *après-yachting*, Nioulargo Week is the place to be. If you intend to visit St-Tropez at the end of October, don't count on getting a berth there until Nioulargo Week is over.

MARINES DE COGOLIN

Approach

A large marina and associated apartment complex in the SW corner of Golfe de St-Tropez.

Conspicuous The apartment blocks of Cogolin and Port Grimaud are easily identified at the end of the gulf. The yellow building on the end of the jetty at Pte de Bertaud torpedo firing range is conspicuous. Closer in the harbour breakwater and the white light tower at the entrance will be seen, but it is impossible to see the entrance proper until right up to it.

By night Use the light at Pte de Bertaud torpedo firing range, Iso.WRG.4s9-6M. The white sector covers the safe approach into Golfe de St-Tropez on 227°–243°. The harbour entrance is lit, Fl(2)R.6s10M, and a light is exhibited at the entrance to Bassin la Brigantine, Fl.G.2s1M.

Dangers With strong easterlies blowing into the gulf a swell piles up at the entrance and difficulties can be encountered when you turn side-on to the swell to enter.

Mooring

Details 1526 berths with 270 berths for visitors. Maximum LOA 35 metres.

Berth Go on the *quai d'accueil* and report to the *capitainerie* for a berth. There are laid moorings tailed to the quay.

Shelter Good all-round shelter although a strong *mistral* can make some of the berths in the Port Public uncomfortable.

Authorities Port captain and marina staff. A charge is made.

Facilities

Services Water and electricity at every berth. Several shower and toilet blocks around the marina.

Fuel On the quay by the *capitainerie*.

Repairs A 35-ton travel-hoist and slipways. Covered storage ashore. Mechanical and engineering repairs. GRP and wood repairs. Electrical and electronic repairs. Sailmakers. Chandlers.

Provisions Some provisions can be obtained in the marina. Better shopping in a supermarket outside the marina, about 15 minutes walk away. Ice available.

Eating out Numerous restaurants and bars around the marina open in the summer.

Other Post office. Bank. Hire cars. Occasional buses to St-Tropez.

General

The large marina is part and parcel of an apartment complex that fringes it. I'm not sure whether it is just all too big, not imaginative enough, or that Port Grimaud next door outshines it, but it doesn't have a lot of appeal over and above being a secure harbour with all facilities. It is not to be confused with the village of Cogolin, a centre of carpet and fabric weaving some 2½ miles away, from which it takes its name.

Rivière Giscle

The river running out between Marines de Cogolin and Port Grimaud. The depths at the entrance vary, but are normally 1–1·5 metres, sometimes more, going to 2–2·5 metres further in. Shallow-draught craft can get into here and berth alongside the bank. There is a light at the entrance, Q.9M. In the near future it is planned to dredge the river and entrance and to create 120 berths along the banks.

PORT GRIMAUD

Approach

The marina immediately N of Marines de Cogolin.

Conspicuous The apartments and houses of Grimaud are difficult to distinguish from the distance, but closer in the lower and more broken profile of Grimaud will be seen and the breakwater protecting the entrance identified.

By night The entrance is lit, Fl.G.4s10M and Fl(2)R.6s6m.

185

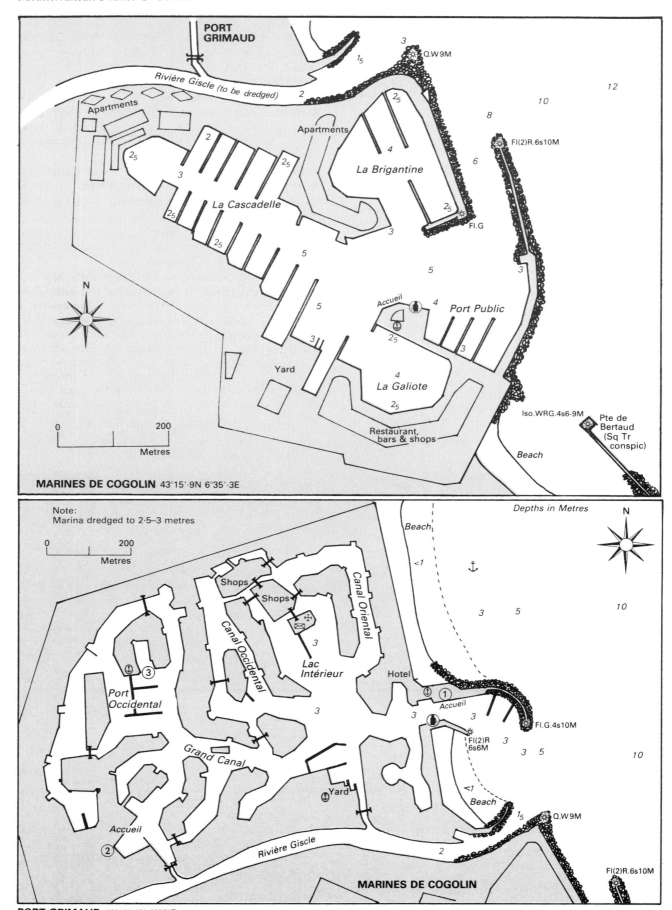

PORT GRIMAUD

Rivière Giscle (to be dredged)

Apartments

Apartments

La Brigantine

La Cascadelle

Q.W 9M

Fl(2)R.6s10M

Fl.G

N

Accueil

Port Public

Yard

La Galiote

Restaurant, bars & shops

Iso.WRG.4s6-9M

Pte de Bertaud (Sq Tr conspic)

Beach

0   200
Metres

MARINES DE COGOLIN 43°15′·9N 6°35′·3E

Note:
Marina dredged to 2·5–3 metres

0   200
Metres

Depths in Metres

N

Beach

Shops

Shops

Canal Oriental

Canal Occidental

Lac Intérieur

Hotel

Port Occidental

Accueil

Fl.G.4s10M

Grand Canal

Fl(2)R 6s6M

Yard

Beach

Q.W 9M

Accueil

Rivière Giscle

MARINES DE COGOLIN

Fl(2)R.6s10M

PORT GRIMAUD 43°16′·4N 6°35′E

Dangers With strong easterlies blowing into Golfe de St-Tropez a swell heaps up at the entrance. In gale force conditions entry may be dangerous.

Mooring

There are three different basins within Port Grimaud as a whole.

Grimaud 1 1100 berths with 207 berths for visitors. Maximum LOA 55 metres. Berth at the *quai d'accueil* just inside the entrance to Port Grimaud and report to the *capitainerie* for a berth. There are finger pontoons or laid moorings tailed to buoys. Shelter is good inside the village proper, but berths on the outer mole are uncomfortable with easterlies and could be untenable in gale force easterlies.

Grimaud 2 616 berths with 53 berths for visitors. Maximum LOA 14 metres. Berth at the *quai d'accueil* in the SW corner of the village (see plan) and report to the *bureau* for a berth. There are laid moorings tailed to the quay. Shelter in here is excellent.

Grimaud 3 200 berths with some visitors' berths. Maximum LOA 20 metres. Berths allocated on application. Excellent shelter.

Authorities Port captain and marina staff. A charge is made.

Facilities

Services Water and electricity (220 and 380v in Grimaud 1) at every berth. Shower and toilet blocks around the marina.

Fuel On the quay at the entrance.

Repairs A 30-ton travel-hoist and slipway up to 60 tons. A 20-ton hoist and 10-ton crane. Mechanical and engineering repairs. Some GRP and wood repairs. Electrical and electronic repairs. Sailmakers. Chandlers.

Provisions Good shopping for provisions including a small market in the summer. Ice available.

Eating out Numerous restaurants open in the summer.

Other Post office. Bank. Hire cars.

General

Just over twenty years ago there was little here except swampy ground at the head of the gulf. Port Grimaud was envisaged and built along the lines of a Provençal village, suitably sanitised, and though it looks real enough from the distance, once inside it is evident it is not. It is a shining example of what can be accomplished in the way of sympathetic development if the architects and planners try. However an apartment in Grimaud costs a lot and a quick glance around soon confirms one's opinions that unless you have a bit of money put by, you won't be able to afford to stay here other than in a boat for a night or

Port Grimaud. Approach looking W.

two – though I might add it is no more expensive than some architecturally hideous resorts along the coast.

The village is built around a series of canals and basins so that those with an apartment can moor their boat at the bottom of the garden. Arched bridges cross the canals here and there, and the planners have made much of it inaccessible to cars giving parts a wonderful tranquillity. The planners even added a church to foster a community spirit.

STE-MAXIME

Approach

Conspicuous The concentration of apartment blocks at Ste-Maxime is easily identified. Closer in a belfry in the town and the large single-arched bridge over the Rivière Preconcil are conspicuous. The breakwater and the light tower at the entrance are easily seen.

By night The entrance is lit, Q(3)G.4s12M and Fl.R. 2s1M. The central pier inside the harbour is lit, N corner F and S corner F.R.

Mooring

Details 389 berths in the Port Public. Maximum LOA 15 metres.

Berth Go on the *quai d'accueil* on the end of the central pier and report to the *capitainerie* for a berth. There are laid moorings tailed to the quay.

Shelter Good all-round shelter although strong SW winds can make some berths uncomfortable.

Authorities Customs. Port captain and marina staff. A charge is made.

Anchorage A yacht can anchor off to the W of the marina in 3–5 metre depths on sand and weed.

Facilities

Services Water and electricity at every berth. A shower and toilet block.

Fuel On the central pier.

Repairs A 10-ton crane and slipway. Some mechanical and engineering repairs. Some GRP and wood repairs. Electrical and electronic repairs. Sailmakers. Chandlers.

Provisions Good shopping for all provisions in the town. Ice available.

Eating out Numerous restaurants around the waterfront and in the town.

Other Post office. Banks. Hire cars. Buses around the coast.

General

Ste-Maxime is a quieter more sedate place than its sister, St-Tropez, across the other side of the gulf. In the summer the town centre is closed off and made into a pedestrian precinct so you can wander around the town without having to tackle the frenetic driving of the French. There is nothing much older than the late 19th century in the town, since it was not safe to build around the shores before this because of piracy, unless there was a garrison fort nearby to protect you as at St-Tropez. Like Grimaud and Cogolin, the old Ste-Maxime is set back from the shore so the inhabitants could see the pirates coming and get out of the way with their valuables.

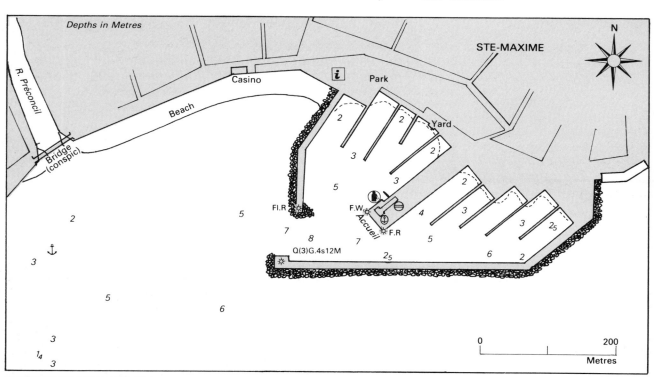

STE-MAXIME 43°18'·4N 6°38'·4E

Note There is a plan to build a motorboat marina some 400 metres up the Rivière Préconcil. Access will be restricted by the 4 metres air height under the bridge. The architect of the project, François Spiery, is the same architect who designed Grimaud, so motorboat owners can look forward to somewhere out of the ordinary to head for.

Calanque de Madrague

In settled weather a yacht can anchor off the beach in the large bay E of Ste-Maxime. Care needs to be taken of La Fourmigue, a rock just above water on the western side of the entrance. Anchor in 2–5 metres on sand and weed, good holding once through the weed. The anchorage is entirely open to the S.

PTE DES SARDINAUX

The point E of Calanque de Madrague with reefs and shoal water off it in the northern approaches to the Golfe de St-Tropez. See the introduction to Golfe de St-Tropez, page 000, for details.

SAN PEIRE-LES ISSAMBRES

Approach

The marina is 1½ miles N of *Les Sardinaux* beacon at the N end of Baie de Bougnon.

Conspicuous From the S the marina breakwater and the light structure on its end can be identified. A large white hotel immediately W of the marina is conspicuous. From the N the marina cannot be seen until around Pte de la Garonne. A beacon, YB, on the extremity of the reef off La Garonne, will be seen.

By night The harbour entrance is lit, Oc(2)WG.6s 11/8M and Fl(2)R.6s4M. The white sector of the sectored light shows the safe approach on 289°–356°.

Dangers

● Care needs to be taken of Sèche à l'Huile and Les Sardinaux off Pte des Sardinaux.

● Pte des Issambres: a reef with above and below-water rocks extends to the E for nearly 300 metres from the point.

● Pte de la Garonne: a reef runs out from the point with a beacon, YB, marking the end.

● With strong SE winds a swell heaps up at the entrance to the harbour and care must be taken in the entrance. With the *mistral* care also needs to be taken in the approach and entrance.

Mooring

Details 446 berths with 110 berths for visitors.

Berth at the *quai d'accueil* just inside the entrance and report to the *capitainerie* for a berth. There are laid moorings tailed to the quay.

San Peire-Les Issambres. The harbour and entrance looking SE.

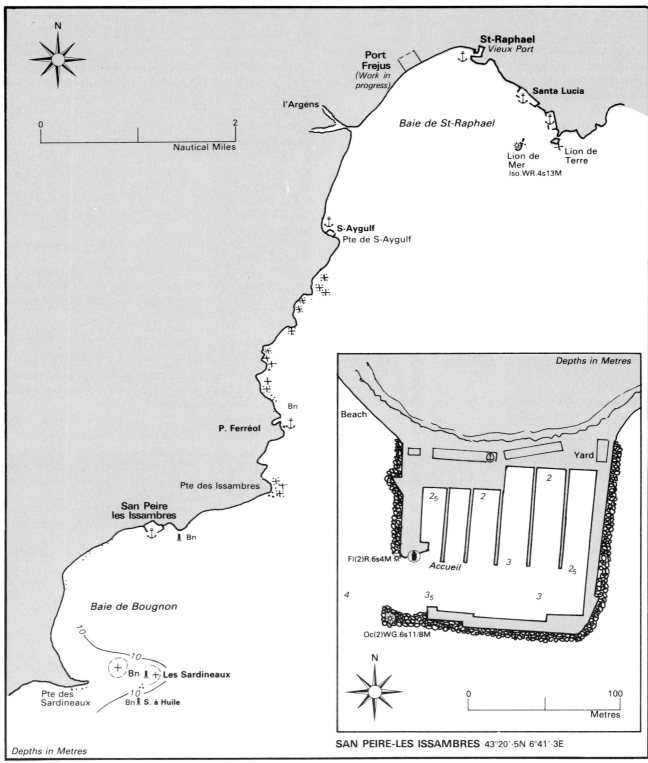

PTE DES SARDINEAUX TO ST-RAPHAEL

Shelter Good all-round shelter although strong south-easterlies make some berths uncomfortable.

Authorities Port captain and marina staff. A charge is made.

Anchorage In calm weather a yacht can anchor off to the W of the marina in 2–5 metres on sand and weed.

There is invariably a swell here making it uncomfortable and with any onshore winds the anchorage should be vacated.

Facilities

Services Water and electricity at every berth. A shower and toilet block.

Fuel On the quay at the entrance.

Repairs A 12-ton hoist and some covered storage afloat. Some mechanical repairs. Chandlers.

Provisions Some provisions at the marina in the summer. Ice available.

Eating out Several restaurants and bars nearby open in the summer.

General

The marina, built near the resort of San Peïre-sur-Mer-Les Issambres, to give it its full name, is set in a small bight on a wooded shore. Large pines make it a pleasant shaded spot in the summer with a good sandy beach nearby. It is a quiet and relaxed place compared to the Golfe de St-Tropez and would be more so were it not for the incessant traffic on the main coast road behind the marina.

PORT DE FERREOL

Approach

A very small harbour ¾ of a mile N of Pte des Issambres. Care needs to be taken of a reef running out from Pte de la Calle and of the rocky ledge on the N side of the entrance. With moderate to strong easterlies a swell piles up at the narrow entrance and entry should not be attempted.

Mooring

Details 136 berths with 12 berths for visitors.

Berth Go onto the pontoon at the entrance until allotted a berth.

Facilities

Water and electricity at or near all berths. Provisions and restaurants nearby.

General

The harbour, situated in a steep-sided inlet, is an attractive little place, but best visited in calm weather because of the difficulties entering and manoeuvring inside.

Port Tonic

A very small quay and basin just N of Férréol. It is reached by a buoyed channel and has 2–3 metres in the approach and outer part of the basin. Small motorboats are stored ashore and craned into the water for the day and out again at the end. Repair facilities ashore.

PORT DE ST-AYGULF

Approach

A small harbour tucked under the N side of Pte de St-Aygulf.

Conspicuous From the S the concentration of buildings on the wooded Pte de St-Aygulf can be identified. The wooded headland is the last rocky bit of coast before the flat sandy shores of Baie de St-Raphaël. From the S the harbour breakwaters cannot be seen until around Pte de St-Aygulf.

By night A Q.R light is exhibited on the outer breakwater.

Dangers
● Off Pte des Louvans, about ½ a mile S of Pte de St-Aygulf, a reef, Roche Portanier, extends out for about 300 metres from the coast.
● With moderate to strong easterlies there is a confused swell at the entrance that makes entry difficult.

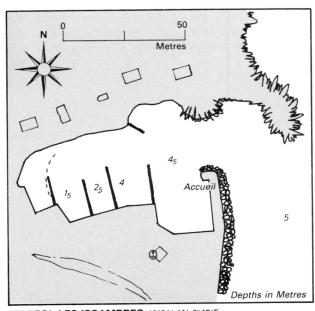

FERREOL-LES ISSAMBRES 43°21′·1N 6°43′E

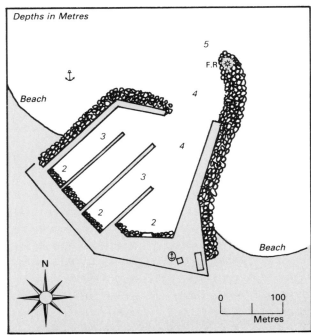

ST-AYGULF 43°23′·5N 6°43′·8E

Mooring

Details 229 berths with 24 berths for visitors. Maximum LOA 15 metres.

Berth on the *quai d'accueil* on the S breakwater and report to the *capitainerie* for a berth. There are laid moorings tailed to the quay.

Shelter Good shelter although strong easterlies could make the harbour uncomfortable.

Authorities Port captain. A charge is made.

Anchorage In calm weather a yacht could anchor off to the N of the harbour in 2–5 metres on sand, mud and weed. Open to southerlies and easterlies.

Facilities

Services Water and electricity at every berth. A shower and toilet block.

Fuel On the coast road behind the marina.

Repairs A 20-ton crane, but limited hard standing. Some mechanical repairs. Chandlers.

Provisions Most provisions can be obtained in the village.

Eating out Several restaurants and bars nearby.

General

The old fishing harbour has been converted into a pleasure-craft harbour with the addition of another breakwater. Development inland has been fairly discreet so that the place is not overwhelmed by large buildings.

FREJUS

A new marina under construction just under 1 mile SW of St-Raphaël Vieux Port.

Approach

The dome of the cathedral behind the Vieux Port at St-Raphaël will be seen and the new marina lies SW of here. Eventually the apartment blocks around the new marina are likely to be conspicuous.

Mooring

Details The marina is to have 750 berths with 50 berths for visitors. Maximum LOA 30 metres. Projected depths are 7 metres in the approaches, 3·5 metres in the outer harbour, and 2–3·5 metres in the inner basin.

Berth The *quai d'accueil* is just inside the entrance.

Facilities

All services are planned including water and electricity, a shower and toilet block, fuel, and a 60-ton travel-hoist.

General

The marina is under construction and there is still some way to go to its completion. What the marina will look like when it is finally completed remains to

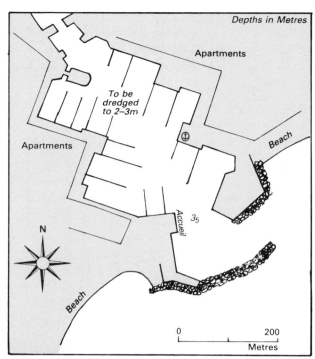

PORT DE FREJUS: PLANNED FINAL FORM *Work in progress* 1990 43°25′N 6°45′E

be seen. Eventually the developers want to have a marina which has large green expanses dotted about it and there are even plans to fill the old Roman port with water. The marina is open for business although not all ancillary features are installed.

ST-RAPHAEL VIEUX PORT

Approach

The old harbour of St-Raphaël lies close to the heart of the town.

Conspicuous Le Lion de Mer and Lion de Terre, the two jagged rocky islets on the eastern side of the entrance to Baie de St-Raphaël, are easily identified. Once into the bay the spire and dome of the cathedral can be distinguished amongst the high-rise buildings around the shore. Closer in the white light tower at the entrance to the Vieux Port is easily identified.

By night Use the light on Lion de Mer, Iso.WR.4s13M. The red sector covers Lion de Terre on 249°–275°. The entrance to the Vieux Port is lit, Fl(3)G.12s10M.

Dangers With the *mistral* entry can be difficult.

Mooring

Details 250 berths with 10 berths for visitors.

Berth where directed. The harbour is crowded in the summer and you will probably have to go to the marina at Santa Lucia.

Shelter Good all-round shelter.

Authorities Customs. Port captain. A charge is made.

The cathedral by the old harbour at St-Raphaël.

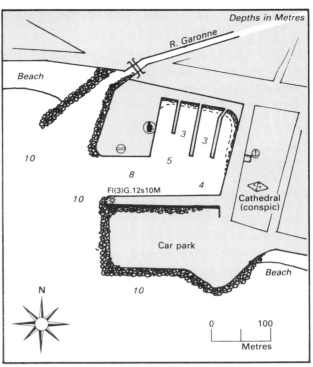

ST-RAPHAEL VIEUX PORT 43°25'·4N 6°45'·9E

Facilities

Services Water at every berth.

Fuel On the W quay.

Repairs A 10-ton crane, but limited hard standing.

Provisions Good shopping for all provisions nearby.

Eating out A wide selection of restaurants in the town.

Other Post office. Banks. Hire cars. Buses and trains along the coast.

General

Its a pity there is so little room in the Vieux Port as you are right in the heart of St-Raphaël and not in the suburbs as you are in the marina down the coast. There are not a lot of things you 'must' see, just a bustling town with lots of cafés and shop windows. You can take a peep into the cathedral and perhaps a longer visit to the Museum of Underwater Archaeology to the NE of the harbour. The museum has a collection of finds from the 5th century BC to the 5th century AD recovered from the sea floor in the vicinity and some interesting exhibits including one on the preservation of wood brought up from the depths.

St-Raphaël is a seaside extension of Fréjus which in Roman times was by the sea. The silt brought down by the river has over the centuries extended the shoreline seawards so that the Roman port which once held a hundred galleys in Augustus' time is now a mile from the sea. Fréjus was founded by Julius Caesar in 49 BC and by Augustus' time it had grown to a city with a population of 25,000 and was the most important garrison town on the coast. Little is left of the town. What was not buried under the silt or destroyed by Saracen pirates, was filled in by local farmers.

In the 19th century the eccentric Alphonse Karr, the pamphleteer, critic, one-time editor of *Le Figaro*, novelist, and wit, 'discovered' St-Raphaël and wrote urging his friends to come here: 'Leave Paris, come and plant your walking stick in my garden; the next day you will find that roses have grown from it'. Karr is attributed with the famous phrase that was to be used internationally to describe political promises: 'plus ça change, plus c'est la même chose'. A number of prominent writers, amongst them Alexandre Dumas and Guy de Maupassant, and the composer Hector Berlioz, joined Karr at St-Raphaël and built villas around the coast.

Although considered eccentric, Karr's friends thought he had gone over the top when he opened a flower shop and sent flowers around Europe by rail. Only when the business boomed and he could count royalty and heads of state amongst his customers was it seen that a prosperous new industry, that flourishes to this day, had arrived on the Côte d'Azur.

ST-RAPHAEL – PORT DE SANTA LUCIA

Approach

A large marina, with two separate basins and entrances, on the E side of Baie de St-Raphaël.

Conspicuous Once up to Lion de Mer and Lion de Terre, the high wall along the long outer breakwater of the marina will be seen. The light towers at the two entrances are easily identified.

By night The entrances are lit. Bassin Sud, Oc(2)WR.6s10/7M; the red sector covers Lion de Mer and Lion de Terre on 057°–082° and 130°–040°. Bassin Nord, Fl.G.4s9M and Fl.R.4s.

Note There is a deep-water passage between Lion de Mer and Lion de Terre. A YB buoy with a ▼ topmark and a YBY buoy with a ✗ topmark, mark the shoal water off Lion de Terre

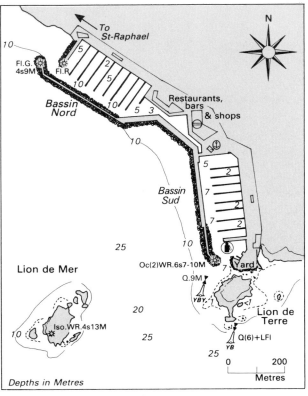

ST-RAPHAEL: SANTA LUCIA 43°24′·7N 6°46′·9E

Mooring

Details 1600 berths with two quays for visitors.

Berth at the *quai d'accueil* just inside the entrance (both Bassins Sud and Nord) or where directed. There are laid moorings tailed to the quay.

Shelter Excellent all-round shelter.

Authorities Customs. Port captain and marina staff. A charge is made.

Facilities

Services Water and electricity at every berth. Shower and toilet blocks in Bassins Sud and Nord.

Fuel On the quay near the entrance in Bassin Sud.

Repairs A 36-ton travel-hoist and a 10-ton hoist. Some covered storage. Mechanical and engineering repairs. GRP and wood repairs. Electrical and electronic repairs. Sailmakers (Hood Sails in Fréjus). Chandlers.

Provisions Most provisions can be obtained at the marina. Better shopping in St-Raphaël about 15 minutes walk away. Ice available.

Eating out Numerous restaurants and bars at the marina.

Other Exchange office. Hire cars. Buses and trains at St-Raphaël.

General

The marina on the outskirts of St-Raphaël is a quiet place under the apartments lining the coast. It is about 15 minutes walk from the town and its attractions, though the marina itself provides most facilities and has a pleasant 'boaty' feel to it despite its size.

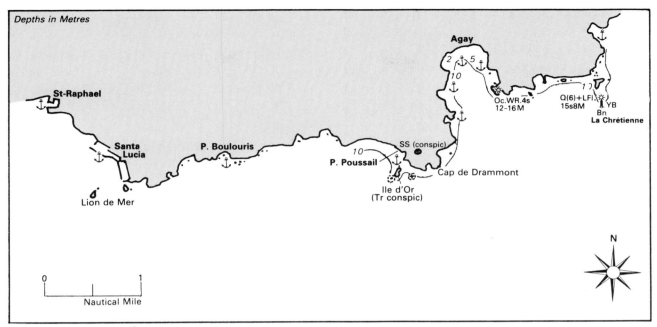

ST-RAPHAEL TO RADE D'AGAY

The Esterel

The Esterel massif along with the Maures massif to the west are two of the oldest groups of rocks, geologically speaking, in France. The red volcanic porphyry of the Esterel was pushed up before the Alpine massif to the east, but has been steadily eroded by wind and water so it is not as high as the Alpine massif. It is cut by gorges and eroded into weird and wonderful shapes. From seawards the gorges and valleys drop dramatically down into the sea and the coast is peppered with knobbly jagged rocks. The red porphyry gives a wonderful red glow to the whole landscape that contrasts vividly with the blue of the sea.

Until recently the Esterel was covered in pine and cork oak, but in 1964 a disastrous fire destroyed much of the forest. Reafforestation has proved difficult, not only because of the large area to be replanted, but also because of a disease that has blighted newly planted trees. Dense *maquis* now covers much of the ground and in the summer imparts that pungent oily aroma characteristic of the plants of the *maquis*.

There are a number of anchorages around the Esterel that can be used depending on the weather, but no real all-round shelter can be found until the harbours in Golfe de la Napoule.

Ile d'Or and its conspicuous tower in the western approaches to Rade d'Agay.

Boulouris In the bay immediately E of Pte des Cadeous there is a tiny private harbour. There are 1–2 metre depths inside, but berths are not normally available for visitors.

Le Poussail A small harbour on the coast opposite Ile d'Or. There are rarely berths available for visitors. However in calm weather or light easterlies a yacht can anchor off the harbour in 5–8 metres on mud and weed.

Ile d'Or A red craggy islet with a conspicuous square tower on it off Cap de Drammont. Cap de Drammont an old signal station is conspicuous on the summit.

RADE D'AGAY TO ILES LERINS

La Chrétienne beacon in the eastern approaches to Rade d'Agay.

RADE D'AGAY

Approach

A deep and wide bay entered between Cap de Drammont on the W and Pte de la Baumette on the E.

Conspicuous From the W the tower on Ile d'Or and the signal station on Cap de Drammont are conspicuous. From the E *La Chrétienne* beacon, the signal station on Cap de Drammont, and the lighthouse on Pte de la Baumette are conspicuous.

By night Use the light on *La Chrétienne* beacon, Q(6)+LFl.15s8M, and the light on Pte de la Baumette, Oc.WR.4s16/12M. The red sector of the light on Pte de la Baumette covers Ecueil des Vieilles on 260°–294°.

Mooring

Anchor near the head of the large bay in 5–10 metres. The bottom is mud and weed, good holding once through the weed. In SE winds yachts tend to cluster on the eastern side and in SW winds on the western side. With strong southerlies, particularly SE winds, the anchorage becomes untenable.

Note There is a small harbour in the NW corner, but it is mostly shallow and in any case crowded with local boats.

Facilities

There are restaurants and bars ashore and some provisions can be obtained.

General

The anchorage here has been used since ancient times and large numbers of Roman amphorae have been found on the seabed. In World War II Agay was the site chosen to land 20,000 troops of the 36th American division in August 1944, part of the Allied operation to liberate France. The event is commemorated by a memorial on Cap de Drammont. Nowadays it is the inhabitants of the villas around the shores and the naturists who flock to secluded coves and crevices who make use of Agay, apart from the not inconsiderable numbers of yachts in the summer.

Note There are plans to build a small marina of 350 berths at Agay, but to date nothing has been finalised.

Ecueil des Vieilles

A rocky islet and reef 1 mile E of Pte de la Baumette. A beacon, *La Chrétienne*, YB with a ▼ topmark, is sited at the extremity of the reef and shoal water. It is lit, Q(6)+LFl.15s8M. Although local yachts cut across inside the beacon, the prudent course is to keep to seawards of it.

Anse d'Anthéor

A cove just N of Ecueil des Vieilles. It affords some shelter from light westerlies, but is open to the S and E.

Cap Roux

A ragged red rock headland running down from the spectacular peaks of Pic du Cap Roux inland. A yacht can anchor on the N or S side of Cap Roux in calm weather, but with any onshore winds the anchorages should be vacated.

La Figueirette. The harbour and entrance looking SE. Note the distinctive light tower at the entrance.

FIGUEIRETTE-MIRAMAR

Approach

A small marina tucked under the steep slopes of Cap de l'Esquillon.

Conspicuous From the W, once around the craggy Cap Roux, the housing estate and small marina will be seen. A television transmitter on Pic de l'Ours inland is conspicuous. From the N the buoy off La Vaquette rock is easily identified. Closer in the breakwater and the sculptured white light tower at the entrance will be seen.

By night Use the light on *La Vaquette* buoy, Q(3)10s and the lights at the entrance, Fl(3)WG.12s13/10M and F.R. The white sector shows the safe approach on 275°–348°.

Dangers
• La Vaquette is a rock just awash some 500 metres off Cap de l'Esquillon. It is marked by a buoy, BYB with a ♦ topmark; it is lit, Q(3)10s. An underwater rock with 1·6 metres over it lies between La Vaquette and the coast.
• With strong easterlies a swell piles up at the entrance to the harbour making entry difficult.

Mooring

Details 235 berths with 47 berths for visitors. Maximum LOA 15 metres.

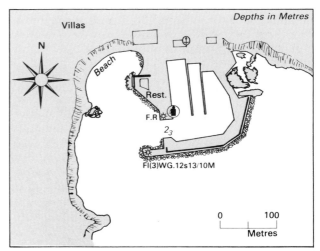

LA FIGUEIRETTE 43°29′N 6°56′E

Berth where directed or go onto the fuel berth and report to the *capitainerie* for a berth. There are laid moorings tailed to the quay.

Shelter Good all-round shelter though strong SE winds could make it uncomfortable.

Authorities Port captain and marina staff. A charge is made.

Facilities

Services Water and electricity at every berth. A shower and toilet block.

Fuel On the quay at the entrance.

Repairs An 8-ton crane, but limited hard standing. Some covered storage.

Eating out A restaurant at the marina and several around the shore.

General

The marina has been built with an associated holiday village on the slopes above the coastal cornice. It is a pleasant enough place with most of the villas built discreetly around the slopes.

LA GALERE

Approach

A small marina which is part of the up-market apartment complex behind it.

Conspicuous The marina with its striking honey comb apartments behind it is easily identified under Pte de la Galère. The white light tower at the entrance is conspicuous.

By night A night approach is not recommended although the entrance is lit. The buoy off Pte-St-Marc is lit, Fl(2)G.6s. The harbour entrance is lit, Q.R.7M and Iso.W.4s.

La Galère. Looking down on the harbour from the steep slopes behind.

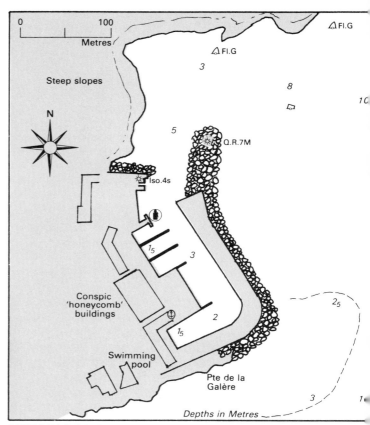

PORT DE LA GALERE 43°30′N 6°57′·4E

Dangers
- Care needs to be taken of La Vaquette rock.
- Roche du Port: an underwater rock with 0·8 metre over it lying about 300 metres off the coast ESE of Pte de l'Aiguille. It is unmarked.
- The channel into the harbour is marked by two green conical buoys. The buoy off Pte-St-Marc is lit: Fl(2)G.6s.
- With strong easterlies entry to the harbour is difficult and could be dangerous.

Mooring

Details 220 berths with 20 berths for visitors. Maximum LOA 12 metres.

Berth Where directed or go on the fuel quay and report to the *capitainerie* for a berth. There are laid moorings tailed to the quay.

Shelter Good all-round shelter.

Authorities Port captain and marina staff. A charge is made.

Facilities

Services Water and electricity at every berth. A shower and toilet block.

Fuel On the quay near the entrance.

Repairs A 10-ton crane, but limited hard standing. Chandlers.

Provisions Some provisions available. Ice available.

Eating out Several restaurants at the marina.

General

Like Figueirette-Miramar, La Galère is part of the apartment complex ashore, a select and architecturally ambitious project intended to blend into the jagged landscape of the Esterel. In this it succeeds tolerably well.

Golfe de la Napoule

Between the Esterel massif and the Iles de Lérins is the Golfe de la Napoule with the city of Cannes in the NE corner. From seawards the shoreline is built up from La Napoule right around to the tip of Pte de la Croisette E of Cannes. The wooded slopes of the Esterel in the SW and the wooded Iles de Lérins stand out prominently against the man-made skyline. In the summer the gulf is dotted with sails like white punctuation marks on a blue background. There are five large marinas around a 5 mile stretch of coast, as well as several smaller harbours; over 6000 yacht berths by my reckoning in the Golfe de la Napoule alone.

Pte de l'Aiguille

The craggy point that drops precipitously down to the sea at the SW corner of the gulf. The bight on the N side of the point is a popular anchorage in the summer. Anchor in 10–15 metres as close to the beach as possible. The bottom comes up quickly from 10 metres. The bottom is mud and weed, poor holding until through the thick weed. There is limited shelter from southerlies although some swell tends to creep around the point. Provisions and restaurants in Théoule-sur-Mer.

THÉOULE-SUR-MER

Approach

A small harbour in the SW corner of the gulf.

Conspicuous The marina and viaduct at La Rague is easily identified and closer in the breakwater of Théoule-sur-Mer will be seen.

By night The entrance is lit, Oc(2)WR.6s9/6M. The white sector shows the safe approach to the harbour on 335°–265°.

Mooring

Details 183 berths. Maximum LOA 13 metres.

Berth where directed or on the fuel quay and report to the *capitainerie* for a berth.

Shelter Good shelter although strong NE winds might make some berths uncomfortable.

Authorities Port captain. A charge is made.

Facilities

Services Water and electricity at every berth. A shower and toilet block.

Fuel On the quay at the entrance.

Repairs A 3-ton crane and a slipway, but limited hard standing. Chandlers.

Provisions Good shopping for provisions in the village.

Eating out Numerous restaurants around the waterfront.

Other Post office. Bank. Buses along the coast.

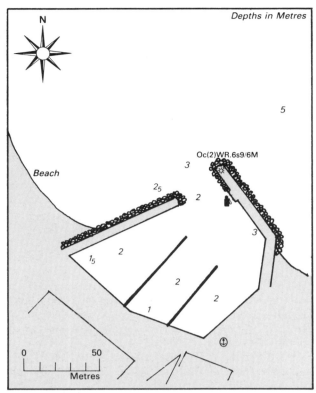

THEOULE-SUR-MER 43°30'·5N 6°56'·4E

General

The former little fishing village of Théoule is now a select resort with some up-market and rather lovely villas around the steep slopes. If you can get a berth in the small harbour, it is one of the most pleasant spots to be in the gulf, a quiet oasis away from the noise of the bigger and more lively resorts.

LA RAGUE

Approach

Conspicuous The railway viaduct (six arches) that runs over the marina is conspicuous. On the slopes just N of the harbour a château-like building is also conspicuous. Closer in the marina breakwater and the white light tower at the entrance are easily identified.

Note The marina at Mandelieu-La Napoule just N of La Rague will also be seen in the approach, though it is not easily confused with La Rague.

By night The entrance is lit, Iso.G.4s10M and Fl.R.2s2M.

Mooring

Details 526 berths with 130 berths for visitors. Maximum LOA 30 metres.

Berth on the *quai d'accueil* on the end of the central pier and report to the *capitainerie* for a berth. There are laid moorings tailed to the quay.

Shelter Excellent all-round shelter.

Authorities Port captain and marina staff. A charge is made.

Facilities

Services Water and electricity at every berth. A shower and toilet block.

Fuel On the quay at the entrance.

Repairs A 30 ton travel-hoist. Some covered storage. Mechanical and engineering repairs. GRP and wood repairs. Chandlers.

Provisions Some provisions available at the marina. Better shopping in La Napoule nearby. Ice available.

Eating out Several restaurants in the marina.

Other Post office and banks in La Napoule. Hire cars. Buses to Cannes.

General

Not a lot goes on in La Rague apart from boats and messing about in boats. It is about 15 minutes walk to La Napoule and the Henry Clews Museum in the restored castle on the water's edge.

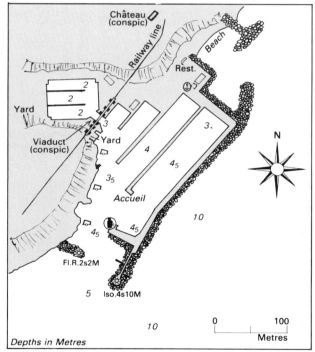

LA RAGUE 43°31'N 6°56'·4E

Mandelieu-La Napoule. The harbour and entrance looking NW.

MANDELIEU-LA NAPOULE

Approach

The marina is situated immediately N of La Rague.

Conspicuous The conical peak of Piton de San Peyré just inland from the marina stands out well. At the NE end of the marina a group of cream and white apartment blocks, the beginning of the chain of buildings extending around to Cannes, is conspicuous. Closer in the castle at the entrance is conspicuous.

By night The entrance is lit, Fl(3)G.12s10M and Oc(2)R.6s2M. In the summer the castle is floodlit and shows up well.

Note A line of buoys to port marks the channel into the harbour.

Mooring

Details 1130 berths with 200 berths for visitors in the Port Public. Maximum LOA 35 metres.

Berth On the *quai d'accueil* on the pier just inside the entrance and report to the *capitainerie* for a berth. There are laid moorings tailed to the quay.

Shelter Excellent all-round shelter.

Authorities Port captain and marina staff. A charge is made.

Facilities

Services Water and electricity (220 and 380v) at every berth. A shower and toilet block.

Fuel On the quay close to the *capitainerie*.

Repairs A 70-ton travel-hoist and 8-ton crane. Mechanical and engineering repairs. GRP and wood repairs. Electrical and electronic repairs. Sailmakers. Chandlers.

Provisions Some provisions available in the marina and better shopping in La Napoule. Ice available.

Eating out Restaurants in the marina and others around the waterfront.

Other Post office. Banks. Hire cars. Buses and trains along the coast.

General

La Napoule is the seaside development of the down-to-earth working town of Mandelieu to the NW of the marina. The attraction at Mandelieu-La Napoule is the restored 14th-century castle. When Henry Clews, the rich son of a New York banker, first set eyes on the ruined towers, he fell in love with the place and from 1919 until his death in 1937 he rebuilt it, though not without adding some of his own Disney-like touches. The castle is now a mixture of Romanesque, Gothic and Henry Clews.

In the grounds and rooms of the castle are Henry Clews' own sculptures, many of which seem to have been inspired by medieval sources. The banker's son has been called one of America's best sculptors and though there is no doubt about his technical abilities, the sculptures are perhaps too technically perfect and

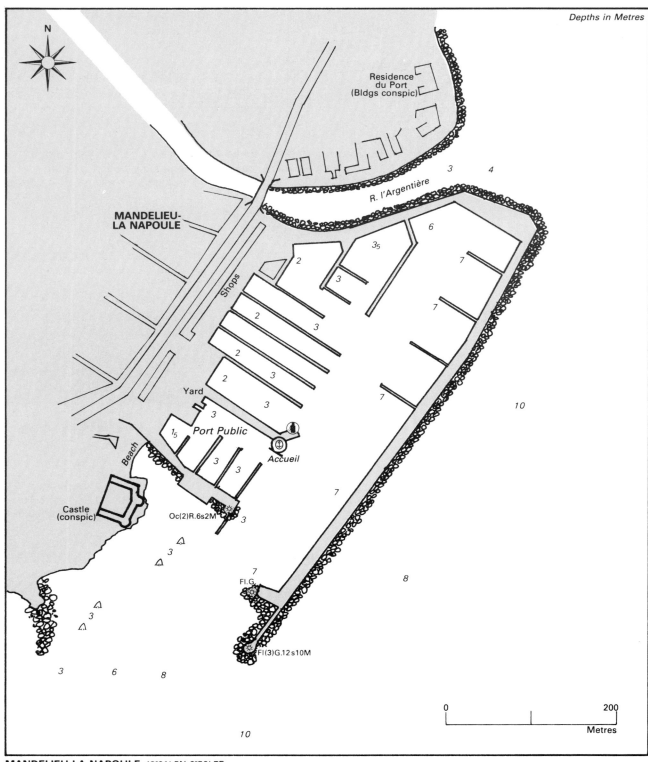

N

Residence
du Port
(Bldgs conspic)

R. l'Argentière

3   4

MANDELIEU-
LA NAPOULE

Shops

2

6

3₅

2

7

3

2

7

3

2

3

7

Yard

2

3

10

3

Port Public

1₅

Accueil

3   3

7

Beach

Castle
(conspic)

Oc(2)R.6s2M

3

3

7
Fl.G.

3

8

3

3

Fl(3)G.12s10M

3   6   8

10

0   200

Metres

MANDELIEU-LA NAPOULE 43°31'·5N 6°56'·7E

lack something. Vitality? The capacity to indelibly impress one? Have a look at them and make up your own mind. The Henry Clews Museum is open to the public and is well worth a visit, as much for the beautifully laid out gardens and the chance to wander around the castle, as for Henry Clews' sculptures.

CANNES MARINA

Not to be confused with Port de Cannes, this marina is primarily a motorboat harbour lying inland up the Rivière la Siagne. Access to this marina is restricted not only by the depths in the river, but also by the air height under the bridges across it. Least depth, 1·5 metres. Maximum air height, 4 metres.

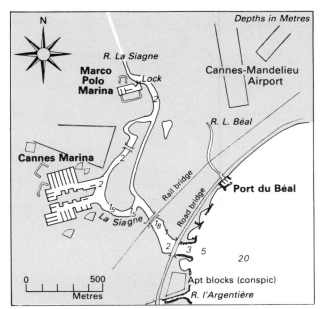

CANNES MARINA AND MARINA MARCO POLO
43°32'·1N 6°56'·3E (Cannes Marina)

Approach

The entrance to the Rivière la Siagne lies approximately 300 metres N of the marina at Mandelieu-La Napoule on the N side of the cream and white apartment blocks conspicuous in the approach to Mandelieu-La Napoule. A road bridge crosses the river right at the entrance with a maximum air height of 4 metres. From the road bridge proceed up the river to the rail bridge and pass under the eastern arch. Depths here are around 1·8 metres dropping to 1·5 metres in places after the bridge. The river forks with the port-hand channel leading to Cannes Marina.

Caution There are 3 metre depths in the entrance dropping to 2 metres on the other side of the road bridge. With moderate or strong onshore winds seas break at the entrance and entry should not be attempted.

Note There is a speed limit of 3 knots in the river and in the marina.

Mooring

Details 1700 berths with visitors' berths. Maximum LOA 12 metres.

Berth on the *quai d'accueil* on the W side of the central pier and report to the *capitainerie*. There are laid moorings tailed to the quay.

Authorities Port captain and marina staff. A charge is made.

Facilities

Services Water and electricity at every berth. A shower and toilet block.

Fuel None in the harbour. Go to Mandelieu-La Napoule.

Repairs A 5-ton crane and slipways. Some mechanical repairs. GRP and wood repairs in the yard nearby. Chandlers.

Provisions Some provisions available locally.
Eating out Several restaurants nearby.

General

The marina is part of the vast apartment complex around it and though the river lends charm to the place, the apartments do not.

Marina Marco Polo

A small marina approximately half a mile upstream of Cannes Marina. A lock regulates entry to the basin on the W bank of the river. Like Cannes Marina, the basin here is part of an apartment complex.

Port Inland

A large basin just upstream from Marina Marco Polo in the old La Siagne canal. There are berths for 1000 boats up to a maximum LOA of 9 metres. Water and electricity at all berths. Good facilities for hauling and repairs ashore.

Port du Béal

A small harbour immediately E of the entrance to the Rivière la Siagne. The harbour sits at the entrance to the Rivière le Béal which has a road bridge across it. There are 1·5–2 metre depths in the harbour though it is liable to silting from the river running into it. The approach to the harbour is difficult in onshore winds. Most of the berths are occupied by local boats and there is rarely space for visitors.

PORT DE CANNES

Approach

The harbour sits in the NE corner of the gulf. From the W the Iles de Lérins just SE of the harbour stand out as, unlike the rest of the coast, they are not built upon.

Conspicuous The white dome of the observatory on the slopes behind Cannes and the tower on the summit of the ridge behind are conspicuous. Closer in the harbour breakwater with the old lighthouse on the elbow and a higher square white light tower on the end of the outer breakwater are conspicuous. At the entrance *Le Sécant* beacon will be seen.

By night The entrance is lit, VQ(3)R.2s8M and *Le Sécant* beacon, Oc(3)G.12s4M.

Note Sailing craft do not have automatic right of way over power craft in the approaches to the port. A good lookout should be kept for the tripper boats running to Iles de Lérin which charge in and out of the harbour, despite a 3 knot speed limit.

Mooring

Details 802 berths with 200 berths for visitors. Maximum LOA 60 metres.

Port de Cannes.

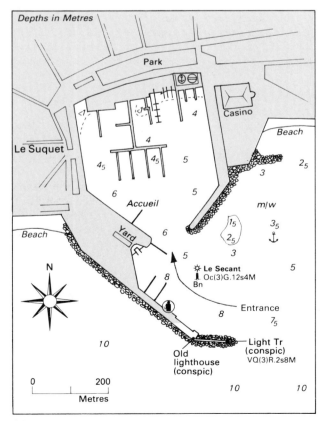

Depths in Metres

Park

Casino

Beach

Le Suquet

Accueil

m/w

Beach

Yard

N

☆ **Le Secant**
⚓ Oc(3)G.12s4M
Bn

Entrance

Light Tr
(conspic)
VQ(3)R.2s8M

Old
lighthouse
(conspic)

0   200
Metres

CANNES 43°32′N 7°01′E

Berth on the *quai d'accueil* just inside the inner entrance and report to the *capitainerie* for a berth. There are laid moorings tailed to the quay or to buoys.

Shelter Good shelter although strong SE winds can make some berths uncomfortable.

Authorities Customs. Port captain and marina staff. A charge is made.

Anchorage A yacht can anchor to the N of the entrance in 2·5–5 metres. Care needs to be taken of a shoal patch with 1·5 metres least depth approximately 100 metres E of the extremity of the northern breakwater. The bottom is mud and weed, reasonable holding once through the weed. With even light southerlies the anchorage is very rolly.

Facilities

Services Water and electricity (220 and 380v) at every berth. A shower and toilet block.

Fuel On the quay near the entrance.

Repairs A 45-ton travel-hoist and slipways up to 60 tons. Mechanical and engineering repairs. GRP and wood repairs. Electrical and electronic repairs. Sailmakers. Chandlers.

Provisions Good shopping for all provisions and a market nearby. Ice available.

Eating out A wide choice of restaurants nearby from the humble to the chic and expensive.

Other Post office. Banks. Hire cars. Buses and trains along the coast. Tripper boats to Iles de Lérins.

General

The Ligurians and the Romans were here, the Abbots of Lérins built a tower to protect the inhabitants, the Templars and Knights of St John strengthened the defences, but Cannes fortunes really started when Lord Brougham was stranded here in 1834. Lord Brougham, the Lord Chancellor of England, was on his way to the Italian Riviera with his sick daughter when he was turned back at the River Var because of a cholera epidemic. The House of Savoy was stopping all travellers from France in an attempt to stop the epidemic from reaching Italy and so Lord Brougham was forced to wait in a small inn at Cannes. The charms of the small fishing village grew on him and he decided he didn't need to travel on to the Riviera at all – he would build a villa here in Cannes.

Lord Brougham did just that, building the *Villa Eleonore Louise*, named after his daughter who sadly died before it was finished. Cannes soon became his second home as Patrick Howarth describes in *When The Riviera Was Ours*: 'He regularly spent his winters there, writing books on politics, philosophy and history, and analysing the habits of bees. He found that in Cannes there were only three days out of 111 on which he could not carry out certain experiments with light which interested him, whereas at Brougham Hall in Westmorland at the same time of year, there were only about three days out of 111 on which he could.' Lord Brougham persuaded a number of his friends to move to Cannes and build villas there so that by the time he died in 1868 the population had increased from 3000 to 10,000.

One of the important changes to Cannes that Lord Brougham was responsible for was the construction of the harbour. He was a good friend of King Louis-Philippe and in 1840 persuaded the king to provide funds for its construction. In 1859 a society for organising yachting regattas was formed, naturally enough with Lord Brougham as president, and in 1860 the first regatta was held. Cannes was given, rather patronisingly, the title of the 'Cowes of the Mediterranean' and became a popular port of call for yachts cruising the Mediterranean. However the harbour was still not entirely safe. Guy de Maupassant cruising in his beloved *Le Bel-Ami* called Cannes '... a dangerous port, unsheltered... where all vessels are in peril'. After modifications to the harbour in 1904, Cannes was a safer harbour and Lord Cavan after a lengthy Mediterranean cruise gave it the thumbs up in his *With the Yacht, Camera, and Cycle in the Mediterranean*: 'This harbour has been greatly improved during the last three or four years. Only four years ago, when I stayed there, it was not uncommon to find yachts moored with their sterns on the mole, laying side by side with one, or possibly two colliers discharging coal. All this has been greatly improved; yachts now have their separate berths, as the mole has been considerably extended.' A new mole built in 1904 was named the Jetée Albert-Edouard in honour of the Prince of Wales, a regular visitor to Cannes.

The harbour neatly divides Cannes into two. On the west is the Cannes of the Cannois, and to the east the English enclave with large villas and wide boulevards. By the harbour is the large winter casino, an elegant building not built without some opposition by the resident English clergy. The opening of the summer casino at the end of Pte de la Croisette in 1929 heralded a newer, brasher era for Cannes, the very name of it, Palm Beach, was designed to attract rich American clientele. The Wall Street crash dented early optimism, but by the mid-1930s rich Americans were spending again. In 1939 the first Cannes film festival had to be abandoned suddenly with the onset of World War II and it was not until 1947 that the festival was held again and quickly grew to become the premier film festival in Europe. Held in May every year, if you are a committed film buff, then Cannes is the place to be.

Today Cannes is a crowded resort, its streets choked with traffic and its hotels full to overflowing. I have ambivalent feelings towards the place. In the harbour you are at least in the centre of things with the old quarter nearby. But stray too far and you will be exhausted by the crowds, asphyxiated by the exhaust fumes of the cars, and unless you choose carefully, appalled by the food passed off as French cuisine. Cannes is a city where you have to pick and choose what you do and where you go with care.

GRASSE

Up in the hills behind Cannes sits Grasse, a small hill town best known for its perfume industry. Every year when the wild mimosa flowers in the hills around Grasse, it is cut and packed off to the perfume houses for the extraction of its essential oils. Not only mimosa, but jasmine, roses, and orange blossom are also collected to extract the oils, the neroli, combined according to secret formulas to produce those miniature bottles which cost so much.

Some of the cost can be explained by what goes on in Grasse. It takes around a ton of blossoms to produce one kilogram of neroli. When the perfume houses have added other exotic ingredients which might include musk from Tibetan deer, ambergris, patchouli oil from the East Indies, ginger from India, vanilla pods, sandalwood from the Pacific Islands, then the cost of those little bottles goes up and up. And then there is all that advertising ....

The perfume industry in Grasse began in the 16th century when perfumed gloves became fashionable. Prior to this the town was well known for producing quality leather goods and especially gloves. Perfumes for the gloves were produced from the wildflowers that grow abundantly in the vicinity, particularly mimosa, and the famous names in the perfume industry were gradually built up so that by the 18th and early 19th century the perfume houses of today were well established. In the early days perfumes were produced by distillation or *enfleurage*. Distillation involves simply boiling the flowers up in water and when the steam is condensed, the aromatic oils and water separate. The oils can then be carefully poured off. *Enfleurage* involves laying the flowers on a layer of grease which absorbs the aromatic oils. The oils are then removed from the grease by washing with alcohol. Modern methods employ fractional distillation at different temperatures using a variety of organic solvents to extract the oils.

You can visit a number of the perfume houses in Grasse: Fragonard in Boulevard Fragonard, Galimard in Route Cannes, and Moulinard in Boulevard Victor Hugo. Most of the houses have organised tours which show you exhibits of the old as well as the new methods of extracting the oils. And of course at the end of the tour you have the opportunity to buy a sample.

PORT PIERRE-CANTO

Approach

A marina taking the overflow from Cannes situated just over half a mile E of the old harbour.

Conspicuous The large white building of the Palm Beach casino on Pte de la Croisette is conspicuous. Closer in the outer breakwaters and the white light tower at the entrance are easily recognised.

By night The entrance is lit, Oc.WG.4s13/8M and Oc(2)R.6s6M. The white sector of the sectored light shows the safe approach to the harbour on 010°–100°.

Warning Entry to the harbour can be difficult in a *mistral* which sends a swell into the entrance. When a *mistral* is blowing an inflatable air barrier may be put across the entrance to reduce the amount of swell entering the Avant Port, and a yacht must wait for this to be opened.

Mooring

Details 650 berths with 100 berths for visitors. Maximum LOA 70 metres.

Berth at the *quai d'accueil* just inside the entrance and report to the *capitainerie* for a berth. There are laid moorings tailed to the quay. Very large yachts use their own anchors in the Avant Port.

Shelter Good shelter except for the Avant Port which can be very uncomfortable in a strong *mistral*. An air barrier is used to lessen the effects of the *mistral*.

Authorities Customs. Port captain and marina staff. A charge is made.

Facilities

Services Water and electricity (220 and 380v) at all berths. Mail service. A shower and toilet block.

Fuel On the quay at the entrance to the inner harbour.

Repairs A 70-ton travel-hoist, 15-ton and 6-ton cranes, and a slipway. Mechanical and engineering repairs. GRP and wood repairs. Electrical and electronic repairs. Sailmakers. Chandlers.

Provisions Most provisions are available in the marina, otherwise there is better shopping in Cannes itself. Ice available.

Port Pierre Canto. The upmarket marina, described as 'le plus luxueux' on the coast, just around from the more chaotic Port de Cannes.

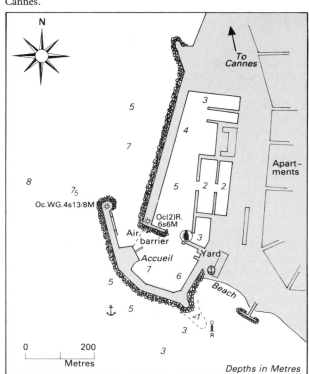

PIERRE-CANTO 43°32'·5N 7°02'E

Eating out Several restaurants and bars in the marina.

Other Post office and banks in Cannes. Hire cars.

General

The marina is very much an up-market place compared to the more work-a-day harbour at Cannes itself. It has the more placid air of the suburbs, away from the hurly-burly of the *centre-ville*, and Palm Beach casino is a short walk away should you feel like a flutter. It is about 15 minutes pleasant walk around the waterfront to Cannes if you don't happen to have a car waiting for you.

Port du Palm Beach. The very small and shallow harbour off the conspicuous Palm Beach casino.

Port du Palm Beach

A small harbour immediately S of Port Pierre Canto. There are only 1–2 metre depths in the harbour. Most berths are occupied by local boats and there is rarely a berth free for visiting yachts. In calm weather a small yacht can anchor off between Pierre Canto and Palm Beach in 2–3 metres. Care needs to be taken of an underwater obstruction, marked by a red can buoy, off the elbow of the breakwater of Pierre Canto.

Port de Mouré-Rouge

A small harbour on the E side of Pte de la Croisette. There are 2 metre depths at the entrance, but only 1–1·5 metre depths inside. It is crammed full of local boats.

Note There are plans to construct a 500-berth marina here though at the time of writing nothing has been finalised.

Iles de Lérins

Two low islands connected by shoal water to Pte de la Croisette. Both Ile Ste-Marguerite and Ile St-Honorat have a number of anchorages around them depending on the wind and sea. Between the two islands and between Ile Ste-Marguerite and Pte de la Croisette there are channels that can be used by yachts drawing 2·5–3 metres. Although at first sight the channels look terrifyingly shallow, in the summer the numerous local yachts using these short-cuts soon inspires confidence in the depths available.

The Passages

● Between Ile Ste-Marguerite and Pte de la Croisette: From the W head on a course of between 110°–130° for Fort Royal. There are least depths of 3·5–4 metres on a course of 120° on Fort Royal. Off Fort Royal head due E. From the E keep about 250 metres off the island and once Fort Royal is abeam change course to 290°–310°.

● Between Ile Ste-Marguerite and Ile St-Honorat: From W and E keep approximately 300 metres off Ile Ste-Marguerite. The dangers are all to the S of this channel.

ILE STE-MARGUERITE

The larger of the two islands. From the W Fort Royal, a château-like fort on the NW corner is conspicuous. At the NW end a beacon, YBY with a Ⅹ topmark, marks the extremity of the reef running out from Pte Bataignier. At the E end of the island there is the low-lying Ile de la Tradelière which can be difficult to identify until close to it.

Anchorages

Port de Ste-Marguerite This is not really a harbour, but an anchorage off the jetties used by the tripper

207

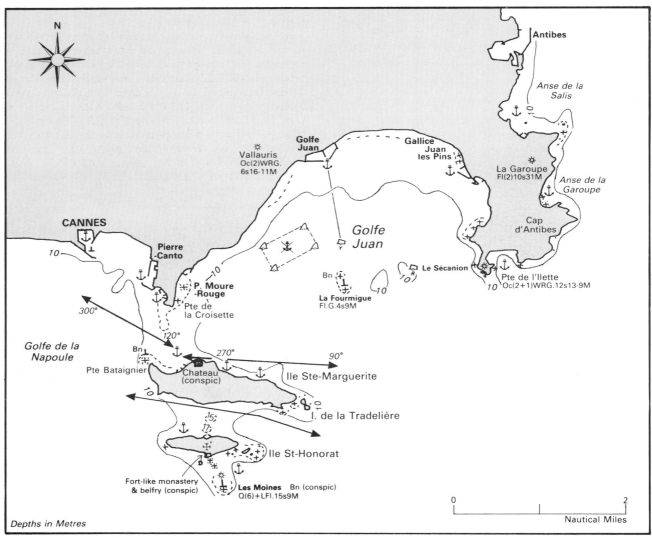

CANNES TO ANTIBES

Ile Ste-Marguerite. Fort Royal and *Bataignier* beacon looking E towards the passage between Ile Ste-Marguerite and the coast.

boats from Cannes. A yacht should not attempt to go alongside these jetties as they are constantly in use by the tripper boats. There are mostly depths of less than 2 metres off the jetties in any case. Anchor off the jetties or to the E of them in 3–5 metres on mud and weed. Keep well clear of the jetties to allow the tripper boats room to manoeuvre. The anchorage is sheltered from SW–SE, but open to the NW–NE. Ashore there is a restaurant and snack bar.

North anchorage To the E of Fort Royal there is a wide bight affording good shelter from southerlies and some shelter from light westerlies. Anchor in 3–10 metres tucked in as close to the island as possible. There are good depths until very close to. The bottom is sand, mud and thick weed, good holding once through the weed. The anchorage is remarkably peaceful in the evening for all its proximity to the hubbub of Cannes, though it is crowded in the daytime with local yachts.

Ile de la Tradelière In calm weather or light NW winds a yacht can anchor between Ile de la Tradelière and Pte Carbonel. Anchor in 4–6 metres on sand, rock and weed, uncertain holding. The anchorage is popular with sub-aqua divers.

South anchorages In calm weather a yacht can anchor off the S side of Ile Ste-Marguerite where convenient. Anchor in 3–10 metres on sand, rock and weed.

FORT ROYAL

Ile Ste-Marguerite is dominated by the fort on its north side. Not long after it was built in the 17th century by Richelieu, the fort received its most famous prisoner, the 'Man in the Iron Mask'. In fact the mask was not iron, but velvet, though this does not detract one bit from the mystery of who he was. His identity has never been established for sure, but there have been numerous theories. Among the popular candidates are the following: that he was the illegitimate son of Louis XIV; Louis' twin brother born several hours after him; a minister of the Duke of Mantua who attempted to trick the king in negotiations over Piedmont; an accomplice of Madame de Brinvilliers, a notorious poisoner; and a black sheep of the nobility. There are a number of other candidates who are less likely, but more intriguing. One is that he was the doctor who performed the autopsy on Louis XIII and found him incapable of producing offspring, the doctor's son indiscreetly releasing the state secret and being imprisoned for his indiscretion. Another tale tells of a son sired by the 'Man in the Iron Mask' and a woman prisoner, the son immediately being whisked away to Corsica to foster parents. To be 'entrusted' in French is 'remis de bonne part', in Italian it is 'di buona parte', and so the tenuous argument goes, the child was the great-grandfather of Bonaparte.

The 'Man in the Iron Mask' ended his years in the Bastille. M. de St-Mars, the governor of Fort Royal whose special charge was the mysterious prisoner, didn't find life very entertaining on the island and eventually wrangled the post of Governor of the Bastille in 1698. His prisoner went with him and spent his final years there until he died in 1703. In the 19th century Marshal Bazaine, the disagreeable general who surrendered Metz in the Franco-Prussian War was imprisoned here from 1873–74. He escaped by bribing the guards, though the authorities attempted a cover-up by saying he had climbed out the window and down a rope – not the cleverest cover-up since it was common knowledge that the corpulent Marshal would have the greatest difficulty getting his overweight figure through a window.

The fort and the cells, including the rather gloomy one the 'Man in the Iron Mask' is said to have inhabited, are open to the public. There is also a small museum and aquarium within the fort.

ILE ST-HONORAT

The smaller of the two islands with the fortress-like monastery of St-Honorat on its southern side. The monastery is conspicuous from a considerable distance off when approaching the islands from the W or E. The spire of the newer church of the monastery is also conspicuous. Off the S side of the island a reef runs out for some 800 metres. A beacon, Les Moines, YB with a ⚑ topmark, near the extremity of the reef is easily identified. It is lit, Q(6)+LFl.15s9M. Off the eastern end of the island there is a scattered group of rocks and a low islet, Ile St-Féréol.

Anchorages

Port aux Moines (Port de St-Honorat) A miniature harbour on the N side of Ile St-Honorat. There are 2·5 metre depths in the entrance, but mostly 1·5 metre and less depths inside. The harbour is used by the tripper boats running from Cannes, and yachts normally anchor off outside. Despite the fact that cables are shown running across the channel between Ile Ste-Marguerite and Ile St-Honorat, local yachts anchor everywhere. Anchor in 4–8 metres on mud and weed, reasonable holding once through the weed. The anchorage is open to the W and E and is tenable in light southerlies only. Despite being so exposed it is a popular spot in the summer and the channel between the two islands bristles with masts.

Ile St Féréol Local yachts anchor tucked under the S end of Ile St Féréol. In calm weather feel your way carefully into here and anchor where convenient. The water is wonderfully clear and the bottom looks sandy with some rock.

Roches d'Ilon A group of rocks close off the S side of the island. In calm weather local yachts anchor NW of the rocks.

THE MONASTERY

In the 4th century St-Honorat, a founding father of French monasticism, decided to settle on the tiny island of Lerina to live a life of solitude. It proved to be a fruitless exercise as his popularity was such that his followers soon discovered where he was and joined him on the island. Relenting, he founded a monastery, and in time it came to be one of the most powerful and influential in the land. It produced some twenty saints and a staggering 600 bishops. One of the saints was St Patrick who studied at the monastery for nine years before embarking on the task of converting the heathen Irish and founding numerous monasteries in Ireland.

In its heyday the monastery's territory spread for a considerable distance along the mainland coast and in the 7th century included a hundred large estates and priories. The fortified tower that is so conspicuous from seaward was built in 1073 by Aldebert, Abbot of Lérins, as a defence against the increasing raids by Saracens. The tower now has a flight of steps up to the door, but was originally reached by a ladder that

Ile St-Honorat. The fortified abbey and church looking NW.

Fort Royal from the anchorage on the N side of Ile Ste-Marguerite. It was here that the mysterious Man in the Iron Mask was imprisoned from 1687 to 1698.

was drawn up into the tower. The monastery declined through the Middle Ages from attacks by Saracen pirates and Genoese adventurers. In the 7th century there were 4000 monks in residence on the island. By the end of the Middle Ages there were less than a thousand and by 1788 only four monks remained and the monastery was closed. After the French Revolution it was bought by a *Comédie Française* actress, but in 1859 it was reconsecrated and 10 years later was taken over by the Cistercian order.

Apart from the fortified tower, most of the other original buildings have been swallowed up in the 19th century rebuilding the Cistercians undertook. The entire island still belongs to the Cistercian order and monks still live here. Numerous signs remind visitors that they should dress and behave appropriately. In the day the island is a favourite excursion spot for the Cannois and visitors to Cannes, but after the last tripper boat has departed a remarkable calm descends on the island. It almost feels like holy ground again.

Note Around Ile Ste-Marguerite and Ile St-Honorat there are boats sailing, puttering along under engine, towing water-skiers, fishing, and everywhere you look boats at anchor. Marvellously at day's end most of these boats return to one of the nearby marinas and where there were perhaps forty or fifty boats, by dusk there will be five or ten.

Golfe Juan

The small gulf, really a large bay, hemmed in by Pte de la Croisette and Cap d'Antibes. On the western side the Iles de Lérins protect the gulf from the worst of the swell from the W–SW. Golfe Juan is peppered with rocks and shoal patches and is fringed by shoal water around the coast.

La Fourmigue A rock almost dead in the middle of Golfe Juan with a conspicuous green beacon with a ▲ topmark and Fl.G.4s9M light. The above-water rock is fringed by a reef running approximately N and S of the rock.

Le Sécanion A reef with 5 metres least depth over it approximately ¾ of a mile E of La Fourmigue. It is marked by a red buoy with a ■ topmark. Between La Fourmigue and Le Sécanion there is a shoal patch with 6 metres least depth over it.

Wreck and sewerage outfall buoy Half a mile N of La Fourmigue there is a wreck and sewerage outfall marked by a yellow buoy.

Marine reserve On the western side of the gulf there is an area marked by four yellow buoys with X topmarks where fishing and anchoring are prohibited.

PORT DE GOLFE-JUAN

Approach

Conspicuous The coast right around Golfe Juan is covered with high buildings making it difficult to detect just where the harbour is from the distance.

The beacon on La Fourmigue is conspicuous and closer in the harbour breakwaters and a white light tower at the entrance will be seen.

By night The light at Vallauris half a mile W of Port de Golfe-Juan shows the two safe passages into the gulf on either side of La Fourmigue: Oc(2)WRG.6s 16-11M. The red sector covers La Fourmigue and Le Sécanion over 309°–336°; the white sectors show the safe approach on 305°–309° and 336°–342°. The light on Pte de l'Ilette shows the red sector over Les Moines and La Fourmigue and Le Sécanion: Oc(2+1)WRG.12s13-9M. Red sectors over 045°–056° and 070°–090°. La Fourmigue is lit, Fl.G.4s9M. The harbour entrance is lit, Iso.R.4s10M and Iso.G.4s.

Dangers
● See Golfe Juan and Iles de Lérins for details on off-lying rocks and reefs.
● In strong SE winds a swell piles up at the entrance and can make entry difficult.

Note While work is in progress on the new basin to the E care should be taken at the entrance. In the future it is likely the lights at the entrance will be changed.

Mooring

Details 847 berths with 299 berths for visitors. Maximum LOA 22 metres. When the new basin is complete the capacity of the harbour will be approximately doubled.

Berth on the pontoon just inside the entrance and report to the *capitainerie* for a berth. For the Nouveau Port the *quai d'accueil* is on the end of the central pier dividing the two harbours. There are laid moorings tailed to the quay or to buoys.

Shelter Good all-round shelter.

Authorities Customs. Port captain and marina staff. A charge is made.

Facilities

Services Water and electricity at every berth. A shower and toilet block.

Fuel On the quay near the root of the breakwater.

Repairs A 7-ton crane and several slipways, but limited hard standing. Mechanical and engineering repairs. GRP and wood repairs in the yards nearby. Electrical and electronic repairs. Chandlers. The service facilities will no doubt be expanded on the completion of the Nouveau Port.

Provisions Most provisions can be obtained nearby. Ice available.

Eating out Restaurants and bars nearby.

Other Post office. Bank. Buses along the coast. Tripper boats to the Iles de Lérins.

General

Compared to Port de Pierre-Canto just around the corner, Port de Golfe-Juan is a more homely, messy sort of place. Behind the marina the town is a delightful mixture of a working town, old iron-balconied houses, dusty streets, and shops with few concessions to tourism. This is changing with the de-

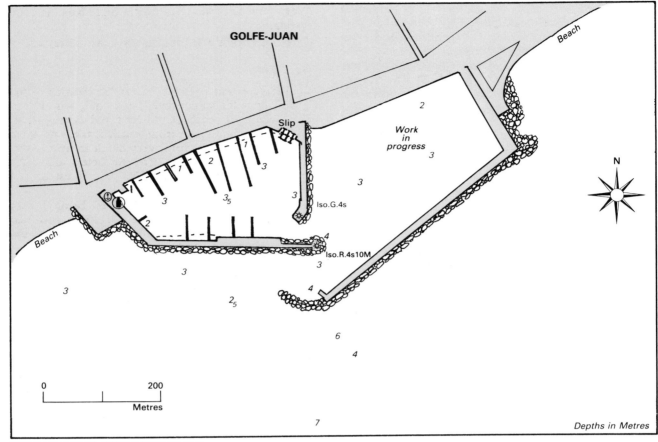

GOLFE-JUAN

PORT DE GOLFE-JUAN 43°34′N 7°04′·5E

velopment of the new basin adjacent to the older Port de Golfe-Juan and the development of the waterfront, though not without some opposition from the locals.

Golfe Juan is chiefly remembered as the place where Napoléon first landed on his return from Elba in 1815. A small plaque on the waterfront records the event. One can imagine the surprise of the local fishermen when Napoléon stepped ashore from the brig *L'Inconstant* and tricolours and cockades were distributed. His famous pledge at Golfe Juan, that 'the eagle, with the national colours, will fly from steeple to steeple as far as the towers of Notre Dame', must have sounded absurd at the time. Things didn't begin well. The envoy he sent to the garrison at Antibes to ask for help was flung into prison. Yet Napoléon pulled it off with his bullish charisma, persuading even the force sent to capture him to come over to his side, and for the 'Hundred Days' he again ruled France.

Note The new basin adjacent to Port de Golfe-Juan is still under construction at the time of writing, though the outer breakwater and the quays are all in place. The positions and numbers of pontoons and the final depths it is dredged to remain to be seen. It will be operational in 1991, though it will be a while before all the ancillary services are in place.

GALLICE-JUAN-LES-PINS

Approach

The fashionable marina tucked into the E side of Golfe Juan.

Conspicuous From the SW La Garoupe lighthouse, a tall square white tower on the summit of Cap d'Antibes, is conspicuous. In Golfe Juan the beacon on La Fourmigue and the red buoy marking Le Sécanion are easily identified. The harbour is situated where the apartments and villas extending around Golfe Juan end and the green wooded slopes of Cap d'Antibes begin. Closer in the harbour breakwater and the white light tower at the entrance are easily seen.

By night Use La Garoupe light, Fl(2)10s31M. Vallauris light, Oc(2)WRG.6s16-11M, shows the safe approach between Le Sécanion and Cap d'Antibes on the white sector over 305°–309°. Pte de l'Ilette light, Oc(2+1)WRG.12s13-9M, covers Les Moines and La Fourmigue and Le Sécanion with its red sectors over 045°–056° and 070°–090°. The entrance to Gallice Juan-les-Pins is lit, VQ(3)G.2s9M. Port Crouton immediately S of Gallice Juan-les-Pins is lit, Q(9)15s9M and Fl(2)R.6s6M. To the NW of the entrance a beacon marking a water-ski ramp is lit, F.Bu and F.Vi.

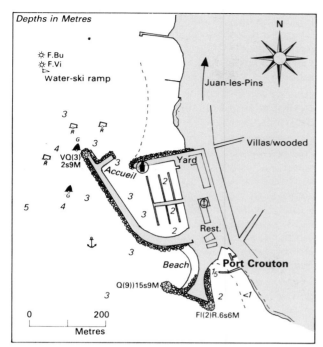

GALLICE JUAN LES PINS 43°33'·8N 7°07'E

Dangers
- In a strong *mistral* care is needed in the approach and entrance.
- To the NW of the entrance there is a water-ski ramp. It is lit, F.Bu and F.Vi.

Note The channel into the harbour is marked by several buoys. Three red can buoys mark the port side and two green conical buoys the starboard side of the channel. The buoys are lit, weak Fl.G and Fl.R. Do not rely on the buoys always being in place or on their lights working.

Mooring

Details 526 berths with visitors' berths available. Maximum LOA 20 metres.

Berth on the *quai d'accueil* just inside the entrance and report to the *capitainerie* for a berth. There are laid moorings tailed to the quay.

Shelter Good all-round shelter.

Authorities Port captain and marina staff. A charge is made.

Anchorage A yacht can anchor off the marina to the S in 3–5 metres on mud and weed.

Facilities

Services Water and electricity (220 and 380v) at all berths. A shower and toilet block.

Fuel On the quay at the entrance.

Repairs A 30-ton travel-hoist. Mechanical repairs. Some GRP and wood repairs. Electrical and electronic repairs. Chandlers.

Provisions Some provisions can be obtained at the marina. Better shopping in the town about 15 minutes walk away. Ice available.

Eating out Several restaurants and bars in the marina.

Other Post office and banks in the town. Hire cars.

General

To a large extent Juan-les-Pins is the creation of the American millionaire Frank Jay Gould, who in the 1920s acquired much of the land and developed it, keeping the pine forest from which it takes its name largely intact. The resort is very much an up-market, secluded sort of place, where the hotels and villas discreetly scattered through the pine forest do not scar the landscape.

Juan-les-Pins and Cap d'Antibes became very much an American enclave in the 1920s and 30s. Gerald and Sara Murphy, who bought a villa on the cape and called it *Villa America*, were largely responsible for publicising the charms of the place. The list of visitors who stayed with them reads like a roll call of the greatest American creative talent of the period: John Dos Passos, Archibald MacLeish, Gertrude Stein, Alice B. Toklas, Robert Benchley, Dorothy Parker, Ernest Hemingway, and Scott and Zelda Fitzgerald. Scott Fitzgerald set his novel *Tender is the Night* on the cape and dedicated it to Gerald and Sara Murphy. Gausse's Hotel des Etrangers in *Tender is the Night* is thought to be the Hotel du Cap d'Antibes, although others suggest that the Hotel Belles Rives fits Fitzgerald's description better: '... palms cool its flushed facade, and before it stretches a short dazzling beach... it's bright tan prayer-rug of a beach'.

As much as anyone else, the Fitzgeralds contributed to the wild reputation Juan-les-Pins gained in this period. Patrick Howarth in *When the Riviera was Ours* describes a few of the episodes of one summer: 'At a restaurant in St Paul-de-Vence Zelda threw herself down the well of a stairway after Isadora Duncan openly admired her husband. Early one morning a French farmer found both Scott and Zelda asleep in a car at a point on the railway track where they would shortly have been run down by a train. At a dinner party given by the Murphys Fitzgerald threw a fig soaked in sherbet at a countess, socked Archibald MacLeish on the jaw, and hurled three Venetian glasses over the garden wall.'

The writers and artists were followed by the stars of the screen and the stars of politics and other assorted personalities. It is still a fashionable resort, though a quieter one than when the Fitzgeralds frequented the cape.

PORT DU CROUTON

The old fishing harbour on the SE side of Gallice Juan-les-Pins. The small harbour has mostly less than 1 metre depths. Local boats moor all around the Y-shaped breakwater and on laid moorings in the middle.

CAP D'ANTIBES

The low wooded cape is easily recognised by La Garoupe lighthouse. There are a number of anchorages around the cape that can be used depending on the wind and sea.

CAP D'ANTIBES

La Garoupe lighthouse on Cap d'Antibes looking NE.

Pointe de l'Ilette On the E side of the point there is an anchorage sheltered from northerlies. The lighthouse and white building on the point and Tour Graillon, a round stone tower N of the point, are conspicuous. Care needs to be taken of the reef fring-ing the point for up to 200 metres. Sèche de St-Pierre, a detached shoal with 3·5 metres least depth over it, lies 400 metres off the point. Anchor in 8–15 metres on sand, rock and weed, not everywhere good holding.

Anse de la Garoupe A cove on the E side of Cap d'Antibes affording shelter from westerlies and light SE winds. Anchor in 6–10 metres on sand and weed.

Anse de la Salis A large bay between Pte Bacon and Antibes town. Care needs to be taken of the shoal water and rocks off Pte Bacon. There is a small islet in the bay which is easily identified. The bay affords some shelter from westerlies and from light SE winds. Anchor where convenient in 4–12 metres on mud and weed, good holding once through the weed. There are restaurants and bars around the shore and Antibes with all its facilities is on the W side of the bay.

Port de la Salis A small harbour in the southern corner of Anse de la Salis. There are 2 metre depths at the entrance and 1–1·5 metre depths inside. The harbour is normally crowded with local boats and there are usually no berths available for visitors.

VAUBAN-ANTIBES

Approach

Conspicuous La Garoupe lighthouse, a tall white square tower on the summit of Cap d'Antibes, is conspicuous from some distance off. Fort Carré on the N side of the entrance to the harbour is conspicuous from the E. A belfry and tower in the old town are also conspicuous. The harbour breakwater is easily identified, but the entrance is not immediately obvious. Closer in the light tower at the entrance will be seen.

By night Use La Garoupe, Fl(2)W.10s31M. The harbour entrance is lit, Fl(4)WR.12s16/12M, and Fl(2)G.6s on the buoy, and Iso.G.4M on the inner breakwater. The sectored light at the entrance shows the safe approach in the white sector on 160°–328°. A directional light within the harbour shows the safe passage through the entrance, DirQ.WRG.9-7M. The white sector covers 191·5°–194·5°. The various basins within the harbour are lit.

Dangers With strong E–NE winds there is a confused sea at the entrance and care is needed.

Mooring

Details 1134 berths with 170 berths for visitors. Maximum LOA 65 metres.

Berth on the *quai d'accueil* or the fuel berth and report to the *capitainerie* for a berth. There are laid moorings tailed to the quay or to buoys.

Shelter Good all-round shelter. Antibes is one of the most popular harbours along the coast for yachts wintering over in the south of France.

Authorities Customs. Port captain and marina staff. A charge is made.

214

Cap d'Antibes looking NE.

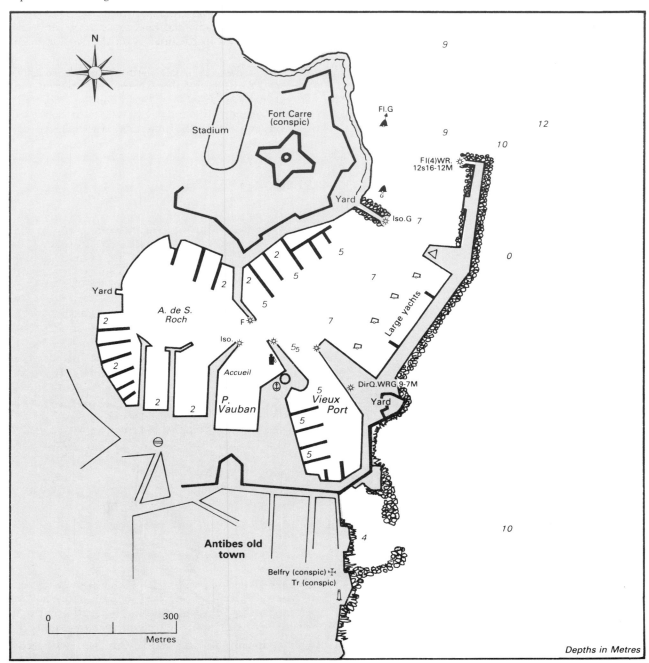

N

9

Fort Carre
(conspic)

Fl.G

Stadium

9

12

10

Fl(4)WR.
12s16-12M

Yard

G

Iso.G   7

10

2

5

2

5

0

Yard

2

2

5

7

A. de S.
Roch

5

2

F

7

Iso.

2

5 5

Large yachts

Accueil

5 5

DirQ.WRG.9-7M

P.
Vauban

2

Vieux
Port

5

Yard

2

2

5

5

Antibes old
town

10

4

Belfry (conspic)
Tr (conspic)

0   300

Metres

Depths in Metres

VAUBAN-ANTIBES 43°35′N 7°08′E

Antibes. The entrance looking W. Note Fort Carré standing prominently over the harbour.

Antibes. Entrance to the Vieux Port.

Note At the entrance in the Bassin de Grande Plaisance there are berths for 19 large yachts from 17 metres up to 65 metres. The basin is administered by the IYCA with its own *capitainerie* on a pier near the entrance.

It is planned to build a new marina due N of Fort Carré. The extension to Vauban-Antibes will double the berthing capacity to around a total of 2300 berths.

Facilities

Services Water and electricity (220 and 380v) at every berth. Telephone connections can be made at some berths. Shower and toilet blocks around the marina.

Fuel On the quay by the *capitainerie*.

Repairs 120-ton and 45-ton travel-hoists. Mechanical and engineering repairs. Steel and aluminium

Above Bonifacio citadel in the evening light looking from Calanque de Catena. *Left* The Riviera Corniche. The lower cornice cut into the cliffs along the coast is conspicuous from seawards.

Anchorage near Théoule-sur-Mer at the northeastern end of the Esterel.

Nice. Bassin Olympia.

Ajaccio. The waterfront of the Vieux Port.

Below The medieval castle at La Napoule rebuilt in 1937 by the talented if eccentric American Henry Clews. It now houses a collection of his sculpture open to the public.

fabrication. GRP and wood repairs. Electrical and electronic repairs. Sailmakers. Chandlers. Freight forwarding agencies.

Provisions Good shopping for all provisions nearby. Market in the old town. Ice available. Just about everything can be delivered to your boat from everyday groceries to personalised chocolates.

Eating out A wide choice of restaurants nearby.

Other Post office. Banks. Hire cars, motorbikes, and bicycles. Buses and trains along the coast. Internal and international flights from Nice.

General

Antibes, along with Marseille and Nice, is one of the oldest towns along the coast, founded as a trading post by the Phocaean Greeks. It was a small walled town that they called Antipolis, the 'city opposite' or across from Nice on the other side of the bay. In medieval times it was called Antiboul and was the easternmost outpost of the kings of France, looking across the Baie des Anges to Nice, the westernmost outpost of the Dukes of Savoy. Fort Carré was built in the 17th century to defend the town and the kingdom and remains an imposing piece of military architecture.

The young Napoléon Bonaparte was installed as commander here in 1794 and brought his family along, though times were still tough for the Bonapartes as Archibald Lyall amusingly recounts in his *The South of France*: 'Even for a general, pay arrived very irregularly in the revolutionary years, and his mother, the celebrated Madame Mère, for all that she was the widow of a nobleman of Ajaccio, had to wash the family linen in the neighbouring stream, while his sisters, princesses-to-be, stocked the larder by raiding the fig trees and artichoke beds of the angry farmers around.' Any tolerance the citizens may have had for Napoléon was exhausted by the time of his return from exile in 1815. The envoy he sent to the garrison at Antibes to ask for help was unceremoniously thrown into prison.

Antibes. Bassin de Grande Plaisance on the outer mole. A row of little ships costing amounts that read like French telephone numbers.

The old town of Antibes retains the feeling of a harbour town and a working town despite the large numbers of tourists that descend on it in the summer. Though every second building seems to be a restaurant or a tourist shop on Antibes' high street, behind it the working town of Antibes survives, though now largely devoted to servicing the yachts crowding the harbour. The harbour itself has been developed with this purpose in mind – to provide a base with all services for yachts large and small – rather than being just another fashionable harbour to be seen in on the Côte d'Azur. In this it succeeds in a remarkably sympathetic way.

MARINA BAIE DES ANGES

Approach

Conspicuous The four huge pyramidal apartment blocks around the marina are conspicuous from some distance off. Closer in the harbour breakwater and a white light tower at the entrance are easily identified.

By night The entrance is lit, Fl.G.4s9M and Oc(2)R.6s7M. The inner entrance is also lit with a weak F.R.

Dangers With strong easterlies there is a confused swell at the entrance and entry can be difficult.

Mooring

Details 527 berths with 53 berths in the Port Public for visitors. Maximum LOA 18 metres.

Berth on the *quai d'accueil* on the N side of the harbour and report to the *capitainerie* for a berth. There are laid moorings tailed to the quay.

Shelter Good shelter although strong easterlies can make some berths in the Port Public uncomfortable.

Authorities Port captain and marina staff. A charge is made.

Facilities

Services Water and electricity (220 and 380v) at all berths. A shower and toilet block.

Fuel On the quay near the *capitainerie*.

Repairs A 50-ton travel-hoist. Mechanical and engineering repairs. GRP and wood repairs. Electrical and electronic repairs. Chandlers.

Provisions Good shopping for provisions in the marina. Ice available.

Eating out Numerous restaurants and bars around the marina.

Other Post office. Exchange office. Hire cars. Buses and trains along the coast. Internal and international flights from Nice airport nearby.

General

My first reaction to the gigantic apartment blocks, the brain-child of architect André Minangoy, was one of horror and anger that some of the other architectural monstrosities seen elsewhere along the coast had been created here on an even larger scale. The terraced pyramidal buildings snaking around the

217

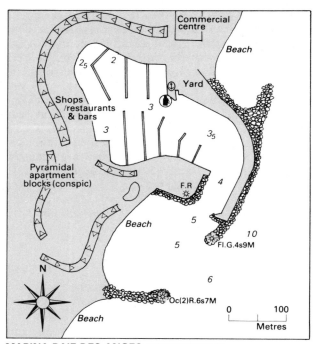

MARINA BAIE DES ANGES 43°38'·2N 7°08'·5E

Baie des Anges. The massive pyramidal apartment blocks that dominate the landscape on the W side of bay.

marina don't just stand out, they obliterate the landscape. But on closer acquaintance the outlines are softened by the trees and shrubs on the terraces and around the marina. Much as I hate to admit it, the huge complex works tolerably well and is quite a pleasant place to be in. And you have to admire the attempt to make a sort of modern 'hanging gardens of Babylon' on a huge scale.

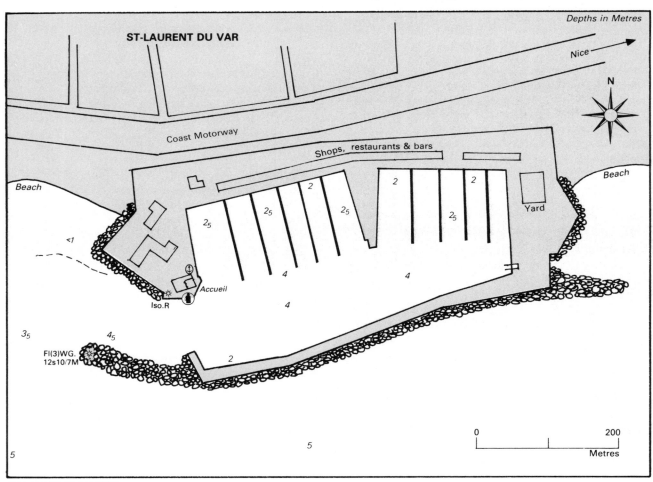

ST-LAURENT DU VAR 43°39'·3N 7°11'E

Cros de Cagnes

A small harbour off Cagnes-sur-Mer just W of Nice Airport. A solid white light pylon is conspicuous. There are 2 metre depths in the entrance and 1–2 metre depths inside. The harbour is crowded with local boats and there is usually no room for visiting yachts.

Note There are plans to build a 1000-berth marina here, though no plans are yet available and no date has been set for work to start.

ST-LAURENT DU VAR

Approach

A large marina situated just to the W of the Rivière Var and Nice Airport.

Conspicuous The airport with planes constantly taking off and landing identifies the general location. The cluster of buildings at St-Laurent du Var can be identified and closer in the breakwater and a white light tower at the entrance will be seen.

By night The entrance is lit, Fl(3)WG.12s10/7M, with the white sector covering the safe approach on 310°–090°. The inner entrance is lit, Iso.4s and Iso.R.4s (strip lights).

Dangers With strong southerlies a swell piles up at the entrance making entry difficult.

Mooring

Details 1063 berths with 212 berths for visitors. Maximum LOA 23 metres.

Berth at the *quai d'accueil* just inside the entrance and report to the *capitainerie* for a berth. There are laid moorings tailed to the quay or to buoys.

Shelter Good all-round shelter.

Authorities Port captain and marina staff. A charge is made.

Facilities

Services Water and electricity at every berth. Shower and toilet blocks.

Fuel On the quay at the entrance.

Repairs A 50-ton travel-hoist and several slipways. Mechanical and engineering repairs. GRP and wood repairs. Electrical and electronic repairs. Sailmakers. Chandlers.

Provisions Most provisions can be obtained at the marina. Better shopping in the town. Ice available.

Eating out Restaurants and bars in the marina.

Other Post office and banks in the town. Hire cars. Buses and trains along the coast. Internal and international flights from Nice Airport on the other side of the river.

General

It is difficult to find something to like about St-Laurent du Var. The planes taking off and landing at the airport thunder loudly overhead making conversation difficult. Cars thunder along the coastal motorway further adding to the din. The air smells thickly of exhaust fumes and spent aviation fuel. The marina and its facilities are really the best thing about the place and you can't deny that you can step off a flight just about onto the deck of your boat if it is kept here.

The Rivière Var was until 1860 the frontier between France and the House of Savoy. Travellers from France had to ford the river upstream. Tobias Smollett on his journey in the south of France described how six guides with long poles guided the coach to the other side. A little later in the 1780s James Smith, a botanist, recorded how 'If any person be lost, the guides are hanged without mercy.' I'm glad that similar punishment is not meted out to the writers of yachtsmen's guides.

Pablo Picasso. *La Paix Vallauris.*

PICASSO

At the end of the Second World War, Pablo Picasso returned from Paris to his beloved Mediterranean. He was the undisputed king of modern art, but in the chaos in the wake of the war, even the king had difficulty finding somewhere to work and materials to work with. To his aid came the enlightened director of the Antibes Museum in the old Grimaldi Castle on the waterfront of Antibes who allowed him to use the museum to work in.

Amongst the dusty exhibits Picasso set to work at a furious rate drawing and painting. He was inspired by his return to the Mediterranean to turn to Greek mythology. Fauns, centaurs, satyrs, bulls, owls, flautists, dancers, and Odysseus and the sirens figure prominently in his work from this period. As canvas was unobtainable he painted on hardboard. Picasso was also inspired by his new-found love, Françoise Gilot, who was a model for many of the paintings. Picasso was sixty-five when he came here and Françoise was in her twenties. The love affair had a sad ending as she left him in 1953 with the cruel remark that she did not want to be married to a historical monument.

When Picasso moved from Antibes to Vallauris, he left nearly the entire output of his time here on permanent loan. Later he added other works and some 200 examples of his ceramics from Vallauris. His work, as well as the room he used for a studio, is open to the public and the Picasso collection here is one of the few in the world that is so complete over a period in the great artist's life.

The museum contains other works as well. One of the most touching is Nicholas de Stael's *Still Life with a Blue Background*. Not long after he finished it the tormented de Stael committed suicide in Antibes.

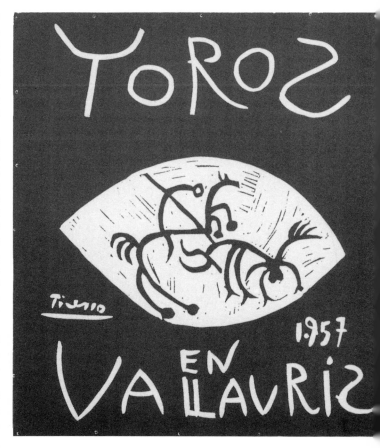

V. The Riviera

The French Riviera is a name much used and misused, so that popularly it has come to mean anywhere between Marseille and La Spezia in Italy. Geographically the French Riviera is the region of the pre-Alps from Nice to Menton, a region extending across the national border into Italy where the pre-Alps extend around to Genoa. The name 'Riviera' has been adopted by geographers to describe a region where high mountains shelter a coast from the worst effects of the winter, for any region that has a mild climate all year round without extremes of hot or cold; though tourist departments use the name more optimistically when somewhere like Britain's southern coastline is described as the English Riviera. Tobias Smollett was one of the first to bring the Riviera and its climate to the attention of the English when he tantalised them with his *Travels Through France and Italy* (1766) that contained descriptions like '... from the 1st to the 25th February, fine weather, clear sky, mild and warm in the day, wind easterly, sharp and piercing in the evening. Almonds, peaches, and apricots in blossom.'

The region described in this chapter is not only geographically defined, but historically defined as well. From 1388 until 1860, Nice and the coast to the east of it belonged to the House of Savoy, in effect to Italy. When Smollett arrived in Nice in 1763 he described it as being an Italian town, and it was referred to by other travellers arriving after him as a part of Italy. Not until the latter half of the 19th century was it to be described as French.

For the yachtsman the French Riviera described here merges gradually into the Italian Riviera. In Monaco the Italian *lira* is used as commonly as the French *franc* and signs and menus are likely to be in Italian as often as they are in French. By the time you get to Menton the coast is only nominally French, the sights and sounds are of Italy.

Weather

The prevailing wind in the summer is a sea breeze blowing from an easterly direction, between NE–E–SE, which gets up in the morning and dies down at night. It rarely gets above force 4–5 and you

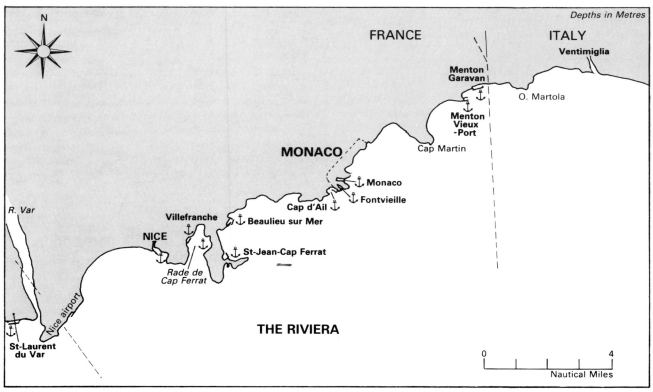

THE RIVIERA

get those lovely windless mornings where the sea is like a huge oily expanse shrouded in a misty haze. The high mountains along the coast shelter it from the worst effects of the *mistral* and although some sea is pushed along the coast, it is nothing like that encountered further west.

NICE

Approach

From the W the outer suburbs of Nice, stretching around the shore of Baie des Anges, will be seen. The airport just E of the river Var is easily identified by the numerous planes taking off and landing there. From the E the harbour is easily seen once around Cap de Nice.

Conspicuous The white observatory on Mont Gros behind the harbour and the Mont de Château de Nice, a wooded knoll immediately W of the harbour, are easily identified. Closer in a memorial carved into the cliff face of Mont de Château and the square lighthouse at the entrance to the harbour are conspicuous.

By night Use the light on Cap Ferrat, Fl.3s25M and the light at the entrance, Fl.R.5s20M. Closer in the starboard-hand light will be seen, Fl.G.4s7M. The entrance to the commercial port is lit, Fl(2)R.6s7M and Fl(2)G.6s6M. The entrance to the inner harbour is lit, Fl.R.4s7M and Fl.G.4s7M.

Dangers With strong southerlies there is a confused swell at the entrance making entry difficult, though rarely dangerous.

Note Yachts do not have automatic right of way over powered or commercial craft in the approaches and the harbour. At all times a yacht should keep well clear of commercial craft.

Mooring

Details 470 berths with 20 berths for visitors, though in practice more visitors are squeezed in.

Berths There are few berths to go around, and a lot of visiting yachts in the summer, so you will be lucky to find a berth available. Berth on the *quai d'accueil* at the entrance to Bassin des Amiraux and report to the Yacht Club de Nice to see if there is a berth available. If not you will be directed to the *capitainerie* where a berth on the commercial quay will be found if possible. A berth may also be found at the Club Nautique de Nice de la Tour Rouge on the N side of the entrance, though this is unlikely in the summer.

Shelter Good shelter in Bassin Lympia.

Authorities Customs. Port captain. YCN offices on the E side of Bassin des Amiraux.

Note When the new commercial port near the airport is completed, cargo boats will use this port leaving more room for yachts in Bassin Lympia. The ferries will continue to use the old harbour.

Facilities

Services Water and electricity at YCN berths.

Nice. Conspicuous monument at the base of Mont de la Château near the harbour entrance.

Fuel Nearby. Large amounts can be delivered by tanker.

Repairs 6 and 12-ton cranes and a slipway, but limited hard standing. Mechanical and engineering repairs. GRP and wood repairs. Electrical and electronic repairs. Sailmakers. Chandlers.

Provisions Good shopping for all provisions nearby. A market in the town and a fish market near the harbour. Ice available.

Eating out A wide choice of restaurants nearby.

Other Post office. Banks. Hire cars. Buses and trains along the coast. Ferries to Corsica. Internal and international flights from Nice Airport.

General

Nice is the capital of the Riviera and is considered by many to be the queen city of the coast, the classiest resort of them all, and the only place to be seen in. After Marseille it is the second largest city on the French Mediterranean coast and the fifth largest in France.

Nice began life around 350 BC as a small trading post of the industrious Phocaean Greeks. Under the Romans it was eclipsed by nearby Cimiez, but around the 10th century it expanded under the Dukes of Provence and soon became the most important harbour town along this stretch of coast. In the 14th century squabbles between Charles of Anjou and Charles of Durazzo over Nice left the way open for Amadeus VII, Count of Savoy, who had secretly made contact with the Governor of Nice, to seize the town and adjoining territory and incorporate it into the lands of the House of Savoy. The townspeople were evidently well pleased with their new sovereign and he was greeted with much celebration, his path strewn with flowers and the houses decorated with rich tapestries, as he rode into Nice to formally claim his new territory. Nice and the coast to the east was to remain part of the House of Savoy until 1860 when it was incorporated into France.

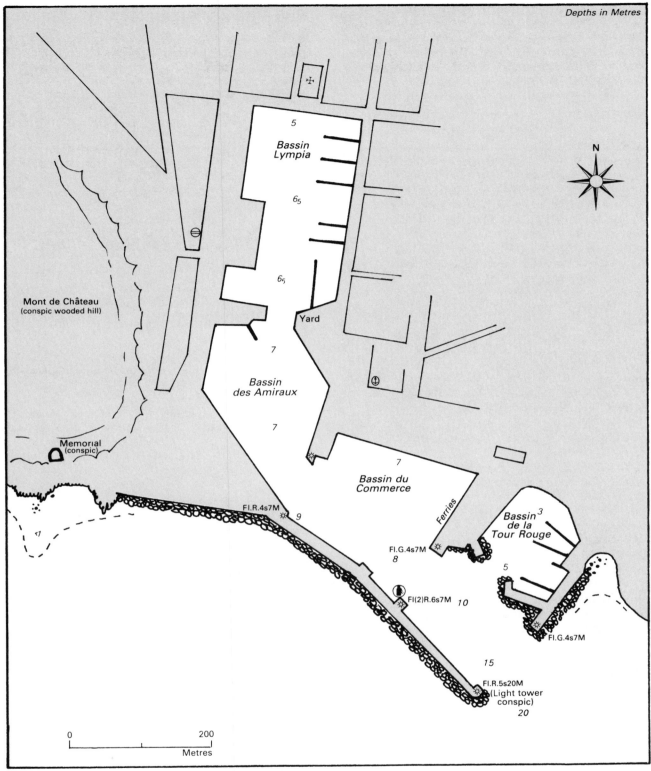

Depths in Metres

Bassin
Lympia

5

6₅

6₅

Mont de Château
(conspic wooded hill)

Yard

7

Bassin
des Amiraux

7

Memorial
(conspic)

7

N

Bassin du
Commerce

7

Fl.R.4s7M   9

Ferries

Bassin
de la
Tour Rouge

3

Fl.G.4s7M
8

5

Fl(2)R.6s7M   10

Fl.G.4s7M

15

Fl.R.5s20M
(Light tower
conspic)
20

0   200
Metres

NICE 43°41′·5N 7°17′·1E

Nice has many claims to fame, but the enduring one of this century is as a tourist resort. From Tobias Smollett who spent most of 1763 in a ground-floor apartment from where he walked to the sea to bathe every day, (an unheard of practice that attracted crowds to see this mad Englishman taking to the water), to the present day when thousands of holiday makers jet into Nice airport every day, the city has been seen as the original, the centre and the hub, of tourism in the south of France.

For all its concentration of tourist activities, it does not rely solely on tourism. Light industry, cultivated flowers, exhibition and conference halls, and since 1966, a university, diversify Nice's interests away from the purely pleasurable. The old harbour reflects this with its mixture of cargo ships, ferries, fishing boats, and yachts, without the latter being the principal occupiers of quay space. To find this working harbour in the tourist capital of the south of France, hemmed in by purely pleasure-craft harbours on either side, is a pleasant and unexpected surprise.

Rade de Villefranche

Immediately E of Nice lies the deep and steep-sided bay of Villefranche. The slopes rise up precipitously from the bay and for the most part are not heavily built upon with pleasing patches of green dotted around the bay. From the W the steep-to Cap de Nice is easily recognised. From the W and E the white hexagonal lighthouse on the tip of Cap Ferrat

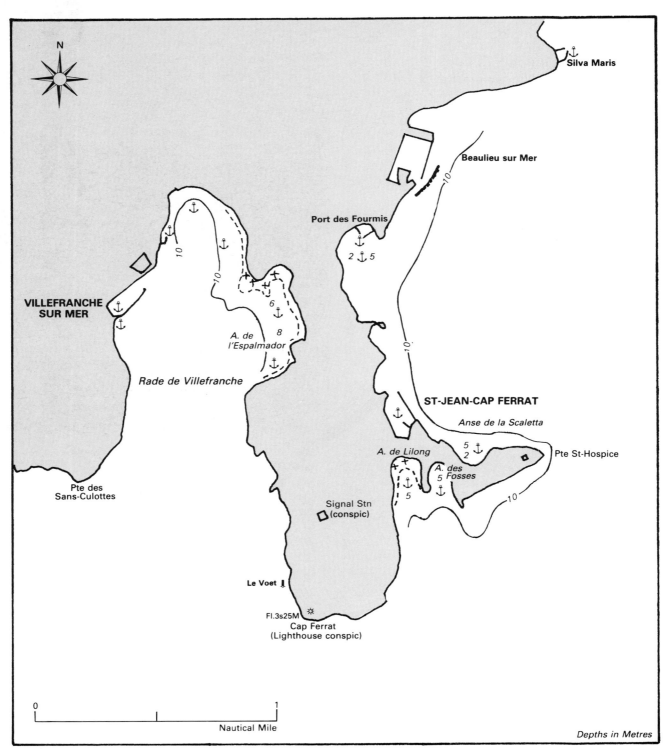

RADE DE VILLEFRANCHE AND CAP FERRAT

and a white signal station on its summit are conspicuous. On the W side of the bay there is a marina at Villefranche and around the bay there are a number of anchorages.

VILLEFRANCHE

Approach

Conspicuous Once into Rade de Villefranche the citadel on the W side is conspicuous and the marina sits just under it.

By night Use the light on Cap Ferrat, Fl.3s25M, and the light at the harbour entrance, Q.WR.12/8M. The white sector shows the safe approach into Rade de Villefranche on 335°–009° (and also over 286°–311°).

Note There are several unlit mooring buoys in the middle of the bay.

Mooring

Details 320 berths with some visitors' berths. Maximum LOA 16 metres.

Berth where directed or go onto the fuel quay and report to the *capitainerie* for a berth. There are laid moorings tailed to the quay or to buoys.

Shelter Excellent all-round shelter.

Authorities Port captain and marina staff. Customs in the small northern harbour. A charge is made.

Facilities

Services Water and electricity at every berth. A shower and toilet block.

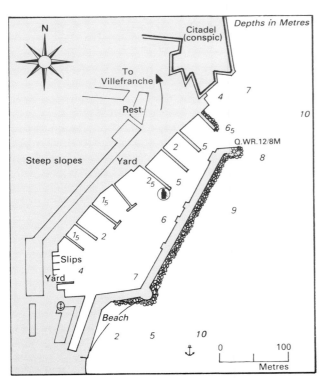

VILLEFRANCHE SUR MER 43°42′N 7°18′·5E

Villefranche. The marina looking from the citadel on the slopes above the entrance.

Fuel On the end of the pier in the middle of the harbour.

Repairs 5-ton and 10-ton cranes and a 40-ton slipway. Mechanical repairs. Some GRP and wood repairs. Sailmakers. Chandlers.

Provisions In the village about 10 minutes steep walk up the hill.

Eating out Several restaurants by the marina and others along the waterfront by the small N harbour.

Other Post office. Banks. Buses and trains in the town.

General

Villefranche is a relaxed resort that retains much of the architecture and character of centuries gone by. The narrow streets run higgledy-piggledy up and down, joined by paths and shaded by mature trees. The citadel next to the harbour was built by the Duke of Savoy in 1560 to guard the port and the

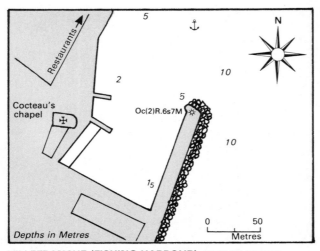

VILLEFRANCHE (FISHING HARBOUR) 43°42'·2N 7°18'·8E

rade, and remains more or less intact with pleasant walks through it and good views over the bay from its ramparts. Within the citadel there is a museum devoted to the sculptures of Volti.

Down by the small harbour to the north is the Chapel of St Peter, a fisherman's chapel that was given to Jean Cocteau in 1957 to decorate. His simply outlined figures traced in a geometrical fashion make a refreshing change from the density of frescoes that usually greet one in Catholic churches. Along the waterfront from the chapel, virtually side by side, are most of the resort's restaurants with wonderful views out over the water to Cap Ferrat.

North harbour

Immediately N of the citadel is the small fishing harbour of Villefranche. The mole of the harbour is lit on the extremity, Oc(2)R.6s7M. On the inside of the mole there are 1·5–2 metre depths. The harbour is packed with fishing boats and local craft and there is not normally a berth available here. On the Quai Courbet at the entrance to the harbour there are 2 metre depths some 20 metres off and craft sometimes anchor with a long line to the quay. Most yachts anchor off to the N of the harbour in 10–15 metres on mud and thick weed.

ANCHORAGES IN RADE DE VILLEFRANCHE

Villefranche Anchor in the bight to the S of the marina in 5–10 metres on mud and thick weed, reasonable holding once through the weed. This anchorage normally has some swell rolling into it and in moderate to strong southerlies is untenable. Its chief merit is being close to the facilities in and around the marina.

NW corner In the NW corner of the *rade* anchor in 10–15 metres on mud and thick weed, reasonable holding once through the weed. The bottom comes up abruptly from the 15 metre line. Open to southerlies. There are numerous restaurants nearby at Villefranche.

Villefranche. One of the most peaceful marinas on the Riviera.

Anse de l'Espalmador The most popular anchorage on the E side of the bay. Here there is the best shelter from the prevailing SE breeze. Care needs to be taken of Roches du Rube with 1·3–1·8 metres over, at the northern end of the anchorage. Anchor where convenient in 4–12 metres on mud and thick weed, reasonable holding once through the weed. The bottom comes up abruptly from the 10 metre line. Like most of the anchorages in Rade de Villefranche some swell always seems to penetrate into here even when it is apparently flat calm outside – not dangerous but enough to make you aware it is there. With strong southerlies it is untenable. Restaurants ashore.

Anse de Passable A small cove under Anse de l'Espalmador affording indifferent shelter.

Note There is a speed limit of 5 knots in Rade de Villefranche that is strictly enforced by the *gendarmerie*.

PTE DE ST-HOSPICE

On the E side of Cap Ferrat the comparatively low-lying Pte de St-Hospice squiggles out from the coast.

The anchorage in Anse de l'Espalmador.

A tower is conspicuous on the green and wooded extremity and a number of large and very private villas are scattered over it. There are several anchorages around it that can be used depending on the wind and sea.

Anse de Lilong A cove on the W side of Pte de Lilong. Anchor in 4–8 metres in the middle of the cove on sand, mud and weed, reasonable holding once through the weed. The bottom comes up quickly from 4–5 metres to less than 1 metre some distance off the coast. Open to the S.

Anse des Fosses The cove on the E side of Pte de Lilong. Anchor in 5–8 metres on sand and weed. Open to the S.

Anse de la Scaletta A cove on the N side of Pte de St-Hospice. Anchor in 4–8 metres on sand and thick weed, poor holding in places. Shelter from moderate southerlies and westerlies, otherwise open to the N and E. The facilities of St-Jean-Cap Ferrat are not too far away.

ST-JEAN-CAP FERRAT

Approach

Conspicuous From the S and E the tower on Pte de St-Hospice is conspicuous. Closer in a clock tower in the town will be seen and the breakwater and the light tower at the entrance are easily identified.

By night The entrance is lit, Fl(4)R.12s9M, and the inner entrance Iso.G and F.R.

Dangers

In strong easterlies there is a confused swell at the entrance making entry difficult.

Mooring

Details 560 berths with 30 berths for visitors. Maximum LOA 30 metres.

Berth at the *quai d'accueil* on the W quay just inside the entrance and report to the *capitainerie* for a berth. There are laid moorings tailed to the quay.

Shelter Excellent all-round shelter.

Authorities Port captain and marina staff. A charge is made.

Anchorage In the summer yachts anchor off the breakwater of the marina and to the N of the entrance. If you are anchoring off here be careful not to obstruct the approach to the entrance.

Facilities

Services Water and electricity (220 and 380v) at all berths. A shower and toilet block.

Fuel On the quay near the entrance.

Repairs A 30-ton travel-hoist and an 8-ton crane. Mechanical repairs. Some GRP and wood repairs. Chandlers.

Provisions Good shopping for all provisions nearby. Ice available.

Eating out Numerous restaurants and bars along the waterfront.

Other Post office. Banks. Hire cars.

General

On Cap Ferrat and around St-Jean-Cap Ferrat are some of the most elegant villas and the finest gardens along the coast. This gives it a green and shaded aspect, lacking in some of the more built-up areas, and the area has attracted its fair share of the wealthy, the titled, and the simply eccentric. As well as King Leopold II of Belgium, the Duke of Connaught, and a Rothschild or two, the eccentric Somerset Maugham lived here from 1927 until his death in 1968. The Villa Mauresque on the cape became his permanent home because, Maugham said, life in the south of France was more convivial than life in the country of his birth. It also shielded him from the censure that homosexuals had heaped on them before the war, and the trial of Oscar Wilde – Maugham was twenty-one at the time – which must have always been on his mind. In the Villa Mauresque he entertained lavishly and an invitation to one of his dinner parties was much sought after. He appears to have been a kindly man, if stern at times. One puzzling thing is that the Riviera does not appear as a setting in any of his major books – he apparently decided to keep the landscape for his own private appreciation.

PORT DES FOURMIS

A small and mostly shallow harbour tucked under Pte des Fourmis. There are 2–2·5 metre depths in the entrance and 1–1·5 metre depths inside. Feel your way carefully into here as the bottom is uneven, and go bows-to the outer mole. All berths are private, but you may be lucky enough to find one free. Enquire at the yacht club at the root of the mole for a berth. The harbour is a most attractive place sitting under the Villa Kerylos on Pte des Fourmis.

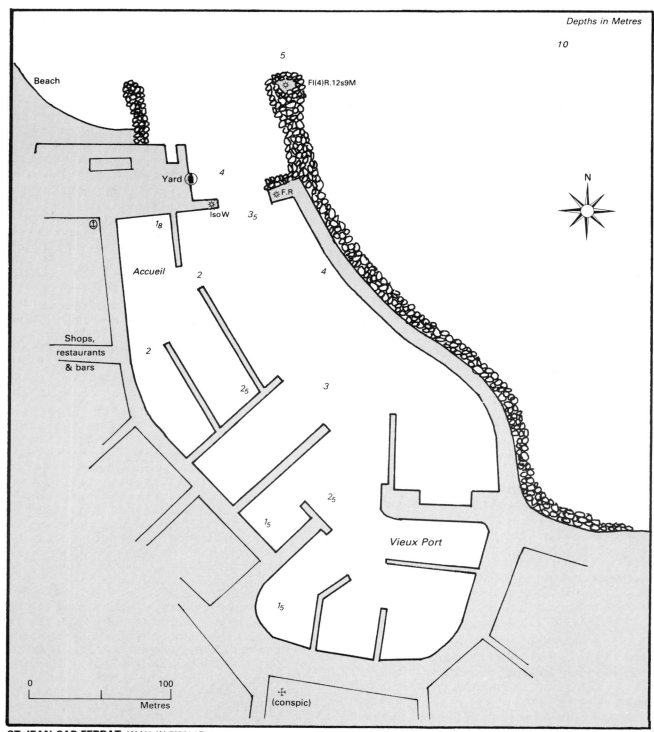

Depths in Metres

10

5

Beach

Fl(4)R.12s9M

Yard

4

IsoW

F.R

3₅

1₈

Accueil

2

4

Shops,
restaurants
& bars

2

2₅

3

2₅

1₅

Vieux Port

1₅

1₅

0   100

Metres

(conspic)

N

ST-JEAN-CAP FERRAT 43°41'·4N 7°20'·1E

VILLA KERYLOS

Sitting prominently on Pte des Fourmis is the fac-
simile of a Greek villa built by M. Théodore Reinach
at the beginning of the century. Reinach was ob-
sessed with things Greek, and with the help of the architect Poutremol and a team of archaeological experts he built the extraordinary villa on the point. He
imported Carrara marble and exotic hardwoods for
the construction and had furniture and frescoes

recreated from examples on Greek ceramics and
mosaics.

The result of all this is a splendid reconstruction
which, if not always accurate, at least gives dilettante
Helenophiles the feel of what a Greek villa might
have been like. A peristyle with Ionic columns
frames a pool in an open courtyard with the rooms
opening off it. There is a *salon* with a beamed ceiling

The Villa Kerylos on Pte des Fourmis. Theodore Reinach built it according to his and other experts' views of what an ancient Greek villa would look like.

and a household altar to the gods, and off it a dining room with couches where Théodore would recline while eating his favourite Greek food. Amongst all the reproductions are numerous originals. Hidden away discreetly are some of the 20th-century pleasures and conveniences Théodore decided he couldn't do without. Apart from electricity and hot and cold running water, he concealed a piano in a wooden chest and a bidet is also cunningly concealed. I'm sure the ancients would have approved.

BEAULIEU-SUR-MER

Approach

The marina sits on the W side of the Baie de Beaulieu at the edge of the high limestone cliffs that continue on around to Monaco.

Conspicuous The high limestone cliffs with the lower and middle cornices cut into them are distinctive from some way off. The lower cornice with its tunnels and viaducts is conspicuous and where it 'disappears' into the buildings of Beaulieu, the outer breakwater of the marina will be seen. The light towers at either end of the breakwater are easily identified.

Note A yacht should make for the Passe Principale, the northern entrance where there is 4 metres least depth. The Passe Secondaire, the southern entrance, has less than 2 metre depths through a buoyed channel and should not be used except by shallow-draught craft.

By night The outer breakwater is lit at either end, Iso.G.4s8M and Q.R.10M. The inner entrance is lit, Fl.R.4s4M and Fl.G.4s4M. Note that Port de Silva-Maris, less than a mile NE, is also lit, Fl(2)R.6s8M.

Dangers In moderate to strong easterlies a swell piles up at the entrance to Passe Secondaire and it should not be used, even by shallow-draught craft. The Passe Principale is safe in all weather.

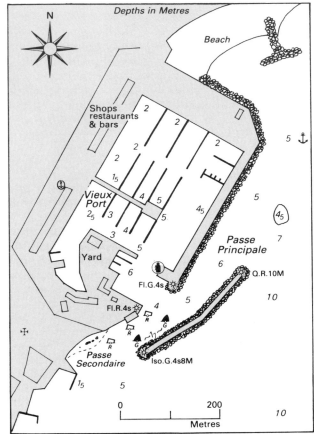

BEAULIEU SUR MER 43°42'·5N 7°20'·3E

Note There is an area off the harbour marked by four yellow buoys where anchoring and fishing are prohibited.

Mooring

Details 776 berths with 152 berths for visitors. Maximum LOA 30 metres.

Berth where directed or go onto the end of the central jetty and report to the *capitainerie* for a berth. There are laid moorings tailed to the quay or to buoys.

Shelter Good all-round shelter.

Authorities Customs. Port captain and marina staff. A charge is made.

Facilities

Services Water and electricity at all berths. A shower and toilet block.

Fuel On the quay near the entrance.

Repairs 35-ton and 100-ton travel-hoists and slipways. Mechanical and engineering repairs. GRP and wood repairs. Electrical and electronic repairs. Sailmakers. Chandlers. Admiralty charts and British publications available from Com. Michael Healy, Le Silmar, 10 rue Jean Bracco. ☎ 93-01-15-72.

Provisions Some provisions in the marina, better shopping in the town nearby. Ice available.

Eating out Numerous restaurants around the waterfront and in the town.

Other Post office and banks in the town. Hire cars. Buses and trains along the coast.

General

Hemmed in by the high mountains behind, Beaulieu claims to have more hours of sunshine than elsewhere on the coast and the warmest winter climate on the Riviera. It is an elegant resort with some wonderful Victorian and Edwardian edifices built by the English visitors who adopted Beaulieu for their own. There has been little high-rise development to obliterate the landscape and the town is well worth a visit, not to see anything in particular, but simply for the old-world ambience it radiates. Along the waterfront between Beaulieu and St-Jean-Cap Ferrat there is a wonderful pedestrian promenade away from the main road, about an hour's peaceful walk.

Wandering around Beaulieu you will come across a street named in honour of the proprietor of the *New York Herald*, James Gordon Bennett. Bennett spent much of his life in Europe between Paris and Beaulieu where he lived in the *Villa Namouna* – when he was not on his yacht *Lysistrata*. The yacht, designed by G. L. Watson and built in 1900, complete with a Turkish bath, was the scene of many of Bennet's extravagances. He abhorred playing cards and when his crew came on board, he had their luggage searched for the offending item; if a pack was found he inflicted the devious punishment of removing the four aces and then returning the pack to the luggage. He also disliked beards and would not allow anyone on board with one. In Monte Carlo he is said to have arrived at his favourite restaurant, a modest

Beaulieu. A shaded elegant resort that claims more sunshine hours than anywhere else on the Riviera.

establishment, to find it full, whereupon he bought it and when he had finished his meal, gave the restaurant to the head waiter as a gift. This eccentric man, whose name became an exclamation for anything outrageous, died peacefully in Beaulieu in 1918.

Port de Silva-Maris (Port d'Eze-sur-Mer)

A small private harbour just under a mile NE of Beaulieu. The entrance is lit, Fl(2)R.6s8M. It is part of an apartment complex and no provision is made for visiting yachts.

CAP D'AIL

Approach

A marina sited adjacent to the border with Monaco.

Conspicuous From the W the skyscrapers of Monaco under the bald slopes of Tête de Chien, a conical peak, are easily identified. The Oceanographic Museum at Monaco and the 9 large arches of the St-Louis Stadium behind the marina are conspicuous. Closer in the breakwater of the marina and the masts of the yachts inside will be seen.

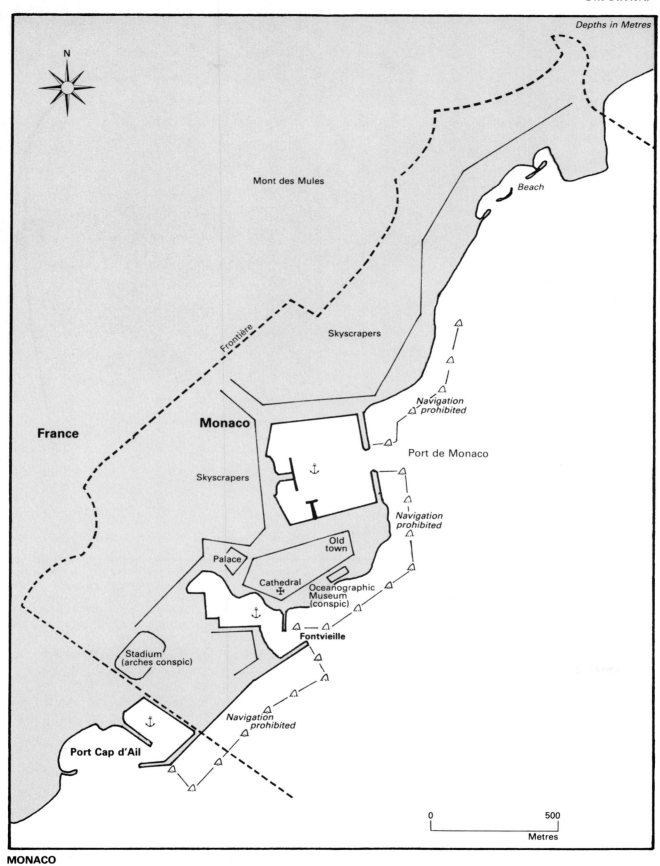

MONACO

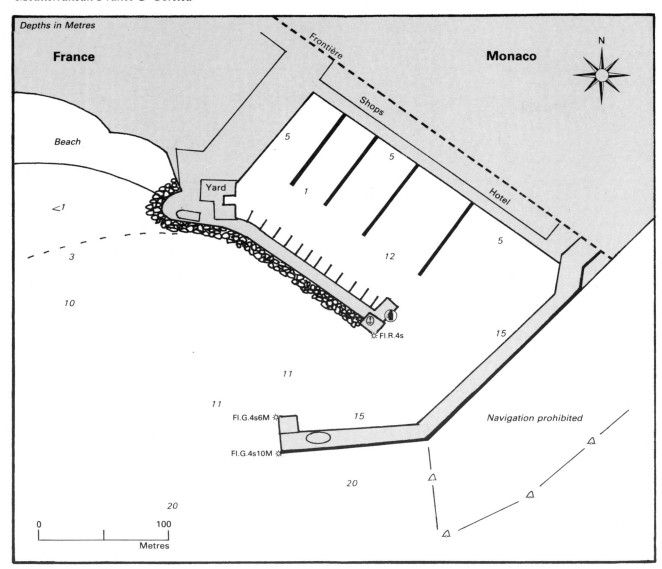

PORT DE CAP D'AIL 43°43′·5N 7°25′E

By night Use the light at the heliport, Mo(MC)30s 10M, and the lights at the entrance, Fl.G.4s10M and Fl.R.4s5M.

Dangers A reef extends off Cap d'Ail for about 200 metres and a yacht should not take a short-cut across the cape when coming from the W.

Mooring

Details 253 berths with 53 berths for visitors.

Berth where directed or go onto the fuel quay at the entrance and report to the *capitainerie* for a berth. There are finger pontoons and laid moorings tailed to the quay.

Shelter Good shelter although strong SW winds cause a surge making some berths uncomfortable.

Authorities Port captain and marina staff. A charge is made.

Facilities

Services Water and electricity (220 and 380v) at all berths. A shower and toilet block.

Fuel On the quay at the entrance.

Repairs A 50-ton travel-hoist and slipway. Mechanical and engineering repairs. Electrical and electronic repairs. Chandlers.

Provisions Good shopping for provisions nearby. Ice available.

Eating out Numerous restaurants nearby.

Other Post office and banks nearby. Hire cars. Buses and trains along the coast. The heliport with connections to Nice is close by.

General

Cap d'Ail is really an extension of Monaco into French real estate. The border between France and Monaco is behind the hotel and shops at the marina and you are literally at the back door to all the sights and sounds of the principality.

Lord Beaverbrook, the Canadian newspaper magnate, spent many of his last years here in a villa where, according to Patrick Howarth, 'he spent much of his time in the swimming pool, only his

Cap d'Ail. The marina built right in the backyard of Monaco.

straw hat showing above the surface as a male secretary read to him the day's leading articles in *The Times*.' He was joined on occasion by Churchill who was made honorary mayor of Cap d'Ail. Beaverbrook himself was honoured by the citizens who named the centre of Cap d'Ail, the 'Place Beaverbrook'.

Monaco

From a point immediately east of Cap d'Ail to just before Pte de la Veille under Cap Martin, sits the tiny semi-autonomous state of the Principality of Monaco. It is just under a square mile in area. From the distance the epithets used to describe Monaco, a 'little Manhattan' and a 'toy-town New York', describe what it looks like well. In fact the wall of high-rise buildings extends out to either side and around the actual boundaries of Monaco, but the concentration of modern skyscrapers around the harbour at Monte Carlo readily identifies the place at once.

A yacht heading for Monaco should remember it is not France and take down the courtesy *tricolore*. It is polite to have a Monegasque flag, a red and white bicolour, before entering Monaco, though nothing drastic will befall you if you don't have one. Nor do you need to fly a yellow 'Q' flag. Monaco has its own *gendarmerie* who patrol the small patch of water off the principality and strictly enforce the prohibited areas.

Ashore there are a number of laws which differ from those in France. The most important of these is that no bathing costumes, bare chests (that includes men) or bare feet are allowed once you step ashore or off the beaches. No campfires are allowed either, but since there are precious few places to light a fire, it is hardly applicable. Monaco has its own police force and everything is strictly enforced. Outrageous behaviour that you might get a 'ticking-off' for over the border will be stringently dealt with in Monaco. Incidentally French currency is used as well as Italian *lire*, which is handy if you have come from Italy and have Italian currency left over.

History

Monaco is the oldest monarchy in Europe where the monarch still has the major say in what goes on. It is, in effect though not in appearances, a medieval kingdom that through luck and skillful manipulation by its rulers, has survived into the 20th century.

It all started when the Grimaldi family bought Monaco from the Genoese in 1308. It has remained in their hands to this day, though not without some ups and downs. In the 16th century Jean II was assassinated by his brother Lucien who was in turn assassinated by his nephew. Later in 1604 Honore I was ignominiously thrown into the sea by the Monegasque to express their disapproval of his policies. Under Honoré II a period of Spanish rule was imposed, followed by a period of French rule which only ended in 1815 when the Treaty of Paris handed the by now much diminished kingdom back to the Grimaldis. Honoré V managed to run his little kingdom into debt and when Charles III inherited it he sold off Roquebrune and Menton to France, thus reducing the size of the principality to its present-day dimensions.

Despite selling off part of the principality's real estate, Charles III was still faced with a large debt. Taking a leaf from places like Baden-Baden which had a thriving casino, he established a casino in Monaco. It was not a success at first. It is recorded that in one week in March 1857 only one visitor tried his luck at the casino – and he won two francs. Not until François Blanc obtained the concession to the casino in 1863 did things begin to look up. In 1868 the railway from Nice to Monaco was opened and the crowds started to flock in. In 1869 all rates and taxes were abolished, an act which was to significantly enhance the prosperity of Monaco in later years by attracting large sums to this convenient tax haven. The situation exists to this day for the native Monegasque who pay no taxes.

With the success of the casino, Monaco quickly developed a reputation for high living, fast money and loose women. In 1866, John Addington Symonds wrote in his diary with Victorian prudishness that 'The croupiers are either fat, sensual cormorants, or sallow, lean-cheeked vultures, or suspicious foxes.... The men of the gaming bank show every trace of a dissolute youth and a vile calling, of low sensuality and hardened avarice.' (Quoted in *When the Riviera was Ours*). Despite the Symonds of this world and attempts by the clergy to have the casino closed, its reputation grew until the site it was built upon, Monte Carlo, and the word 'casino', became synonymous. The English, in particular, considered Monte Carlo their own, and by Edwardian times it had become the place to go to and be seen at on the Riviera.

The notoriety of Monte Carlo Casino attracted a considerable number of confidence tricksters and hangers-on, as well as producing a large number of losers. The casino operated a system known as *viatique*, the name given to the one-way ticket home for a person who had lost everything at the tables. Anyone issued with a *viatique* was banned forever from the casino, and to ensure they did not get back in, a complex card-index system was kept and a number of expert physiognomists employed. One such, a Monsieur Le Broq, was said to be able to recognise some 50,000 faces. The casino also gave birth to anecdote and song. The song, *The Man who Broke the Bank at Monte Carlo*, is said to have been written about Charles Deville Wells, a confidence trickster who in one run of good luck, turned £400 into £40,000 in three days. Alas he died impoverished after serving eight years for fraud. Other myths of the tables, such as the *Greek Syndicat* which operated on the baccarat tables, have a substantial element of truth. One of its members, Nico Zographos, when he died in 1953,

left five million pounds, all of it, he said, won at baccarat. The rich and the hopeful, the famous and the notorious, politicians and the shadowy figures behind politics, royalty and those with dubious titles, mixed freely at Monte Carlo in one long all-singing-and-dancing party.

After the Second World War the austerity measures imposed by many governments severely curtailed the amount of currency that could be taken out of a country and the casino was not the high-rolling place it had been. In 1949 Prince Rainier III succeeded to the throne and he set about changing the economy of Monaco. For the casino he looked to Las Vegas and trundled in one-armed bandits. He organised and promoted festivals, shows and sports tournaments. He built conference centres to attract businessmen. When he married the film star Grace Kelly in a fairy-tale romance, he captured the popular imagination and put Monaco back on the map as the place to be on the Riviera, not just to be at the casino, but also for the non-stop entertainment and cosmopolitan atmosphere. The rich and famous returned to Monaco and though it was not the Monaco of old, it was again a fashionable place to be.

Ashore

There is much to do and see ashore and the following list is an indication only.

Monte Carlo Casino All roads in Monaco seem to lead to the casino and it is easily reached from Fontvieille or Port de Monaco.

The old town On the rock between Fontvieille and Port de Monaco sits the old town of Monaco. Narrow cobbled streets and shady squares crisscross the old walled town and if there is even a light breeze it is a pleasantly cool spot.

Prince's Palace There are guided tours in the summer when the Prince is not in residence. The square off it has fine views over the sea and Fontvieille.

Oceanographic Museum One of the finest in the Mediterranean. Established by Prince Albert I, a passionate oceanographer who used his private yachts, the *Hirondelle* and later the *Princess Alice*, for deep-sea exploration and research. The results of his work and some of his finds are displayed along with ongoing research. There is a large aquarium with one of the best collections in Europe of Mediterranean and tropical fish and crustaceans. There is also a vast collection of shells and a collection of curios made from marine animals. The director of the museum is Jacques Cousteau and a small theatre shows his films continuously through the day.

Cathedral A neo-Romanesque affair with some early paintings of the Nice School.

Zoo Above the marina at Fontvieille.

Tropical Gardens On a rocky promontory with a large collection of cacti and other succulents.

Prehistoric Museum Close to the tropical gardens. Interesting and well laid-out displays of prehistoric finds in the region.

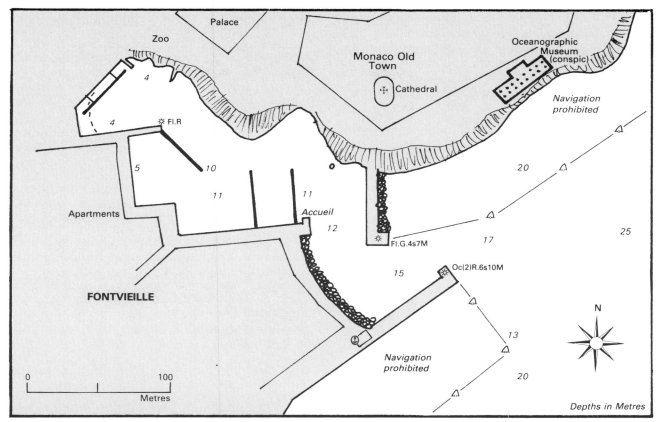

FONTVIEILLE 43°43'·7N 7°25'·4E

Observatory Caves Close to the tropical gardens. Thought to be a dwelling place of prehistoric man.

Museum of Dolls and Automata A wonderful collection of dolls from the 18th century to the present day, and 19th-century automata that are set in motion several times a day.

FONTVIEILLE

A new marina tucked under the cliffs on top of which Old Monaco is built.

Approach

Although there are sufficient landmarks to identify where the harbour is, the entrance is difficult to identify until you are right up to it.

Conspicuous From the W the 9 large arches of St-Louis II Stadium and the Oceanographic Museum on the E side of the entrance are conspicuous. From the E Port de Monaco will be seen and the Oceanographic Museum is conspicuous. Even close off the harbour the overlapping breakwaters present what appears to be a solid barrier. Head towards the light tower until the entrance opens up.

By night Use the light at the heliport Mo(MC)30s 10M and the lights at the entrance, Oc(2)R.6s10M and Fl.G.4s7M.

Dangers With strong southerlies and easterlies there is a confused swell reflected off the breakwaters which makes entry difficult. In anything approaching gale force onshore winds the entrance could be dangerous.

Note Between Cap d'Ail Marina and the entrance to Fontvieille there is a line of yellow conical buoys approximately 150 metres off the coast, inside which entry is prohibited. Likewise from Port de Monaco to the entrance at Fontvieille there is a line of yellow buoys inside which entry is prohibited.

Mooring

Details 170 berths with 10 berths for visitors. Maximum LOA 35 metres. In practice in the summer there are more berths available.

Berth Go alongside the *quai d'accueil* just inside the entrance and report to the *capitainerie* for a berth. The harbour is very crowded in July and August, but the marina staff will do their best to fit you in somewhere. There are laid moorings tailed to the quay or finger pontoons.

Shelter Good all-round shelter although there can be a surge in the outer half of the harbour with southerly gales.

Authorities Port captain and marina staff. A charge is made.

Facilities

Services Water and electricity (220 and 380v) at or close to all berths. A shower and toilet block.

Fuel In Port de Monaco.

Repairs No hauling facilities. Chandlers.

Provisions Most provisions can be found locally. Ice available.

Eating out Restaurants around the marina.

Other Post office. Banks. Buses and taxis to La Condamine and Monte Carlo. Hire cars. Monaco Heliport is adjacent to the marina.

General

Fontvieille was developed comparatively recently as an area of light industry, though the industry is so light in places it is barely discernible. Fontvieille is dominated by the Louis II Stadium conspicuous from seawards, and the park between Cap d'Ail marina and the marina at Fontvieille. In the park a rosery is touchingly dedicated to the late Princess Grace. Around the marina there is a large modern apartment complex with a shopping mall underneath.

The most attractive feature of Fontvieille Marina is the rocky limestone cliffs on the eastern side which have been left intact and provide a spectacular rugged contrast to the man-made surroundings that dominate Monaco. Prince Rainier III keeps his own yacht, a comparatively modest sailing boat bristling with practical ideas that reflect his genuine love of sailing, at Fontvieille instead of in the public gaze at Port de Monaco. And if you hear strange grunts and hoots and other jungle sounds while in the marina, it is not your imagination, but emanates from the small zoo above the northern end of the harbour.

PORT DE MONACO

Approach

Conspicuous From the distance the concentration of buildings including numerous skyscrapers behind the port are conspicuous. The Oceanographic Museum is conspicuous. From the E a horizontal building as opposed to the predominantly vertical ones is conspicuous on the waterfront immediately E of the harbour. Closer in the breakwaters and entrance are easily identified.

By night The entrance is lit, Oc.G.4s11M and Oc.R.4s11M.

Note The pilot station for the port operates on VHF channels 16, 12 and 6. Call sign is Monaco Radio.

Fontvieille marina. Looking down from the old town.

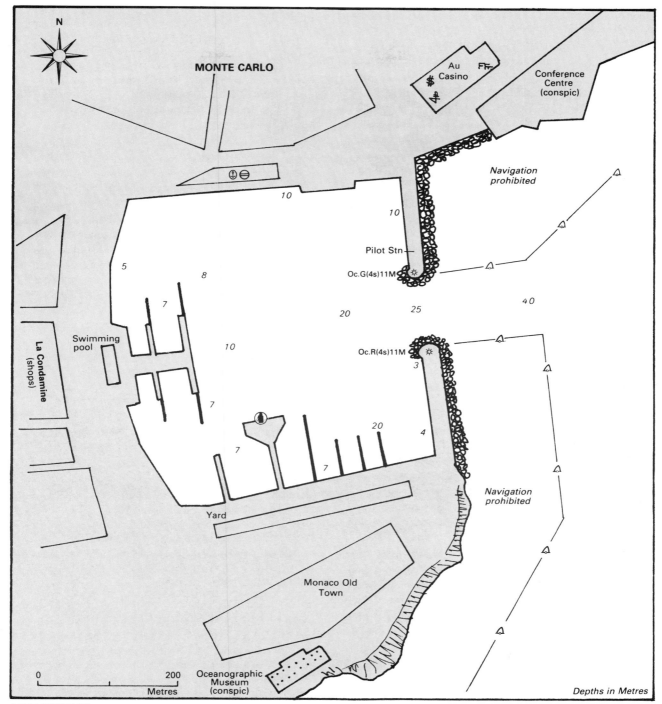

PORT MONACO 43°44′·1N 7°25′·5E

Mooring

Details 700 berths with 60 berths for visitors. Maximum LOA 140 metres.

Berth Report to the pilot station at the head of the northern breakwater where you will be allotted a berth if one is available. The harbour is a popular destination in the summer and berths are few and far between. Large yachts should book a berth well in advance. Small and medium-sized yachts can go to Fontvieille or Cap d'Ail if Port de Monaco is full. Some berths have laid mooring lines tailed to the quay. Large yachts must use their own anchors.

Dangers With southerlies and easterlies there is a confused reflected swell off the entrance. With gale force onshore winds the entrance could be dangerous.

Note A line of yellow buoys extends from the entrance of Fontvieille to the entrance of Port de Monaco and around the coast to the NE of the northern breakwater. Entry is prohibited inside this line of buoys.

Monaco. In the western approach the stadium with its arched colonnade is conspicuous. Cap d'Ail marina is on the left of the picture.

Shelter Shelter from all but easterlies. With moderate to strong easterlies there is a considerable surge in the harbour with the N quay getting the worst of it.

Authorities Customs. *Gendarmerie.* Port captain and staff. A charge is made.

Facilities

Services Water and electricity (220 and 380v) at or close to all berths. Telephone connections can be made. Shower and toilet blocks.

Fuel On the pier on the S side of the harbour.

Repairs 15-ton travel-hoist, 10 and 20-ton cranes, and slipways up to 100 tons. Mechanical and engineering repairs. GRP and wood repairs. Electrical and electronic repairs. Sailmakers. Chandlers.

Provisions Good shopping for provisions in La Condamine. Ice available.

Eating out Numerous restaurants of all types and categories nearby.

Other Post office. Banks. Hire cars. Buses around Monaco. Trains along the coast. Heliport at Font-vieille with regular connections to Nice.

General

Port de Monaco was built by Prince Albert I at the beginning of the century, no doubt to keep his own yacht-cum-research-vessel safe, rather than to encourage luxury yachts to visit Monaco. Prince Albert I was interested in the casino and its profits only to the extent it provided him with funds to further his oceanographic research, and when his royal duties forced him to mix with the rich and the titled, I like to think of him pining for his floating laboratory and the open sea as he smiled and made the appropriate responses.

Although the harbour was regularly visited by yachts large and small between the wars, it was not until the 1950s and 60s that the real competition began to get a berth for the season at Port de Monaco to display yachts which were more like little ships. The undisputed king of the harbour, indeed he was referred to as the 'uncrowned king of Monaco', was Aristotle Onassis and his much loved yacht *Christina*. Onassis had become a major shareholder in the casino, the Winter Sporting Club and a number of hotels, and on *Christina* he threw the most opulent and prestigious parties of the Principality. *Christina* was the benchmark for other rivals to aim at and the competition was bizarre at times. When Stavros Niarchos heard that Onassis had his bar seats covered with whale's scrotum he had his own bar seats covered with the same odd material. Larger and newer yachts were constructed to rival the *Christina*, but few could and even fewer could match Onassis' extravagance ashore and afloat. Until Prince Rainier forced Onassis out in the 1960s, he considered that Onassis' shareholdings in Monaco threatened the independence of the principality, the Greek shipping magnate was the undisputed king of the harbour.

Today the port is still on the super-yacht circuit, though I was interested to see that there were more large sailing yachts here than motor yachts. Certainly if you can get a berth it is worth putting up with the often uncomfortable harbour to be in the middle of Monaco.

THE CASINO

When Odile suggested we go to the casino one hot June morning, I really couldn't be bothered getting dressed up in a tie and jacket to gain entry. I put on shorts and a T-shirt and said I would make a tour of the back streets and shop fronts while she tried her luck on the roulette tables. Had I known the liveried staff would have let me in without a tie and jacket, had I worn a reasonably neat pair of trousers and a shirt, and had what is quaintly described as a 'desirable physiognomy', I would have been less slothful and my first visit to the casino would not have been confined to the main gambling hall and its serried rows of one-armed bandits.

The main gambling hall, up the impressive marble steps of the entrance, under a *belle époque* glass roof, and surrounded by glass cases with the costumes from various operas inside, is in striking contrast to the rattle and clatter and electronic chimes of the one-armed bandits. However much the old devotees of Monte Carlo were horrified when the first machines were installed in 1949, at least some of them have adapted and become addicted to electronic gambling. A grand old dame, all of seventy years young, bedecked in pearls and an elegant dress, sat next to

Monaco. The Oceanographic Museum set into the cliffs in the old town is conspicuous in the approaches to the principality.

me at an electronic blackjack machine with all the concentration she could muster, keenly watching the digital cards come up, punching the 'deal' button, and in half an hour worked her way through £100 worth of ten franc pieces. In fact old age pensioners were much in evidence, most of them patently not as well off as the grand dame, but nonetheless getting through ten franc pieces at a consistent rate. There were the young as well. I watched a young Vietnamese teenager in jeans and leather jacket sit in rapt concentration at an electronic roulette table and loose £120 in under an hour – I counted the wrappers of the bundles of ten franc pieces he left behind.

The present casino was designed by Charles Garnier, also the architect of the Paris Opera House, and was built in 1879. Additions were made up until 1910, but essentially it remains the building envisaged by Garnier. The style inside is of that era, when society was emerging from strict Victorian values and starting to kick up its heels. In the bar off the main salon the ceiling is covered in plump naked ladies lying around puffing on cigars and cigarettes. Gilt mirrors panel the walls. From the windows of the bar you have one of the best views out over the sea and plush red velvet chairs to rest from the exertions of electronic gambling.

Off the main salon and its machines are the roulette tables, but first you have to register and present your passport to show you are over 21, and to have your physiognomy assessed. Although a tie and jacket are not required by day, you must be neatly attired. Odile passed through to the tables while I, though not because of my physiognomy I was assured, contented myself losing heavily on the machines. Odile, with a run of luck on *carré* calls, was winning and returned periodically to subsidise my losses and to tell me how much nicer it was to gamble on the real thing. Fortunately I was to return, properly attired, to savour the quietness of the tables punctuated by the *rien ne va plus* of the croupier before the wheel is spun. No fortunes are made or lost in these rooms though I saw thousands of francs being wagered at a time.

The big-time gambling goes on in the *Cercle Privé*, a private club behind closed doors. Perhaps here, as in the days of old, a gentleman might walk out into the gardens and put a bullet through his head after losing everything he had. This caused the authorities a good deal of trouble and a certain Captain Weihe, a German naval officer, wrote a book in which he asserted that the bodies of the suicide victims were stuffed into cracks in the limestone under the foundations of the casino, until the smell became too great and the bodies were taken out into the bay, weighted, and consigned to the deep.

If you are on a winning streak it is worthwhile remembering that the casino has always made money. It got Charles III out of debt; provided Albert with the funds for his oceanographic research; in the 1920s it was among Sir Basil Zaharoff's interests and the shady arms dealer and manipulator of international affairs only took on things that made money; after World War II Onassis had a majority shareholding and it is estimated to have made him a great deal of money. It is owned, and always has been, by the innocuous sounding *Société des Bains de Mer*, the shares held by various syndicates and individuals. The principality now holds a controlling majority so that a Zaharoff or an Onassis can no longer threaten

Port de Monaco looking E.

Monaco. Often described, for obvious reasons, as a 'little Manhattan'.

the lifeblood of Monaco. The *Société* owns not only the casino, but also the Winter Sporting Club, the Summer Sporting Club at Monte Carlo beach, the beaches, and a number of hotels. It is the single largest employer and pays over forty per cent of the wages in Monaco. I didn't mind making a contribution to the *Société* and Monaco's wage packet for the elegance of the casino and it is, after all, an entertaining way to contribute. But don't forget, they always make a profit.

CAP MARTIN

Between Monaco and Menton, the blunt Cap Martin juts out with the elegant Hôtel Cap Martin on its tip. The hotel and also an old signal station on the summit of Cap Martin are conspicuous. In the last century the cape was one of the most exclusive places on the Riviera, but its popularity declined in the 20th century. It was off here that the architect Le Corbusier, the father of modern architecture, was drowned in 1965. Some critics of the modern architecture that Le Corbusier spawned have cruelly suggested it was not before time.

On either side of Cap Martin there are anchorages that can be used depending on the wind and sea.

Roquebrune Anchor in the bay where convenient in 6–12 metres on sand and thick weed. Care needs to be taken of the rocky ledge extending some distance out from the coast in places. Limited shelter from the N and E.

Carnolès Anchor in 3–6 metres on mud and weed. Really only suitable in calm weather.

Menton

The Vieux Port and the marina at Menton-Garavan sit right on the Italian border. In the case of Menton-Garavan, the border, a deep ravine in the limestone cliffs, is a mere 700 metres E of the marina.

MENTON VIEUX PORT

Approach

Conspicuous The buildings of the old town piled up one another and the cathedral and spire in the town are conspicuous. Closer in the high wall of the outer mole of the harbour, the small fort at the root of the mole, and the square light tower at the entrance, are easily identified.

By night Use the light on the end of the mole of the Vieux Port, VQ(4)R.3s10M.

Dangers
● In the approach from the E care should be taken of the reef extending out from Capo Mortola. The extremity is marked by a conical buoy, YB with a ▼ topmark.
● With strong easterlies a swell piles up at the entrance making entry difficult.

Mooring

Details 440 berths with 50 berths for visitors. Maximum LOA 25 metres.

Berth where directed or go onto the N mole and report to the *capitainerie* for a berth. There are laid moorings tailed to the quay or to buoys.

Shelter Good shelter except from strong SE–E winds which make the harbour uncomfortable .and could make some berths dangerous.

Authorities Customs. Port captain. A charge is made.

Anchorage A yacht can anchor off to the NE of the harbour in 6–8 metres on sand and weed, good holding once through the weed.

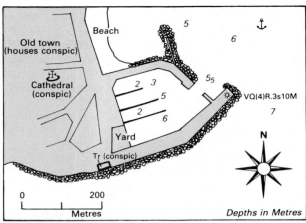

MENTON VIEUX PORT 43°47'N 7°31'E

Facilities

Services Water and electricity at or close to all berths. A shower and toilet block.

Fuel At Menton-Garavan or in the town.

Repairs Small yachts can be hauled out on a slipway. Some mechanical repairs. Chandlers.

Provisions Good shopping for all provisions in the town. Ice available.

Eating out Numerous restaurants along the waterfront and in the town.

Other Post office. Banks. Buses and trains along the coast and to Italy.

General

The Vieux Port is the best place to be for a short visit, being close to all the amenities and sights of the town. The town is only nominally French, in all other respects it looks and feels like an Italian town on the wrong side of the border.

Menton was one of the most popular resorts for the English in the 19th and early 20th centuries, being particularly recommended for its climate which was believed to be beneficial for chest complaints. Katherine Mansfield spent her last years here before she died at an early age from tuberculosis. She knew she was dying and wrote this poignant letter to John Murray from Menton:

'The wind of the last days has scattered almost the last of the fig leaves and now through those candle-shaped boughs I love so much there is a beautiful glimpse of the old town.... I've just been for a walk on my small boulevard and looking down below at the houses all bright in the sun and housewives washing their linen in great tubs of glittering water and flinging it over the orange trees to dry. Perhaps all human activity is beautiful in the sunlight. Certainly these women lifting their arms, turning to the sun to

Menton-Ville and Vieux Port (on the left). The approach looking W.

shake out the wet clothes were supremely beautiful. I couldn't help feeling – and after they have lived they will die and it won't matter. It will be alright....

Wander with me 10 years – will you darling? Ten years in the sun. Its not long – only 10 springs'.

(From Raison's *The South of France*.)

MENTON-GARAVAN

Approach

Conspicuous The marina sits just to the W of the border between France and Italy, a deep ravine that splits the cliffs in two. A large white building is conspicuous at the bottom of the ravine and a viaduct spans it at the top. Closer in the breakwater and a white light tower with a red top at the entrance can be seen, as well as the masts of the yachts inside.

By night The entrance is lit, Fl(2)R.6s10M and Fl.G.4s2M.

Dangers Care is needed in strong southerlies when a yacht must turn side-on to the swell when entering.

Mooring

Details 800 berths with 144 berths for visitors. Maximum LOA 40 metres.

Berth at the *quai d'accueil* just inside the entrance and report to the *capitainerie* for a berth. There are laid moorings tailed to the quay.

Shelter Excellent all-round shelter.

Authorities Customs. Immigration. Port captain and marina staff. A charge is made.

Facilities

Services Water and electricity at all berths. A shower and toilet block.

Fuel On the quay at the entrance.

Repairs 20 and 100 ton travel-hoists and a slipway. Mechanical and engineering repairs. GRP and wood repairs. Electrical and electronic repairs. Sailmakers. Chandlers.

Provisions Most provisions can be obtained in the marina. Better shopping in Menton-Ville about 15 minutes walk away. Ice available.

Eating out Numerous restaurants and bars at the marina. Others along the waterfront and in Menton-Ville.

Other Exchange office. Hire cars.

General

The marina offers better shelter and facilities than Menton Vieux Port, but is a little way out of town. From here the Italian Riviera stretches around the Ligurian coast to Genoa and while it has much the same sort of Riviera-type climate, it's character is distinctly Italian and quite different to the French Riviera.

Menton-Ville. More Italian than French.

Menton Garavan looking across to Italy.

243

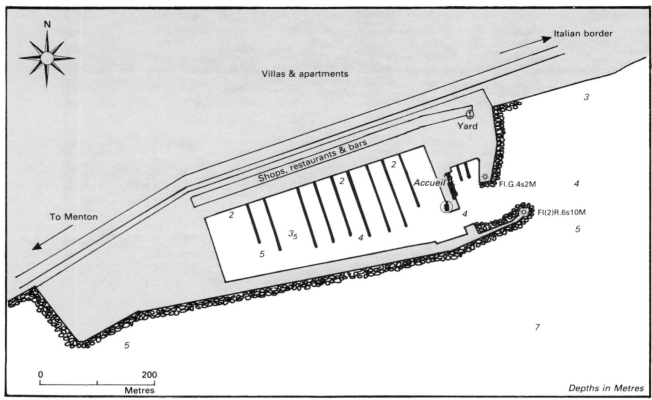

MENTON-GARAVAN 43°47′N 7°31′E

FROM MENTON

Many yachts will continue along the Italian Riviera from here: it is 14 miles to San Remo, the nearest large Italian harbour and from there a yacht can coast from harbour to harbour all the way around to Genoa. Alternatively Corsica sits over the horizon: Calvi is 92 miles and Bastia 118 miles from Menton.

VI. Corsica

The island of Corsica lies some 100 miles off the French coast, tucked in closer to Italy than it is to France. It's not surprising that the geographical distance gives it a quite different character to the French Mediterranean coast, a difference reinforced by the geography of the island. The high jagged granite mountains inevitably figure in any description of the island. In Dorothy Carrington's preeminent book on Corsica, naturally enough called *Granite Island*, she describes her first view of Corsica like this: 'The mountains surged into the sky, behind, beyond, above one another, ending in rows of cones and spikes and square-topped knobs like gigantic teeth. Their lower slopes, smothered in vegetation, looked uninhabited and impenetrable.'

For the yachtsman arriving in Corsica, the mountains provide one of the most impressive backdrops to a coast in the western Mediterranean. In places the mountains are the coast. The proximity of the mountains to the coast can cause a few problems for the yachtsman. Where the mountains drop straight down into the sea and keep going so there are considerable depths right up to the coast, any seas are reflected off it to cause a confused swell up to a mile offshore, though usually less. Winds are channelled through mountain gaps and funnelled off the high slopes causing severe gusts in places. And the high slopes are the perfect breeding ground for katabatic winds. The weather and the sea are in this respect like the land, savage and severe, and merit considerable respect.

The four parts of this chapter are arranged as follows:

West Corsica – Calvi to Propriano
South Corsica – Propriano to Porto Vecchio
East Corsica – Porto Vecchio to Bastia
North Corsica – Bastia to Calvi

I have started at Calvi as most yachts heading for Corsica from France make for this port first, and proceed in an anticlockwise direction right around the island.

Weather

In general there is more wind and sea on the W coast of Corsica than on the E. Having said this, I have to add the rider that at times the wind can gust down on the E coast with great force and can raise a vicious sea. The high mountains tend to stop the wind and force it around the edges or through mountain gaps, giving rise to strong gusts in some places and near calms in others. This occurs on the W coast as well as the E where the wind hits the coast at an angle.

WINDS

On the W coast the prevailing summer wind is a westerly sea breeze which gets up in the late morning and dies down in the evening. It normally blows anything from force 3–6. The sea breeze blows from the W in the middle of the island and is deflected by the mountains so it fans out to blow from the SW towards the northern half of the island and from the NW towards the southern half. At Calvi and L'Ile Rousse it blows constantly from the SW while at Bonifacio it blows constantly from the NW. Close to the coast the wind is much channelled by the land so it blows into bays and around or across headlands.

At night a land breeze may set in from the E although again it blows down valleys and around obstructions so that its direction can be anywhere between SE and NE. At times a katabatic wind will fall down off the mountains with great force in the evening or night.

On the E coast a light sea breeze blows onto the coast, mostly from a SE direction. However this sea breeze may be overcome by the stronger sea breeze on the W coast and when the *libeccio* or *mistral* blows, the wind penetrates over and through the mountains to gust down onto the E coast.

Around the N and S of Corsica the wind is channelled and funnelled with often vicious results. Around Cap Corse there will inevitably be a confused sea with any sort of wind, though it rarely precludes passage around it. With a strong *libeccio*, *mistral*, *tramontane*, or southerly gales, Cap Corse is a place to keep well away from. In the Straits of Bonifacio westerlies are channelled in between Corsica and Sardinia to produce stronger winds than those outside it. Easterlies are likewise channelled. Unlike Cap Corse, there are abundant places to shelter in the Straits of Bonifacio, so the strong winds are not as worrying.

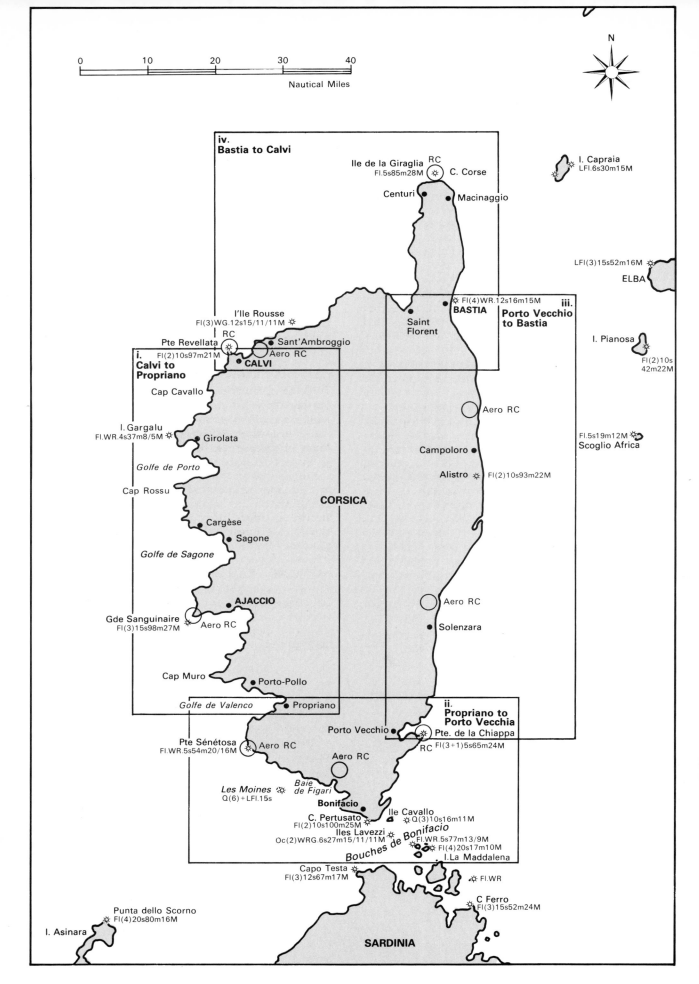

Nautical Miles

0 10 20 30 40

N

iv.
Bastia to Calvi

Ile de la Giraglia RC
Fl.5s85m28M ☼ C. Corse

I. Capraia
LFl.6s30m15M

Centuri Macinaggio

LFl(3)15s52m16M ☼
ELBA

I'lle Rousse
Fl(3)WG.12s15/11/11M ☼

☼ Fl(4)WR.12s16m15M **iii.**
BASTIA **Porto Vecchio**
to Bastia

Saint
Florent

I. Pianosa

Fl(2)10s
42m22M

Pte Revellata RC
☼ ☼ ● Sant'Ambroggio
Fl(2)10s97m21M Aero RC
● **CALVI**

i.
Calvi to
Propriano

Cap Cavallo

Aero RC

I. Gargalu
Fl.WR.4s37m8/5M ☼ ● Girolata

Campoloro ●

Fl.5s19m12M ☼
Scoglio Africa

Alistro ☼ Fl(2)10s93m22M

Golfe de Porto

Cap Rossu

CORSICA

● Cargèse
● Sagone

Golfe de Sagone

AJACCIO

Aero RC

Gde Sanguinaire ☼
Fl(3)15s98m27M Aero RC

Solenzara ●

Cap Muro
● Porto-Pollo

Golfe de Valenco ● Propriano

ii.
Propriano to
Porto Vecchia

Porto Vecchio ● ☼ ● Pte. de la Chiappa
RC Fl(3+1)5s65m24M

Pte Sénétosa ☼ Aero RC
Fl.WR.5s54m20/16M

Aero RC

Les Moines ☼ *Baie*
Q(6)+LFl.15s *de Figari*

Bonifacio

Ile Cavallo
C. Pertusato ☼ Q(3)10s16m11M
Fl(2)10s100m25M Iles Lavezzi Fl.WR.5s77m13/9M
Oc(2)WRG.6s27m15/11/11M ☼ ☼ Fl(4)20s17m10M
Bouches de Bonifacio I.La Maddalena

Capo Testa ☼ ☼ Fl.WR
Fl(3)12s67m17M

C Ferro
☼ Fl(3)15s52m24M

Punta dello Scorno
☼ Fl(4)20s80m16M

I. Asinara

SARDINIA

The libeccio and the mistral

The sea breeze is often augmented by the *libeccio* and occasionally in the summer by the *mistral*, though the latter is more often associated with the spring and autumn.

The *libeccio* blows from the W to SW and can blow anything up to force 7 or 8, though normally less. It is often a warm wind associated with cloud cover and sometimes rain. Normally it blows for anything from three days to a week and along the W coast it raises considerable seas when it has been blowing for a day or two.

The *mistral* blowing out of the Golfe du Lion has fanned out to blow from the W–SW by the time it reaches Corsica. It will usually reach Corsica a day or so after it has begun to blow off the Rhône delta, when the depression that caused it has moved across to the Gulf of Genoa. In contrast to the *libeccio*, the *mistral* is a dry, colder wind blowing out of a clear sky. It can blow with great force, up to force 10 or 11 on occasion, though normally force 7–8 in the summer, and it pushes huge seas onto the exposed W coast.

Both the *libeccio* and the *mistral* blow across Corsica and down onto the E coast. In places, especially at Porto Vecchio and Bastia, there can be severe gusts, locally called *raggiature*, down the valleys. There is often some confusion over nomenclature on the E coast when a *mistral* may be called a *libeccio* and vice versa. For instance any wind blowing from the NW and bringing rain is called a *mistral noir*, whether it is a *mistral* in origin or not. From Cap Corse down to Bastia the *mistral* is warmed as it crosses the land, so it is called a *libeccio*, while in Calvi the same wind is called a *mistral*.

Other winds

Tramontane A N–NE wind blowing off the Italian coast. It is usually associated with cloud and rain and can often blow at gale force. It is associated with a depression passing across Italy to the Adriatic.

Gregale A NE–E gale that occasionally blows in winter, though its full effect is felt much further S.

Sirocco The torpid southerlies that occasionally blow, sometimes at gale force, from the S.

Ponente Any westerly breeze.

Maestrale Any fresh NW breeze.

WEATHER FORECASTS

Daily weather forecasts are posted at all marinas, often in English as well as French, or there is the new *Antiope* video text forecasts which are constantly updated.

Telephone services (In French)
Calvi ☎ 95 65 01 35
Ajaccio ☎ 95 21 05 91. Tape recording ☎ 95 20 12 21.
Bastia ☎ 95 36 22 97. Tape recording ☎ 95 36 05 96.

VHF radio At 0733 and 1233 local time the weather forecast from Grasse Radio is transmitted at Ajaccio on channel 24, Porto Vecchio on channel 25, and at Bastia on channel 24.

The weather forecasts on *France-Inter* on 1829 metres (164 kHz) at 0645 and 2005 local time are easily picked up all around the coast. The areas concerned are Golfe de Gênes, Ouest Corse and Est Corse.

The Italian weather forecast on *Radio Due* on 1035 or 846 kHz at 0700, 1535 and 2235 local time are also useful. The areas concerned are Mar di Corsica, Mar Ligure, Tirreno Settentrionale and Tirreno Centrale.

MAGNETIC ANOMALIES

Off the E coast of Corsica magnetic variations up to and over 5° exist that have caused many yachtsmen, myself included, to wonder what was going on. Care needs to be taken over your navigation in this area.

RESTRICTED AREAS

There are numerous areas around the coast where anchoring and fishing (including spear-fishing) are prohibited. These areas are all clearly marked on the charts and some are marked by yellow conical buoys. Many of these areas where anchoring and fishing are prohibited have been established to protect marine life, a concerted effort on the part of the authorities to conserve and restore the marine environment. Given that Corsica has less pollution and more marine life than many other parts of the Mediterranean, the foresight of the authorities is to be applauded.

NOMENCLATURE

Around Corsica the capes, bays, islands etc., have been variously named by the Genoese, the French and the Corsicans themselves. Consequently there is a mixture of languages for the nomenclature. I have used the names in common usage.

Passage planning

From France most yachts set out for Calvi on the NW corner of Corsica. From Ile de Porquerolles it is 116M, from St-Tropez 102M, from Antibes 95M and from Monaco 92M. Calvi is easy to enter by day and night and the anchorage affords good protection from the prevailing winds. However there is no reason why a yacht cannot make for Ajaccio or Macinaggio, though the latter can be dangerous in strong NE–E winds.

Before setting off to or from Corsica, it is essential to monitor what the weather is doing and to get a 24-hour weather forecast. If a *mistral* rushes down the Rhône valley and fans out towards Corsica while you are on passage, exceptionally large seas can build up in a short time. On passage a listening watch should be kept for warnings of a *mistral*. On passage from Corsica to France, if a *mistral* gets up, it may be necessary to alter course to a harbour on the French Riviera or in Italy, afterwards working westwards along the coast to your destination.

Brief synoptic history

The following chronological list of events is not meant to be complete, more of a quick reference guide to put things in historical perspective.

BC
- *3000* Evidence of megalithic inhabitants.
- *1400* Toreens invade Corsica spreading west from Porto Vecchio and controlling the southern half of the island.
- *565* BC Greeks from Phocaea found a colony at Aleria on the east coast.
- *295* Romans take Aleria and establish themselves in Corsica, though the interior is not conquered.

AD
- *200* Christianity takes a hold on the island.
- *430* Vandals attack coastal towns and control the island by 460.
- *534* The Byzantines under Belisarius drive out the Goths and Corsica becomes part of the Byzantine Empire.
- *581* Lombards invade and in 725 Corsica becomes part of the Lombard Kingdom of Italy.
- *712* Saracens begin raids which continue right up until the 12th century. In the south a number of coastal towns are under Saracen control.
- *1000* Saracens retreat and the north is controlled by local seigneurs.
- *1077* Pisans make Corsica a protectorate and embark on an extraordinary church building programme, many of which remain to this day.
- *1133* Genoa disputes Pisa's rights to Corsica and gradually acquires territory. The Pisans are finally ousted in 1284.
- *1330* Aragon attacks the Genoese cities and again in 1335, but is repulsed.
- *1358–9* Anti-seigneurial rebellion led by Sambocuccio.
- *1376–1401* Arrigo della Rocca, supported by Aragon, rebels against the Genoese.
- *1380* Genoese found Bastia.
- *1453* Genoa assigns Corsica to the Bank of St George, a Genoese corporation with its own army, who impose a tough military rule on the island.
- *1553–59* The French with Sampiero Corso invade and control Corsica, except for Calvi and Bastia. Corsica is returned to the Genoese in 1559.
- *1564* Sampiero Corso supported by Catherine de' Medici rebels against the Genoese again and controls Corsica until 1567.
- *1567–1729* Corsica again controlled by the Genoese though there is much ill-feeling amongst the Corsicans.

- *1729–69* The Corsicans rebel and the Genoese retreat to the coastal towns.
- *1738–41* The French crush the rebellion. French troops leave in 1741.
- *1745–48* The British intervene, though not to any great effect.
- *1748* French troops arrive again and stay until 1752.
- *1755* Pasquale Paoli elected General of the Nation. He controls much of Corsica except for a number of coastal cities.
- *1769* Paoli defeated by the French and goes into exile in England. Napoléon Bonaparte is born at Ajaccio on the 15th of August.
- *1769–89* Corsica under French control.
- *1789* The French Revolution is mirrored in Corsica with the establishment of a Constituent Assembly.
- *1790* Paoli is welcomed back to Corsica, but by 1793 has quarrelled with the Assembly and proclaims Corsica independent.
- *1794* The British aid Paoli and an Anglo-Corsican Kingdom is proclaimed.
- *1796* The British leave and Paoli again goes into exile.
- *1796–1815* Corsica is a part of France under Napoléon.
- *1815* Corsicans are made French citizens.
- *1860* British tourists discover Corsica, principally Ajaccio.
- *1914–18* Corsicans fight alongside the French.
- *1931* Large police operation cleans up most of the bandits that have been terrorising the island.
- *1939–45* Local partisans liberate Bastia in October 1943.

CORSICANS TODAY

One of the first things people ask about Corsica is whether there is any danger from the Corsican separatist movement, the *Front de libération de la Corse* or FLNC. While the FLNC attacks tourist targets, it does not attack tourists. When I was last in Corsica the train between Calvi and Bastia was held up by the FLNC in order to distribute leaflets describing their ideas and aims. No-one was hurt and after the leaflets had been distributed the train was allowed to continue on its way.

The separatist movement, though supported in its general aims by the Corsicans, treads a thin line between support and alienation. In recent years the balance has swung away from the FLNC as tourism declined because of adverse publicity and naturally enough the Corsicans pockets were hurt. Ask most Corsicans what they think of the FLNC and they will answer that while they agree there should be more autonomy for Corsica and less direction from Paris, they do not want the total separation urged by the more radical proponents of the FLNC. Still, around the countryside the slogans of the FLNC are daubed

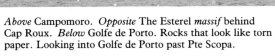

Above Campomoro. *Opposite* The Esterel *massif* behind
Cap Roux. *Below* Golfe de Porto. Rocks that look like torn
paper. Looking into Golfe de Porto past Pte Scopa.

Bonifacio citadel looking up from the harbour.

Campomoro.

Roccapina Cove. You need a calm day and an iron nerve to get in here. Prudence and a LOA of no more than 8 metres is counselled.

on rocks and walls and the signposts are disfigured and in some cases pockmarked by bullets.

I mention the FLNC because it is usually uppermost in people's minds and because the media, especially the French media, make so much of it. Most dubbed movies in France give the bad guys a Corsican accent such is the extent of the stereotype of Corsicans as gun-toting separatists. In reality your impressions of Corsica and the Corsicans will include next to nothing of them. Nor will the Corsicans you encounter around the coast conform to the usual stereotypes that paint them as a dark and gloomy people, difficult to befriend and slow to smile. On the contrary most of them have an Italianate gaiety, the young males especially have that irritating machismo found in Italy, while the women have emerged from Corsican kitchens to display their dark beauty in the cafés and boulevards. On the whole they are a friendly and mostly helpful people without being self-seeking or servile. However inland, especially in some of the smaller villages off the beaten track, the Corsicans do have more reserve than their coastal cousins and are less open to strangers.

One of the things a yachtsman should do on arrival in Corsica is purchase the Corsican flag, the *Tête de Maure*. Apart from the fact it is a nice courtesy to fly a regional flag, the *Tête de Maure* makes a pleasant change from the coloured bands and stripes and star combinations of most other national flags found in the world. The enigmatic emblem of a Moor's head in profile with a white bandanna was first used by Corsican rebels in the 18th century. They had taken it from the coat of arms of Aragon which contained four Moor's heads with bandannas, a commemoration of a triumph over the Saracens. Pasquale Paoli in turn adopted the Moor's head and it was then used for everything from the flags and banners of independent Corsica to its coins. Through all the subsequent history of Corsica it has remained the emblem of the island and most yachts visiting Corsica fly it under the *tricolore*.

Corsican cuisine

'And what about the food,' a friend asked me, 'is it still as bad as ever?' Corsican cuisine has not enjoyed a good reputation in past years, though happily, in my experience, those times are gone. One of the reasons is that it is difficult to find real Corsican products in the restaurants and paradoxically that is no bad thing. Corsican specialities produced outside of the Corsican home have tended to be second rate versions of the real thing: the cured hams are dry and stringy, the sausages are fatty and tasteless, and the famous *charcuteries* made from wild boar are hard and dry and over priced. The cheeses are better, but no match for cheeses from the mainland. Where Corsica does shine is in the seafood department.

The fish soup made in Corsica benefits from a variety and fresh ingredients. Though I don't expect anyone to agree, especially the Marseillais, I rate Corsican fish soup above that served up in restaurants along the mainland coast. As in France, the fish soup arrives with toasted bread, garlic, *rouille*, and grated cheese, and is virtually a meal in itself. Fish comes fried or grilled and often with a sauce derived from France. If you are in the money, crayfish and lobster are generally available.

More traditional Corsican cooking revolves around stews, though these are rarely available in restaurants. Most of the meat dishes offered are *à la Française* and none the worse for that. Spit-roasted wild boar is often mentioned as a Corsican delicacy, but it is not often on offer in restaurants. The only boar I tried in Corsica turned out to be pork and not game at all. I didn't bother with tracking down the elusive Corsican cuisine after that, but chose what looked appetising rather than what I felt I should sample – and on the whole I was not disappointed.

WINES

Like Corsican cuisine, Corsican wines have not enjoyed a good reputation in the past. Happily steps were taken some time ago to improve methods and standards and though today Corsica is not renowned for its wines, for the average tippler the wines are more than adequate. Some of the reds I sampled were particularly good robust wines.

The wines are graded as *Appellation d'Origine Controlée* from the vineyards of Ajaccio, the Balagne, Patrimonio, Porto Vecchio, Sartène, Cap Corse, and Figari. *Appellation Régionale A. O. C. Vin de Corse* wines come from the vineyards at Golo and the eastern coast. The wines of Patrimonio, Sartène, and Cap Corse are the ones usually singled out as the best of the bunch. In general the reds are superior to the whites which can be rather acidic.

GOING INLAND

Inland Corsica is as wild as it looks from seawards and even a short trip into the interior will be repaid with quite magnificent scenery. Buses run infrequently between the main villages and towns. The actual distances are not a good measure of how long a journey will take as the roads must often twist and wind around mountain valleys and average speeds can be low. For instance the distance from Bonifacio to Ajaccio is approximately 140 kilometres, but the bus takes around four hours, an average speed of 35km per hour. Hire cars are available in the larger towns and resorts, but hire charges are expensive, possibly because of the rough roads the cars must traverse.

In the north, the narrow-gauge railway, built in 1897, but modernised in 1983, provides spectacular views and a sedate pace to enjoy them. The railway runs from Bastia to Ponte Leccia where it divides, one line running down to Corte and Ajaccio, and the other running across to L'Ile Rousse and then down to Calvi.

Useful books

YACHTING GUIDES

South France Pilot – La Corse, Robin Brandon, Imray, Laurie, Norie & Wilson. Detailed descriptions of harbours and anchorages, aerial and sea-level photography, with folded chart.

The Tyrrhenian Sea H. M. Denham, John Murray. Out of print and out of date but with interesting historical notes.

Le Syndicat des Ports de Plaisance de Haute Corse issues a helpful booklet on the marinas north from Calvi and around to Campoloro. A booklet, *Guide Côtier Sud-Corse*, covering marinas in the south, is also available.

GENERAL

Granite Island – A Portrait of Corsica, Dorothy Carrington, Longman Penguin. A wonderful and very readable classic on Corsica. It is not a guide book, but will tell you more than most guide books about Corsica.

Blue Guide – Corsica, Roland Gant, A. & C. Black. A good guide book on things to do and see.

Corsica, Ian Thompson, David & Charles

Corsica – A Traveller's Guide, John Lowe, John Murray. A new guide to Corsica, sour in tone and disappointing in content.

West Corsica – Calvi to Propriano

CALVI

Approach

Conspicuous From the S and W Punta la Revellata can be recognised, but the lighthouse will not be seen until almost directly N of it. From the N and NE the lighthouse on Punta la Revellata, a square white tower with a black top, is conspicuous. From the NE the solid sprawl of red-roofed villas at Sant'Ambrogio is easily identified. Closer in the solid walls of the citadel at Calvi and the old town is unmistakable.

By night Use the light on Punta la Revellata, Fl(2) 15s24M. Closer in use the light on the citadel (Oc(2) G.6s10M), on the extremity of the mole of the commercial harbour (Q.G.9M), and at the entrance to the marina (Fl.R.4s7M). A night entry is straightforward.

Dangers With westerlies there are strong gusts out of Golfe de la Revellata and across the marina and the anchorage.

Note Care needs to be taken of ferries and trip boats coming and going from the harbour.

Mooring

Details 350 berths with 180 berths for visitors. Maximum LOA 45 metres.

Berth Where directed or go onto the *quai d'accueil* on the end of the pier just inside the entrance and report to the *capitainerie* for a berth. Large yachts go onto either side of the mole at the entrance. There are laid moorings tailed to the quay or to buoys.

Shelter Excellent all-round shelter.

Authorities Customs. Port captain and marina staff. A charge is made.

Note The marina is packed to capacity in July and August and while the staff will do their best to find you a berth, do not rely on being able to find one.

Anchorage In the anchorage off the breakwater of the marina there is good shelter from all winds except NE, which anyway are rare in summer. Anchor in 3–6 metres on a sandy bottom, good holding. Because of the gusts into the anchorage ensure that an

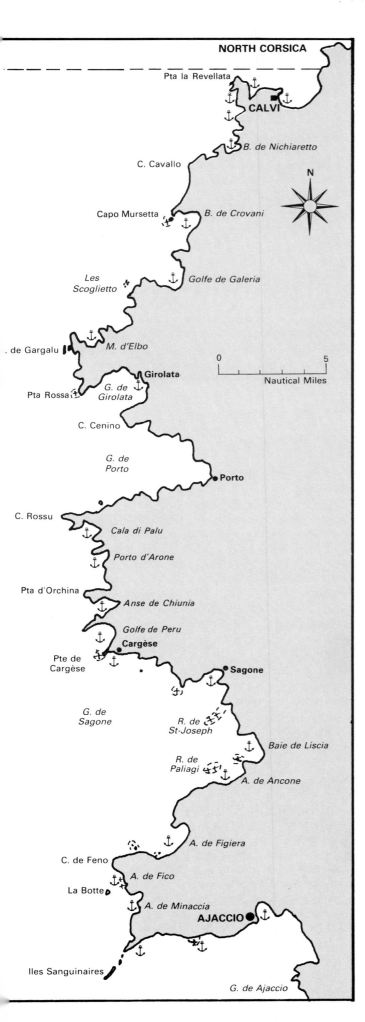

NORTH CORSICA

- Pta la Revellata
- **CALVI**
- *B. de Nichiaretto*
- C. Cavallo
- *B. de Crovani*
- Capo Mursetta
- *Les Scoglietto*
- *Golfe de Galeria*
- . de Gargalu
- *M. d'Elbo*
- **Girolata**
- Pta Rossa
- *G. de Girolata*
- C. Cenino
- *G. de Porto*
- **Porto**
- C. Rossu
- *Cala di Palu*
- *Porto d'Arone*
- Pta d'Orchina
- *Anse de Chiunia*
- *Golfe de Peru*
- **Cargèse**
- Pte de Cargèse
- **Sagone**
- *G. de Sagone*
- *R. de St-Joseph*
- *Baie de Liscia*
- *R. de Paliagi*
- *A. de Ancone*
- *A. de Figiera*
- C. de Feno
- *A. de Fico*
- La Botte
- *A. de Minaccia*
- **AJACCIO**
- Iles Sanguinaires
- *G. de Ajaccio*

0 — 5 Nautical Miles

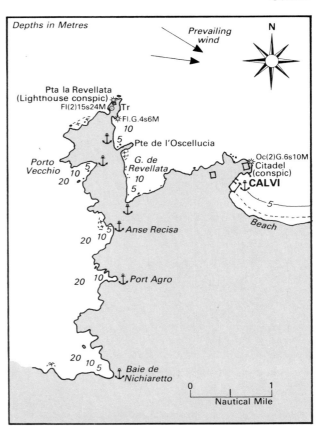

Depths in Metres — *Prevailing wind* — N

APPROACHES TO CALVI AND ANCHORAGES AROUND PTA LA REVELLATA

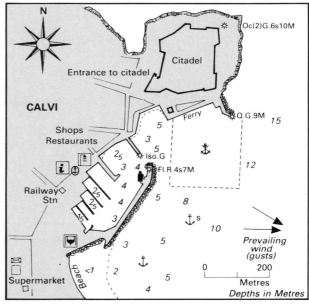

CALVI 42°34′N 8°46′E

adequate scope of chain is laid out. The holding has been described as poor, but on snorkling over the two anchors I had laid out, I found them both to be well dug in.

Note

● It is prohibited to anchor in the area off the commercial port where the ferry must manoeuvre to get in and out (see plan).

Pte la Revellata. The lighthouse is more conspicuous than it appears in the photograph.

Calvi. The citadel looking from the anchorage off the marina.

• In July and August large numbers of yachts use the anchorage at Calvi and a mass of masts extending SE from the marina breakwater will be seen in the approaches. At night less than 50% of the yachts display anchor lights, so considerable care is needed.

Facilities

Services Water and electricity at every berth. A shower and toilet block near the *capitainerie*.

Fuel On the quay in the marina.

Repairs A small mobile crane and a slipway. A 25-ton travel-hoist is to be installed. Mechanical repairs. Chandlers.

Provisions Good shopping for all provisions. Ice available.

Eating out Numerous restaurants around the waterfront and in the town.

Other Post office. Banks. Hire cars and motorbikes. Buses along the coast. Train to L'Ile Rousse. Ferry to Nice. Flights to Europe.

General

Rising up from the sea and the land as if hewn from the solid rock it sits on, the citadel dominates Calvi from whichever direction you look. The walls and ramparts look impregnable. The entrance is a narrow curving tunnel with a drawbridge and portcullis. Over the entrance is the motto: *Civitas Calvi semper fidelis*, a motto honouring the fidelity of the citizens of Calvi to Genoa. Inside the walls of the old houses lean over the narrow cobbled streets in a pleasantly dilapidated way and the only activity is from the tourists labouring their way upwards and the cars and vans of the French Foreign Legion hurtling around the corners to their base in the fort at the top.

The citadel dates from the 13th century though the site was occupied and fortified long before this. From around 500 BC the Phoenicians and later the Greeks used the anchorage at Calvi and established small colonies here. The Romans moved in and established a trading post they called Sinus Caesiae around the 1st century AD and were here until the Vandals destroyed the colony in the 5th century. Not until the 11th century under the Pisans did Calvi really get started again and the citadel was built in 1268. Just ten years later the citizens of Calvi rebelled and asked the Genoese for protection. The town was to remain loyal to Genoa until it was handed over to the French in the 18th century. One of the worst batterings the citadel got was in the 16th century when the French fleet, helped by the Turks, twice attacked Calvi. Though heavily outnumbered the citizens fought back fiercely and succeeded in driving the French off and for their valiant deeds acquired the motto inscribed over the entrance.

But in 1794 the citadel fell to the English and the strategy of one of her most famous sons, Horatio Nelson. Paoli had returned from exile in London and the English had pledged to help him regain power in Corsica. To take Calvi, Nelson decided not to attack from the sea, an almost impossible task, but to land artillery on the Revellata peninsula and haul it overland to the hill overlooking the citadel. After four weeks, 11,000 rounds of shot and 3000 shells, Calvi surrendered. It was here that Nelson lost his right eye when splinters of stone from an enemy shell landing nearby wounded him.

The citadel is not much frequented and is not at all reconstructed as any sort of tourist toy-town attraction. In a way it looks like it never recovered from the pounding Nelson gave it. In contrast the town around the harbour buzzes and sizzles with tourists. Cars struggle through the swarms of people on the streets and waiters nonchalantly dodge the cars to ferry cold drinks to customers doing nothing much at all. Calvi fosters an indolence that is catching and I stayed longer than anticipated.

BAIE DE LA REVELLATA

On the E side of Punta la Revellata there is a good anchorage sheltered from W–SW winds on either side of Punta di l'Oscellucia. Anchor in 3–10 metres on the N side of Punta di l'Oscellucia or 5–10 metres on the S side. The bottom is sand, rock and weed, bad holding in parts. There are strong gusts into the anchorage, but little swell gets in. Apart from yachts anchored in here, the place is deserted.

Anchorage can also be obtained at the S end of Golfe de la Revellata in 5–10 metres.

PORTO VECCHIO

A bay on the W side of Punta la Revellata. It is only tenable in calm weather or in light N–NE winds, being completely open to westerlies. The *libeccio* sends a heavy swell in here. Care needs to be taken in the approach of above and below-water rocks on the S side of the entrance. Inside anchor near the head of the bay in 5–10 metres on sand, rock and weed.

Anse Recissa

A not very well sheltered cove just under a mile S of Porto-Vecchio. Care needs to be taken of a reef on the N side of the entrance. Anchor in 10–15 metres and at the merest hint of a *libeccio* get out.

Port Agro

A small *calanque* just S of Recissa. Suitable in calm weather only as it is entirely open to westerlies. Anchor in 5–10 metres on sand, rock and weed. It was here that Nelson landed his guns and troops in 1794 to attack Calvi from landwards.

Baie de Nichiaretto

A large bay just over 3 miles to the S of Punta la Revellata. It is open to the NW–W and is not well sheltered from the SW, though in a light or moderate *libeccio* it is tenable. The best anchorage is in the cove on the S side in 5–10 metres on sand, rock and weed. In calm weather a yacht can anchor at the head of the bay in 6–10 metres on sand and weed.

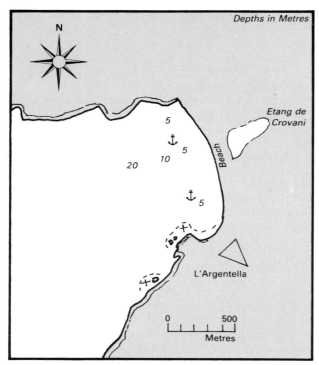

BAIE DE CROVANI 42°28′N 8°40′E

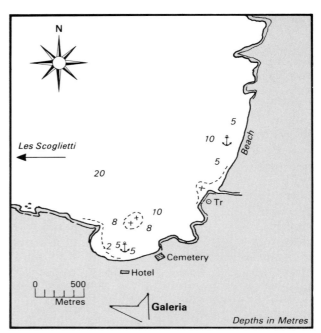

GOLFE DE GALERIA 42°25′N 8°39′E

Cap Crovani

A steep bold cape that is easily recognised by the disused signal station on its summit.

Baie de Crovani

A large bay under Capo Mursetta. The islet immediately S of the cape is easily identified. The bay is open to westerlies which send a swell in. In calm weather anchor in 5–10 metres in the SW corner. The bay is surrounded by high mountains with a sandy beach around the head of it. The small village of L'Argentella will be seen at the southern end of the bay. The village is named after a lead and silver mine nearby (*l'argent* – silver) and no doubt the inhabitants were being optimistic about the quantities of silver to be found. As it turned out, the seam expired and the mine is now disused.

Golfe de Galéria

A large bay S of Baie de Crovani. The group of rocks, Les Scoglietti, running out from the coast off the southern entrance, is easily identified. The bay offers reasonable protection from moderate SW winds, though some swell creeps around into here. It is open to the W–NW. Once into the bay care needs to be taken of a reef with 1·8 metres least depth over it, lying in the middle of the entrance to the anchorage on the S side (see plan). Anchor in 5–8 metres off the hotel on the shore. The bottom is sand and weed, good holding once through the weed.

Ashore most provisions can be obtained in Galéria or a mini-market close to the eastern end of the bay and there are several restaurants and bars.

In calm weather a yacht can anchor off the beach to the N of the Genoese tower on the rocky spit by the shore. Anchor in 5–7 metres off the long sandy beach, but be ready to get out in the event of westerlies.

Caution Though the cove off Galéria is tenable in moderate SW winds, with a strong *libeccio* a swell rolls in and there are gusts into the bay making it a dangerous place to be.

Anse de Focalara

An open bay 2 miles S of Les Scoglietti. In calm weather anchor off the small beach. The surroundings are spectacular.

Marina d'Elbo

In the SE corner of the bay to the E of Punta Palazzo, a ravine continues down into the sea to form a spectacular mini-*calanque*. In the approach a Genoese tower on the E side of the *calanque* is conspicuous as is a large rock off the entrance. Care needs to be taken of an underwater rock approximately 350 metres due W of the entrance, and for this reason the anchorage should be approached on a SE course. The distinctive red rock can be passed a short distance off and the reef running out from the eastern entrance point left to port (see plan).

Anchor fore and aft in 5–7 metres off the small beach at the head. The bottom is sand and weed. Reasonable protection from W–SW winds, but open NW–NE.

The *calanque* is a gem, a slit in the mountains that go straight up, or so it seems, to some 600 metres (nearly 2000ft), though it appears to be more. Marina d'Elbo is popular in the summer, not only with yachts cruising the coast, but also with the tripper boats which include it on their itinerary.

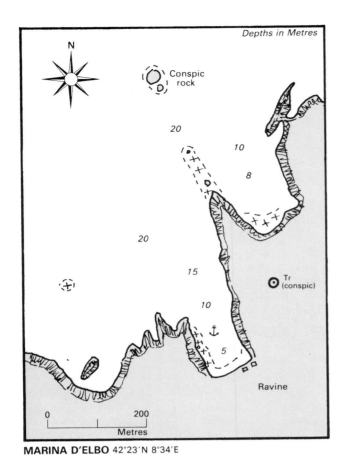

MARINA D'ELBO 42°23′N 8°34′E

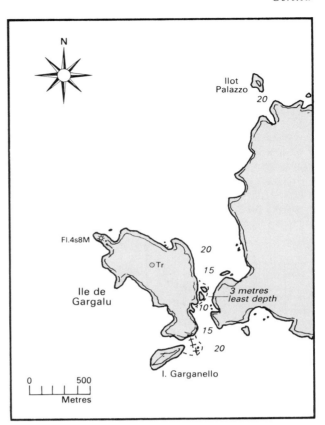

GARGALU PASSAGE

Ile de Gargalu and the passage between it and the coast looking
SE. Note the tower on Ile de Gargalu.

Ile de Gargalu

Ile de Gargalu is separated from Punta Palazzo by a narrow channel with a least depth of 3 metres and in calm weather is navigable with care, though local yachts charge through the passage with apparent disdain. The passage through the channel is spectacular with red rock cliffs on either side and clear turquoise water under the keel.

Ile de Gargalu, a craggy red island is easily identified from the N or S. The Genoese tower on the summit of the island is conspicuous. From the N the approach to the channel is straightforward. From the S a group of above and below-water rocks off Ile de Gargalu need to be avoided and the approach to the channel should be made on a NW course.

LA SCANDOLA NATURE RESERVE

From Marina d'Elbo a line taken east of south across the coast cuts off La Scandola nature reserve. Everything to the west is a nature reserve with a large number of species of birds, including several rare species, breeding here. The last bald buzzards in Europe are said to be here. Some 127 species of birds have been recorded in Corsica and of these 112 breed on the island. Amongst the species frequenting La Scandola are the sea eagle, kestrels, osprey, cormorants and Audouin's gull.

At La Scandola efforts have been made to accommodate tourism and the interests of the locals without endangering the ecology of the area. It is prohibited to camp or light fires and to fish in the area, particularly spear-fishing even without bottles. Between man and his effects, whether the noise and disturbance he causes or the more long-lasting effects such as the forest fires that devastate areas of Corsica in the summer, the guardians of La Scandola have their work cut out. Local fishermen have agreed not to work the waters off here. Visiting yachtsmen must respect the efforts being made here or they may well find themselves banned from the area in the future.

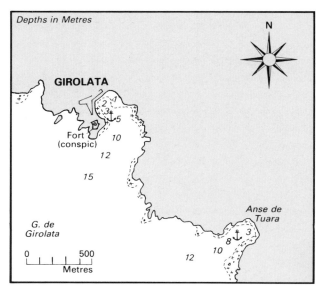

GIROLATA AND ANSE DE TUARA

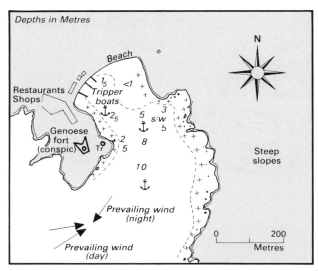

GIROLATA 42°21′N 8°37′E

PORT GIROLATA

Approach

Port Girolata is not actually a port but a sheltered cove at the W end of Golfe de Girolata. The approach is straightforward and free of dangers.

Conspicuous From the N Ile de Gargalu is easily recognised and the approach around Punta Rossa (Punta Muchilina) into Golfe de Girolata is straightforward. From the S Cap Rossu with a tower on its summit is easily recognised. Once into Golfe de Girolata the Genoese fort on a low headland at the entrance to the cove is conspicuous. However care should be taken not to confuse this fort with the tower on the low headland at Porto in Golfe de Porto.

Port Girolata. The approach with the conspicuous fort at the entrance.

The Genoese fort at the entrance to Port Girolata looking from the anchorage.

By night There are no lights.

Dangers When the *libeccio* is blowing heavy seas pile into Golfe de Girolata and the wind is funnelled by the high land on either side right into the head of the gulf.

Mooring

Anchor fore and aft tucked as far into the cove as possible. Alternatively take a long line ashore to the W side with an anchor out to the E–NE. The bottom is hard sand and weed, not the best holding, so make sure the anchor is properly in. In the evening and in the night a N–NE wind will often blow down the valley into the anchorage, sometimes with considerable force. If there are yachts anchored fore and aft and yachts swinging to an anchor, the confusion when the wind turns in the evening is considerable. Its good entertainment as long as the wind is not blowing too strongly.

Shelter Good shelter from all but a strong *libeccio*. If tucked right up into the NW corner there is all-round shelter, but otherwise a swell is pushed into the outer half of the anchorage making it uncomfortable and possibly dangerous.

Dangers Care must be taken of the shallow patch in the NE of the anchorage and of the rocks bordering the W side. When the anchorage is crowded, which it always is in the summer, the temptation to squeeze into the W side or the NE corner should be resisted.

Note In the season a number of tripper boats include Girolata on their itinerary. They use the jetties in the NW corner and access to these jetties should not be obstructed. I have seen small yachts moored close to the jetties swirled into others from the wash of the tripper boats when they arrive and leave which they do at near maximum throttle. When the last tripper boat has left for the evening shallow-draught craft can use the jetties as long as they are off before the first boats arrive in the morning.

Facilities

Ashore there are a number of restaurants and bars catering entirely for waterborne clientele. Limited supplies, including bread, are available from two small shops, though prices are naturally over and above the norm as everything must arrive by boat.

General

Shut off from the land by the mountains and ravines behind, Girolata looks to the sea as it always has done. The Genoese built a fort here to defend one of the few places their galleys and small ships could shelter from the prevailing westerlies. The galleys of the time were not deep-draught boats, usually drawing a little over a metre, so they could tuck right up into the corner of the anchorage out of the *libeccio*. The fort was to keep the sea route along the coast clear of pirates and corsairs and not to take possession of the surrounding country, which anyway was of little value and militarily almost impossible to contain.

After the Genoese left Girolata it was populated by fishermen and in the 20th century a motley collection of characters that Dorothy Carrington describes as '... a dozen or so Corsicans, without a road in a weird confusion of Biblical and Bohemian simplicity, gardening, hunting, and selling food and drink to passing fishermen, off-beat tourists and artists, and gangsters cheating the law'. The community exists now on the more prosperous pickings of visitors on tripper boats and yachts, and in the summer their numbers are considerable. The anchorage is packed over and beyond capacity and the tripper boats are crowded with happy holidaymakers only too eager to touch solid ground if the trip has been a rough one, get some food inside them, and most likely loose it on the trip back.

Anse de Tuara

A small bay to the SE of Girolata suitable in calm weather only as it is entirely open to westerlies including SW. In calm weather anchor in 5–6 metres taking care of above and below-water rocks fringing the edge of the bay. The bottom is sand, rock and weed, not everywhere good holding.

Golfe de Porto

The gulf with the small fishing village of Porto at the head is described in gushing prose in most of the tourist literature: '... the most spectacular place in the Mediterranean', '... one of the most spectacular and scenic places on the coast', '... a unique and dramatic beauty', or prose in a much similar vein. The prose may be a little overdone as it struggles to catch some of the moody and savage beauty of the gulf, but for the yachtsman the place is a nightmare in anything other than a flat calm. With the prevailing westerlies a swell is pushed into the gulf and rebounds off the steep coast to produce a confused sea that heaps up on itself from different directions.

The gulf is one of those places best seen from the land or, dare I say it, from the deck of a tripper boat. It is without doubt a spectacular place where the rock literally thrusts up out of the sea and keeps on going up to finish in jagged granite pinnacles and razor-backed ridges. The sun catches the red rock in different ways to create a natural light show, now picking out a rock that looks like torn paper and now softening hard barren granite into something almost malleable. It needs to be a calm day for the yachtsman to appreciate it or he or she may come away with a less benevolent view of the gulf.

There are a number of anchorages around Golfe de Porto, though no really safe ones. Use the following with discretion depending on the wind and sea.

Anse de Lignaggia A bay immediately E of Pte Scopa. Keep at least 200 metres off Pte Scopa to avoid an underwater rock off it and proceed into the bay. Anchor in 8–12 metres on sand, rock and weed. Open W–SW–S.

Anse de Gradelle A small cove just under 2 miles E of Pte Scopa. It is tucked under a rocky headland and gives some protection from NW–W winds, though it is open SW. Care needs to be taken of off-lying rocks on either side of the entrance. Anchor in 3–5 metres off the small beach.

Anse de Caspio A small cove immediately E of Gradelle, though not as well sheltered from the NW–W. Anchor in 3–5 metres on sand and rock off the beach.

Marine de Bussagna A large bay to the N of Porto village. It is open to all westerlies and a heavy swell rolls in with winds from this direction. Care needs to be taken of a reef off the above-water rocks off the beach. Anchor in 5–10 metres where convenient off the beach.

Porto The village at the head of the gulf is readily identified by the Genoese tower on a rocky outcrop by the village. There is no shelter to be had from

Looking into Golfe de Porto, the end of Ile de Gargalu is in the left of the photograph.

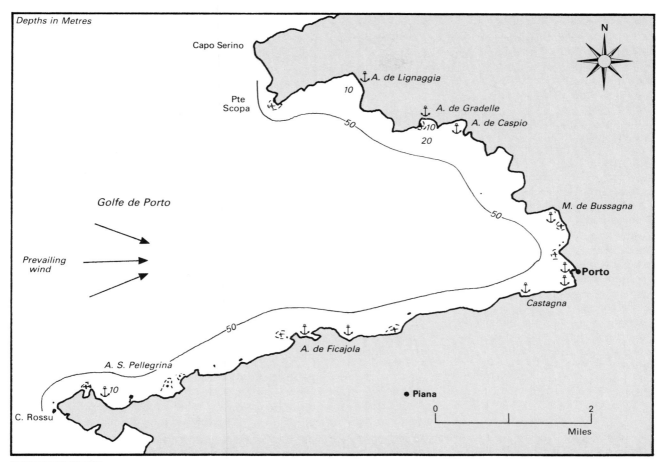

Depths in Metres

Capo Serino

Pte Scopa

Golfe de Porto

Prevailing wind

A. de Lignaggia

A. de Gradelle

A. de Caspio

M. de Bussagna

Porto

Castagna

A. de Ficajola

A. S. Pellegrina

C. Rossu

● Piana

N

10

50

10

20

50

50

50

10

0   2

Miles

GOLFE DE PORTO

westerlies here and a yacht should not attempt to anchor off in anything other than calm weather. On the N side of the rocky outcrop there is a short quay for the tripper boats.

In calm weather anchor off the beach on the S side of the rocky outcrop in 6–12 metres on sand and gravel, not the best holding. A swell rolls in with westerlies and just about any other wind direction as well.

Ashore there are numerous hotels, restaurants and bars, and most provisions can be obtained. Porto has become an important tourist base for exploring the surrounding coast, though it retains much of its original character. Why the Genoese should call the place 'Porto' is baffling unless it was because they could get their boats up the River Porto that flows into the sea on the S side of the tower. Local fishing boats use the river and once inside there is excellent all-round shelter.

Poztu di a Castagna A small cove tucked under Pta Capicciolo to the WSW of Porto. The cove offers some shelter from the SW, but naturally enough the locals from Porto have taken advantage of this and most of the cove has permanent moorings down for local boats, leaving little room for a yacht to anchor.

Anse de Ficajola A small bay approximately halfway between Cap Rossu and Porto. The village of Piana sits high on the slopes, around 500 metres high, above the bay. The bay offers some shelter from the SW, but with moderate to strong winds a swell rolls in and there are gusts off the land. There are a number of laid moorings in the bay. Anchor in 6–10 metres on a sandy bottom. The fit can attempt the climb up to the village where some provisions can be obtained.

Golfe de Porto. Rocks that look like torn paper. Looking into Golfe de Porto past Pte Scopa.

Anse San Pellegrino

On the N side of Cap Rossu there is a large bay suitable in calm weather. Anchor in 10–12 metres near the head of the bay to the E of the tower on Cap Rossu. With westerlies a swell rolls in.

Cap Rossu

This high cape, as its name suggests, is a distinctive reddish-brown colour. A tower on top of the cape is conspicuous from the N and S and helps to distinguish it from Capo Senino on the N side of Golfe de Porto, also a red cape, and Pta Rossa on the N side of Golfe de Girolata, yet another red cape.

Cala di Palu

A large bay directly under Cap Rossu. It is open to the W–SW so is really only suitable in calm weather. Anchor in 10–15 metres in the cove at the N end or on the E side. The bottom comes up quickly.

Port Leccia

An attractive cove just under Cala di Palu that offers some shelter from light SW winds, but is otherwise open to westerlies. Anchor in 8–10 metres on sand and weed.

Porto d'Arone

A large bay under Pte Tuselli. Keep to seaward of the isolated rock off the point as a reef connects it to the point itself. Anchor in 3–6 metres off the beach. The bottom is sand, good holding. Ashore a number of villas have been built.

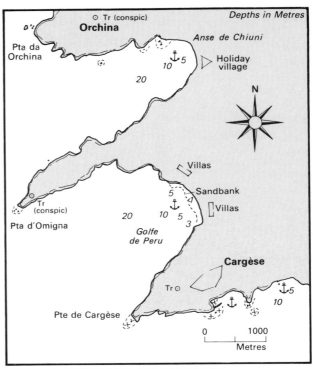

ANSE DE CHIUNI AND GOLF DE PERU

Anse de Chiuni

A large bay under Pta d'Orchino. The Genoese tower on the S side of the entrance, Torre d'Omigna, is conspicuous. Care needs to be taken of the rocks bordering the N side of the bay. Anchor off the beach in 4–8 metres on sand. Open to the W–SW when a swell rolls in. There is a holiday village at the head of the bay.

Golfe de Peru

A large bay under Pta d'Omigna. The Genoese tower on the point and the houses of Cargèse on the saddle of the ridge on the S side of the bay readily identify it. The bay is open to westerlies when a swell rolls in. Anchor off the beach in 5–8 metres on sand and weed. Care needs to be taken of shallows off the beach in places. There are villas around the bay and in the summer the beach is crowded with visitors to Cargèse.

CARGESE

Approach

The harbour and anchorage tucked in behind Pte de Cargèse is easily identified by the buildings of Cargèse on the saddle of the ridge running inland from the point itself.

Conspicuous Apart from the houses of the village, the tower on Pta d'Omigna stands out well. Closer in a tower on Pte de Cargèse will be seen. The breakwater of the small harbour is easily identified.

By night There are no lights.

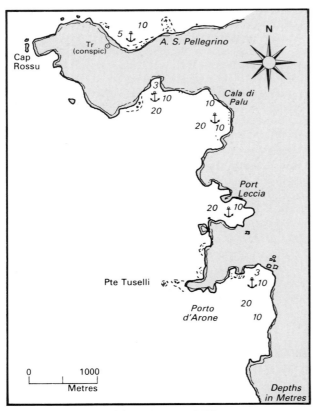

CALA DI PALU AND PORTO D'ARONE

Pte d'Omigna and it's conspicuous tower looking N from Anse de Chiuni.

Dangers

• The reef off Pte de Cargèse should be given a good offing as it is difficult to see, especially when there are whitecaps.

• From the E and SE care must be taken of an underwater rock with 1·3 metres least depth over it off the eastern entrance to the bay.

• In the closer approach stay well clear of the reef running out from the root of the breakwater.

Mooring

Go stern or bows-to the breakwater if there is room. The recent addition to the mole provides space for a few more yachts. In the near future three pontoons will be secured to the coast and will provide additional berths. Alternatively anchor in 4–8 metres off the entrance to the harbour tucked in as far as practicable. The bottom is sand, rock and weed, reasonable holding.

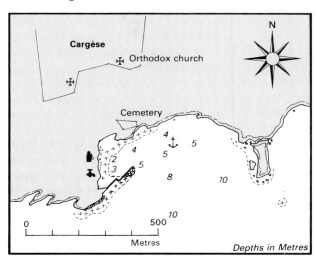

CARGESE 42°08′N 8°36′E

Shelter Reasonable shelter from the W–SW if you are tucked behind the breakwater. With strong SW winds the harbour is uncomfortable and in a southerly gale could be dangerous.

Note There are plans to construct a marina at Cargèse, but at present improvements are proceeding slowly with the breakwater extension and the installation of pontoons.

Facilities

Water and fuel in the village. Good shopping for provisions, and restaurants and bars in the village. Post office and bank.

General

Something about Cargèse seems out of step with the Corsican landscape. Not until you have looked at the village for a while, and at the church in the village, do you realise there is a flavour of the eastern Mediterranean here, and more than that, solid architectural testimony as well. The church in the village is typical Orthodox such as you might find in any Greek village and inside the ornate iconostasis and icons with candles burning in front of them are pure Greek Orthodox. Not surprisingly the village has Greek origins.

In the late 17th century a community of Maniote Greeks from the Gulf of Kolokythia on the bottom of the Peloponnesus, fleeing from Turkish occupation, approached the Genoese for help. Genoa promptly gave them land in Corsica in the hope the Greeks would help them subdue the troubled colony. The original land given to the Greeks was Paomia, a village inland from Cargèse near Vico. The Greeks planted vines and olive trees, and soon prospered much to the envy of the local Corsicans. Friction grew between the colonists and the locals and in 1715 and again in 1729 the village was attacked by the Corsicans. In 1731 the Greeks took refuge in Ajaccio

Cargèse. The village and harbour looking N.

when their village was burned to the ground. When
the French took possession of Corsica in 1768 the
Greeks were given Cargèse for the loss of Paomia and
again they set about cultivating the land and building. In 1793 the Corsicans again forced them to
return to Ajaccio, but by the end of the century they
had returned. Slowly relations with the local Corsicans improved and so the Greek community has
remained here, though much intermarried since
those early days.

The old envies and differences have died over the
years and the two religious groups, Greek Orthodox
and Catholic, live side by side with the Catholic
church just across from the Greek Orthodox.

ROCCA MARINA

In the large bay immediately E of Cargèse there is
shelter from W–NW, but it is open to southerlies.
Anchor in 3–6 metres off the beach on sand and
weed. Care needs to be taken of off-lying above and
below-water rocks off the coast.

SAGONE

Approach

Care is needed in the approach because of the off-
lying reefs around the bay. By day this is straightforward, but it should not be attempted at night.

Conspicuous From the W the low-lying rock, Rocher
Marifaja, will be seen and closer in Pta de Trill can
be identified. Give the point a reasonable offing to
clear the reef and shoal water off it. Once into Baie
de Sagone a number of hotels around the beach and
the tower on the W side of the bay will be seen.

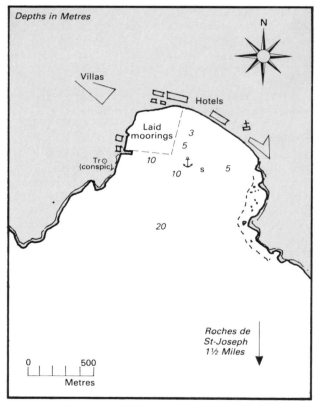

BAIE DE SAGONE 42°06′N 8°42′E

From the S it can be difficult to identify just where
the bay is until close in and the hotels and tower can
be seen.

Dangers
● Care needs to be taken of the reef off Punta de
Trill which can be difficult to see even in calm
weather.

Sagone. The pier looking from the anchorage.

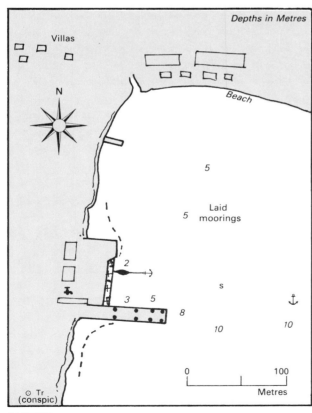

SAGONE

● Care needs to be taken of Rochers de St-Joseph, a reef extending SW from the eastern entrance to Sagone. Although the sea breaks on the reef, it can be difficult to spot until close to, especially at dusk. A back-bearing of 207° on Cap de Feno shows the safe approach line into the bay.

Mooring

Anchor to the E of the short mole in 6–10 metres on a sandy bottom, good holding. There are numerous local boats on laid moorings in the bay. The prevailing SW wind blows into the bay, though it does not blow home, so it is a good idea to put out a stern anchor to hold the bows into the swell after the wind dies in the evening. A yacht can go stern or bows-to behind the short mole, but the wind blowing into the bay usually causes a surge here and you will be more comfortable anchored fore and aft in the bay.

Shelter Reasonable shelter from the NW–W and though open to the SW, the wind does not usually blow home. A N–NE wind will often blow in the evening. With a strong *libeccio* Sagone is not a good place to be, though the local boats stay on moorings through the summer.

Facilities

Water ashore. Most provisions can be obtained in a supermarket near the mole or in the village. Restaurant by the mole and others around the beach.

263

General

The bay is an odd place. My first impressions were of an untidy resort around a fine sandy beach and I was ready to dislike the large hotels scarring the landscape. But somehow the hotels shrunk in size after an hour or two and didn't seem as obtrusive.

The history of the place is a chequered one and little remains to remind you of its former importance. Towards the end of the Roman era a bishopric was established here. During the period of the Pisan protectorate a cathedral was built and its ruins can be found by the river. Two ancient statue-menhirs were incorporated into it as cornerstones and as Dorothy Carrington points out, this was not for lack of stone or craftsmanship, but to demonstrate the triumph of the new faith over the old. Sagone suffered from numerous Saracen raids and this coupled with its malarial site led to its decline. The bishopric was moved to Vico and later to Calvi.

Perhaps reading this sad history caused me to view the place benevolently and not to begrudge the place its modest tourist trade. That and the friendly fisherman who showed me where to anchor, assured me it was good holding, and advised me to put a stern anchor out to hold *Tetra* into the swell.

Baie de Liscia

The large bay in the easternmost part of Golfe de Sagone. The tower on Pte Locca at the N entrance and the tower on Pte Palmentojo at the S entrance are readily identified. Care needs to be taken of the reef close to the islets off Pte Palmentojo. The bay is open to the W but some shelter from SW winds can be found in the SE corner.

Anchor in 6–10 metres in the SE corner. Care must be taken here as the depths come up quickly to 1 metre and less some distance off the coast. Alternatively in calm weather anchor in the NE corner in 5–10 metres taking care of a reef running out from the shore.

Ashore in the NE corner there are several hotels. There is also the Castle of Capraja, one of the strongholds of the Cinarche family who ruled over part of Corsica from the 13th to the 16th century. From their rough stone castles and forts this family fought not only the Genoese, but also feuded amongst themselves, so it is not surprising that hardly one of them lived out his natural term without coming to a sticky end either from the Genoese or from a relative.

Récif de Paliagi

Care needs to be taken of this reef lying just over 1 mile WSW of Pte Palmentojo. The reef and shoal water covers a sizeable area, but is readily identified. In calm weather it shows up as a discoloured patch and with any swell running the sea breaks on it.

Golfe de Lava

A large bay in the S of Golfe de Sagone. In calm weather a yacht can anchor in Port Provençal in the NE corner. It is easily recognised by the houses of the holiday village ashore. Care needs to be taken of a reef lying 200 metres to the W of the cove, but otherwise entrance is straightforward. Anchor in 5–10 metres off the beach on sand and weed.

In moderate SW winds some shelter can be found in Anse de la Figiera in the S of Golfe de Lava. A number of rocks and a small islet will be seen and a yacht can anchor under here in 4–7 metres on sand and weed. Do not attempt to pass between the islet and the coast as the passage is obstructed by a reef. good distance off.

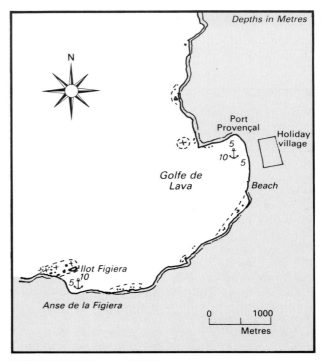

GOLFE DE LAVA 41°49′N 8°39′E

Anse de Fico

A small cove under Capo di Feno suitable in calm weather only, being entirely open to the W. Care needs to be taken of a reef with 2 metres least depth over it lying 500 metres WSW of the northern entrance.

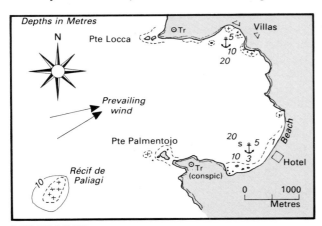

BAIE DE LISCIA 42°03′N 8°44′E

La Botte

A steep-to islet easily identified. Off La Botte and in the vicinity of Capo di Feno large confused seas heap up with prolonged westerlies and it is best to keep a good distance.

Anse de Minaccia

A large bay to the S of Fico and like it, suitable in calm weather only.

Iles Sanguinaires

This group of islands extends SW from Pte de la Parata at the northern entrance to Golfe d'Ajaccio. The largest island, Grande Sanguinaire, is easily recognised by the lighthouse on it, a white tower and dwelling; Fl(3)20s25M light. There is also a tower on the S of the island. A tower on Pte de la Parata is also easily identified. Yachts can take a short-cut between Pte de la Parata and the northernmost of the islands, Ile di Porri, where there are 7·5 metre least depths in the fairway. In strong westerlies care is needed as the waves heap up and break in the passage. However I have been through here after a NW gale with a 4–5 metre swell running and though not to be recommended, it is not as bad as it looks.

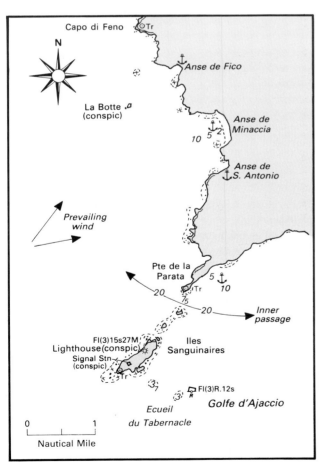

CAPO DI FENO TO ILES SANGUINAIRES

If going around the outside of the islands care needs to be taken of Ecueil du Tabernacle, a reef to the ESE of Grande Sanguinaire with 3 metres least depth over it. It is marked by a light buoy with a ■ topmark, Fl(3)R.12s light. Care also needs to be taken of the above and below-water rocks extending some 600 metres off the end of Grande Sanguinaire.

The name of the group, the 'blood thirsty' islands presumably describes their peril to sailors entering the Golfe d'Ajaccio. They have that sort of appearance being jagged rocks surrounded by needle-like rocks and reefs, an appearance reinforced for me during the aftermath of a gale by the large swell beating on them and sending plumes of spray into the air.

Pte de la Parata

In calm weather a yacht can anchor under Pte de la Parata where there is some shelter from the NW–W, but with strong westerlies from any sector a swell rolls around into here making it most uncomfortable.

Anse de Barbicaja

A shallow bight midway along the N side of Golfe d'Ajaccio. Anchor in 5–8 metres to the E of the reef running out from the coast. Reasonable protection from the NW–W, but entirely open to the S. There are hotels and restaurants ashore.

AJACCIO

Approach

The gulf and the two marinas here are accessible in all weather and although there are dangers to navigation close to the coast, there are none in the gulf itself.

Conspicuous The concentration of buildings around the city centre and the surrounding apartment blocks in the suburbs are easily identified from some distance off. Two chimneys with red bands and two large hangars are conspicuous at the N end of the city. Closer in the solid walls of the citadel and the mole sheltering the Vieux Port show up well and the older houses of Ajaccio will be seen. The light tower on the end of the mole of the Vieux Port is conspicuous. The breakwater of the new marina Port de l'Amirauté (Port des Cannes) will not be seen until right up to the Vieux Port.

By night Use the light on the citadel, Fl(2)WR.10s 20/16M. The red sector covers Ecueil de la Guardiola over 045°–057°. Closer in the lights on La Guardiola, Fl.R.2·5s2M, and Ecueil de la Citadelle, Fl(4)R.15s 7M, will be seen. The entrance to the Vieux Port is lit, Oc.R.4s8M, as is the jetty for the ferries, Jetée des Capucins, Fl.RG.4s7M. The entrance to Port de l'Amirauté is lit, Fl.R.2s, and Fl(4)Vi.15s1M on the elbow of the breakwater.

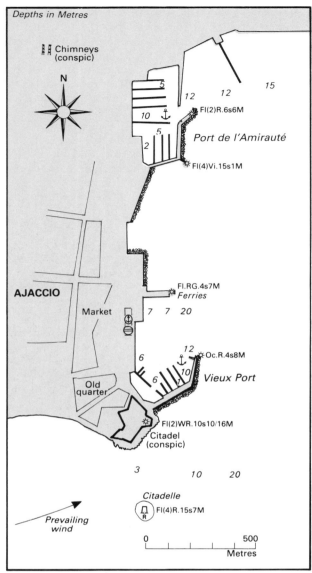

AJACCIO AND APPROACHES 41°55′N 8°45′E

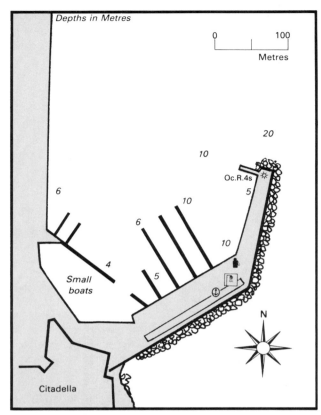

AJACCIO: VIEUX PORT

Dangers

● On the N side of the gulf care needs to be taken of the reef off Pte Scudo; of La Botte, a rock and reef marked by a small beacon; of Ecueil de la Guardiola, a reef marked by a sturdy red tower with a ■ topmark; and Ecueil de la Citadelle, a reef marked by a red tower.

● On the S side of the gulf care needs to be taken of the reef off Pte de la Castagna; the isolated reef La Campanina marked by a red tower off Pte de Sette Nave; the reef off Pte de Sette Nave; and the isolated reef, Ecueil Dorbéra, S of Pte de Porticcio, which also has a reef off it.

Mooring

Vieux Port

Details 250 berths with 63 berths for visitors. Maximum LOA 50 metres.

Berth where directed or go onto the fuel quay and report to the *capitainerie* for a berth. There are finger pontoons or laid moorings tailed to the quay or to buoys.

Shelter Good shelter although strong southerlies cause a surge. The coming and going of tripper boats also causes some wash which is uncomfortable.

Port de l'Amirauté

Details 648 berths with 78 berths for visitors. Soon to be expanded to 803 berths with 255 berths for visitors.

Berth where directed. Most berths are on finger pontoons.

Shelter Good all-round shelter.

Authorities Customs and Immigration at the ferry jetty. Port captain and staff in the Vieux Port and Port de l'Amirauté. A charge is made in both marinas.

Facilities

Services Water and electricity at or near every berth in the Vieux Port and l'Amirauté. Shower and toilet blocks in the Vieux Port and l'Amirauté.

Fuel On the quay in the Vieux Port and l'Amirauté.

Repairs 20 and 40-ton mobile cranes at the Vieux Port, but limited hard standing. A 50-ton travel-hoist at l'Amirauté. Mechanical and engineering repairs. Most GRP and wood repairs. Electrical and electronic repairs. Sailmakers. Chandlers.

Ajaccio. The citadel looking NW.

Ajaccio. Approach to the Vieux Port looking NW.

Provisions Good shopping in the town for all provisions. There is a daily market on the waterfront near the Vieux Port. Ice available in the Vieux Port and l'Amirauté.

Eating out Restaurants of all types in and around the old town. Several restaurants close to l'Amirauté.

Other Post office. Banks. Hire cars and motorbikes. Buses along the coast. Train to Bastia. Ferries to Nice and Toulon. Flights to Europe.

General

Ajaccio is the capital of Corsica and it feels like it. Cars and motorbikes hurtle around the narrow streets or more commonly inch forward in the all too common traffic jams the narrow streets cause. Pedestrians battle it out with the cars. Restaurants and souvenir shops line the streets. Vendors of balloons, candied nuts, fluffy stuffed toys, and badly made African statuettes tout from restaurant to bar to restaurant. Ajaccio hustles and bustles and it all comes as a bit of a shock after the quieter and less crowded places along the coast. But none of this should be taken as a vituperation of the city.

Ajaccio, apart from the anonymous modern apartment blocks on the outskirts, is divided between the old town and the new. The old town adjacent to the citadel was built during Genoese rule and it has a distinct Italianate feel to it. The six and seven-storey houses seem to lean over the narrow cobbled streets and shut out the sun. Washing hangs from balconies

AJACCIO: PORT DE L'AMIRAUTE (PORT DES CANNES)

and dark doorways reveal glimpses of small courtyards. The citadel on the point was built by the Genoese in 1554 and the oldest parts of the city date from around this time. The new city was a product of the 19th century and to a large extent, a British product in the same way many of the resorts along the Riviera were. It comes as a bit of a surprise to hear Ajaccio included along with Cannes, Nice, Menton and other resorts in the south of France, but that is what it was in the 19th century and much of its popularity can be traced to the endeavours of a certain Miss Thomasina Campbell.

Miss Campbell was a Scottish spinster of a certain age who arrived in Corsica in the 1860s and had a large villa built in Ajaccio. She was one of those eccentric lady travellers who sniffs at danger and hardship, who met and dined with Corsican bandits while recording the flora of the countryside. She enthused about Ajaccio and its healthy winter climate and the beauty and charm of the interior and recorded her experiences in a book, *Southward Ho*, a no-nonsense unromantic account of her travels. She befriended Edward Lear, a writer of more romantic prose, as well as of nonsense in his *Nonsense Rhymes*, whose *Journal of a Landscape Painter in Corsica* records in words and watercolours the savage and untamed aspects of the island. Other Victorian expatriates soon arrived and built themselves villas in Ajaccio. These new buildings in the Victorian style of Cannes and Menton and the other resorts, laid out on wide streets with large gardens, contrast vividly with the high narrow houses side by side in the old town. There is even an Anglican church built largely by the efforts of Miss Campbell.

While the resorts on the mainland prospered, Ajaccio faded from the genteel imagination to become the rather seedy capital of Corsica. After World War II Ajaccio was well nigh forgotten as a resort. Dorothy Carrington records an amusing conversation she had in the 1950s with the director of the Syndicat d'Initiative when she arrived in Ajaccio: '.... "I'm so very delighted to see you! The English have always favoured us.... We had many English visitors here before the war, but now the bandits have disappeared, we are less attractive to you."' Now the English are back and so are other Europeans, though not in the sort of numbers the locals would like to see. While having a coffee on the waterfront in June, black clouds began to gather and in ten minutes it had begun to pour with rain. 'Mon dieu', the patron said to nobody in particular, 'if the summer goes on like this, we will all starve.'

THE NAPOLEONS

Napoléon Bonaparte was born in Ajaccio. The city has erected statues to him, named the main thoroughfare, the Cours Napoléon, after him, made the Napoléons' house into a museum, and traded on his name and fame wherever possible. Restaurants and bars are called the *Napoléon* or the *Bonaparte* not just in Ajaccio, but all over Corsica. Yet the twist in the tale is that after Napoléon left Ajaccio at the

Napoléon as a rather grumpy looking first-consul in Ajaccio.

children every educational advantage to rise above their station. None could have foreseen what the results of the scholarship to the French military academy at Brienne and the Ecole Militaire in Paris would do for the young Napoléon.

Napoléon left Ajaccio in 1779 and acquitted himself honourably, though not brilliantly, to become a lieutenant of the artillery at the age of sixteen. The French Revolution in 1789 saw the return of Pascal Paoli from exile, though he soon squabbled with the revolutionary government and again declared Corsica independent. The Bonapartes were now on the wrong side and a target for Paoli's patriots. The house in Ajaccio was attacked and looted, forcing Letiza and the younger children (Carlo had died in 1785) to flee and hide in the *maquis*. The family was rescued by Napoléon and brought to Toulon, its fortunes in tatters. By 1795 the French were again in control in Corsica, Paoli was back in exile, and Letiza and her elder son Joseph were again in residence in the family home in Ajaccio. Napoléon saw the house again only once, on a brief visit on his way to France from Egypt in 1799. Letiza had already moved to Paris and no Bonaparte was to live here again.

The attack on the family house and its subsequent looting by his fellow Corsicans must have scarred Napoléon badly. His family was hounded from their native land and their reputation blackened, their fortunes apparently destroyed. Not until his final exile on St Helena did Napoléon recall the scent of *maquis* of the Corsican countryside, and perhaps too much has been made of what may have been an offhand comment. His request to be buried in Ajaccio only if he could not be buried in Paris gives his birthplace a mean second place. Nor are any of the statues of Napoléon there at his request, though he was fond enough of commissioning them in other places. They were all erected after his death and tell us little about the man. The statue outside the Hôtel de Ville of Napoléon as the First Consul, incongruously attired in a toga with four lions around his feet, can bear little resemblance to one of the greatest soldiers the world has seen. In the end Ajaccio was his birthplace, but not his home; nor, it appears, in his thoughts very often, nor his final resting place.

tender age of nine in 1779, he returned only once and far from honouring the city of his birth, he spurned it.

Napoléon was born to Carlo and Letiza Bonaparte in 1769. Carlo Bonaparte was a lawyer, a restless and ambitious though apparently thriftless man who in 1769 was working in Corte as secretary to Pasquale Paoli. With the defeat of Paoli at Ponte-Nuova, Paoli fled to England and the Bonapartes, Letiza heavy with child, made a perilous journey on mules over the mountains to Ajaccio. The family moved into the house now on show as a museum, though they occupied only the first floor, and Carlo set about rebuilding his career. He cultivated the newly arrived French authorities including the military governor, Comte de Marboeuf, and succeeded in gaining educational privileges for his children and the status of a delegate of the Corsican estates for himself. The Bonapartes, it seems, were determined to give their

Porticcio

A calm weather anchorage on the E side of Punta di Porticcio. Care needs to be taken of the rocks off the point and Ecueil Dorbéra, a group of above-water rocks S of the point. Anchor in 8–10 metres taking care of the shoal water that extends a considerable distance off the shore. A hotel and restaurants ashore.

Anse Sainte Barbe

An anchorage hemmed in by rocks and reefs on the N side of Pte de Sette Nave. It affords good protection from the W–SW, but is open to NW–N. The Genoese tower on the point and the red beacon tower

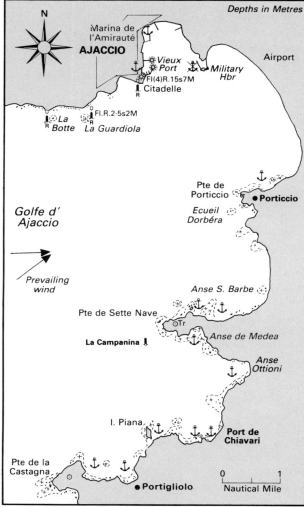

AJACCIO TO PTE DE LA CASTAGNA

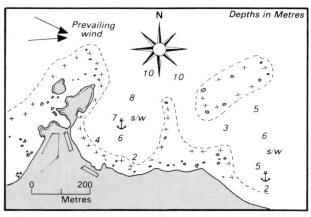

ANSE SAINTE BARBE 42°51′N 8°46′E

on La Campanina are conspicuous. In the approach care needs to be taken of the rocks and reefs off the shore and also of an isolated rock just under the water, 0·3 metres over, approximately 500 metres off the coast due N of the tower. The approach to the anchorage should be made on a southerly course after keeping well clear of the coast.

Anchor off the beach in 6–8 metres on sand and weed. Do not approach too close to the beach as the depths come up quickly from 3–4 metres to less than a metre over a rocky shelf. There is a holiday village ashore with a restaurant and bar on the beach.

A yacht can also anchor to the E of the above-water rocks bordering the eastern side of Sainte Barbe. Anchor in 4–5 metres off the beach on sand and weed.

Anse de Medea

A cove on the S side of Pte de Sette Nave. The prevailing westerlies blow in here so it is really a calm-weather anchorage. Keep well off the coast and approach it on a northerly course. Anchor in 4–5 metres on sand and rock. A number of villas have been built around the slopes.

Anse Ottioni

A bay a mile to the SE of Medea that can be used in calm weather. It is entirely open to the W. Anchor in 5–7 metres on sand near the head of the bay.

Port de Chiavari

A large bay immediately SSW of Ottioni. Care needs to be taken of the above-water rocks and the reef off the W side of the bay and the reef extending out from the coast on the N of the bay. Reasonable protection from the W–SW, but open to the NW–N. In the middle of the bay a group of above and below-water rocks extends out from the shore. Anchor to the W of these in 7–10 metres or to the E in 5–7 metres. The bottom is sand, rock and weed. There are a few villas ashore.

Ile Piana

To the W of Chiavari there is an islet, Ile Piana, just off the shore. A yacht can tuck in behind the eastern side where there is good shelter from W–SW winds. Care is needed in the approach to keep well clear of the reef fringing the islet, particularly to the NE of it where it extends nearly 100 metres off. Anchor in 5–10 metres on sand, rock and weed.

Anse de Portigliolo

A bay approximately a mile E of the conspicuous Genoese tower on Pta de la Castagna. It is open to the W. Anchor in 5–6 metres taking care of the above and below-water rocks fringing the coast. Ashore there is the small village of Portigliolo.

Anse de la Castagna

The bay on the N side of the point with the conspicuous Genoese tower on it. Pte de la Castagna itself is fringed by reefs to the W and SW for some 500 metres off the coast. When entering the bay care needs to be taken of an underwater rock (0·2 metres over) in the middle, approximately 200 metres off the beach. Anchor in 8–10 metres on the W side of the bay on sand and weed. A number of villas have been built around the slopes.

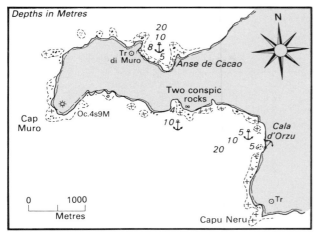

ANSE DE CACAO AND CALA D'ORZU

Anse de Cacao

A bay on the N side of Cap Muro giving good shelter from W–SW. From the S and W the lighthouse on Cap Muro, a white square tower with a black top, is conspicuous. The Genoese tower on the W side of Anse de Cacao is also conspicuous. Care needs to be taken of the reefs bordering Cap Muro on the NW, W and SW for up to 600 metres off the coast. In the approach to the anchorage care needs to be taken of the reef running out for 250 metres on the eastern side of the bay. Anchor near the head of the bay off the miniature beach in 6–10 metres on sand and weed. The bay is somewhat forbidding, being surrounded by low cliffs and steep slopes, the only relief being the miniature beach.

Weather note The prevailing sea breeze from Cap Muro and along the coast to the S is a westerly breeze tending to the NW.

Cala d'Orzu

A large bay under Cap Muro. There is reasonable shelter here from westerlies, though the anchorage is completely open to the S. There are two anchorages. Anchor off the beach on the NE side where several villas have been built. Care needs to be taken of the reef off the N coast and an isolated underwater rock 100 metres off the beach in the N of the bay. Anchor in 3–5 metres on sand, rock and weed.

The alternative anchorage is in a cove to the WNW of the first anchorage. Two large round rocks sitting on the E side of the entrance to the cove are conspicuous. Care needs to be taken of an underwater rock (0·7 metre over) approximately 250 metres off the coast to the SW of the entrance. A group of above-water rocks and a reef runs out from the E side of the cove. Anchor in 4–5 metres on a rocky bottom, questionable holding. The cove should only be used in calm weather or light NW winds.

Baie de Cupabia

A large bay to the E of Orzu. A Genoese tower on Capu Neru is conspicuous. The bay gives some shelter from light westerlies, but strong westerlies send a swell in here. Anchor off the beach in 3–5 metres on sand and weed.

Cap Muro looking N. The tower is conspicuous.

271

PORTO POLLO

Approach

From the W the anchorage and village cannot be seen until around Pte de Porto Pollo. The tower on Capu Neru is conspicuous, but the tower at Porto Pollo itself will not be seen. Closer in the line of rocks running out for some 800 metres from Pte de Porto Pollo will be seen and these should be given a good offing. From the S the buildings of Porto Pollo are easily identified.

Mooring

Anchor off the village in 6–10 metres clear of the permanent moorings. The bottom is sand and weed, patchy holding in places, so make sure your anchor is through the weed and holding properly. Good shelter from the prevailing W–NW winds, although there are gusts into the bay. With SW winds go to Campomoro.

Facilities

Water and fuel ashore. Good shopping for most provisions, and restaurants and bars in the village.

General

Porto Pollo sits on a golden stretch of beach and both its situation under gentle wooded and cultivated hills and the beach itself have meant a transition from fishing village to a modest tourist resort. Hotels and holiday homes have been built around the coast and along the east side of Pte de Porto Pollo, the western slopes of the point being too windy with the prevailing westerlies. The village is an attractive place with a cheerful feel to it in the summer, though I suspect it is rather desolate in the winter when the summer residents depart.

A taxi can be arranged here to go to Filitosa about 5 miles away, though the marina at Propriano is a more secure place to leave your boat for a visit.

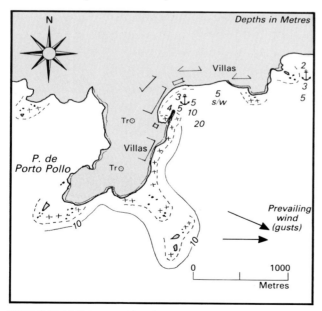

PORTO POLLO 41°42′N 8°48′E

FILITOSA

From as early as 4000 BC megalithic monuments to the dead were raised all over Europe and the Mediterranean. Many of them are well known: the stone circle at Stonehenge, the processional menhirs at Carnac, the stone temples and catacombs of Malta, and the tholoi-like figures of the Balearics and southern Spain. Many sites are not as well known from as far north as the Orkneys, through France, to the Mediterranean islands, as far west as the Caucasus and as far south as Palestine. Megalithic art was widespread and practiced by diverse races and religions, though all of it relates to the veneration of the dead and a belief in an afterworld. Sometime around 3000 BC this megalithic faith reached Corsica and was to flower into a potent art form and into an intriguing variation on the megalithic menhirs.

Filitosa was one of the centres of Corsican megalithic art and it was here that Roger Grosjean with the help of Dorothy Carrington identified the megalithic origins of the menhirs until then thought to be naive Greek or Roman work. The statues and burial tombs are much much older than this. The figures stand over a rocky incline in a shaded and wooded valley. The figures themselves stand two to two and a half metres high. The most famous of the figures, Filitosa V, is armed with a sword and a dagger, and he is clothed in what looks like a cloak. But it is the face just emerging from the rock that is most compelling; a powerful face with a cruel mouth and piercing eyes. It is the faces that set the Corsican statues apart from other megalithic art in Europe. The sculptors of these statues were not just leaving a monument to the dead, but were sculpting dead warriors and leaving a monument to a specific man. As Dorothy Carrington so ably describes, 'The head, hardly damaged, was astonishingly, disturbingly, realistic: the prominent brow, coarse nose, heavy jaw and small tight mouth make up the physiognomy of brutal power, the likeness it seemed of some formidable warrior, some prehistoric Tamberlane.'

Mystery still surrounds the megalithic statues of Filitosa and the other places in Corsica where similar examples have been found, just as mystery still surrounds Stonehenge, Carnac, Malta, and the other centres of megalithic art in Europe and the Mediterranean. Explanations stretch from the old masterrace theory, usually the Egyptians or the Celts are mentioned, to the theories of the credulous who attribute the statues to beings from outer space and attribute complex astronomical meanings to the stones. But though megalithic art seems to be of one type, there is sufficient variation in form and in the dates it originated, for it to be simply the early expressions of man to venerate the dead and the spirits of the afterworld.

Production of the megalithic statues ended around 1500 BC with the arrival of the Toreens. This warlike group apparently subdued the statue-builders and like all conquerors, set about rearranging the sites to their own taste. One interesting theory put forward by Roger Grosjean is that the statues armed with swords and daggers are portraits of the Toreens killed in battle, trophies erected by the megalithic people. The newly arrived Toreens were builders, but not sculptors, and it is they who erected the tombs similar to the Sardinian *nuraghs* on the site at Filitosa.

Filitosa can be reached from Porto Pollo or from Propriano, the latter being the safest place to leave a boat.

South Corsica – Propriano to Porto Vecchio

PROPRIANO

Approach

Propriano lies at the very end of Golfe de Valinco which has Porto Pollo on the N side and Campomoro on the S.

Conspicuous The long white sandy beach running from Propriano around to Portigliolo shows up well. Closer in the buildings of the town and the breakwater of the commercial harbour are easily identified. A belfry in the town and the white light tower at the commercial harbour are conspicuous. The marina breakwater cannot be seen until you are right up to the commercial harbour. The entrance to the marina is difficult to see, but it is obvious where it is.

By night Use the light on the commercial mole, Oc(3)WG.12s15/12M. Closer in use the light on the commercial mole, Iso.G.4s10M, and the light at the entrance to the marina, Fl(3)G.12s6M.

Dangers
• Care needs to be taken of the above-water rocks and reef off Cap Lauroso about ¾ of a mile WSW of the commercial harbour.
• Care needs to be taken of an underwater rock (1·1 metre over) approximately 150 metres NW of the

light tower at the commercial harbour and another underwater rock (1·5 metres over) approximately 90 metres N of the tower. Above and below-water rocks fringe the coast to the S of these rocks.
• With strong westerlies there is an awkward swell at the entrance to the marina, though it is unlikely to be dangerous.

Mooring

Details 380 berths with 320 berths for visitors. Maximum LOA 32 metres.

Berth where directed or in a vacant spot on the outer pontoon and report to the *capitainerie*. There are finger pontoons or laid moorings tailed to the quay or to buoys. Larger yachts go stern-to the quay on the W side of the marina.

Shelter Good all-round shelter though NE gales (rare in the summer) might cause some disturbance inside.

Authorities Customs. Port captain and marina staff. A charge is made.

Note There are plans to expand the marina by building a basin opposite the existing harbour. There are no plans to begin construction in the near future.

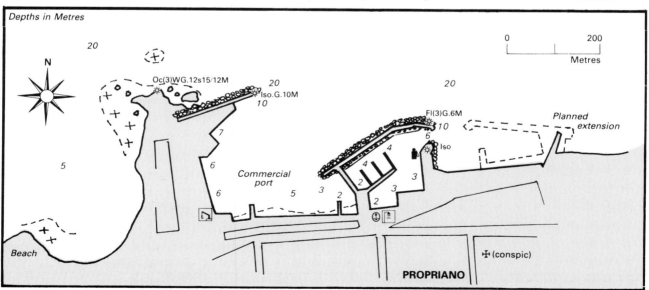

PROPRIANO 41°41′N 8°54′E

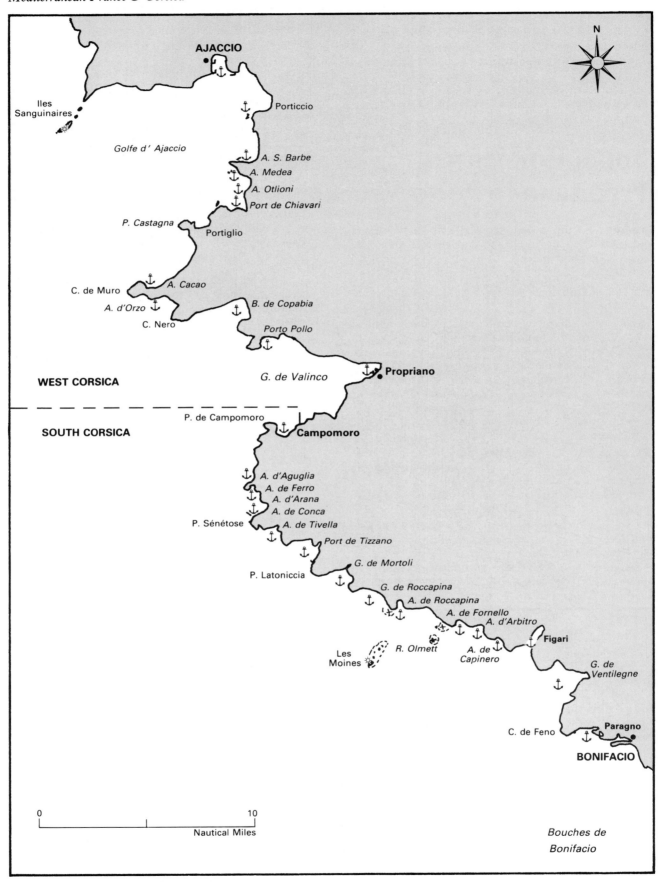

N

AJACCIO

Iles
Sanguinaires

Porticcio

Golfe d' Ajaccio

A. S. Barbe
A. Medea
A. Otlioni
Port de Chiavari

P. Castagna

Portiglio

C. de Muro   *A. Cacao*

A. d'Orzo

C. Nero   *B. de Copabia*

Porto Pollo

WEST CORSICA   *G. de Valinco*   **Propriano**

SOUTH CORSICA   *P. de Campomoro*   **Campomoro**

A. d'Aguglia
A. de Ferro
A. d'Arana
A. de Conca
P. Sénétose   *A. de Tivella*

Port de Tizzano

G. de Mortoli

P. Latoniccia

G. de Roccapina
A. de Roccapina
A. de Fornello
A. d'Arbitro
Figari

Les   *R. Olmett*   *A. de*   *G. de*
Moines   *Capinero*   *Ventilegne*

C. de Feno   **Paragno**

BONIFACIO

0   10

Nautical Miles

*Bouches de
Bonifacio*

Facilities

Services Water and electricity at every berth. A shower and toilet block.

Fuel On the quay near the entrance.

Repairs A 12-ton crane can haul yachts onto the quay at the root of the commercial mole. Most mechanical repairs. Chandlers.

Provisions Good shopping for provisions nearby. Ice available.

Eating out Restaurants and bars in the town.

Other Post office. Banks. Hire cars. Bus to Ajaccio and Bonifacio.

General

Tucked into the end of the Golfe de Valinco, surrounded by green hills that slope gently up to the high mountains behind, and with a white sandy beach stretching right around the gulf, Propriano attracts its fair share of tourists in the summer. The fishing village has been turned upside down to provide hotels, restaurants, bars and boutiques for the summer visitors and it fairly hums with the sound of its new cottage industry. Yet like Porto Pollo, this vigour has a charm of its own. Perhaps the vigorous celebration is a palliative for the rigours of the past and the not-so-distant past as well.

Propriano is mostly a new place, the original fishing village was destroyed repeatedly in the 16th and 17th centuries by the Turks and it was not until a hundred years ago that Propriano got started again. Most of the houses date from this period and the new edifices of the tourist trade are plainly visible amongst the older houses. Even in the 1950s Propriano had an uncertain reputation as Dorothy Carrington records. She was staying in the small village of Olmeto and her hosts had warned her of the violent reputation of the place, of innocent locals murdered in drunken revelry, of innocent tourists robbed and then murdered, of a local fisherman who killed the coastguard who had him convicted of fishing with dynamite, a catalogue of violent crimes. Originally I wrote that it no longer has this reputation, but in April 1990 the FLNC blew up a restaurant and holiday village in the vicinity, though no one was hurt. It seems Propriano is determined to hold onto its violent reputation.

CAMPOMORO

Approach

This large bay is tucked under Pte de Campomoro at the southern entrance to the Golfe de Valinco. The Genoese tower on the point is conspicuous from all directions.

Dangers Care needs to be taken of the above and below-water rocks fringing Pte de Campomoro. On the W side a reef to the SW of the tower extends 550 metres from the coast. On the E side of the point a chain of rocks extends out in a NE direction. The latter are easily identified.

Propriano. View from the marina.

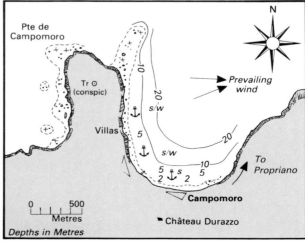

CAMPOMORO 41°38′N 8°49′E

Pte de Campomoro looking NE. The tower on the summit of the point is conspicuous.

Mooring

Anchor in the SW corner or off the SW side of the bay. The SW corner is the best place as there are convenient depths of 4–10 metres outside the permanent moorings. Off the W side a yacht will have to anchor in deeper water, 8–20 metres depending on where there is space. The bottom is sand and thick weed, good holding once through the weed and into the sand.

Shelter Good shelter from westerlies, even moderate NW winds to which the bay is partially open. Open to the N.

Facilities

Some provisions can be obtained ashore and restaurants and bars open in the summer.

General

The small village of Campomoro that straggles around the beach is dwarfed by the steep bare slopes rising up behind it. It is an attractive place on the edge of the beach with tall palm trees dotted about which give it an almost North African feel. On the slopes behind is the Château Durazzo, presumably belonging to the same Durazzo family of Fozzano who feuded violently for over a century with their neighbours, the Carabella, a vendetta recorded in Prosper Merimée's novel *Colomba*.

Campomoro.

ANSE D'AGUGLIA TO CALA LONGA

Anse d'Aguglia

A small inlet on the N side of Pte d'Eccica. The islet off Pte d'Eccica shows up well. The inlet is open to westerlies and is only suitable in calm weather. Care needs to be taken of the above and below-water rocks fringing the entrance. Anchor in 8–10 metres on sand, rock and weed.

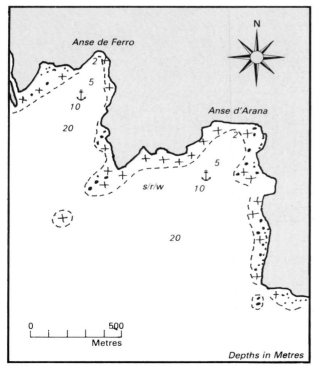

ANSE DE FERRO AND ARANA

Anse de Ferro

A cove on the S side of Pte d'Eccica sheltered from the NW but open to the W–SW. Although there is a narrow passage between Pte d'Eccica and the coast, it is bordered by reefs and inadvisable. In the approach to Anse de Ferro care should be taken of the above and below-water rocks bordering the coast and of an underwater rock (0·5 metre over) approximately 400 metres SW of the eastern entrance point. Anchor in 5–8 metres on sand and weed.

Anse d'Arana

A cove immediately S of Ferro. Care needs to be taken of the reef and isolated underwater rock running out SW between the two coves. Anchor in 4–5 metres on sand, rock and weed, taking care of the above and below-water rocks fringing the coast. Shelter as for Ferro.

Anse de Conca

A cove affording shelter from the NW and SW, but open to the W. With the prevailing NW wind it affords reasonable shelter. The cove lies tucked into the E beyond the conspicuous white rocks of Scoglio Bianco. Care needs to be taken of two underwater rocks in the approach. The first lies 100 metres off a conspicuous rock to the N of the entrance. The second (1·8 metres over) lies 500 metres W of the southern entrance point (see plan). Anchor in 5–7 metres on sand. The bay is an attractive place with rocky slopes sparsely covered with *maquis* and clear turquoise water over a sandy bottom.

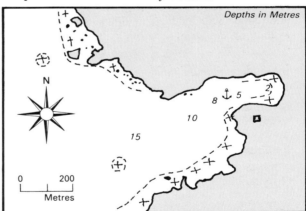

ANSE DE CONCA 41°34′N 8°48′E

Scoglio Bianco

An anchorage tucked behind the conspicuous white blotchy rocks of Scoglio Bianco which make up Pointe de Sénétosa. The Genoese tower above the point is conspicuous. The rocky cove is sheltered from the W–SW and even from light NW winds. Care needs to be taken of an underwater rock 200 metres off Pte de Sénétosa, not to be confused with the 4 metre patch off the entrance. Anchor in 7–10 metres on sand, rock and weed. The deserted bay is surrounded by rounded white and grey rocks, hence its name, that have been sculpted by the wind and sea into weird and wonderful shapes.

277

Scoglio Bianco. The Henry Moore sculpted anchorage.

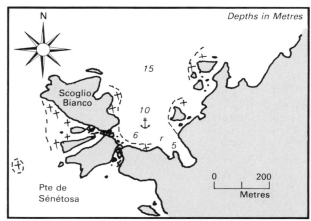

SCOGLIO BIANCO 41°34′N 8 °47′E

Pointe de Sénétosa

This point with the lighthouse off Pte Aquila is easily identified by the lighthouse and other man-made clutter on it. The lighthouse itself is conspicuous with twin white towers on a white dwelling. The aero RDF beacon, a lattice tower, and two large wind generators are also conspicuous. On the summit is the Genoese tower.

Care needs to be taken of the above and below-water rocks off the point and also the isolated underwater rock off Pointe de Sénétosa itself.

Anse de Tivella

A small cove tucked into the E of Pte Aquila. It provides some shelter from NW winds, but is open to the W–SW. It can be recognised by the green valley running inland from it. Anchor in 5–8 metres on sand and weed.

Cala Longa

A narrow inlet immediately SE of Tivella. Care needs to be taken of an underwater rock approximately 200 metres off the coast midway between Tivella and Cala Longa. The inlet is very narrow and bordered by a reef on its eastern side. Anchor in 5–8 metres on sand in the 'basin' before the inlet narrows.

Cala di Tizzano

An inlet on the N side of Pte Latoniccia. Good shelter from the prevailing westerlies can be found here except for strong SW winds. The numerous villas built on the slopes around the inlet make it readily identifiable. Care needs to be taken of an underwater rock (1·5 metres over) lying approximately 200 metres S of the western entrance to the inlet.

Inside the inlet the depths shelve quickly to less than a metre in the northern half, and a number of moorings for local craft have been laid in the middle. Consequently a yacht must anchor where it can, the best place being in 4–5 metres on the W side. The bottom is sand with some rock and weed, but generally good holding. Limited provisions can be obtained ashore and a restaurant and bar open in the summer. Not far inland at Palaggiu there is a major site of the megalithic culture with a large number of menhirs, 258 of them, and it may be possible to arrange a taxi or to hitch a lift from Tizzano to the site.

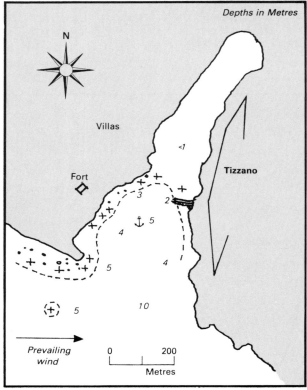

CALA DI TIZZANO 41°32′N 8°41′E

Golfe de Murtoli

A large bay under Pte Latoniccia. The islet off the point, La Botte, is conspicuous from the N and S.

278

La Botte, easily identified from the N and S, off Pte Latoniccia.

There are several anchorages in the bay depending on the wind and sea.

With NW winds anchor in the cove on the N side in 8–10 metres on sand. Alternatively anchor at the N end of the beach in the NE corner in 7–10 metres on sand. With SW winds anchor in the cove on the E side in 5–10 metres. With strong westerlies none of the anchorages are really tenable.

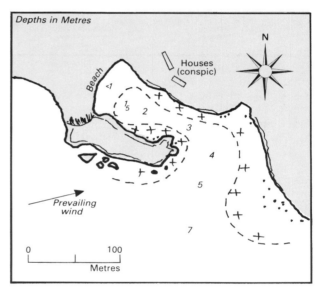

ROCCAPINA COVE

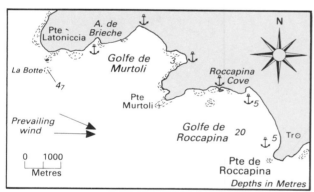

GOLFE DE MURTOLI AND ROCCAPINA

Golfe de Roccapina

A large bay immediately SE of Murtoli. Care needs to be taken of the rocks and reef extending out from the point between Murtoli and Roccapina. There is also a group of low-lying rocks on the W side of the bay that can be difficult to see. Anchor at the NW end of the long sandy beach in 5–10 metres on sand. This is a fair-weather anchorage only and when the prevailing westerlies get up you must be prepared to move.

Roccapina cove

In the N of Golfe de Roccapina, to the W of the beach, there is a minute cove. It should be stressed that you need an iron nerve and calm weather to get in here. A small yacht, 8 metres or less and drawing less than 1·5 metres, could get into this entrancing place. In the gulf a large two-storeyed stone house stands out prominently and the cove is right underneath it. You will need someone up front to con you in. Anchor fore and aft as there is not room to swing. From halfway in the bottom comes up gradually to the beach. In *Tetra* (10 metres and drawing 1·6 metres), I nudged in until I just touched bottom to drop the anchor and then backed off. One of the problems here is turning to get out, though smaller craft than *Tetra* should have fewer problems. Nonetheless much prudence is counselled.

Anse de Roccapina

A small bay to the E of Golfe de Roccapina, on the E side of Pte de Roccapina. The Genoese tower on the W side of the bay and two craggy peaks (Lion de Roccapina), just inland, are conspicuous. In the entrance there is a group of above-water rocks easily

279

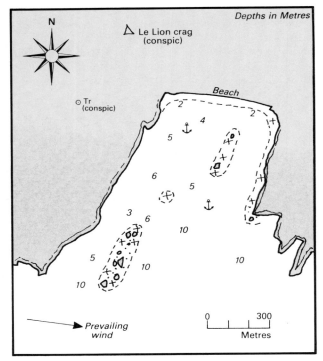

ANSE DE ROCCAPINA 41°29′N 8°56′E

recognised and there is another above-water rock in the NW of the bay. Approximately midway between these two groups of rocks there is an underwater rock that must be avoided (see plan).

The best anchorage is in the NE of the bay in 3–6 metres on sand, good holding. However in the summer the anchorage is very popular and you will have to anchor wherever you can. Good shelter from all but southerlies and quite magnificent wild surroundings.

Les Moines

A group of rocky islets lying between 2½ and 4 miles off the coast. The outermost islet has a solid black tower on it with a yellow top and is conspicuous from a considerable distance off. It is lit, Q(6)+LFl.15s 11M. When closer in the inner and outer group of islets will be seen. Between Les Moines and the coast there is a reef and shoal water, Ecueil d'Olmeto, at a distance of approximately 1½ miles off the Genoese tower on Pte d'Olmeto. This reef can be difficult to see until close to it. Closer in to the coast there is an above-water rock, Le Prêtre, and a reef.

While the prudent course is to go outside Les Moines beacon, the passage between Les Moines and Ecueil d'Olmeto is safe and deep. In calm weather the passage between Le Prêtre rock and Ecueil d'Olmeto is perfectly feasible, though due caution should be exercised and a lookout stationed forward.

Anse de Fornello

A bay lying to the E of Pte d'Olmeto. The Genoese tower, Torre d'Olmeto, is easily identified at the western entrance to the bay. Care needs to be taken of an underwater rock (1·5 metres over) in the entrance. Keep to the W side of the bay to avoid it. An-

chor in 3–5 metres on sand near the head of the bay. The bay is only open S and affords good shelter from the prevailing W–NW breeze.

Anse d'Arbitro

A small cove a mile to the W of Fornello. The coast between Fornello and Arbitro is fringed by above and below-water rocks so keep a good distance off. Anchor just inside the entrance to Arbitro in 4–5 metres as there is an underwater rock right in the middle and a reef running out from the beach. Good shelter from all but southerlies.

Anse de Capinero

A large bay just to the E of Ilots Bruzzi, a group of rocky islets easily recognised off the western entrance to the bay. The bay affords good shelter from NW–W winds and is the best place to be if the anchorage behind the islet at Figari is crowded. Care needs to be taken of the reef running S for approximately 500 metres from Ilots Bruzzi and of a reef approximately 300 metres SW of the eastern entrance point. Anchor near the head of the bay in 3–5 metres on sand and weed. There are a number of villas around the slopes and the sandy beach is popular in the summer.

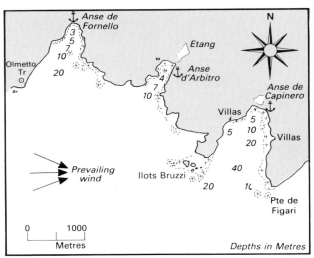

ANSE DE FORNELLO, ANSE D'ARBITRO, ANSE DE CAPINERO

BAIE DE FIGARI

Approach

The approach to this deep bay and the bay itself, has rocks and reefs scattered all about it. However with due care, particularly in a breeze when whitecaps make it difficult to pick out some of the rocks, the approach is not perilous, though it may be a little nerve-racking.

Conspicuous Torre di Figari, the Genoese tower on the W side of the entrance, is conspicuous from the W and S.

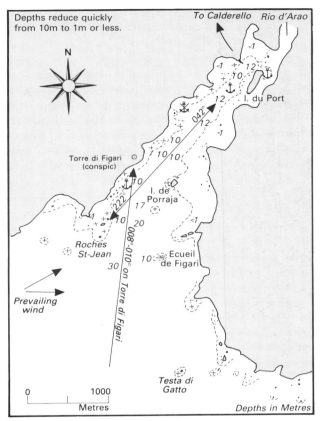

BAIE DE FIGARI 41°27′N 9°03′E

Torre di Figari at the entrance to Baie de Figari. A bearing of 008°–010° on the tower leads into the bay clear of the dangers in the approaches.

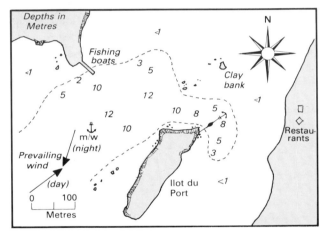

FIGARI: ILOT DU PORT

Entry Keep well off the coast and when Torre di Figari bears 008°–010° head towards it on this course. This will keep you well clear of Ecueil de Figari and the rocks (Roches St-Jean) and isolated underwater rock off the W entrance point. When the rocks of Roches St-Jean come onto a back-bearing of 222° proceed on this course (042°) into the inlet. Ilot de Porraja is easily identified and is a helpful reference point as is Ilot du Port once you are past Porraja. Past Porraja two small red buoys show the W side of the channel, though they cannot always be relied upon to be in place.

Dangers
● Testa di Gatto a low-lying rock and reef lying approximately 600 metres off the coast in the southern approach to Figari. Though the sea breaks upon it, it is difficult to spot in a breeze when whitecaps obscure it.
● Ecueil de Figari, a low-lying rock and reef off the eastern entrance to Figari. Also difficult to see if there are whitecaps.
● An underwater rock (0·2 metre over) approximately 550 metres N of Ecueil de Figari. Difficult to see with whitecaps.
● An underwater rock (0·3 metre over) approximately 500 metres SW of Roches St-Jean. It is difficult to pick out even in calm weather.
Note An entry course of 008°–010° on Torre di Figari is clear of all these dangers.

Anchorage
● In 3–6 metres just S of Torre di Figari. The bottom is sand, mud and weed, good holding. This anchorage provides some shelter in light westerlies, but is open to the SW–SE.
● In the channel W of Ilot du Port in 10–12 metres. The bottom is sand, mud and thick weed, good holding once through the weed. For larger yachts (over 14–15 metres) or if the anchorage behind Ilot du Port is crowded, this is the only place to anchor. With moderate westerlies it is tenable, but in strong SW winds it would be untenable.
● Behind Ilot du Port. Entry behind the island requires care and should be carried out with someone up forward conning you in. A clay bank with less than half a metre over it fringes the anchorage on the N, extending around it to the E and S. The bank is easily identified and a yacht should creep around Ilot du Port keeping to mid-channel between the reef fringing the islet and the shallow clay bank. On the E side of the islet the depths come up quickly from 3–4 metres to less than a metre. Anchor where possible

with a long line to the islet or put a stern anchor out. The bottom is sand, clay and weed, good holding. In the evening the prevailing westerlies will often die down and a N–NE breeze will blow through the night, though usually with no great strength. The anchorage has a number of permanent moorings which severely limit the space available, however if you can get in here there is all-round shelter.

Note
● It is now prohibited to anchor in the cove on the W side of Figari, approximately 800 metres NE of Torre Figari. It has been designated as a marine reserve.
● Though there are 3 metre depths off the end of the short pier opposite Ilot du Port, a notice on the pier expressly forbids its use by pleasure craft.

Facilities
Two restaurants ashore near Ilot du Port.

General
The large bay pricked by spiky rocks and reefs has a forlorn beauty to it. The land around it is not the spectacular mountain scenery found elsewhere, but it has its own savage beauty. Unfortunately it sits directly under the flight path of Figari airport on the flat land at the head of the bay and this taints the peace and quiet of the place. I don't want to sound too mean-mouthed about Figari, but it had been built up in my mind as one of the safest and most tranquil anchorages along this stretch of coast. It is safe if you can squeeze in behind Ilot du Port. It is not tranquil when passenger jets roar just overhead.

Golfe de Ventilegne
A small gulf immediately SE of Figari. Care needs to be taken of Testa di Gatto when coming from the W. In calm weather a yacht can anchor in the bay in the N of the gulf in 3–5 metres on sand and weed. With the prevailing westerlies a swell rolls in here.

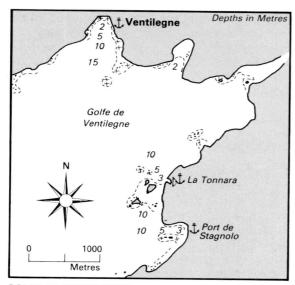

GOLFE DE VENTILEGNE

Iles de la Tonnara
An anchorage behind several rocky islets on the E side of Golfe de Ventilegne that affords reasonable shelter from the prevailing westerlies. Care needs to be taken of a reef (1 metre depths, with a 3·5 metre patch around it) lying approximately 350 metres NW of the islets. The islets themselves are fringed by above and below-water rocks. Enter the anchorage on a course of due S after rounding the off-lying reef.

Anchor in 4–5 metres on sand, rock and weed. Ashore there are a number of houses of the small fishing village. A restaurant and bar open in the summer. The village, La Tonnara, was once a base for the long nets, the *tonnara*, that were laid in the summer to trap tunny and swordfish on their migration W.

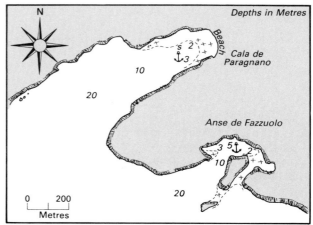

CALA DE PARAGNANO AND FAZZUOLO 41°24′N 9°08′E

Anse de Stagnolo
A fine-weather anchorage in a cove under La Tonnara. Anchor in 4–5 metres on sand. Open to the W.

Cap de Feno
A rocky cape with a small lighthouse on it. The lighthouse, a white tower with a black top, is easily identified; Oc.4s19M light. Care should be taken of the reefs off the cape.

Cala de Paragnano
A deep inlet under Cap de Feno. It provides reasonable shelter from moderate westerlies though it can be uncomfortable. Anchor in 3–6 metres near the head of the inlet on a sandy bottom. The very end is obstructed by a reef and on the N side a shallow shelf extends a considerable distance out. The beach is popular with the locals and visitors to Bonifacio in the summer.

Anse de Fazzuolo
A spectacular *calanque* with an islet in the entrance. Reasonable shelter from light westerlies, though a reflected swell off the sides makes it uncomfortable. It is not tenable in strong westerlies. Entry is on the N side of the islet, the S side is obstructed by a reef.

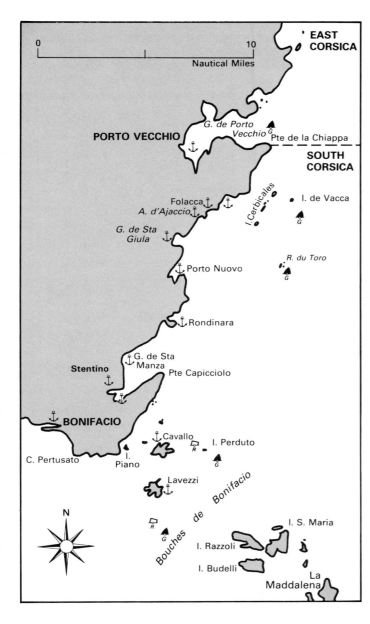

BONIFACIO

Approach

The harbour is in a *calanque* on the SW corner of Corsica. It is literally a slit in the chalk cliffs that is difficult to see until you are close up to it. Fortunately the houses of the old town of Bonifacio on top of the cliffs are easily identified and the entrance lies immediately to the W.

Conspicuous From the S and W the lighthouse on Cap Pertusato, a square white tower and dwelling, stands out clearly. From the N the lighthouse on Cap de Feno, a white tower with a black top, is conspicuous. The houses of the old town on top of the cliffs are readily identified with the restored Genoese tower and 'l'escalier du roi d'Aragon', a stairway cut into the cliffs, conspicuous. Closer in the light tower on the W side of the entrance will be seen.

By night Use the light on Cap de Feno, Oc.4s19M, and on Cap Pertusato, Fl(2)10s25M). The entrance is lit, Iso.R.4s5M. Once inside, the harbour is lit at the dogleg, Oc(2)R.6s5M and Fl.G.4s5M. The fuel jetty inside is lit, Oc.G.4s7M.

Dangers With strong westerlies there is a confused swell at the entrance although once inside it is calm.

Note When approaching the entrance keep a good lookout for ferries and the local tripper boats that are constantly coming and going.

Mooring

Details 250 berths in the Port de Plaisance.

Berth where directed or in a vacant spot and report to the *capitainerie* for a berth. There are laid moorings tailed to the quay or to buoys.

Shelter Good all-round shelter.

Authorities Customs. Port captain and marina staff. A charge is made.

Anchorages On the N side of the *calanque* are two inlets. The first, Calanque de l'Arenella is shallow for the most part, though yachts can anchor fore and aft in the entrance. The second, Calanque de la Catena, is deep for most of its length and offers good shelter. Yachts anchor here with a long line to the W side of the inlet where there are iron rings in the rock. The bottom is hard sand and mud and thick weed, not the best holding, so make sure your anchor is well in before taking a line ashore. Though the wind tends to gust in here, no sea enters.

Facilities

Services Water and electricity at every berth. A shower and toilet block.

Fuel On the quay on the S side.

Repairs A 30-ton crane, but only limited hard standing. Mechanical repairs. Chandlers.

Provisions Good shopping for all provisions by the harbour. Ice available.

Eating out Numerous restaurants around the waterfront from the humble to starched pink tablecloths and waiters in penguin suits.

Anchor in 3–5 metres with a stern anchor out or a line to the shore. The *calanque* is often included on the itinerary of the tripper boats from Bonifacio which erodes its charm a little.

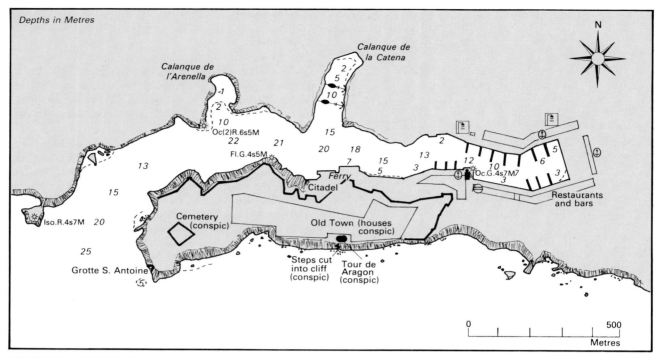

BONIFACIO 41°23'N 9°09'E

Other Post office. Bank. Hire cars. Buses to Ajaccio and Porto-Vecchio. Ferry to Santa Teresa in Sardinia. Flights to Europe from Figari in the summer.

General

Tucked away in the southern folds of the mountains on a limestone plateau, Bonifacio is both a part of and apart from the rest of Corsica. The geology is what initially separates it from the rest of Corsica. The striated limestone cliffs have been eaten away under the old town so that the outermost houses are perched on a huge natural balcony over the sea itself – not somewhere I could live and feel secure looking down on all the sections of cliff that have fallen into the sea in the past. At the base of the cliffs caves have been scooped out by the action of the sea, one of which is conspicuous at the entrance to the *calanque*. The *calanque* itself is a marvel, a slit in the cliffs that turns in on itself to form one of the most memorable natural harbours in the western Mediterranean and more than likely a harbour known to mariners in antiquity.

Bonifacio has been identified with the harbour of the Laestrygonians in the *Odyssey* and it matches the description well. If Homer was describing places known to Mycenaean navigators, and despite recent theories this still seems to be the case, then it is likely this natural harbour was used as a stepping-stone between France and northern Corsica and Sardinia and Italy. Homer describes the place like this:

'a curious bay with mountain walls of stone
to left and right, and reaching far inland,
a narrow entrance opening from the sea
where cliffs converged as though to touch and close.'
(Translation by Robert Fitzgerald.)

Bonifacio harbour looking down from the citadel.

Odysseus' fleet was safely 'sheltered here, inside the cavern of this bay', though Odysseus moored his own ship at the entrance, in Calanque de l'Arenella perhaps. Homer's description of the surrounding countryside would do as well today, 'No farms, no cultivated land appeared', but it was populated by a people known to Odysseus as the Laestrygonians and so he sent three men to investigate. One of these was ripped apart and eaten on the spot while the other two were chased by the Laestrygonians to the harbour. Here they rained boulders down on the ships and speared the unfortunate men in the water; all but Odysseus and his crew who escaped out to sea. The gory behaviour of the Laestrygonians described by Homer may enlarge on fragments of travellers' tales of the barbaric inhabitants of the interior of Corsica.

Artifacts found in Bonifacio indicate that it has been inhabited more or less continuously from the Neolithic period and it may be that the description of the Laestrygonians is our one and only reference to the Toreens or to the pre-Toreen inhabitants.

Bonifacio was utilised by the Romans, but it was not until 828, when Count Bonifacio was returning from an expedition against the Saracens that the site got its first real fortifications and its name. By the 12th century the Genoese ruled Bonifacio and most of what we see today is Genoese in origin. For this reason Bonifacio looks more Italian than French, something it shares with the other Genoese strongholds at Calvi and Bastia. You can walk up to the citadel, through the entrance and drawbridge (the mechanism for lifting the drawbridge is still in place), through the zigzag tunnel and into the old town. The houses of the old town, four or five storeys high, shut out the light from the narrow cobbled streets and when the prevailing westerlies blow, the dust and litter and the odd awning are swirled through the streets and over into the *calanque*.

While the old town has changed little, the port area has grown in response to the tourism that has arrived in recent years, though the changes are friendly enough and detract little from the place. Edward Lear's watercolour of Bonifacio in the 19th century already shows a considerable number of buildings around the shores of the *calanque*, though now the masts of modern yachts fill the harbour, and not the yardarms and spars of sailing craft from an earlier era.

THE GREAT SIEGE

The citadel built by Count Bonifacio on the top of the cliffs occupied a natural defensive position with cliffs on all sides except the landward side. The Genoese further fortified the site and transported serfs to the town, since volunteers were reluctant to emigrate to this lonely outpost surrounded by enemies on the land and water. The citadel was attacked at various times, but the most serious attempt to take the town was mounted in 1420 when the King of Aragon attacked it. The story of the siege reads like an heroic epic.

Corsica was controlled by a pro-Aragonese faction and only Calvi and Bonifacio belonged to Genoa. Alfonso V of Aragon decided to subdue the troublesome cities, and on his arrival in Corsica with a large fleet, Calvi surrendered leaving Bonifacio alone true to Genoa. In August he sailed his fleet of eighty ships into the harbour and began the siege. The Aragonese set up mortars and cannons and began to bombard the town. The Aragonese troops also had muskets, a new invention just on the military scene, which terrified the townspeople who had no firearms or cannons of their own. There were in fact no Genoese troops at Bonifacio, only the townspeople. They fought back with bows and arrows, javelins, rams, stones, boiling water and molten lead; literally anything they could throw at the Aragonese. Miraculously they repelled the experienced troops of Aragon and withstood the siege. One can see Alfonso of Aragon, master of Sicily and Sardinia, shaking his head in bewilderment at this pinprick of Genoa repulsing his troops.

After three months the citadel was out of food and the inhabitants were reduced to eating bark off the trees. A truce was arranged and the townspeople agreed to surrender in forty days if no help had come from Genoa. Thirty-two child hostages were given to the Aragonese as a sign of good faith. In desperation the townspeople built a boat and lowered it down the cliffs to summon help from Genoa. In December it was learnt that help was on its way. By the agreed fortieth day the relief forces from Genoa had still not arrived and Alfonso demanded that the citadel be handed over. An extension of the truce was arranged and that night the church bells rang out and shouting was heard on the ramparts. In the dawn the Aragonese saw troops marching around the walls. The townspeople, and there were now more women and children fighting than men, had dressed in the armour of the dead and appeared to the Aragonese as the relief force. So the battle was renewed.

Just after Christmas seven Genoese ships appeared on the horizon and made straight for the harbour and the Aragonese ships blocking it. The townspeople helped the ships break through and supplies were landed. Five days later the ships broke out and sailed back to Genoa. Though nothing really substantial had been gained, the spirit of the Aragonese was broken. This insignificant outpost had defied some of the most seasoned troops of Christendom for nearly five months. The news of mutiny at Calvi in which the inhabitants rebelled and massacred the Aragonese troops stationed there further disheartened Alfonso's army, and on the 5th of January 1421 Alfonso sailed away with just his child hostages to show for his efforts.

Les Bouches de Bonifacio

The channel between Corsica and Sardinia, the Strait of Bonifacio, is fringed by islands, rocks, reefs and shoal water on both sides. At first glance the area looks a navigator's nightmare, and so it is. But on closer acquaintance and a little familiarity with the area, the jigsaw puzzle of dangers can be sorted out, and among the islands and rocks will be found some enchanting anchorages. The area is best tackled in calm weather. By lunchtime the prevailing westerlies will have got up and the whitecaps only complicate the navigator's problem of spotting reefs just awash or just below the water. In calm weather the crystal clear water allows you to identify the dangers and with transit and clearing bearings you can get safely in and out of most of the anchorages.

Weather note The Strait of Bonifacio tends to funnel and increase the strength of winds so that a friendly force 4 on the Corsican or Sardinian coast becomes a not so friendly force 5–6 in the strait. If gales are predicted for the area it is best to run for cover and wait

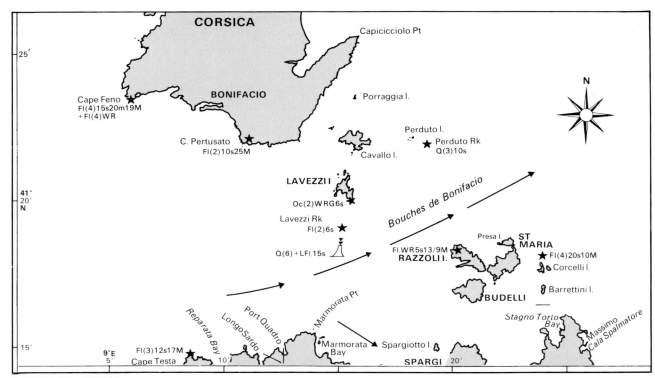

BONIFACIO STRAIT

for another day before tackling the anchorages on the Corsican side of the strait. Depending on the wind direction, Bonifacio or the harbours and anchorages around Sardinia afford good all-round shelter.

Currents The prevailing westerlies set up an E-going current through the strait of 1–2 knots depending on the wind strength. Likewise prolonged easterlies set up a W-going current, though this tends to be less than the normal E-going current.

Grande Passe des Bouches The main deep-water route through the strait and the one used by commercial shipping passes to the S of the solid beacon on Ecueil de Lavezzi, in fact S of the buoy (S cardinal, YB and a ▼ topmark, Q(6)+LFl.15s light about ¾ mile S of the beacon. The beacon on Ecueil de Lavezzi is conspicuous from some distance off from just about anywhere in the strait. It is a solid black tower with a red band, 18 metres (59ft) high, with 2 vertical balls as topmark, though the latter tends to be obscured by a wind generator whirring away. The beacon is lit, Fl(2)6s9M. The passage is limited on the S side by Razzoli Island.

ILES LAVEZZI

Approach

The island lies in a maze of rocks, reefs and shoal water. From the W and S the beacon on Ecueil de Lavezzi is conspicuous. Between the beacon and Ile Lavezzi there is a deep-water passage free of dangers in the fairway. Approaching Iles Lavezzi from the W, the memorial to the wreck of the *Semillante*, a

Lavezzi lighthouse looking N.

pyramidal structure on the SW of the island, is conspicuous. From the S the lighthouse, a square white tower with a red band and a white dwelling is easily identified. The lighthouse will also be seen from the E.

Caution Although the beacon on Ecueil de Lavezzi is lit and Iles Lavezzi is lit on the SE corner, Oc(2)WRG.6s18-14M, on no account should a night approach be made to the island and the anchorages around it.

Note Although it is possible to pass between the N end of Iles Lavezzi and Ile Cavallo, this passage is not to be recommended. There are numerous reefs and rocks to be avoided and with even a slight ruffle on the water these can be difficult to spot.

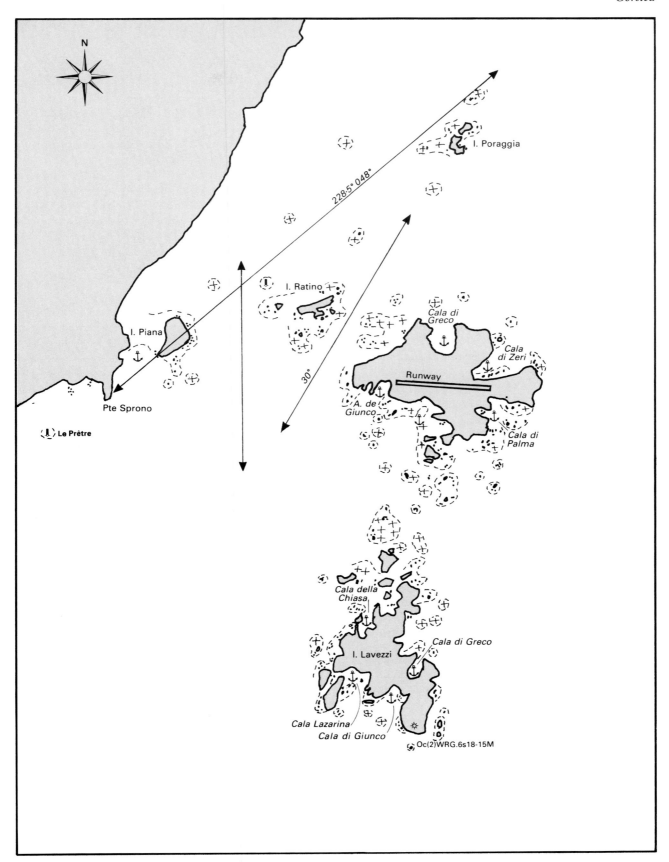

I. PIANA, I. LAVEZZI, I. CAVALLO AND PASSES

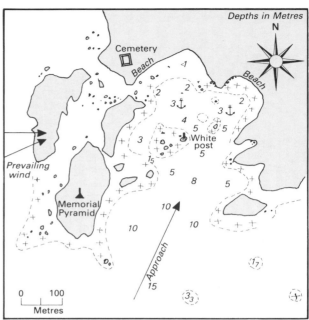

LAVEZZI: CALA LAZARINA

The memorial to *La Semillante* at the entrance to Cala Lazarina.

Anchorages

Note The bottom in the anchorages is sand, rock and some weed, mostly good holding.

Cala Lazarina Offers the best protection from the prevailing winds and is consequently the most popular in the summer. In July and August it is literally packed over and beyond capacity. Make for the memorial to the *Semillante* and off the above-water rocks SSE of the memorial, head on a course of 030° for the small beach in the NE corner. At the entrance a white post marks a group of rocks to be left to port. Someone has helpfully painted a white arrow on the rocks to overcome any confusion. Anchor where convenient or possible. The best place is on the W side with a stern anchor out. Nearly all-round shelter inside.

Cala di Giunco An open bay just E of Cala Lavezzi. It offers poor protection from westerlies. Head on a course of 020° for the white-walled cemetery at the head of the bay and then turn N and anchor where convenient.

Cala di Greco A small cove on the E side of Ile Lavezzi. It has good shelter from westerlies but is open to the E–NE. Approach it from the NE on a course of 213° with the E entrance point in line with the cemetery. A reef runs out from the W entrance point and a reef and above-water rocks obstruct the head of the cove. Inside the cove put an anchor out and take a long line to the W side if westerlies are blowing. Alternatively anchor in 5–6 metres just inside the entrance. There is an alternative anchorage in the cove to the NW in 6–7 metres.

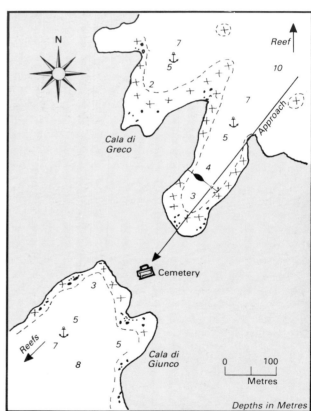

LAVEZZI: CALA DI GRECO AND CALA DI GIUNCO

Cala della Chiasa A small cove on the NW of Iles Lavezzi. Entrance is from the W between Iles Lavezzi and an islet to the N of the cove and then due S into the cove itself. Anchor fore and aft or with an anchor out and a long line to the W of the cove. Good shelter from westerlies if tucked right inside.

288

Ile Lavezzi. Cala della Chiasa.

Facilities

There is a place to dump rubbish in Cala Lazarina, but really it is better to take it away with you.

General

This low rocky island, almost bereft of vegetation and surrounded by rocks sculpted into rounded shapes along the lines of giant Henry Moore sculptures, is both a beautiful and mysterious place. The mystery comes from the memorial to the wreck of the frigate *La Semillante* in 1855 and the two cemeteries for the dead washed up on the shores of Lavezzi. The story of the shipwreck and the aftermath is both puzzling and strange.

La Semillante was on its way to the Crimean War packed with French troops, some 773 beings including the crew. The ship foundered in a gale off Lavezzi at midday on the 15th of February, 1855, and everyone on board was drowned. Over the days following the shipwreck, the bodies of the drowned were washed ashore on Lavezzi in such a mangled condition that only one, an officer, could be identified. So it is that the crosses of the graves are not named, though in the eastern cemetery a plaque records the names of the officers. Alphonse Daudet who visited the island shortly after the tragedy and described it in his *Lettres de mon Moulin* (*L'Agonie de la Semillante*), tells of his encounter with the sole oc-

cupant of the island who had witnessed the shipwreck and subsequent horror. He was a leper, a shepherd on the island, and to tell the story he had to hold his upper lip with one hand so he could relate, only just intelligibly through his deformed mouth, the events he had seen. Daudet concluded that the horror of it had caused the poor man to lose his wits.

For me the perplexing thing is that not one person survived. Out of the 773 people on board, a few must have been able to swim or to cling to spars or barrels washed off the ship. But none did. The island is now a nature reserve though the lighthouse keeper is allowed to keep cows and cattle, and one very friendly donkey who comes down to the beach to see what has been brought in the way of picnic lunches. Quite sensibly it is prohibited to light fires, camp, or pick wildflowers. A number of plots of land have been fenced off around the island to see what the vegetation will revert to when not grazed by cows or trampled by sightseers.

The other occupants of the island are sea birds, including giant sea gulls remarked upon by Daudet as the guardians of the souls of the dead from *La Semillante*. And a bird in the night with a call like a baby crying, a cry that echoed around the bay and caused the yachts at anchor to try to pinpoint it with spotlights. All that could be seen was the occasional flash of white wings arcing through the night.

ILE CAVALLO

Ile Cavallo lies directly N of Iles Lavezzi, connected by a bridge of rocks, reefs and shoal water. As I have already mentioned, the passage between Iles Lavezzi and Ile Cavallo is not to be recommended.

The passage between Ile Cavallo and Ile Ratino lying just off the W side is practicable in calm weather. Proceed on a NE or SW course through the middle of the passage with an experienced lookout forward conning you through. The passage should not be attempted in other than calm weather.

Approach

From the S, Iles Lavezzi and the memorial to the *Semillante* and the lighthouse are readily identified. The prudent course is to go around the E side of Iles Lavezzi keeping well outside the rocks fringing the coast. From the N, Ile Poraggia, the buoy (YBY with a ⟊ topmark) NW of Ile Perduto, and the beacon (BYB with a ♦ topmark) marking Ecueil de Perduto are readily identified.

Anchorages

Note The bottom in the anchorages is sand, rock and some weed, mostly good holding.

Cala di Palma A cove on the SE of the island. The approach is surrounded by above and below-water rocks and should be made with an experienced lookout forward. A bearing of 342° on a small red cupola behind the beach shows the way in. Anchor in 3–4 metres where convenient. Good shelter from westerlies and from the NE, but open E–SE.

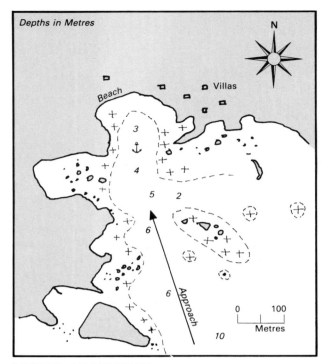

CAVALLO: CALA DI PALMA

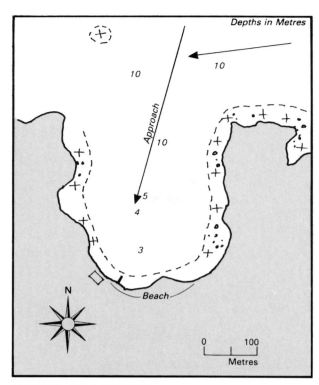

CAVALLO: CALA DI GRECO

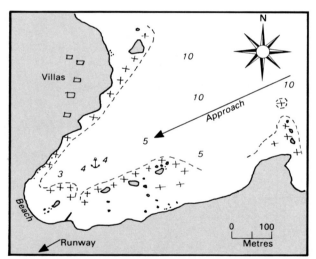

CAVALLO: CALA DI ZERI

Cala di Zeri A cove on the NE of Ile Cavallo. Care needs to be taken of a rock approximately 250 metres N of the entrance and of the underwater rock just off the rocks running out from the E entrance point. The SE half of the bay is rock bound. Anchor in 4–5 metres in the bay or in 5–10 metres just inside the entrance. Good shelter from westerlies, but open E.

Cala di Greco A cove on the N of the island. Care needs to be taken of a rock approximately 300 metres N of the E entrance point and of a 1·5 metre patch just off the entrance. Anchor in 4–6 metres on a sandy bottom. Good shelter from westerlies and southerlies, but open N.

Anse de Giunco A small cove in the SW corner. From the W head on a course of 035° for the beach. Care needs to be taken of the rocks on the eastern side of the approach. Anchor in 3–5 metres. Poor shelter from westerlies.

Facilities
A small landing-craft type ferry belonging to the summer residents of the island goes to Corsica, but it is not for the use of itinerant visitors. There is a private landing strip on the island.

General
Unlike Iles Lavezzi, Ile Cavallo is populated in the summer by the owners of the up-market villas on the island. Occasionally one of these prosperous souls will be seen flying to or from the island or zipping about in a *Riva* or equivalent runabout. However the residents do not have it all their own way – recently one who had built a small private harbour without authority was fined and ordered to restore the shoreline to its original condition.

The stone of the island was quarried by the Romans in the 3rd and 4th centuries AD and around the shores lie numerous columns, hewn intact from the island, and a little inshore the quarry itself. Dorothy Carrington describes the scene from an earlier time, when no villas had been built.
'We landed on the columns themselves; monoliths, twenty feet long and more, rectangular, with waving surfaces like giants' cheese straws. They are piled haphazardly at the water's edge where they were rolled preparatory to embarkation; others lie scattered on the granite slopes that fall in ramps to the

beaches. The Romans evidently evacuated the islands in haste, leaving their wealth in stone behind them. Strangely enough no remains of these granite colossi have been found in the ruins of Corsican towns, where the columns are made of segments of brick, faced with stucco. Cavallo and San Baïnzo must have supplied their half-finished products exclusively to the home market.' *Granite Island* Dorothy Carrington.

Ile Ratino

A small islet off the W side of Ile Cavallo. It is easily recognised in the closer approach. Above and below-water rocks fringe it for some distance off. *Tignosa* beacon, a BY pole with a ⚑ topmark, marks a rock some 400 metres NW of Ile Ratino.

Ile Piana

An islet lying close E of Pte Sprono. A beacon, BRB, marks Le Prêtre rock approximately half a mile SW of Pte Sprono. In settled weather a yacht can pass outside Ile Piana and between *Tignosa* beacon off Ile Ratino and the coast (see Passage de la Piantarella). On the E side of Pte Sprono there is an anchorage suitable in calm weather. Anchor in 5 metres between Ile Piana and the point, on a sandy bottom. A yacht should not attempt to pass to the W of Ile Piana as this passage is obstructed by a reef and shoal water.

Passage de la Piantarella

A safe passage in settled conditions, though it is best attempted the first time in calm weather.

From the W pass outside Le Prêtre rock towards Ile Cavallo. When the islets off Ile Ratino and Tignosa bear 024° (when the islets will be in line with Pta di u Cappiciolu), change course to approximately 010° to pass midway between Ile Piana and Ile Ratino. When the front leading mark (a white wall) on Ile Piana bears 228·5°, head on a course of 048° leaving *Tignosa* beacon to starboard. Very soon the rear leading mark (a white wall) on Pte Sprono will be visible and the two marks should be kept in line. Off Ile Poraggia change course slightly to the NW as the leading marks take you very close to the rocks off the islet.

From the NE keep the leading marks in line on 225° and off *Tignosa* beacon head on a course of 190° until *Le Prêtre* beacon bears due W.

Ile Poraggia

A small islet of broken granite 1 mile to the N of Ile Cavallo. It is surrounded by reefs and shoal water. The islet is easily recognised and there is deep water to the E of it.

Ile Perduto

An islet 1½ miles to the E of Ile Cavallo. The shoal water extending NW from the islet is marked by a yellow buoy with a black band and a ⚑ topmark; the buoy is easily spotted. The passage between the buoy and Ile Cavallo is free of dangers in the fairway.

A reef, Ecueil de Perduto, to the SE of Ile Perduto, is marked by a beacon, BYB with a ⚑ topmark and is readily visible from some distance off. The beacon is lit, Q(3)10s11M. There is deep water to the E of the beacon.

GOLFE DE SANT'AMANZA

Approach

A gulf on the SE corner of Corsica. From the S the rugged ridge forming the SE side of the gulf is readily identified and the rugged red rocks of Pta di u Cappiciolu show up well. Torre de Sant'Amanza, a tower on the ridge, is conspicuous. From the N the entrance to the gulf with the high ridge on the SE side is obvious. A conical peak standing on its own close to the Etang de Balistro is conspicuous from the entrance. Once into the gulf the buildings at the head of the gulf will be seen.

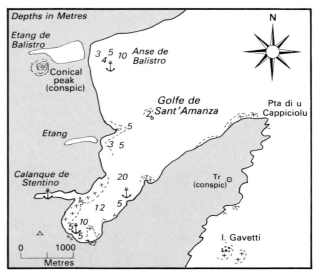

GOLFE DE SANT'AMANZA 41°25′N 9°14′E

Anchorages

● At the head of the gulf in 4–8 metres on sand and weed. Care needs to be taken of the reef and shoal water extending up to 250 metres out from the W side and of the reef in the S corner.
● Calanque de Stentino, a beautiful *calanque* affording all-round protection on the W side of the gulf. A yacht drawing 1·5 metres or less can, with due care, enter the *calanque* through a narrow channel – entry should be made in calm weather only and with an experienced lookout forward. Head on a course of 315° for the short jetty below a white villa and from here on a SW course to avoid the sandbank extending nearly all the way across the *calanque* from the N side. Once past it anchor in 3–6 metres on sand and weed.
● Under Cap Bianco in 2·5–5 metres. Open to the NE–E–SE.
● Balistro, anchor off the long sandy beach in 4–6 metres on sand.

CALANQUE DE STENTINO

Facilities

Restaurants and beach bars at the head of the gulf. Some provisions can be obtained.

General

The gulf is popular in the summer with a lot of campers and camper-vans and considerable numbers of powered dinghies and *bateaux pneumatiques*.

PORT DE RONDINARA

Approach

From the S Pte de Rondinara looks like an island. From the N the tower on Pte Sponsaglia is conspicuous. In the close approach care needs to be taken of the reef running E from the northern entrance point and of a rock just awash about 150 metres off Pte de Rondinara.

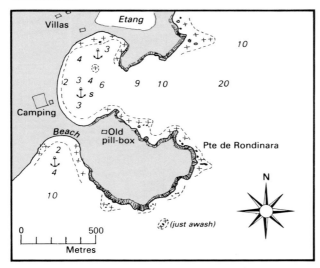

PORT DE RONDINARA 41°28′N 9°17′E

Mooring

Anchor where convenient in 4–6 metres off the beach or in the northern half of the bay in 2·5–4 metres on sand, good holding. Care needs to be taken of a rock just under the water in the N half of the bay – it is difficult to see despite the clarity of the water. There is good shelter from all winds. I have sat out a NE gale in the northern end and though some swell crept around into here, it was not dangerous.

Facilities

Restaurant and beach bar at the camping ground.

General

Apart from offering good all-round shelter, Rondinara is an exquisitely beautiful bay. The water is so clear that you can make out every feature on the bottom. When swimming into the shore I kept thinking I could stand up on the bottom the water was that clear, though when I tried it was a good metre deeper than it looked. Ashore there are a few villas and the new camping ground.

Porto Novo

A large double-headed bay about 2 miles to the N of Port de Rondinara. The tower on Pte Sponsaglia is conspicuous. Care needs to be taken of an underwater rock with 0·8 metre over approximately 100 metres N of the eastern entrance. A yacht can anchor in the W bay off the beach in 3–4 metres on sand and weed. Alternatively anchor in the S bay in 2·5–4 metres taking care of the above and below-water rocks bordering the W side of the bay. The S bay affords the best protection from the SE breeze which often blows.

The area is comparatively deserted with a wooded valley down to the small beach at the head of the S bay.

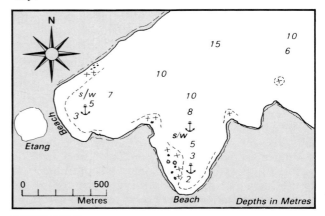

PORTO NOVA 41°30′N 9°17′E

Golfe de Sta Giulia

A large bay just over a mile N of Porto Novo. There are numerous above and below-water rocks and shoal patches making navigation into the bay an interesting exercise preferably carried out in calm weather with an experienced lookout forward – though local yachts charge in and out without, it appears, a care in the world.

The easiest place to anchor is in the SW corner where entry is easy along the S side of the bay. Anchor here in 3–5 metres on sand, good holding. Most local yachts prefer the NW anchorage closer to the amenities ashore and where there is better shelter if you can tuck yourself behind the rocks.

The bay is a busy place. There is a vast *Club Med* complex dominating the NW beach and villas stretch

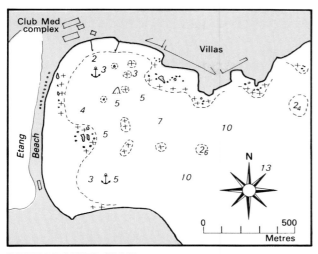

GOLFE DE SANTA GIULIA 41°31′N 9°17′E

Ile du Toro

Two small humpbacked islets to the S of Ile de la Vacca. They are easily identified when coasting N or S. A buoy marks a reef to the E of the islets.

Baie de Palombaggia

A long sandy beach under Pte Cerbicale. In calm weather it is possible to anchor off the beach, though care must be taken of underwater rocks fringing the N end. A number of villas have been built around the slopes above the beach.

Baie de Bona Matina

In calm weather a yacht can anchor on the S side of Punta di a Chiappa off the holiday village in the bay. Anchor in 3–4 metres on sand and weed.

around the northern shore. A hotel and beach huts complete the chain of buildings around to the S side. There are restaurants and bars on the northern side.

Anse d'Aciajo

In settled weather there is an attractive anchorage under Pte d'Aciajo. Anchor in 5–7 metres under the point taking care of the underwater rocks fringing it. Ashore a few villas have been built amongst the pine-covered sand dunes.

Anse de la Folaca

Just above Pte d'Aciajo, a knobbly red rock islet, Ilot de la Folaca, encloses an attractive anchorage. Proceed into the bay on a NW course taking care of the reef running out from Pte d'Aciajo and a reef at the S end of the islet. Anchor in 4–6 metres on sand. The anchorage is really only suitable in settled weather. Ashore a number of villas have been built on the slopes above the beach and sand dunes. A beach-bar opens in the summer.

Iles Cerbicale

A group of islands lying less than a mile off the coast to the S of the entrance to Golfe de Porto-Vecchio. The islands are easily identified by day and a yacht can pass through the channel between the islands and the coast where there are least depths of 19 metres in the fairway. Off the W side of the islands there are several shoal patches including one with 1·3 metres over it, but keeping to the fairway these are easily avoided.

In calm weather a yacht can anchor off the islands where depths are convenient. The islands are a nature reserve and it is not permitted to land on them.

Ile de la Vacca

A small island immediately E of Iles Cerbicale. There is a shoal patch with 4 metres least depth to the SE of the islet marked by a BYB pillar buoy. It is lit, Q(3)10s.

East Corsica – Porto Vecchio to Bastia

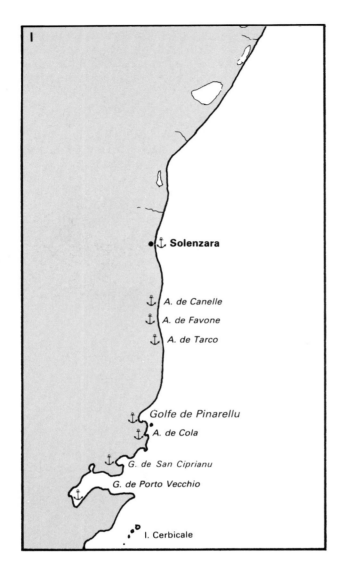

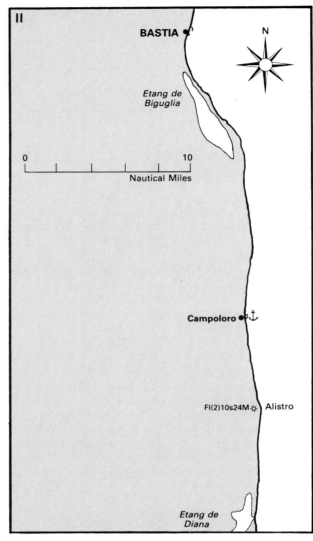

GOLFE DE PORTO VECCHIO

A long gulf with a number of anchorages and the marina of Porto Vecchio at its head.

Approach

The approach is easy in all weather although there is usually a disturbed swell at the entrance with moderate to strong winds from any direction. With westerlies there are strong gusts and confused seas at the entrance, but the sea will be comparatively calm a short distance into the gulf.

Conspicuous From the N the tower on Ile de Pinarellu and the tower on the N entrance of the gulf are conspicuous. From the S Ile du Toro and Iles Cerbicale are easily identified. At the entrance the lighthouse and signal station on Punta di a Chiappa are conspicuous and the light tower on La Pecorella in the middle of the entrance is easily identified.

By night The entrance is well lit. Punta San Ciprianu, Fl.WG.4s11/9M. The green sector covers La Pecorella on 281°–299° and also the shoal water and reef of Banc de Benedetto on 072°–084°. Pta di a Chiappa, Fl(3+1)15s24M. La Pecorella, Fl(3)G.12s 6M.

Entrance In calm weather a yacht can enter the gulf between Punta di a Chiappa and Chiapino, a rock on the S side of the entrance, where there are 9 metres least depths in the fairway. The normal entrance to the gulf is between Chiapino rock and La Pecorella light tower. Alternatively enter between Punta San Ciprianu and La Pecorella.

Pta di a Chiappa. The lighthouse and signal station are conspicuous.

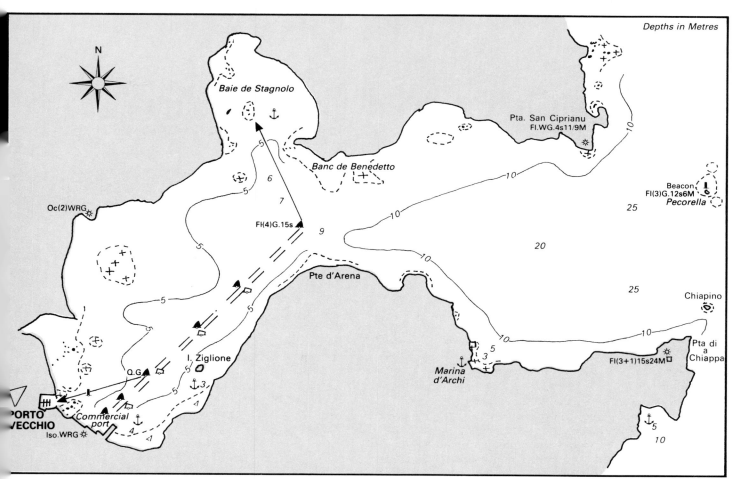

Depths in Metres

Baie de Stagnolo

Pta. San Ciprianu
Fl.WG.4s11/9M

Banc de Benedetto

Beacon
Fl(3)G.12s6M
Pecorella

Oc(2)WRG

Fl(4)G.15s

Pte d'Arena

Chiapino

I. Ziglione

Q.G.

Marina
d'Archi

Fl(3+1)15s24M

Pta di
a
Chiappa

PORTO
VECCHIO

Commercial
port

Iso.WRG

GOLFE DE PORTO VECCHIO

Porto Vecchio marina looking down from the old town.

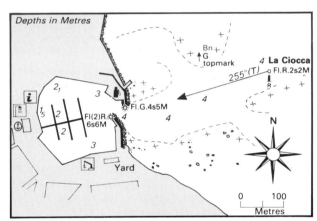

MARINA DE PORTO VECCHIO 41°35'·5 N 9°17'E

Porto Vecchio old town.

Porto Vecchio marina. The approach looking W with La Cioccia beacon prominent in the foreground.

MARINA DE PORTO VECCHIO

Approach

Once into the gulf head for the green conical buoy (with a ▲ topmark) marking the S extremity of Banc de Benedetto. From this buoy a course of 225° takes you to the large green and red pair of buoys marking the channel to the commercial port and the marina. The subsequent buoys are very small and difficult to spot. Off Ilot Ziglione at the second small starboard channel buoy head on a course of 255° for the red light tower on La Cioccia rock. Just NW of La Cioccia, a green triangle on a post marks the N side of the channel. The approach to the marina entrance is now straightforward.

Conspicuous The buoy marking Banc de Benedetto is easily picked out and from here the two buoys marking the entrance channel are also easily picked out. Ilot Ziglione can be identified and the marina and the masts of the yachts inside stand out well. If a ship is berthed at the commercial port to the SE of the marina it stands out clearly.

By night The buoy marking Banc de Benedetto is lit, Fl(4)G.15s. At Pozzoli behind the buoy there is a leading light, Oc(2)WRG.6s14-13M. The white light shows the direction to the buoy on 271·7°–275·2°. From the buoy there is a leading light at the channel into the commercial port, Iso.WRG.4s11-10M. The white light shows the channel. The second small buoy where you head for the marina is lit (Q.G) and La Cioccia is lit (Fl.R.2s2M). The marina entrance is lit,: Fl.G.4s5M and Fl(2)R.6s6M.

Dangers
● Banc de Benedetto with shoal water and a reef partially obstructs the N of the gulf.
● At Pte d'Arena a sandbank projects out into the channel. It pays not to cut the corner too fine here.
● Off the entrance to the marina there is the rock La Cioccia and on the N side of the channel there are above and below-water rocks.

Caution With westerlies there are strong gusts down into the approaches to the marina.

Mooring

Details 430 berths with 130 berths for visitors. Maximum LOA 20 metres.

Berth where directed or go onto one of the visitors' berths on the S side of the marina. There are laid moorings tailed to the quay or to buoys. Yachts are literally packed into here leaving little room to get into and out of berths.

Shelter Good all-round shelter.

Authorities Customs. Port captain and marina staff. A charge is made.

Facilities

Services Water and electricity at every berth. A shower and toilet block.

Fuel On the quay near the entrance.

Repairs 10 and 30-ton cranes in the marina. Mechanical repairs. Sailmakers. Chandlers.

Provisions A mini-market near the marina. Good shopping in the village above, though it is a hot walk up and down. Ice available.

Eating out Numerous restaurants around the marina and in the old village above. It is well worth the walk up to the village to eat in one of the restaurants with a view over the gulf.

Other Post office and banks in the village above and an exchange office in the marina. Hire cars. Buses to Bonifacio and along the east coast from the village.

General

The old walled town and the natural harbour at the head of the gulf has been the site of human settlement for thousands of years. The Toreens, the invaders who took over from the megalithic culture around 1500 BC, are thought to have based themselves at Porto-Vecchio before spreading westwards across the island. The Romans used Porto-Vecchio as one of their east coast ports and when the Genoese arrived, they too exploited the natural shelter of the gulf. The Genoese built the old walled town on the easily defended bluff that we see today. They also built the numerous towers around the adjacent coast to defend and warn the town against enemy attacks.

The old walled Genoese town and the environs of the gulf have not always looked as picturesque and prosperous as they do today. Dorothy Carrington described her stay here some forty years ago like this: 'Porto Vecchio...was still a stagnant, ramshackle place that seemed overwhelmed by its sub-tropical environment. Everything in the town was seedy, but the surrounding countryside was luxurious.' The countryside is still luxurious, to Dorothy Carrington it 'recalled the landscapes in Chinese paintings', but the town is no longer seedy with the new income from tourism.

ANCHORAGES AROUND GOLFE DE PORTO VECCHIO

Marine d'Archi An anchorage off a small harbour in the SE of the gulf. Anchor to the SE of the harbour in 4–5 metres on sand and weed, patchy holding. There is a good lee here from westerlies though there are gusts off the land. There are 2 metre depths at the entrance to the harbour, but for the most part it is rock bound inside.

Marine Vizza An attractive cove suitable in calm weather. Care needs to be taken of rocks extending out from the coast.

Ilot Ziglione There is a pleasant anchorage under this islet sheltered from easterlies. Westerlies blow straight in. Anchor in 4–5 metres on mud and weed, good holding once through the weed. A number of local craft are kept here on permanent moorings. Ashore there is a hotel and villas around the slopes.

Port du Commerce Yachts cannot use the commercial port, but can anchor to the S of the channel. The anchorage is uncomfortable from the short chop set up by westerlies gusting down into it, but tenable. Anchor in 4–5 metres on mud and weed, good holding. Ensure you are well clear of the channel and manoeuvring area for ships entering and leaving the commercial port.

Baie de Stagnolo A nearly landlocked bay on the N side of the gulf. From the green buoy marking Banc de Benedetto head on a course of 340° for a group of whitish rocks in the middle of the bay. Before getting to the rocks head N to the anchorage. Anchor where convenient in 2·5–4 metres on mud, sand and weed, good holding. On the E side of the anchorage the bottom comes up quickly from 2 metres to less than a metre some distance off the shore. With care you can also anchor on the W side of the central group of rocks in 2·5–3 metres. Good all-round shelter although SE winds are reported to send in a swell.

Ashore there are several camping sites and a holiday village. Several restaurant-bars around the shore. The place is most attractive, despite the name, with a long sandy beach around the W side between two lagoons and pine-covered dunes back from the beach.

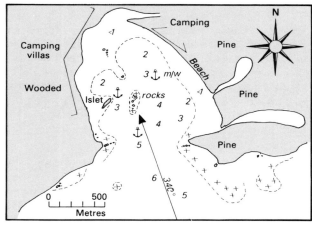

BAIE DE STAGNOLO 41°37'N 9°19'E

Anse de Tramulimacchia Small craft can obtain shelter here though care is needed getting into the bay.

Golfe de San Cipriannu

A large bay immediately N of the entrance to Porto-Vecchio. The red knobbly rocks of Ile Cornuta are easily identified, but Ile San Cipriannu tends to blend into Pte d'Araso when approaching from the S. Care needs to be taken of the reef running out from Punta San Cipriannu at the southern entrance.

Once into the bay anchor in the SW corner in 3–5 metres on a sandy bottom, good holding. There is shelter here from W through S to SE if you are tucked right in. The reef running out from the beach is marked by a small green buoy. A yacht can also anchor at the N end behind the islet in 3–4 metres

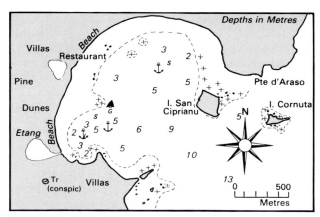

GOLFE DE SAN CIPRIANU 41°38'N 9°22'E

where there is shelter from W through N to NE. Ile San Cipriannu is connected to the N entrance of the bay by a reef and shoal water.

San Cipriannu is a popular place in the summer and several hotels and a camping ground cater for the summer visitors. A number of restaurants and beach-bars open in the summer. Sand dunes covered with pine stretch back from the beach across the flat land to Baie de Stagnolo. The water is that clear you doubt there can be a gap between the keel and the bottom – only swimming down to have a look will convince you.

Anse de Pta Capicciola

Under Pta Capicciola there is an attractive anchorage suitable in calm weather. Anchor in 5–6 metres off the beach taking care of a reef running about 100 metres out from it. A tranquil spot little visited by local yachts.

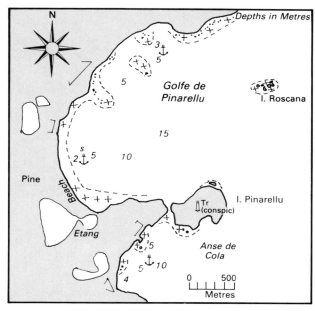

GOLFE DE PINARELLU AND ANSE DE COLA 41°41'N 9°23'E

Anse de Cola

A bay on the S side of Golfe de Pinarellu. Anchor in 5–8 metres in the middle of the bay. Good shelter from westerlies. At the S end of the beach there is a holiday village and villas have been built on the slopes to the N.

Golfe de Pinarellu

A large bay 3 miles NNE of Golfe de San Cyprianu. The tower on Ile de Pinarellu is easily identified. Ile Roscana, a group of rocks in the entrance are also easily identified. Anchor off the beach to the S of the hotel in 3–6 metres on sand, good holding. Good shelter from W through to S. SE winds push a swell into the bay.

Ashore there is a hotel and villas have been built on the slopes around the bay. Restaurant-bars in the summer.

Anse de Tarco

A small cove 2 miles from the towers on Pte et Ile de Fautea. Anchor in 2–3 metres on sand off the beach. Open to all E sectors. There are apartment blocks and villas around the bay.

Anse de Favone

A bay with a number of villas around the shore and a camping site. Anchor in the S of the bay in 3–4 metres on sand, good holding. Care needs to be taken of rocks off the shore. Good shelter from the W–SW, but open to E–NE. Ashore limited provisions can be obtained and a restaurant-bar opens in the summer.

Anse de Cannella

A small cove lying just over 1 mile N of Anse de Favone. Anchor at the N end in 2–3 metres on sand, good holding. Good shelter from W–NW, but open to E–SE. Restaurant-bar ashore.

SOLENZARA

Approach

The marina lies next to the mouth of the Solenzara river and just before the flat plains and *étangs* of the east coast extending N to Bastia.

Conspicuous From the S the buildings and breakwaters of the harbour can be identified from several miles off. From the N Solenzara airfield and watchtowers on the last of the flat coastal strip will be seen. Closer in the outer breakwater and the masts of the yachts inside will be seen. The entrance is difficult to see until close to it.

By night A F.Vi.4M is exhibited on the elbow and a F.G at the entrance. A night approach should be made with care because of the rocks and shoal water at the entrance.

Dangers
● Care needs to be taken of the rocks and shoal water on the western side of the entrance.

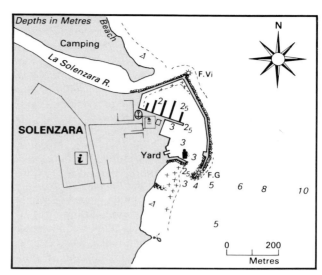

SOLENZARA 41°51′N 9°24′E

● With strong SE winds there is a confused swell at the entrance making entry difficult.
● With strong westerlies there are gusts down into the approaches to Solenzara.

Mooring

Details 450 berths with 300 berths for visitors. Maximum LOA 25 metres.

Berth where directed or on the end of the central pier and report to the *capitainerie* for a berth. There are finger pontoons or larger yachts use their own anchors.

Shelter Good all-round shelter.

Authorities Port captain and marina staff. A charge is made.

Facilities

Services Water and electricity at or near all berths. A shower and toilet block in the marina.

Fuel On the quay near the entrance.

Repairs 12 and 25-ton cranes. Mechanical repairs. Chandlers.

Provisions Good shopping for all provisions in the village nearby.

Eating out Numerous restaurants in and around the village.

Other Post office. Bank. Buses along the coast.

General

Solenzara marina was built from scratch to attract yachts to the east coast of Corsica and somehow bring the magic touch of tourism to this depressed area to provide jobs and incomes. The original plans provided for several jetties with pontoons off them, but from the start just one jetty has sufficed. Yachts did not arrive in the numbers anticipated, though this may change as other marinas to the south become crowded.

The village sits on green and shaded slopes beside the Solenzara river running down to the sea just north of the marina. Though it is hot here in the summer, the place has a pastoral air to it. On the other side of the river there is a camping ground half hidden by numerous trees and with the river on one side and the sea on the other, it gets full marks as camping grounds go.

When I first came here in 1982 there were a large number of prefabricated apartments behind the marina housing refugees from Vietnam. These have now disappeared and so it seems have the refugees, no doubt to other parts of Corsica and to mainland France. There are Vietnamese restaurants in the most unlikely French towns and villages, a phenomenon akin to the ubiquitous Indian restaurants in English towns and villages, though sadly no Vietnamese restaurant exists in Solenzara.

Solenzara to Campoloro

A number of the *étangs* and rivers on this stretch of coast could be navigated by shallow-draught craft, though entry should be made only after ascertaining whether a bar has formed across the entrance and what the depths are over the bar. Etang d'Urbino and Etang de Diane are reported to have mostly 2 metre depths in the entrance and channel, but I have not attempted to enter them. The Tavignano river leading to Aléria is also reported to be accessible to shallow-draught craft.

The best time to explore the *étangs* and river would be in late summer or early autumn when the outflow from the channels has hopefully washed most of the silt from winter storms away. I should hardly need to stress that entry should be attempted only in calm weather.

ALERIA

Between Solenzara and Campoloro the flat coast has numerous *étangs* opening onto the sea. Between the Etang de Sale and Etang de Diane are the ruins of ancient Aléria. They can be reached from Solenzara (32 kilometres) or Campoloro (30 kilometres).

The site was settled as long ago as 560 BC by colonists from Phocaea, just above present-day Izmir in Turkey. These intrepid Greeks, noted for their sea-faring skills, went on to establish other colonies all along the French Mediterranean coast. Aléria, originally Alalia to the Phocaeans, became an important stepping-stone port between the colonies in France and other colonies in Italy. In 278 BC the Carthaginians took Aléria and in 259 BC the Romans ousted the Carthaginians. The subsequent Roman occupation and Roman buildings so obliterated the Greek town that the remains of the Greek buildings were not unearthed until 1955, though it had always been known there was a Greek town along this coast somewhere. The extent and richness of the Greek town proved surprising.

On the outskirts of Roman Aléria the archaeologists discovered a Greek necropolis and from the contents of the tombs, fine pottery and ceramics imported from around the Mediterranean, the importance of the Greek town was established. The Greek newcomers were apparently not troubled by the indigenous Corsicans, but initially they had problems with the Etruscans and Carthaginians. In 540 BC they defeated a combined Etruscan and Carthaginian fleet just off Aléria and thereafter were little troubled until the Carthaginians occupied the region in 278 BC.

The Roman port and town of Aléria was no less important than the Greek one. In the Musée Jérome Carcopino, named after the archaeologist who began the excavations here, there are displayed many of the finds from the site. The rooms of the museum are crammed full of ceramics, glassware, coins, pottery, iron and bronze weapons, all the detritus left from the long occupation of the town. The museum is housed in an old Genoese fort in the village near the site and can be difficult to find. The site itself is not all that impressive as little remains apart from the foundations of buildings. In ancient times it is likely the Etang de Sales lapped at the edges of the town and that the galleys and plump merchant ships were brought into the *étang* by a channel now silted up or possibly up what is now the Tavignano river.

CAMPOLORO

Approach

The marina lies on a straight section of coast between Solenzara and Bastia. It is difficult to see from the distance and cannot be accurately identified until 2 or 3 miles away.

Conspicuous From the S the lighthouse at Alistro, a white tower with a silver top on a small bluff a little inland can be identified. Closer in the harbour and the masts of the yachts inside will be seen. The light tower at the entrance shows up well.

By night From the S use Alistro light, Fl(2)W.10s 24M. The entrance to the marina is lit, Oc(2)WR.6s 9/6M and Fl.G.2s2M. The white sector of the entrance light shows the safe approach on 184°–342°.

Caution The harbour and entrance are prone to silting. The entrance is periodically dredged and normally there is a minimum depth of 2 metres. The dredged channel is marked by small red buoys which are difficult to see at night so some care is needed.

Dangers With strong onshore winds a swell piles up at the entrance making entry difficult and in gale force easterlies dangerous.

Mooring

Details 464 berths with 200 berths for visitors.
Berth Go onto the *quai d'accueil* on the end of the jetty and report to the *capitainerie* for a berth. Most berths have laid moorings tailed to buoys.
Note The harbour was recently being dredged to 3 metres in the approach channel and 2–3 metres at most berths.
Shelter Good all-round shelter.

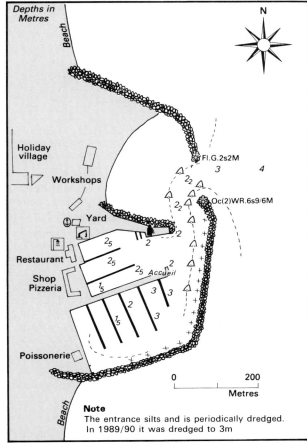

CAMPOLORO 42°20′N 9°32′E

Authorities Port captain and marina staff. A charge is made.

Facilities

Services Water and electricity at every berth. A shower and toilet block.

Fuel On the quay near the entrance.

Repairs 50-ton travel-hoist. Some covered storage. Most mechanical repairs. Some GRP and wood repairs.

Provisions A small mini-market in the marina. A large supermarket near Prunete about 2 kilometres away.

Eating out Two restaurants in the marina.

General

Campoloro was developed as one of several marinas down the east coast in association with a holiday village. The village and marina have a forlorn air to them. A few of the holiday cottages are occupied, the swimming pool has water in it, the tennis courts are swept, the restaurants in the marina are open with clean cloths on the tables, only the people are missing. Through no fault of its own Campoloro seems to have been forgotten.

To be sure there are some people here, but even they have a bit of a fazed look about them. Campoloro was recently given an award for the cleanest beach in Europe and inland the countryside is wonderful. The name Campoloro is taken from the name of the surrounding region, the Valle-de-Campoloro, meaning a field of laurels (*champ de lauriers*).

LA CASTAGNICCIA

In the foothills behind Campoloro, the village of Cervione stands out on a steep ridge. The grey stone houses are precariously perched around a large church, grouped in a defensive huddle with steep slopes on all sides. Cervione is at the very eastern end of a huge chestnut forest, La Castagniccia, extending on up into the mountain valley beside Monte San Petrone as far as Ponte Leccia. It is a wild primeval looking landscape with the gnarled trunks and boughs of the chestnuts rooted in the hard schist of the slopes. Dotted through the forest, almost everywhere you look, are the grey stone houses of hamlets and villages. Despite the primeval appearance of the forest, it is almost entirely man-made.

In the 16th century, the Genoese were anxious to develop agriculture in Corsica, though with the needs of the Genoese and not the Corsicans in mind. They encouraged the cultivation of wheat and olives in the northeast plains for export to Genoa and needed a substitute for the Corsicans' own consumption. The solution was chestnuts. The chestnut grew readily on the steep mountain slopes where wheat could not be grown and the flour made from the chestnuts replaced flour made from wheat. It gave rise to a whole cuisine based around chestnut flour and pork from the pigs that foraged for chestnuts overlooked in the autumn harvest. Today chestnut flour is hardly used at all, though domestic and wild pigs still figure prominently in Corsican cuisine.

The chestnut forest of La Castagniccia bestowed a prosperity on this region that led to a development of cottage industries, including the production of fine rifles, and the isolated mountain slopes also produced an inclination for radical politics. The village of Merosaglia near where Pasquale Paoli was born, is in the centre of the forest, and most of his support was drawn from the surrounding area. The house where this first and greatest fighter for Corsican independence was born is now a small museum with relics of the Paoli family and the remains of Pasquale Paoli, brought from London's St Pancras cemetery, to his birthplace in this forested mountain fastness.

It is well worth making an excursion into La Castagniccia. Many of the small villages are partially deserted now and the chestnuts are no longer harvested, but there are a lot of contented pigs around.

North Corsica –
Bastia to Calvi

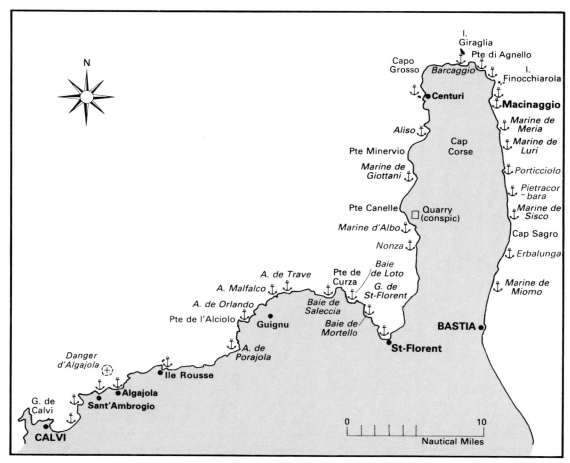

BASTIA TO CALVI

BASTIA

Approach

Conspicuous From the N and S the concentration of buildings in and around Bastia are easily identified. The high breakwater of the commercial harbour stands out well. A belfry in the old town is conspicuous. Closer in the breakwater of the Vieux Port and the two light towers at the entrance are easily identified.

Note In the approach from the S there are a number of unlit mooring buoys and a buoy, BYB, off the airport approximately 2 miles S of Bastia. The buoy is lit, Q(3)10s.

By night The commercial harbour is lit, Fl.G.4s9M and Q.R.7M. The Vieux Port is lit, Fl(4)WR.12s 15/12M and Oc(2)G.6s8M.

Dangers
● With strong winds and gales from the E, there is a confused sea and breaking waves at the entrance to the Vieux Port.

● With strong westerlies there are gusts off the high land in the approaches to Bastia.

Mooring

Berth Go stern or bows-to the quay just around the dogleg of the N mole if there is room. The bottom is mud and rock, patchy holding. Alternatively go stern or bows-to the end of the outer pontoon.

Shelter The best shelter is on the mole. The harbour is prone to a surge with winds from just about any direction. Normally this is merely uncomfortable, but with strong onshore gales the harbour could be dangerous if you are not prepared. It may be possible in this situation to find a berth in the commercial harbour.

Authorities Customs. Immigration. Port captain. A charge may be made in the summer.

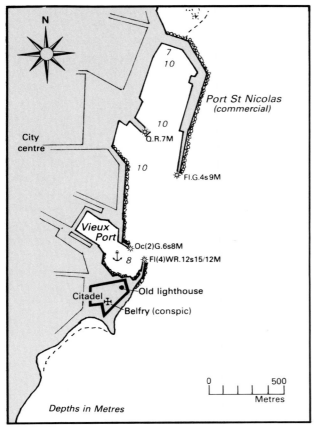

BASTIA 42°42′N 9°27′E

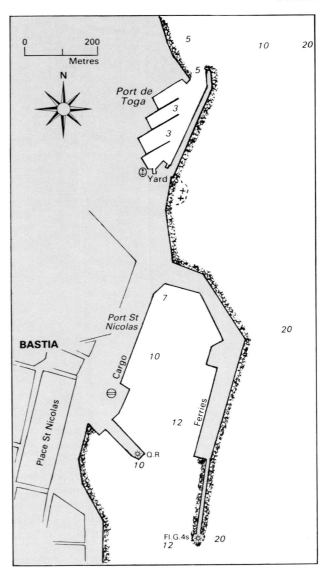

BASTIA: PORT ST NICOLAS AND PORT DE TOGA

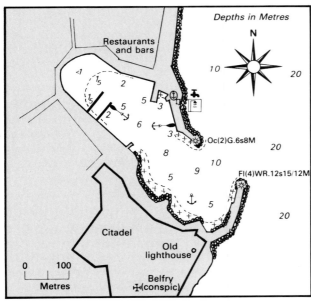

BASTIA: VIEUX PORT

Facilities

Services A tap on the quay. A shower and toilet block near the *capitainerie*.

Fuel A tanker will deliver large quantities in the summer.

Repairs 10-ton slipway. Most mechanical repairs. Chandlers.

Provisions Good shopping for all provisions in the town. Ice available.

Eating out Numerous restaurants around the Vieux Port and others in the town.

Other Post office. Banks. Hire cars. Buses along the coast. Train to Ajaccio and Calvi. Ferries to Marseille, Nice, Genoa and Piombino. Flights to Europe.

General

In the Vieux Port you are right in the middle of the oldest part of Bastia, a proper Mediterranean style harbour surrounded by tall houses with restaurants

Bastia. Vieux Port.

and cafés around the waterfront. It looks like a waterfront scene from the Italian Riviera and in a way it is. Until the Genoese built the citadel on the rocky bluff above the port, there was only the insignificant fishing village of Cardo here. In 1380 the local governor, Leonelli Lomellini, decided to build a citadel and to improve the port. This gave the Genoese a port close to Genoa and strengthened the defences on the east coast. The town was named after the fortress, the *bastiglia*, that defended it.

More than Bonifacio and Calvi, Bastia is an Italianate town. The six and seven-storey houses leaning over the narrow streets have a seediness reminiscent of Genoa. Washing is strung randomly high above the streets. Housewives gossip to each other high above the streets. And the driving definitely has an Italian flair that sends pedestrians scurrying for safety. Above the old town, Terra Vecchia, is the new town, Terra Nova, enclosed by the walls of the citadel. Though the citadel looks imposing from below, once you are inside it, it doesn't have the impregnable feel of Calvi or Bonifacio.

Bastia was the capital of Corsica until Napoléon bestowed that honour on Ajaccio. Bastia lost its prestige and privileges and gradually it lost its trade and industry as well. The town decayed to become a slum by the 20th century and then in World War II it had the unfortunate distinction of being the only Corsican town to be severely bombed. In 1943 the Germans were hurriedly evacuating the last of their troops from Bastia and it became a battlefield between the partisans and the Germans. By a cruel irony, after the last German had left and the townspeople were celebrating the victory, the Americans bombed the town, destroying many of the buildings and killing a number of civilians, in the belief that the Germans still occupied it.

The city has recovered from the neglect of centuries and the damage inflicted during the war. It hums and bustles with an energy sometimes lacking in other Corsican towns. Some of its status was returned in 1975 when it was made prefectural capital of Haute Corse, while Ajaccio is the capital of Corse du Sud. With the development of the fertile east coast, mostly in vines, and of tourism, it has regained some of its former prosperity. Not that this will touch you much in the Vieux Port. Here you are in Genoa only lightly tempered by things Corsican.

PORT DE TOGA

A new marina still under construction to the N of Port St-Nicolas, the commercial port. The marina is virtually finished, but in the winter of 1988–89 the harbourmaster's office and adjoining buildings were blown up, probably by the FLNC, who sometimes hit tourist targets to hurt the local economy. Completion is now envisaged in 1990–91.

Approach

Conspicuous The harbour lies immediately N of Port St-Nicolas. The cranes and gantries in the commercial harbour and any ferries berthed here readily identify it. Closer in the breakwater of Port de Toga will be seen.

By night Use the lights at the Vieux Port and Port St-Nicolas. Lights are to be installed at the entrance to Port de Toga.

Dangers In strong E–NE winds the entrance would be difficult.

Mooring

Details There will be berths for 411 boats. Maximum LOA 25 metres.

Berth Quai d'accueil to be established. Laid moorings to be installed.

Shelter There appears to be good all-round shelter although strong NE winds could make it uncomfortable.

Authorities Harbourmaster and marina staff. A charge will be made.

Facilities

To be established are water, electricity, fuel, and a chandlers. A travel-hoist is to be installed and there is hard standing at the southern end of the harbour.

General

The marina will provide much-needed space for pleasure craft at Bastia which at present has only the limited berths available in the Vieux Port. It is about a kilometre from the centre of Bastia where provisions and restaurants can be found, though no doubt there are plans to provide a mini-market and restaurant(s) at the marina.

Erbalunga

A miniature harbour in a shallow bight off the village of Erbalunga some 5 miles N of Bastia. The old houses of the village are easily identified. The miniature harbour has depths of only 1–1·5 metres and is in any case packed with local craft. Anchor off the village to the SW of the harbour in 4–7 metres on sand. Care needs to be taken of the above and below-water rocks bordering the coast and the harbour. The anchorage is open to all easterlies and to the S.

Most provisions can be obtained ashore and there are restaurants and bars. The old fishing village is a picturesque place built on a rocky spit with a Genoese tower on the end.

Marine de Sisco

A fine-weather anchorage off a small resort. The anchorage is open to all easterlies and to the S. Anchor in 3–5 metres on sand to the S of the river mouth. Restaurant-bars open in the summer.

Marine de Pietracorbara

A shallow cove 1½ miles N of Sisco. A Genoese tower, Torre d'Aquilia, is conspicuous on the S side of the cove. Anchor in 3–4 metres on sand off the beach. The cove is open to easterlies, but affords better protection than Sisco. A hotel ashore.

Porticciolo

A cove 2½ miles N of Pietracorbara. The small village of Porticciolo is easily identified and the anchorage is immediately NW of it. Anchor in 3–5 metres off the beach on a sandy bottom. Open to the E though some shelter from light SE winds can be found. Ashore some provisions can be obtained and there are several restaurant-cafés.

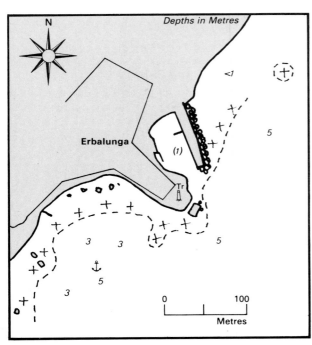

ERBALUNGA 42°46′N 9°29′E

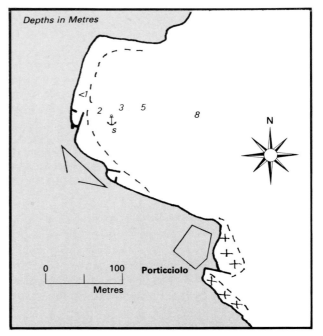

PORTICCIOLO 42°52′N 9°29′E

Note There is a harbour for small boats at the S end of the beach and another on the S side of the cove. The short mole off Porticciolo has 2–3 metres off it, but is rock bound.

Marine de Luri

A shallow bight a mile N of Porticciolo. There is a small harbour for shallow-draught craft drawing less than a metre. Most yachts will have to anchor in the cove S of the harbour. Care needs to be taken of a reef running E for some 200 metres from the point and the harbour breakwater. Anchor in 3–4 metres on sand off the entrance to the harbour. The bottom comes up quickly to less than a metre about 100 metres off the beach. The anchorage is open to the E though the harbour breakwater provides some shelter from NE winds.

Ashore most provisions can be found and restaurant-bars open in the summer. Fuel is available from a petrol station on the road behind the beach.

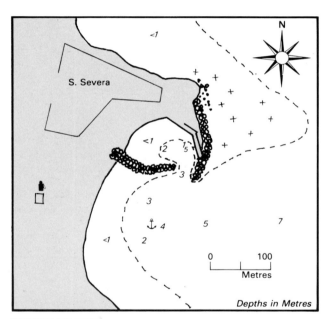

MARINE DE LURI 42°43′N 9°29′E

Marine de Meria

A cove 2 miles N of Luri. An old windmill will be seen on the N side of the cove and closer in a Genoese tower close to the beach. Anchor in 3–5 metres on sand to the S of the tower. Open to the E and S.

MACINAGGIO

Approach

The village and marina are tucked into the S corner of Baie de Macinaggio just around on the E side of Cap Corse.

Conspicuous From the N and S the Genoese tower on the outermost of Iles Finocchiarola is conspicuous.

The beacon on Banc de Ste-Marie will also be seen. An old windmill can be identified on the N side of the bay and closer in the marina breakwater and the buildings of the village will be seen.

By night Use the light on Ile de la Giraglia, Fl.5s 29M, and the light on Banc de Ste-Marie VQ(3)5s. The marina entrance is lit, Oc(2)WR.6s11/7M and Fl.G.2s4M. The white sector of the light shows the safe approach on 218°–331°.

Dangers With strong NE–E winds a swell heaps up at the entrance to the marina making entry difficult and possibly dangerous with onshore gales.

Note The entrance to the marina is narrow and with craft constantly coming and going some care is needed.

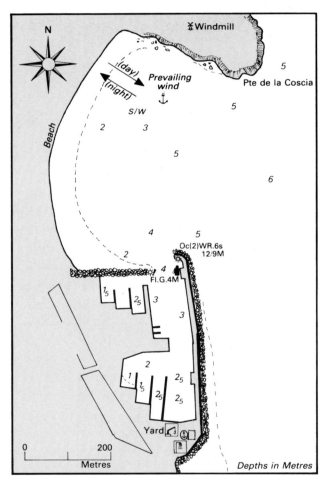

MACINAGGIO 42°57′N 9°27′E

Mooring

Details 500 berths with 200 berths for visitors.

Berth where directed or go onto the central pier where convenient. Large yachts usually go stern-to the quay S of the fuel quay. There are laid moorings tailed to the quay. The bottom of the harbour is black smelly mud and when you pick up a mooring the mud will splatter your topsides and, most likely, the unfortunate soul who picks it up.

Elegance and style anchored off Baie de Macinaggio.

Shelter Good all-round shelter although NE–E gales cause a surge.
Authorities Customs. Port captain and marina staff. A charge is made.

Facilities

Services Water and electricity at or near every berth. In the summer water is rationed and only turned on at certain times of the day. A shower and toilet block.
Fuel On the quay near the entrance.
Repairs A 15-ton hoist. Some mechanical repairs. Chandlers.
Provisions Most provisions can be found in the small village. Ice available.
Eating out Numerous restaurants in the village.
Other Post office. Bank. Bus to Bastia.

General

At Macinaggio the landscape has been moulded into a gentler landscape, rolling hills rather than the razorback ridges of the interior. There are green valleys and cows grazing. The little fishing village of Macinaggio is the seaside settlement of the main village on the slopes inland, the latter at one time the capital of the region of Cap Corse. The fishing village looks much like it did fifty years ago, if old postcards are anything to go by, except for the marina and the forest of masts in front of it, though there has been a harbour here for many years and the anchorage has been known since Roman times. Four kilometres away at Monte Bughiu excavations have revealed a Roman settlement from the 2nd century BC. A small dusty case in the *capitainerie* at Macinaggio contains a few of the artifacts found there.

Not far inland from Macinaggio and close to Rogliano stand the ruins of a castle and fortified towers, the stronghold of the Da Mare family. The Da Mares ruled Medieval Cap Corse, one of the aristocratic seigneurial families who controlled parts of Corsica prior to and during part of the Genoese occupation. The gaunt castle standing on the hillside was destroyed by the Genoese when the Da Mares sided with Sampiero Corso in 1564 in a bid for an independent Corsica, a strange alliance between an aristocratic family and a shepherd's son who had visions of a Corsica ruled by Corsicans. The castle was partially dismantled so it could not be used again and it has a melancholy air to it in this rugged landscape.

Baie de Macinaggio

A yacht can anchor in the bay N of the marina where there is good shelter from W–NW winds. Anchor in 3–5 metres on sand and weed, good holding once through the weed. A line of yellow buoys marks the bathing area where anchoring is prohibited. Make sure you are not obstructing the entrance to the marina. In the evening there is often a light SE breeze, uncomfortable rather than dangerous.

Baie de Tamarone

A bay immediately N of Macinaggio. Good shelter from the prevailing W–NW wind. Anchor in 3–5 metres on sand, rock and weed. The bay is an attractive place with clear water over a sandy bottom and little habitation ashore.

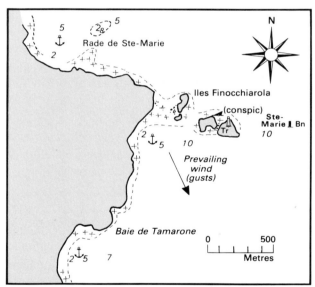

RADE DE STE-MARIE TO BAIE DE TAMARONE

Iles Finocchiarola

These rocky islets extending out from the coast are easily recognised. The Genoese tower on the outermost islet is conspicuous and from the N the remains of a wrecked coaster will be seen on the N side of the islet. The beacon on Banc de Ste Marie is also conspicuous. It is lit, VQ(3)5s. Between the beacon and the outermost islet there are least depths of 10 metres in the fairway, though the clarity of the water makes it look considerably less.

A yacht can anchor under the islets in 3–6 metres on sand and weed. Good shelter from the NW–W wind though there can be gusts off the land.

Ile Finocchiarola and its conspicuous tower.

Note According to *Le Syndicat des Ports de Plaisance de Haute Corse*, Baie de Tamarone, Finocchiarola and Ste-Marie N of Iles Finocchiarola are prohibited anchorages. However in the summer yachts anchor here with apparent impunity. Nonetheless the prohibition should be remembered in case it is enforced in the future.

Rade de Ste-Marie

To the N of Iles Finocchiarola there are three coves affording better shelter from W–NW winds than they would appear to do on the chart. Care needs to be taken of reefs running out from the coast, up to 100–200 metres off in places. Anchor where convenient on sand, rock and weed.

Cap Corse

The bold outline of the extremity of Cap Corse is highest at its western end, sloping gradually to the sea on the eastern side. Ile de la Giraglia, a steep-to island with a conspicuous white lighthouse on the summit, lying ¾ of a mile off the cape, is easily identified. Between Ile de la Giraglia and the coast there are uneven depths with least depths of 3·5 metres in the channel, though the sandy patches show up so brilliantly that you will probably constantly keep checking the depths.

At the western end of Cap Corse, Cap Bianco, as its name suggests, a white cape against the otherwise black rocky coast, and Cap Grosso, with a signal station conspicuous on its summit, are easily identified. At the eastern end of Cap Corse the Genoese tower on Pte d'Agnello is conspicuous.

Cap Corse has an evil reputation in bad weather and deserves to be treated with every respect. Strong winds get up from seemingly nowhere and can make the passage around the cape a rough one. Any wind from the west or east is funnelled around the cape and there are strong gusts off the land. In bad weather it should be given a good offing to avoid the shallows between Ile de la Giraglia and the coast and the shallows off the east coast as far out as the beacon on Banc de Ste-Marie. Confused seas build up over these shallows even in moderate winds and in gale force conditions a yacht is advised to keep 2½ to 3 miles off.

Marine de Barcaggio

A large bay with a sandy beach around it just W of Pte d'Agnello. There is a small fishing village on the shore. The anchorage can be used in calm weather. Anchor off the beach at the eastern end in 3 metres on sand and rock, bad holding. Care needs to be taken of a reef extending up to 300 metres off the centre of the beach with depths of less than a metre in places. Off the village there is a jetty for the local fishing boats. A restaurant-bar opens in the summer.

CENTURI

Approach

The village of Centuri is tucked in behind an islet 2 miles S of Cap Bianco.

Conspicuous From the N the grey stone houses of the village are easily identified, but from the S the houses cannot be easily seen and the islet merges into the land behind. A hotel on the slopes just to the E of the village is conspicuous from the S.

Dangers
● Care needs to be taken of the above and below-water rocks around Ile de Centuri. An isolated reef lies 200 metres NNW of Ile de Centuri.
● The approach to the miniature harbour is obstructed by a reef marked by a red beacon. Approach the harbour on a course of due E and leave the beacon to port.

Mooring

Berth The miniature harbour has berths for a few small yachts only and most must anchor off in the bay W of the harbour. Anchor in 5–8 metres keeping well clear of the rocky reef fringing the coast. The

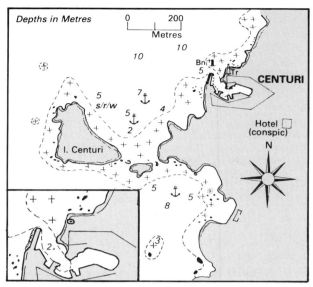

CENTURI 42°58'N 9°19'E

From Centuri Boswell journeyed through the mountains to Sollacro where he met Paoli. Of the first encounter he wrote that 'For ten minutes he walked backwards and forwards through the room, hardly saying a word, while he looked at me, with a steadfast, keen and penetrating eye, as if he searched my very soul.' Paoli's assessment must have been favourable as Boswell was accepted into the household and treated like a bosom friend – Paoli even gave his favourite horse to Boswell for the length of his stay in Corsica.

On his return to England Boswell campaigned vigorously for Paoli's vision of an independent Corsica. His book on his travels, *An Account of Corsica, the Journal of a Tour to that Island and Memoirs of Pascal Paoli*, was published in 1768 and was instantly a best-seller. For several years after, Boswell continued to campaign and to influence the British government to get supplies to Paoli. It was to be Paoli who came to Britain in exile, not Boswell who returned to a freed Corsica. One wonders what the two men said when they met again in such different circumstances.

bottom is sand, rock and weed, mostly bad holding. Depending on the wind and sea a yacht can also anchor on the S side of Ile de Centuri. Anchor in 8–10 metres on sand, rock and weed.

Shelter Generally a settled-weather anchorage as any swell tends to get in here. If there is any likelihood of strong winds a yacht should make for Macinaggio or St-Florent.

Facilities

Water and fuel in the village. Some provisions can be found and restaurants and bars open in the summer.

General

The grey stone houses with grey schist roofs look cheerlessly uniform from seaward, hardly different from the rocky ground they are built upon, but once there the village takes on texture and colour. The fishing village has revived with a modest income from tourism in recent years, though it has not altered substantially. The harbour was apparently built with private money in the 18th century, though for what purpose it is difficult to know.

It was here that Boswell landed in October 1765. The young adventurer was in search of Pasquale Paoli and he chose to land at Centuri rather than Bastia because the latter was held by the French. This adventure of Boswell's was well outside the limits of the average *Grand Tour*, Corsica being considered an anomalous patch of wilderness sandwiched in between grand France and artistic Italy. Boswell showed some courage and fortitude during his stay in Corsica. Apart from fever, rough mountain journeys, and at times little food and warmth, Boswell also had to forego his womanizing for which he was notorious. On his arrival in Centuri he had been told by the Corsican sailors that if he seduced any of their women he could expect 'instant death', and apparently he respected their advice enough to refrain from his normal lifestyle.

Anse d'Aliso

A bay 2 miles S of Centuri. A tower on the coast near the village of Pino is conspicuous to the S of the bay. In the light to moderate prevailing westerlies it affords some shelter. Anchor in 3–5 metres on a sandy bottom. A steep ravine-like valley runs inland from the bay and apart from Pino, there is little habitation around.

Marine de Giottani

A bay 3½ miles S of Aliso, on the S side of the steep-to knoll of Pte Minervio. Coasting from the S the village of Canari with a conspicuous square tower is easily identified and the bay is just over a mile N of here. Care needs to be taken of a rock just awash off the coast at Canari. Close to the bay the houses around the beach will be seen and the miniature harbour on the N side. Anchor in 5–7 metres on sand. Open to westerlies.

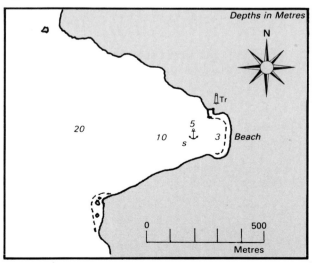

MARINE DE GIOTTANI 42°52'N 9°20'E

Marine d'Albo

A poor anchorage in a cove under the huge quarry on the slopes above. Care needs to be taken of a reef extending some 200 metres off the tower on the S side of the anchorage. Anchor in 5–10 metres off the beach. Restaurant-bar ashore.

Note One of the most conspicuous landmarks from seaward and when entering the Golfe de St-Florent from the S is the huge quarry on the slopes above Marine d'Albo. From the distance the regular rock-cut terraces look like some Inca city removed from South America and planted on the slopes of Corsica. Perhaps it is the same sort of savage mountainous landscape that fosters this impression.

Marine de Nonza

To the S of the quarry, the village of Nonza hangs precariously on a rocky outcrop above the sea, a picturesque place though sadly it doesn't have much in the way of an anchorage. In calm weather anchor in 7–10 metres at the S end of the long beach under the village. Open to all westerlies.

SAINT-FLORENT

Approach

Conspicuous The rock-cut terraces of the quarry above Albo are easily seen from some distance off. Once into the Golfe de St-Florent the lighthouse, a square white tower, and the signal station on Pte de la Mortella, are conspicuous. From here the buildings of St-Florent can be seen and closer in the solid walls of the citadel and a belfry in the town will be seen. The entrance to the marina is not readily obvious, but will be seen when close-to.

By night Use the lights on Pte de la Mortella, Oc.G.4s9M, on Cap Fornali, Fl(2)G.6s7M, and on Pte Vecchiaia, Fl(3)WR.12s10/7M. The red sector of Pte Vecchiaia covers the dangers in the closer approach to St-Florent on 174°–035°. Closer in the light on Tourelle Tégnosa, Fl.R.2s2M, will be seen. The marina entrance is lit, Oc(2)WR.6s9/6M and Fl.G.2s2M. The red sector of the entrance light covers the dangers in the approach on 116°–227°.

Dangers
● Off the entrance to the harbour, a reef Ecueil de la Tégnosa, is marked by a solid red beacon that is readily identified. To the ENE of this reef there is another reef and shoal water – a yacht should keep the beacon to port in the approach to the harbour.
● Strong northerlies pile up a swell at the head of the gulf making entrance to the marina difficult.
● In the spring and autumn there can be a sustained strong katabatic wind blowing down into the gulf in the evening.

Mooring

Details 600 berths with 80 berths for visitors.

Berth where directed or go onto the outside of the central T-pier. There are laid moorings tailed to the quay. The bottom is glutinous mud that gets over everything, including the unfortunate handling the mooring line.

Shelter Good all-round shelter.

Authorities Port captain and marina staff. A charge is made.

Anchorage A yacht can anchor off to the W of the marina in 3–5 metres. The bottom is mud and weed, good holding. The shelter here is adequate in light to moderate westerlies. Although the prevailing wind blows down into the gulf, causing some chop at the head, the wind and chop usually die down in the evening. The best shelter is, unfortunately, the furthest from the town, tucked into the bight immediately under Cap Fornali.

Facilities

Services Water and electricity at or near every berth. A shower and toilet block at the *capitainerie*.

Fuel On the quay near the entrance.

Repairs 20-ton travel-hoist and a 12-ton crane. Most mechanical repairs. Some GRP and wood repairs. Chandlers.

Provisions Good shopping for provisions in the town. Ice available.

Eating out Numerous restaurants on the waterfront and in the town.

Other Post office. Banks. Hire cars. Bus to Bastia. Flights from Bastia, about 20 minutes drive away.

General

In summer St-Florent fairly sizzles as no other resort on Corsica does, with the possible exception of Calvi. Everything seems to be going on at once along the waterfront as crowds promenade up and down, eat vast meals, eat exotic *glaces*, drink exotic drinks, dash off for some rendezvous or look anxiously at their watches as the time of a rendezvous comes and goes, or just sit over an empty glass and watch the others; it's an exhausting business this going on holiday. Yet though St-Florent sizzles, it does it in the most amicable and laid-back way. There is nothing for the hard-bitten old salt to do, but join in and become a St-Florent tourist for a day or two.

The town dates from around the 16th century. A mile inland there was the Roman settlement at Nebbio which during Pisan rule in the 12th century was made a bishopric. The industrious Pisans built a cathedral, Santa-Maria-Assunta, and it still stands, a lonely reminder of Pisan Romanesque and one of the two remaining Pisan cathedrals on the island. The settlement at Santa Maria and its cathedral were abandoned in the 16th century because, it is said, of its malarial site, and the settlement at St-Florent was built close to the Genoese citadel. Why there should be fewer mosquitoes in the marshy land around St-Florent is something of a mystery to me and I suspect the move may have had more to do with moving to a secure site close to the Genoese citadel and close to what was becoming a thriving port under the Genoese mercantile influence.

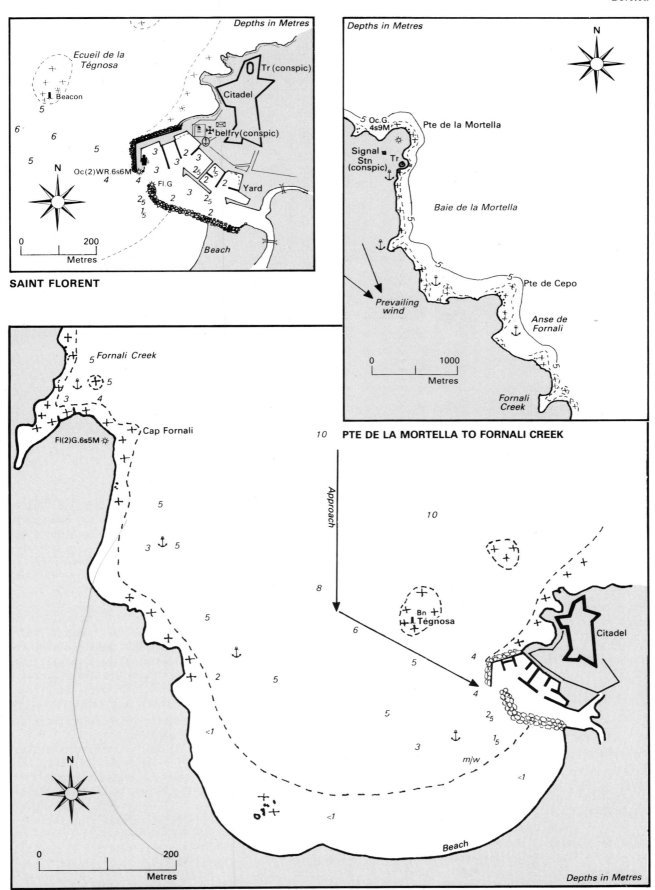

SAINT FLORENT

Depths in Metres

Ecueil de la Tégnosa

Beacon

Tr (conspic)

Citadel

belfry (conspic)

Oc(2)WR.6s6M

Fl.G

Yard

Beach

0   200

Metres

Depths in Metres

N

Oc.G. 4s9M   Pte de la Mortella

Signal Stn (conspic)   Tr

Baie de la Mortella

Pte de Cepo

Prevailing wind

Anse de Fornali

0   1000

Metres

Fornali Creek

PTE DE LA MORTELLA TO FORNALI CREEK

Fornali Creek

Cap Fornali

Fl(2)G.6s5M

N

Approach

Bn Tégnosa

Citadel

m/w

Beach

0   200

Metres

Depths in Metres

APPROACHES TO SAINT-FLORENT

St-Florent. Approach looking SE with *Tégnosa* beacon in the foreground.

Today St-Florent is again thriving. Malaria was wiped out after World War II with DDT and in recent years tourists have arrived in considerable numbers by land and water. The town is one of the most picturesque places on Cap Corse and as I have mentioned, it fairly sizzles with life in the summer. If you need a recommendation treat yourself to a *Colonel*, lemon and vodka sorbet floating in vodka and delightfully cooling, or one of the more exotic creations featuring various ice-creams or sorbets, meringue, raisins, chopped nuts, pineapple and orange, soaked in an alcohol of some description and usually topped with oodles of *chantilly*, the sort of thing that makes dietitians throw up their hands in horror at so many 'bad' things crammed into a single dessert. And a brandy and a *café noir* – why not?

Fornali Creek

A cove immediately N of Cap Fornali. The light tower on Cap Fornali makes identification straightforward. A number of local craft are kept on permanent moorings here and this limits the small amount of space available. In the approach care needs to be taken of the reef off Cap Fornali and of an isolated rock (1·6 metres over) in the middle of the entrance. Anchor in 3–4 metres in the mouth of the cove. Mediocre shelter from the prevailing wind blowing into the gulf.

Anse de Fornali

A bay under Pte de Cepo to the NW of Fornali creek. Care needs to be taken of the off-lying reefs that extend out from the coast on either side of the anchorage. Anchor in 3–6 metres on mud, good holding. Reasonable shelter from the prevailing wind.

Baie de la Mortella

A long bay between Pte de la Mortella and Pte de Cepo. The lighthouse and old signal station of Pte de la Mortella are conspicuous, but the Genoese tower by the water will not be seen in the approach from the N until into the bay. There are several places a yacht can anchor.
● Anchor under the tower in 4–5 metres on sand, rock and weed. Surprisingly good shelter from the prevailing wind is obtained here.
● Anse Fiume Santo, where the river meets the sea. Care needs to be taken of the rocky shelf bordering the coast. Anchor in 3 metres on sand and rock.
● Off the beach at the S end of the bay. A reef projects from the coast on either side of the anchorage. Anchor in 4–6 metres on sand and rock. The prevailing wind tends to blow in here by the afternoon.

THE MARTELLO TOWER

In 1794 Paoli's appeal to the British for help was answered with the dispatch of Lord Hood and the British fleet to Corsica. In February Lord Hood attacked St-Florent and though the town was easily taken after bombardment, the round Genoese tower on Pte de la Mortella refused to surrender and appeared to be impervious to bombardment. A strong force of marines had to be landed before it was finally taken.

The round Genoese tower, now in ruins, so impressed Lord Hood that he had the design and specifications recorded and on his return advised that similar towers be built for the coastal defences of Britain. Many of these towers, now called Martello towers, were built in 1803 against the threat of a French invasion. Ironically the towers were built to thwart the ambitions of a Corsican, Napoléon Bonaparte.

Baie de Loto

To the W of Pte Cavallata is a long sandy beach backed by a razorbacked ridge of hills. In calm weather and light westerlies the anchorage off the beach is popular. Anchor in 4–6 metres on a sandy bottom. Behind the beach are several *étangs* including Etang de Loto.

Marine de Peraldu

A small inlet immediately NW of Loto. There is room for only a few yachts to anchor in 3–4 metres on sand, rock and weed. Ashore several restaurants open in the summer.

In settled weather yachts anchor off the coast between Peraldu and Pte de Curza where there is shelter from light westerlies.

Baie de Saleccia

To the W of Pte de Curza there is a long beach of blinding white sand backed by sand dunes. In calm weather or light westerlies the beach is a popular anchorage. Anchor in 4–6 metres on sand.

Anse de Trave

A cove 3 miles W of Saleccia. Suitable in calm weather only. Anchor in 4–5 metres on a sandy bottom.

Anse de Giugnu

A cove immediately W of Trave. Suitable in calm weather only. Care needs to be taken of a reef running out for 200 metres from the point between two coves and for some distance out from the E side of Giugnu. Anchor in 3–5 metres off the beach on a sandy bottom.

Anse de Malfalco

An inlet 1 mile to the W of Giugnu. Some shelter can be gained from westerlies in here, though the shelter is not as good as it looks. Anchor in 4–5 metres about halfway into the inlet. The bottom is sand and rock. Small yachts drawing 1 metre or less can get further in though care needs to be taken of the rocky reef fringing the edges of the inlet.

Desert des Agriates

Between Golfe de St-Florent and Ile Rousse, the land back from the coast is known as Desert des Agriates, a huge tract of land where there are few villages. From seawards it is a brown rocky landscape folded in on itself, barren except where patches of *maquis* clothe the slopes or a few trees have managed to grow. The absence of villages makes it difficult to give conspicuous landmarks to identify the various anchorages and consequently the navigator must pick out the headlands and bays with some care.

Anse d'Orlando

A bay immediately E of Pte de l'Alciolo. Monte Orlando inland from the point can be identified. There is reasonable shelter from light westerlies tucked in under the point. Anchor in 3–5 metres off the small beach.

Anse de Peraiola

A calm-weather anchorage 2 miles S of Pte de l'Alciolo. Anchor off the beach in 3–5 metres on a sandy bottom. A restaurant-bar opens in the summer.

Anse de Lozari

A large bay 2 miles S of Peraiola suitable in calm weather. Anchor in 3–5 metres off the beach. Holiday villas have been built around the coast and at the W end of the beach there is the village of Lozari.

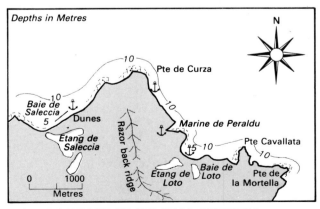

BAIE DE SALECCIA TO PTE DE LA MORTELLA

ILE ROUSSE

Approach

From the W and E the red rock islet of Ile Rousse stands out clearly and is easily identified.

Conspicuous From the W Algajola is easily identified and the islet of Ile Rousse will be seen. From the N and E the islet and the houses of the town will be seen. The lighthouse on Ile Rousse, a round white tower and dwelling, is conspicuous. Closer in the Genoese tower and an ugly white hotel on the islet will be seen though they are not visible from the W until around the islet. The harbour breakwater and anchorage are easily identified.

By night Use the light on Ile Rousse, La Pietra, Fl(3)WG.12s15/11M. The white sector shows the safe approach clear of Danger d'Algajola on 079°–234°. Closer in use the light on the extremity of the breakwater, Iso.G.4s7M and on the fishing harbour, Oc.R.4s7M.

Dangers

• Care needs to be taken of Danger d'Algajola. See the note on page 315.

• Care needs to be taken of an isolated reef 150 metres W of Ile de Pietra (Grande Ile-Rousse). It is difficult to pick out even in calm weather.

Mooring

Anchorage In the summer with the prevailing westerlies most yachts anchor off the town SE of Roches de la Puntella or off the causeway NW of Roches de la Puntella. The latter anchorage is the more secure, but numerous laid moorings restrict the space available. The anchorage off the town is closer to amenities, but is bedeviled by ski-boats and water-bikes making wash and noise.

Berth If there are no commercial craft using the harbour it is possible to go stern-to or alongside the quay. The best place is stern or bows-to the W quay. The bottom is everywhere hard sand with patches of weed and not everywhere good holding.

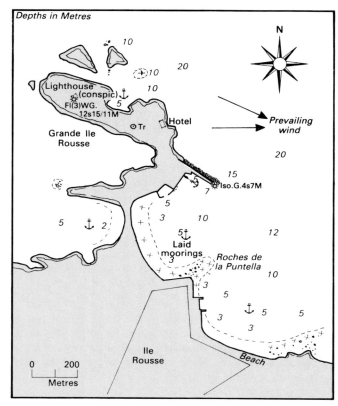

ILE ROUSSE 42°38′N 8°56′E

Shelter In settled weather with the prevailing westerlies, the anchorage and harbour afford good shelter. If the wind turns to the N the anchorages are not tenable. With moderate northerlies there is some shelter tucked into the N corner of the harbour. With strong N–NE winds go to Calvi.

Note In the evening a SE breeze may blow off the land, but it rarely gets up to anything.

Authorities Customs. Port captain. A charge is not usually made in the harbour.

Facilities

Water and fuel in the town. A small chandlers. Good shopping for provisions and a small market in the town in the morning. Numerous restaurants and bars. Post office. Bank. Train to Bastia and Calvi.

General

From the bay Ile Rousse looks an impressive place, a piece of the Riviera transplanted to this unlikely site, but once ashore it soon becomes apparent that the town is a shell thinly populated by locals and a few tourists. Once the tourists have left you get the feeling the locals must rattle around in the town like peas in a pod. The central square is larger than any in Calvi or St-Florent, with a classical facade sheltering the market place; an impressive square, with a name, La Place Paoli, that holds the clue to its origins and to the shape and size of Ile Rousse.

Prior to 1758 there was little here except the Genoese tower on the islet and a few ruins from a small Roman settlement. The origins of the town are

Ile Rousse looking SE.

rooted in Pasquale Paoli's need for a harbour on the west coast and the refusal of the citizens of Calvi to hand over their town and harbour to him. They remained faithful to Genoa, as they always had, so Paoli was forced to build his own town and harbour at Ile Rousse. He planned it along the lines of a grid-city, three streets running parallel with smaller intersecting streets and a large central square. The buildings matched the design: solid, square edifices with somewhat grandiose entrances, out of place on this rocky coast where the local buildings are modest affairs. The town councils of later years continued to expand on Paoli's vision until the town became what it is today, an artificial 18th-century vision marooned in a remote corner of the Balagne.

Yet it is not an unpleasant place, just a little bizarre. The local farmers sit in large elegant cafés to sip their coffee or *pastis* and look distinctly out of place. The tourists add colour and life, but you are always aware that their contribution is fleeting. Perhaps melancholy is the word I am looking for to describe Ile Rousse.

ALGAJOLA

Approach

The anchorage and small harbour lies just under 4 miles W of Ile Rousse. The buildings of the village and the citadel are easily recognised.

Dangers
● Care needs to be taken of Danger d'Algajola.
● Care needs to be taken of the reef fringing the town for some 100 metres and also around the harbour. A rock NW of the town is also fringed by a reef.

Mooring

Anchor off the E side of the town in 3–5 metres on a sandy bottom. There is only shelter from light westerlies here. Small yachts can moor in the harbour with a long line ashore. Care needs to be taken of underwater rocks that fringe the quay and coast.

Facilities

Provisions can be obtained and there are restaurants and cafés.

General

Algajola was one of the original citadels built by the Genoese to secure the west coast. Its fortunes have been varied and it suffered first of all from the rise of Calvi and later from the creation of Ile Rousse by Paoli. It is a pleasant little place that attracts some tourism in the summer.

Danger d'Algajola About 1 mile off the coast to the NW of Algajola lies a dangerous reef (0·8 metres over) and an area of shoal water. The reef merits the title of a 'danger' rather than just a 'reef' or 'rock'. It is marked by a spindly black metal pole, though

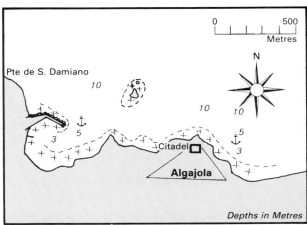

ALGAJOLA 42°37′N 8°52′E

this is often destroyed in winter storms. The reef is easily identified in calm weather and passage between the reef and the coast is straightforward. In a fresh breeze the reef and the metal pole can be difficult to spot and though the inside passage is not dangerous in this weather, considerable caution should be taken.

SANT'AMBROGIO

Approach

From the W the ruined Genoese tower on Pte Spano is easily recognised, though the harbour and holiday village will not be seen until into the bay. From the E the vast belt of the holiday village with conspicuous red roofs will be seen. In the closer approach the harbour breakwater will be seen.

By night The entrance is lit, Fl.G.2s2M and Fl.R.2s 2M. A first-time night approach is not recommended.

Dangers
● From the E care needs to be taken of Danger d'Algajola.
● With strong NE–E winds a swell piles up at the entrance making entry difficult and possibly dangerous.

Note The entrance channel to the harbour is buoyed. Approach the channel on a course of due S and then follow the buoyed channel into the harbour.

Mooring

Details 150 berths with 21 berths for visitors.

Berth where directed or go onto the quay immediately N of the fuel quay. There are laid moorings tailed to the quay. Care needs to be taken of underwater ballasting along the quays.

Shelter Good shelter though strong NE winds cause a surge.

Authorities Port captain. A charge is made.

Note The harbour is very small and yachts over 12 metres should not attempt to enter.

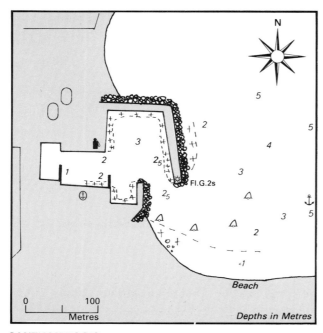

SANT'AMBROGIO 42°36′N 8°50′E

Facilities

Services Water and electricity at or near every berth. A shower and toilet block.

Fuel On the quay.
Repairs 15-ton crane. Some mechanical repairs.
Provisions Most provisions nearby. Ice available.
Eating out Restaurants and cafés open in the summer.

General

The marina at Sant'Ambrogio is really an adjunct to the huge holiday village spreading over the coastal slopes to the east and north. Most of the animation goes on around the marina, on the yachts, the swimming pools, tennis courts, and in the nearby restaurants and bars. In the winter I suspect it is a shell empty of people.

Baie Algajo

In calm weather there are several attractive anchorages in the bay.

• Under Pte Spano in 4–5 metres on sand.
• At Port Algajo at the S end of the bay. Anchor in 2–5 metres on sand.
• On the S end of Pte Carchincu in 5–6 metres.

All of these anchorages are open to the prevailing westerlies and a yacht should go to Calvi when the wind gets up.

Appendix

I. USEFUL ADDRESSES

Tourist offices

United Kingdom
French Government Tourist Office (FGTO),
178 Piccadilly, London W1. ☎ 071-491 7622
USA
FGTO, 610 Fifth Avenue, New York, NY 10020.
☎ (212) 757-1125
FGTO, 9410 Wilshire Blvd, Beverly Hills, CA
90212. ☎ (213) 272-2661
Canada
FGTO, 1840 Ouest rue Sherbrooke, Montreal,
Quebec H3H 1E4. ☎ (514) 931-3855
Australia
FGTO, BWP House, 12 Castlereigh St, Sydney,
NSW 2000. ☎ (612) 231-5244

Associations

Cruising Association, Ivory House, St Katherine's
Dock, London E1 9AT. ☎ 071-481 0881
Royal Yachting Association, RYA House, Romsey
Road, Eastleigh, Hants SO5 4YA. ☎ 0703 629962
Touring Club de France, Service Nautique,
65 Avenue de la Grand Armée, 75782 Paris. Also at
FGTO Piccadilly, London (above).

Inland Waterways

L'Office National de la Navigation, 2 Boulevard de
Latour-Maubourg, 75007 Paris. (For information on
chômages.)

II. USEFUL BOOKS AND CHARTS

Admiralty publications

Mediterranean Pilot Vol II. Covers the S coast of
France and Corsica. NP 46
List of Lights Vol E. Mediterranean, Black, and Red
Seas. NP 78

Yachtsmen's pilots and guides

South France Pilot, Robin Brandon. Imray. The classic guide to the coast. Published in three volumes,
each one containing a folded chart:
South France Pilot
    West – Spanish frontier to Cap Sicié
    East – Cap Sicié to the Italian frontier
    La Corse
Votre Livre de Bord: Méditerranée, Bloc Marine. Distributed in the UK by Imray. Annual publication in
French giving basic data on the harbours in the south
of France and Corsica.

Skipper, Bateaux. Annual publication giving some-
what skimpy coverage of harbours around France. In
French.
Pilote Côtier. Alain Rondeau. Fenwick. Vol. I covers
Marseille to Genoa; Vol. II covers Marseille to Bar-
celona; Vol. III covers Corsica.

Inland waterways

Inland Waterways of France, David Edwards-May.
Imray. The definitive reference and guide.
Cruising French Waterways, Hugh McKnight. Nauti-
cal Books. Good details and information.
Guide Vagnon, Henri Vagnon. Editions du Plaisan-
cier. No. 5 covers the Rhône; No. 7 covers the Canal
Latéral à Garonne and Canal du Midi; No. 9 covers
the Canal du Rhône à Sète. The most practical and
detailed guides with strip-maps, though short on
'extracurricular' details.
Through France to the Med, Mike Harper. Batsford.
Entertaining and informative.
Notes on the French Inland Waterways, Cruising Asso-
ciation booklet.
Through the French Canals Philip Bristow. Nautical
Books. Scanty information and sometimes in-
accurate.
France – The Quiet Way, John Liley. Nautical Books.
More evocative than descriptive with wonderful
photographs.

Other guides

The South of France, Archibald Lyall. Collins Companion Guide. Although originally written more than 25 years ago, it is still one of the best guides around and a treat to read as well.

The Midi, Edmund Swinglehurst. Weidenfeld. A well informed and entertaining guide to the region between the Rhône and Menton.

Michelin Green Guides: *Provence; French Riviera* and *Pyrénées Albigeois* (the latter in French only). The best detailed guides on things to do and see along the coast.

Blue Guide: France, Ian Robertson. A. & C. Black. Normally an excellent series, the guide to France obviously has to skimp to fit the south of France in, but even so it's commentary is sour and sad on the south.

The Rough Guide to France, Baillie, Salmon & Sanger. RKP. Not very detailed, but what there is is good down-to-earth information.

West of the Rhône Freda White. Faber. Although written some time ago, it has much interesting information on the Languedoc-Roussillon region.

General

When the Riviera Was Ours, Patrick Howarth. Century Hutchinson. Entertaining history on tourism on the Riviera.

The French, Theodore Zeldin. Fontana. Erudite and entertaining on the French as opposed to France. Well worth taking along.

The South of France, compiled by Laura Raison. Cadogan. An anthology of writing on the south of France.

Spirit of Place, Lawrence Durrell. Faber. Durrell lives in the Languedoc and this book contains some essays on the south of France.

Isabel and the Sea, George Millar. Century Hutchinson. Tale of a trip through the canals to the Mediterranean at the end of World War II.

The Journeying Moon, Ernle Bradford. Grafton. Readable tale of a trip through the canals and along the coast in a Dutch botter.

Montaillou, Emmanuel Le Roy Ladurie. Penguin. Bringing 14th-century Languedoc history and the persecution of the Cathars alive.

Asterix and the Gauls, Uderzo & Goscinny. Much truth revealed via the comic strips.

For books on Corsica see the introduction to Chapter VII.

Flora

Flowers of the Mediterranean, Oleg Polunin & Anthony Huxley. Chatto & Windus. Comprehensive work with excellent colour photos and line drawings for identification.

Trees and Bushes of Britain and Europe, Oleg Polunin. Paladin.

Marine life

Hamlyn Guide to the Flora and Fauna of the Mediterranean Sea, A. C. Campbell. Comprehensive guide on Mediterranean marine life.

The Yachtsman's Naturalist, M. Drummond & P. Rodhouse. Mainly aimed at northern Europe, but useful for the Mediterranean.

The Natural History of Whales and Dolphins, Peter Evans. A. & C. Black/Christopher Helm. Comprehensive.

Dangerous Marine Animals, Bruce Halstead. The standard reference.

Food

French Provincial Cooking, Elizabeth David. Michael Joseph. The person who introduced the word *Provençal* into British kitchens.

A Table in Provence, Leslie Forbes. Michael Joseph. Evocative and interesting but too nice a book to get grubby in the kitchen.

Mediterranean Cookbook, Arabella Boxer. Penguin.

Mediterranean Seafood, Alan Davidson. Penguin. Excellent reference to seafood in the Mediterranean.

Michelin Red Guides to Hotels and Restaurants, For gourmets and gourmands.

British Admiralty charts

Chart	Title	Scale
French south coast		
149	Rade de Toulon	12,500
	Rade de Villefranche – Monaco and Port of Nice	15,000
150	Marseille	12,500
1506	Plans on the South Coast of France	
	Port Vendres	5,000
	Port La Nouvelle	15,000
	Approaches to Port Vendres	50,000
1705	Cape St Sebastien to Iles d'Hyères	300,000
1780	Barcelona to Naples	1,000,000
2164	La Rhône to Cap Sicié	75,000
	Port de la Ciotat	20,000
2165	Cap Sicié to Cap Camarat	75,000
2166	Cap Camarat to Cannes	60,000
	Saint Raphael	20,000
2167	Cannes to Menton	60,000
	Cannes: Antibes	15,000
2606	Approaches to Sète	50,000
	Port de Sète	10,000
2607	Marseille to Agay Road	146,000
2609	Rade d'Agay to San Remo	146,000
3498	Golfe de Fos	30,000
Corsica		
1131	Island of Corsica	245,000
1213	Bonifacio Strait	50,000
1424	Ports on the south and west coasts of Corsica	
	Bonifacio	7,500
	Ajaccio: Propriano	10,000
	Golfe d'Ajaccio and Golfo de Valinco	60,000
1425	Ports on the north and east coasts of Corsica	
	Macinaggio	10,000
	Bastia	15,000
	Porto Vecchio	25,000
	Approaches to Calvi	50,000

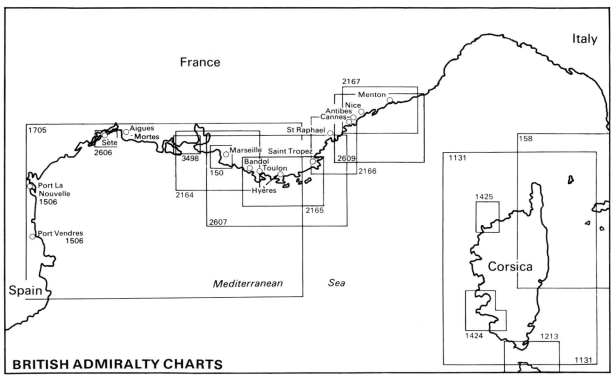

BRITISH ADMIRALTY CHARTS

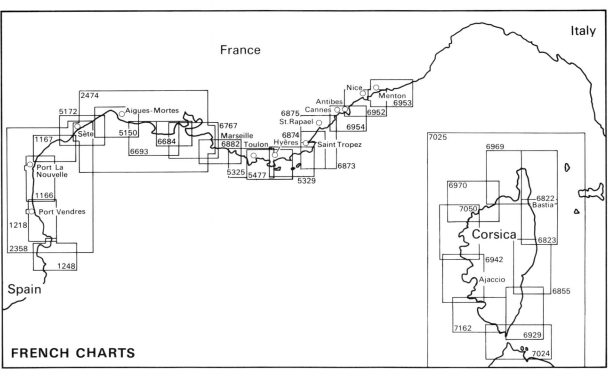

FRENCH CHARTS

French charts

General area charts

1303	Du Cap Creux au Cap Martin	448,300
1865	Côtes de France et d'Italie de Marseille à l'île d'Elbe	448,700
7015	De Gibraltar aux îles Baléares	1,000,000
5017	Bassin Ouest de la Méditerrannée (3e feuille) du méridien de La Calle au méridien de Messine. Côtes d'Italie et de Tunisie, Corse, Sardaigne et Sicile	1,070,000

Coastal charts

1248	Du cap Creux aux îles des Mèdes	50,800
4457	Baie de Figari 10,000	
4708	Baie de Villefranche	7,200
4784	Du cap Pertusato à la pointe de Sénétose	35,700
4786	De la pointe de Sénétose au cap Muro, golfe de Valinco	35,600
5113	Golfe de la Napoule, rade de Cannés	14,400
5122	Golfe Juan, îles de Lérins, Antibes	14,400
5151	Rade d'Hyères	25,000
5175	Parages de Toulon, golfe de Giens	25,000
5176	Environs de Nice, et de Villefranche – Embouchure du Var – Rade de Beaulieu	14,450
5255	Golfe de St Tropez	14,400
5266	Baies de Briande, de Bon-Porte et de Pampelonne	25,000
5325	Du Bec l'Aigle à presqu'île de Giens	50,100
5329	De la presqu'île de Giens au cap Camarat	50,100
5477	Du Cap Sicié au Cap Bénat, rades de Toulon et d'Hyères	50,200
6610	De Bandol au Cap Sicié Rade de Brusc	20,000
6612	De Cassis à Bandol, baie de la Ciotat	20,000
6615	Iles de Port Cros et du Levant (Iles d'Hyères)	25,000
6616	Du Cap Bénat au Cap Lardier, rade de Bormes, baie de Cavalaire	25,000
6632	De Marseille à Menton. Côte Nord-Ouest de Corse	285,000
6684	Golfe et Port de Fos	25,000
6693	Des Saintes-Maries-de-la-Mer à Port-Saint-Louis du Rhône	49,900
6713	Côte Nord-Est de la Corse, canal de Corse	152,000
6739	Golfe de Marseille	17,000
6767	De Fos sur Mer à Marseille	49,900
6821	Côte Ouest du Corse, du cap Corse au Golfe d'Ajaccio	152,000
6822	Abords, Nord de Bastia	50,300
6823	Abords Sud de Bastia	50,600
6850	St-Florent, Centuri, Macinaggio	10,000, 15,000
6851	Ports d'Ajaccio et de Propriano	75,000, 10,000
6855	Du phase d'Alistro a Solenzara	51,000
6856	Abords et port de Bastia	15,000
6838	Abords de Saint-Raphael. De la Pointe des Issambres à la Pointe d'Anthéor	20,000
6839	Etang de Trau	30,000
6843	Du Cabo Creus à Port Barcarès	50,000
6844	De Port Barcarès à l'embouchure de l'Aude	50,000
6863	Du Cap Ferrat au Cap Martin	20,000
6878	Du phare du Titan au Cap Roux	50,000
6881	Abords de Monaco. Ports de la Condamine, de Fontvieille et de Cap d'Ail	7,500
6882	De l'île de Planier à Ciotat	50,000
6907	Etang de Berre	25,000
6911	Port de Porto-Vecchio	15,000
6929	Abords de Porto Vecchio, de l'anse de Favore aux îles Lavezzi	51,200
6942	De Punta d'Orchino au Cap Muro	50,000
6951	De Fos-sur-Mer à Capo Mele	250,000
6952	D'Antibes à Menton	49,600
6953	De Monaco à San Remo	49,600

6954	Du Cap de Drammont au Cap d'Antibes	50,000
6969	Du Cap Corse à le pointe de l'Acciolu Golfe de St Florent	50,300
6970	De Punta di l'Acciolu à Cap Cavallo	50,500
6980	Ile Rousse, Sant'Ambrogio, Calvi	15,000
7002	Ports de Banyuls-sur-Mer, Port Vendres, Collioure, Saint-Cyprien, Port-la-Nouvelle	10,000
7003	Le Cap d'Agde - Embouchure de l'Hérault	15,000
7004	Golf d'Aigues-Mortes Ports de Palavas-les-Flots, Carnon-Plage et des Saintes-Maries-de-la-Mer	15,000
7017	Du Cap Ferrat à Capo Mele	100,000
7024	Bouches de Bonifacio	50,000
7025	Ile de Corse	250,000
7050	De Calvi à Cargèse	50,000
7053	De Sète à la pointe de l'Espiguette	50,000
7054	De l'embouchure de l'Aude à Sète	50,000
7072	Port de Sète	15,000
7088	Du Cabo de San Sébastian à Fos-sur-Mer	25,000
7093	Rade de Toulon	10,000
7096	Port de Bonifacio	5,000
	Baie de Figari	10,000
7162	Du Cap Muro au Cap de Feno	50,000

Navicarte

Carte-Guides Navigation Côtière & Routiers, published by Editions Cartographiques Maritimes (ECM). General scale 1:50,000 with enlarged insets.

French south coast

500	Nice – San Remo
501	St-Raphael – Nice
502	Cavalaire – St-Raphael
502	Toulon – Cavalaire – Iles d'Hyères
504	Marseille – Toulon
505	Port-Saint-Louis – Marseille
507	Port de Bouc – Port Camargue
508	Port-Camargue – Sète
509	Sète – Valras
510	Valras – Port Leucate
511	Port Leucate – Banyuls

Corsica

1006	Calvi – Bastia
1007	Porto – Ajaccio
1008	Propriano – Bonifacio – Maddalena

Routiers (1:250,000)

R1	Marseille – San Remo
R2	Golfe de Gênes (Hyères – Calvi – l'Elbe)
R3	Corse

III. GLOSSARY

General

yes	*oui*
no	*non*
please	*s'il vous plait*
thank you	*merci*
excuse me	*pardon*
it's nothing	*de rien*
where?	*où?*
when?	*quand?*
how?	*comment?*
today	*aujourd'hui*
tomorrow	*demain*
left	*à gauche*
right	*à droite*
big	*grand*
small	*petit*
open	*ouvert*
closed	*fermé*
goodbye	*au revoir*
good morning	*bonjour*
good afternoon	*bonjour*
good evening	*bonsoir*
good night	*bonne nuit*
I understand	*je comprends*
I don't understand	*je ne comprends pas*
OK	*d'accord*
How are you	*Comment allez-vous/ Ça va?*
Fine, thanks	*Très bien, merci*
Excuse me, do you speak English?	*Pardon, Madame/ Monsieur, vous parlez anglais?*

one	*un*
two	*deux*
three	*trois*
four	*quatre*
five	*cinq*
six	*six*
seven	*sept*
eight	*huit*
nine	*neuf*
ten	*dix*
twenty	*vingt*
fifty	*cinquante*
one hundred	*cent*
one thousand	*mille*
Sunday	*dimanche*
Monday	*lundi*
Tuesday	*mardi*
Wednesday	*mercredi*
Thursday	*jeudi*
Friday	*vendredi*
Saturday	*samedi*

In the restaurant

(See the section on *Food* in the Introduction.)

Shopping

apples	*pommes*
apricots	*abricot*
aubergine	*aubergine*
bakery	*boulangerie*
beans	*haricots*
beef	*boeuf*
biscuits	*biscuits*
bread	*pain*
butcher	*boucher*
butter	*beurre*
carrots	*carottes*
cheese	*fromage*
chicken	*poulet*
chocolate	*chocolat*
coffee	*café*
cucumber	*concombre*
eggs	*oeufs*
fish	*poisson*
flour	*farine*
grocer	*alimentation*
honey	*miel*
jam	*confiture*
lamb	*agneau*
lemon	*citron*
meat	*viande*
melon	*melon*
milk	*lait*
oil	*huile*
onions	*oignons*
oranges	*oranges*
peaches	*pêches*
potatoes	*pommes de terre*
rice	*riz*
salt	*sel*
sugar	*sucre*
tea	*thé*
tomatoes	*tomates*
water	*eau*
wine	*vin*

French names and terms found on charts

anse	bay, creek
avant port	outer harbour
baie	bay
balise	beacon
banc	bank
barre	bar
basse	shoal
bassin	basin
blanc	white
bouche	mouth of river or channel
calanque	fjord-like inlet
canal	canal, channel
cap	cape
capitainerie	port/harbour office
château	castle
chaussée	causeway
chenal	channel
col	mountain pass
colline	hill
côte	coast
darse	basin
digue	mole
écueil	shoal, reef
est	east
étang	lake, lagoon
fleuve	river, stream
fosse	ditch
golfe	gulf
grand(e)	great
grau	channel
gros	large
haut-fond	shoal
île	island
îlot	islet
isthme	isthmus
jetée	jetty
lac	lake
maison	house
marais	swamp
marine	marine
mer	sea
môle	mole
mont	mount, mountain
montagne	mountain
mouillage	anchorage
neuf(ve)	new
noir(e)	black
nord	north
nouveau	new
ouest	west
passe	channel
petit(e)	small
pic	peak
plage	beach
plateau	shoal
pointe	point

pont	bridge
port	port
presqu'île	peninsula
quai	quay
quai d'accueil	arrivals/reception quay
rade	roadstead
rivière	river
roche	rock
rocher	above water rock
rouge	red
sable	sand
saline	salt works
sommet	summit
sud	south
torrent	stream, torrent
tour	tower
vieux, vieil, vieille	old

Pronunciation

One important rule to remember is that the consonant at the end of a word is silent. Thus lait (milk) is pronounced *lay*.

Vowels are pronounced as follows:

a	as in f*a*t
e	as in p*e*rt
é	as in g*e*t
è	as in g*a*te
eu	as in b*u*rnt
i	as in mach*i*ne
o	as in g*o*t
ô, au	as in *o*ver
ou	as in s*oo*n
u	as in p*u*ce

Combinations of vowels get more complicated. Consonants are pronounced much as in English except for:

ch	is *sh*
ç	is *s*
h	is silent
th	is *t*
w	is *v*
r	is rolled

Almost any of the small phrase books or dictionaries will get you going. On board I use the small *Hugo* French-English dictionary which has a phonetic guide to pronunciation for the words. French is a difficult language despite the similarities between many English and French words, but any attempt to speak French, even a simple *'Bonjour'*, *'merci'*, or *'Comment ça se dit en français?'*, will be appreciated.

IV. BEAUFORT SCALE

Sea state	Beaufort No.	Description	Velocity in knots	Velocity in km/h	Term	Code	Wave height in metres
Like a mirror	0	Calm glassy	<1	<1	Calm	0	0
Ripples	1	Light airs rippled	1–3	1–5	Calm	1	0–0·1
Small wavelets	2	Light breeze wavelets	4–6	6–11	Smooth	2	0·1–0·5
Large wavelets	3	Gentle breeze	7–10	12–19	Slight	3	0·5–1·25
Small waves, breaking	4	Moderate breeze	11–16	20–28	Moderate	4	1·25–2·5
Moderate waves, foam	5	Fresh breeze	17–21	29–38	Rough	5	2·5–4
Large waves, foam and spray	6	Strong breeze	22–27	39–49			
Sea heads up, foam in streaks	7	Near gale	28–33	50–61	Very rough	6	4–6
Higher long waves, foam in streaks	8	Gale	34–40	62–74			

Sea state	Beaufort No.	Description	Velocity in knots		Term	Code	Wave height in metres
High waves, dense foam, spray impairs visibility	9	Strong gale	41–47	75–88	High	7	6–9
Very high tumbling waves, surface white with foam, visibility affected	10	Storm	48–55	89–102	Very high	8	9–14
Exceptionally high waves, sea covered in foam, visibility affected	11	Violent storm	56–63	103–117	Phenomenal	9	>14
Air filled with spray and foam, visibility severely impaired	12	Hurricane	>63	>118			

V. CONVERSION TABLES

metres–feet

m	ft/m	ft
0·3	1	3·3
0·6	2	6·6
0·9	3	9·8
1·2	4	13·1
1·5	5	16·4
1·8	6	19·7
2·1	7	23·0
2·4	8	26·2
2·7	9	29·5
3·0	10	32·8
6·1	20	65·6
9·1	30	98·4
12·2	40	131·2
15·2	50	164·0
30·5	100	328·1

centimetres–inches

cm	in/cm	in
2·5	1	0·4
5·1	2	0·8
7·6	3	1·2
10·2	4	1·6
12·7	5	2·0
15·2	6	2·4
17·8	7	2·8
20·3	8	3·1
22·9	9	3·5
25·4	10	3·9
50·8	20	7·9
76·2	30	11·8
101·6	40	15·7
127·0	50	19·7
254·0	100	39·4

metres–fathoms–feet

m	fathoms	ft
0·9	0·5	3
1·8	1	6
3·7	2	12
5·5	3	18
7·3	4	24
9·1	5	30
11·0	6	36
12·8	7	42
14·6	8	48
16·5	9	54
18·3	10	60
36·6	20	120
54·9	30	180
73·2	40	240
91·4	50	300

kilometres–statute miles

km	M/km	M
1·6	1	0·6
3·2	2	1·2
4·8	3	1·9
6·4	4	2·5
8·0	5	3·1
9·7	6	3·7
11·3	7	4·3
12·9	8	5·0
14·5	9	5·6
16·1	10	6·2
32·2	20	12·4
48·3	30	18·6
64·4	40	24·9
80·5	50	31·1
120·7	75	46·6
160·9	100	62·1
402·3	250	155·3
804·7	500	310·7
1609·3	1000	621·4

kilograms–pounds

kg	lb/kg	lb
0·5	1	2·2
0·9	2	4·4
1·4	3	6·6
1·8	4	8·8
2·3	5	11·0
2·7	6	13·2
3·2	7	15·4
3·6	8	17·6
4·1	9	19·8
4·5	10	22·0
9·1	20	44·1
13·6	30	66·1
18·1	40	88·2
22·7	50	110·2
34·0	75	165·3
45·4	100	220·5
113·4	250	551·2
226·8	500	1102·3
453·6	1000	2204·6

litres–gallons

l	gal/l	gal
4·5	1	0·2
9·1	2	0·4
13·6	3	0·7
18·2	4	0·9
22·7	5	1·1
27·3	6	1·3
31·8	7	1·5
36·4	8	1·8
40·9	9	2·0
45·5	10	2·2
90·9	20	4·4
136·4	30	6·6
181·8	40	8·8
227·3	50	11·0
341·0	75	16·5
454·6	100	22·0
1136·5	250	55·0
2273·0	500	110·0
4546·1	1000	220·0

Index